BURTON L. WHITE

THE *NEW* FIRST THREE YEARS OF LIFE

*The Completely Revised and Updated Edition
of the Parenting Classic*

A FIRESIDE BOOK
PUBLISHED BY SIMON & SCHUSTER
NEW YORK   LONDON   TORONTO   SYDNEY

FIRESIDE
Rockefeller Center
1230 Avenue of the Americas
New York, NY 10020

FIRESIDE and colophon are registered trademarks of Simon &
Schuster Inc.

DESIGNED BY BARBARA MARKS

Manufactured in the United States of America

20 19 18 17 16 15 14 13 12

Library of Congress Cataloging-in-Publication Data
White, Burton L., 1929–
    The *new* first three years of life/ Burton L. White.
      p.   cm.
    "The completely revised and updated edition of the
parenting classic."
    Rev. ed. of: The first three years of life. New and rev. ed.
c1990.
    Includes index.
    1. Infant psychology.   I. White, Burton L., 1929–
First three years of life.   II. Title.
BF719.5.W45 1995
649'.122--dc20   95-18297
                                       CIP

ISBN 0-684-80419-0

Also by Burton L. White:
Raising a Happy, Unspoiled Child

ACKNOWLEDGMENTS

Throughout my thirty-seven-year research career, I have always had help from others. As the years went by the numbers have grown to thousands of people. I have never, however, formally acknowledged my gratitude for one other kind of essential assistance. Brandeis, MIT, and Harvard have provided the bases that made my research possible over more than twenty years.

In 1976 I represented the United States at meetings of UNESCO. It was quite clear that no other country has ever supported research on the development of children to anywhere near the extent that this country has.

To each of these institutions I am deeply grateful.

To the memory of a wonderful
young man, Mark Howard Berman

CONTENTS

PREFACE

The first edition of this book was written in 1974 and published in 1975. This fourth edition has been completely rewritten to reflect my best understanding of development during the first three years of life. I was delighted to be able to bring this book up to date, and as I expected, writing it has been a labor of love. You see, after all these years of research, thirty-eight to be exact, I am still convinced that no subject is more important than the quality of people, and that what happens during a child's first three years of life makes a unique and powerful contribution to the basic makeup of each new person. To add to all that, I have never lost my enjoyment of babies.

In spite of the revolutionary increase in interest since the 1960s in the events of the first years of life, this book remains the only one based directly on studies of children and parents in their own homes. It is also the only collection of ideas about raising children that has ever been tested (the Missouri New Parents as Teachers Project—1981–1985).

I am fortunate to have been able to conduct research and parent education work with thousands of normal families, visiting their homes on a monthly basis, usually over a period of more than two years. In this work I have been assisted by dozens of talented associates.

The work of the last six years has been particularly useful, as it has allowed me to examine very closely how effective our previous information is with new families just starting to raise children. In the operation of our New Parents as Teachers model program, my colleagues and I have been able to refine our previous views and also fill in many more details of the development and parenting process. For example, I have now concluded that helping a child acquire high level of intelligence and language is surprisingly easy to do in most instances. On the other hand, helping a child to become socially effective and a pleasure to live with has turned out to be considerably more difficult.

I have been enormously impressed with the link between loving but very firm parenting from the time a baby is seven to twenty-two months old, and the maintenance of happiness in a child.

It is very rewarding to be able to provide advice and support to new parents that regularly lead to the miracle of a beautifully developed two-year-old.

And here lies one of the important refinements that has emanated from our recent work. By the time a child reaches fourteen months of age, we have been able to determine whether that child is moving in a direction that augurs well for the first three years or is already well on the way to trouble. By the second birthday, the picture generally has become quite clear. By twenty-seven months of age, I believe it is now rather easy to see the signs that will lead to optimal readiness for school at six years of age or to substantial problems in respect to language, intelligence, and social behaviors.

The last thirty years or so have seen a steady growth of new and useful information about how a child begins to take shape during the first years of life. This information can help parents and their children make the most of the uniquely important early experiences. If you are about to raise your first child, you are in for one of life's special pleasures. I hope this book will enhance the experience. Good luck.

SECTION I

THE SEVEN PHASES OF THE FIRST THREE YEARS OF LIFE

1

BIRTH TO EIGHT MONTHS: GUIDELINES FOR PHASES I TO V

GENERAL REMARKS

Why Separate the First Eight Months from the Balance of the First Three Years?

Reports from many parts of the world indicate that most children, even when raised under substandard conditions, do quite well educationally during their first eight months of life. Neither the child who will achieve superbly nor the one who will be seriously behind by the first grade seems to show any special qualities during the first year of life.*

---

* There are exceptions to this statement. Approximately 15 percent of all children are either born with a significant handicap or acquire one during the first year of life. Also, there are undoubtedly many children born into nightmarish special situations who are considerably worse off. Such exceptional cases are beyond the scope of this book.

In our work we have found that rearing children well becomes much more difficult once they begin to crawl. Another way of expressing this thought is that during the first eight months of life doing what comes naturally usually leads to very good results, but it is rarely enough to ensure the best results for the balance of the first three years.

During the first eight months of life a baby's good development is largely ensured by nature. If parents do what comes naturally and provide a baby with generous amounts of love, attention, and physical care, nature will pretty much take care of the learning process. I do not mean to imply that it is impossible to do a bad job of child-rearing during this period; it is always possible, through stupidity or callousness, to do lasting harm to a child of any age, and especially during the first months of life. Nor do I mean to say that the "normal" course of development during the first eight months of life cannot be improved upon. But it appears that nature, almost as if in anticipation of the uncertainties that beset new parents, has done its best to make the first six to eight months as problem-free as possible. There are, however, two significant hazards during this period that can lead to trouble. They are middle ear disease that interferes with hearing, and the overdevelopment of the "demand cry." I shall deal with both issues at length.

Establishing Goals

If you are not clear about what you are trying to achieve, you have no way to determine whether or not you have succeeded. I have always found that spelling out goals and finding ways to assess to what degree they have been reached is the only starting point that makes sense.

What most parents want out of the early years is a well-developed child, along with a good deal of simple pleasure for both the child and themselves. They also want to avoid unhappiness, anxiety, and of course danger to the child. If optimal early development were incompatible with enjoyment for both the parents and the baby, it would be unfortunate. Happily, that is clearly not the case. Especially in the first months of life, the vast majority of child-rearing activities I'll recommend will lead to both an involved, happy baby and a more contented parent. By the later stages of infancy and toddlerhood, I have found that the well-developing baby is by far the most pleasant to live with and the happiest.

General goals, however, are simply not enough. After you have decided you want a well-developed, happy child, then what? How do you achieve that goal? Indeed, what does it mean? Let's look first at the goals for the first eight months of life.

We recommend that parents work toward three major goals during the first eight months of the baby's life:

1. Giving the infant a feeling of being loved and cared for.
2. Helping her develop specific skills.
3. Encouraging her interest in the world around her.

As we follow the developing child from Phase I through Phase IV, I will refer repeatedly to these basic aims. Let us examine them more closely.

Giving Your Infant a Feeling of Being Loved and Cared For

During the first two years of life all children have a special need to form at least one strong attachment to an older person. Clearly, if a baby is to survive, let alone develop well, protection and nurturance must be available from the very beginning and for a long time thereafter.

During the first eight months of life, social development is comparatively simple. Erik Erikson, the famous personality theorist, called the primary social goal of this period the establishment of a sense of "trust." I believe the term is an appropriate one. *No requirement of good child-rearing is more natural or more rewarding than the tending of your baby in a loving and attentive way in order to establish a feeling of being loved and cared for, or a sense of basic trust.* Although there is little reason to think that an infant of eight months has more than a simple awareness of his mother, most students of human development agree that the basic foundation of a child's personality is being formed in his earliest interchanges with nurturing adults.

Helping Your Infant Develop Specific Skills

Few living creatures are as helpless as a newborn baby. At birth, an infant cannot think, use language, socialize with another human being, run, walk, or even deliberately move around. When on her back she can't lift her head; on her stomach she can barely lift her nose off the surface on which she is lying. The list of things she cannot do is almost as long as the complete list of human abilities.

What *can* a newborn infant do? A newborn infant has a small number of reflexlike sensorimotor abilities. When placed on his stomach he can lift his head high enough to avoid suffocation when left with his nose in the mattress. With a little over two pounds of strength in each hand, he will grasp small objects with them, but only if someone else elicits the behavior in the correct manner. He may glance at and track an object for a few seconds if the object is large enough (more than a few inches in each dimension), contrasts well with the background, is no closer to him than six to eight inches and no farther away than approximately twenty-four inches, and is moving through his line of sight at or near a speed of about one foot per second. As soon as the target stops moving, however, he'll lose interest in it. Moreover, he will behave this way only when he is awake, alert, and inactive, a condition that is likely to exist for only two or three minutes out of each waking hour during the first three weeks of life. In other circumstances you will see very few signs of interest in examining the outside world in those early days.

Newborns are also usually able to locate a small object touching them on or near the lips (rooting behavior), then grasp and suck it. They cry when they are uncomfortable. They blink when their eyes are touched or when they receive a puff of air. They respond with a knee jerk (the patellar response) when an appropriate stimulus is administered.

Of special interest is the baby's startle reflex, which can be a source of needless concern to parents. A newborn will often startle if she is lowered through space abruptly, if she hears a loud noise nearby, or at times even when the light goes on in a dim room. These startles are most likely to occur when the baby is in a quiet rather than an active state. More dramatic, however, is the spontaneous startle, which, as the name implies, needs no external stimulus. During deep sleep, characterized by regular breathing and little or no movement, normal newborns will startle as frequently as every two minutes. During sleep states when the infant is slightly more active, spontaneous startles occur, but less regularly and less frequently. The more activity, the fewer the startles. Both kinds of behavior usually disappear by the end of the third month of life.

From about six weeks of age, a baby becomes increasingly able to deal with the world. From this time on, development proceeds rapidly. By the age of eight months, she has acquired a good deal of control over her body. She can hold her head erect and steady quite easily. She can turn over at will, can sit unaided, and may even be able to crawl across a room. Ordinarily she cannot as yet pull herself to a standing posture, walk, or climb,* but she is quite skillful at using her hands to reach for objects. About 99 of 100 babies have excellent, mature eyesight—better than their fathers' if they are over forty-five years old. The infant can locate and discriminate sounds with admirable accuracy. Socially, she knows full well who her key people are and is likely

---

* Some babies develop much faster than others in these respects. I have seen babies crawl across a room and even pull themselves to a standing position at five months of age. Mercifully, this happens only in about one in five hundred instances. The subject of variability in developmental rates is quite important and I will deal with it at greater length further on.

to have become quite choosy about who picks her up and holds her close. As for intelligence, while she is a long way from being able to process or create ideas, she has acquired two important problem-solving skills: the ability to move an obstacle aside to get at something she wants to grasp, and even more important, the ability to use her cry to get someone to come to her.

This vigorous, extremely attractive young person has, in other words, acquired quite a number of basic skills.

Enjoyable and effective child-rearing during a baby's first eight months is more likely when you know the normal pattern of emerging skills and how to provide opportunities for your baby to use them. I should point out, however, that most of these skills will evolve without any special effort from you. Apparently they are so basic that, except under extraordinarily poor conditions, normal development is assured. A more important reason for encouraging their use involves the third major goal for these first eight months of life.

Encouraging Your Baby's Interest in the Outside World

Whether a child learns to reach for objects at three or four months rather than five or six is probably of no consequence. It has been my experience, however, that *when very young infants are provided with an environment that offers them the opportunity to practice emerging skills, they become more interested in their environment, more alert and more cheerful. In fact, a basic principle of good child-rearing, especially during the first years, seems to be that you should design your child's world so that his day is rich with options for activities that relate to his rapidly shifting interests and abilities.* To create this environment successfully, you need detailed and accurate information as to what those interests and abilities are as the child grows. You will find much of that information in this book.

To sum up, then, during the first eight months of life, a baby should be reared in such a manner that she comes to feel she is deeply loved, that she acquires all the basic skills that can be acquired during those first months, and that her inborn tendency to learn more about and to enjoy the world around her is deepened and broadened.

2

PHASE I: BIRTH TO SIX WEEKS

GENERAL REMARKS

"Helpless as a kitten" is a popular way of describing a newborn baby, but a kitten is considerably more able at birth than a human infant. If the newborn infant had to rely on his own abilities to find nourishment, he would not last long. The newborn baby seems to be only partially prepared for life outside of the womb, and the first four to six weeks of life seem more like a transitional period between two very different modes of existence than a time of rapid development. The new baby is oriented toward seeking comfort rather than exploring the world.

To begin with, life outside the womb depends upon the action of the lungs and several other systems that were not previously in use. In addition, for many infants the birth process itself is physically difficult. The typical extensive sleeping during the weeks after birth would seem to indicate that being born is an exhausting experience.

GENERAL BEHAVIOR DURING THE POSTNATAL PERIOD

Sleepiness and Irritability

Perhaps the most obvious quality babies show during the first weeks of life, aside from total dependence, is sleepiness. In the first postnatal days you can expect your baby to average about two to three minutes an hour of alertness during the day, and less at night. Such periods of wakefulness will lengthen gradually over the next month to an average of six or seven minutes an hour.

Even when your baby is awake, don't expect a great deal of responsiveness to your loving overtures, or for that matter many signs of blissful contentment. On the contrary, the typical newborn is often rather irritable.★ There is nothing personal going on yet. It's not you. Give him nine or ten weeks and he will begin to give you smiles that will knock your socks off. You will just have to be patient for the time being.

Another term of relevance here is "temperament," that part of the personality that a baby brings with her at birth. Some sophisticated research has been performed on this subject under the direction of Herbert Birch of the Albert Einstein School of Medicine in New York. Popularized versions of the results of that work are available, notably Birch, Chess, and Thomas, *Your Child Is a Person* (New York: Bantam Books). The debate about how much of a three-year-old's personality is innate and how much is learned has been around for a long time. In general, those who study temperament tend to emphasize innateness, whereas those who study child-rearing processes, like

---

★ Here and elsewhere it must be noted that my remarks will not be perfectly applicable to all babies. In general during the first six months of life infants behave remarkably alike in many situations and respects. Nonetheless, one of the best-established principles of human development is variability. One characteristic that varies considerably from child to child is irritability. These variations have a substantial impact on both infants and parents, particularly during the first months of life. When a very young infant seems unusually irritable, we say that he suffers from "colic." Life with such a baby is typically much more stressful at first than it is with an "easy" infant. Often children from the same family will differ remarkably from the start in respect to irritability. Colic is a reality for some families and has to be factored into the discussion of early development and parenting, especially in connection with the first six months of life.

me, while acknowledging the importance of innate temperament, attribute the majority of the personality of the three-year-old to the effects of experience, especially those experiences that take place between seven or eight and twenty-four months of age.

Another interesting quality in the newborn's behavior is rapid shifts in mood. Babies move from all-out rage to apparent contentment and vice versa very rapidly. That volatility will continue for the better part of the first year of life. Along with other signs, this volatility seems to suggest that you are not justified in assuming that a baby's emotional life is like yours.

The Fragmented Nature of Infant Behavior

Another rather unusual aspect of the newborn's behavior is its fragmented nature. Offer a six-month-old a small object and he will very probably look at it, then reach out and grasp it. He will then turn it this way and that and in all probability put it in his mouth and gum it for a while. He may then transfer it to his other hand. If you place it in his hand when he isn't looking, he will quickly pay attention to it and begin to explore it in the aforementioned ways. Offer such an object to a newborn, however, and he is not even likely to notice it. You can get him to hold the object, provided you know how to unclench his usually fisted fingers. If you succeed, he will get a good grip on the object, but he won't look at it. His grasp reflex operates in an isolated way during the first two months of life. Once he drops the object, don't expect him to notice that it is gone and look for it. That kind of behavior is a long way off.

From an adult point of view, the behavior of a newborn in respect to a small object may seem puzzling. This behavior is convincingly explained, however, in Jean Piaget's brilliant book, *The Origins of Intelligence in Children* (see Recommended Readings). According to Piaget, a baby's behavior at birth consists mainly of a small number of somewhat clumsy, unfinished, isolated reflexes. These simple bits of behavior—rooting and sucking, grasping, occasionally glancing at nearby objects—are the foundation elements of all later intelligence. There is reason to believe that these behaviors are ancient fragments of what long ago made up useful, organized, instinctive patterns.

In a stunning analysis, documented by detailed descriptions of the evolving behavior of his own three children, Piaget mapped out the emergence of problem-solving and thinking ability in the first two years of life. But problem-solving is far beyond the capacity of the baby in Phase I. Her reflexes are triggered by internal and external stimuli of which she has no awareness. They operate briefly and mechanically and, as far as anyone can tell, are in no way deliberately controlled by her.

During Phase I an infant's reflexes become more reliable and efficient through repeated triggering. In addition, the first signs of coordination among them begin as the baby brings her fist to her mouth increasingly often and gums or sucks it. In this manner, she grasps an object and occasionally brings it to her mouth and gums or sucks it. But let her drop that object and she will give no indication that she knows it exists. Out of hand (or mouth) is out of mind.

These early bits of behavior—the automatic grasping reflexes of the fingers and toes, the rooting responses of the mouth, the coordinated arm and leg movements—are perhaps best understood in the light of the behavior of simpler animals. In our parent education work we show an incredible film about the red kangaroo fetus. Long before its actual birth, the fetus leaves its mother's uterus and passes through the cervical canal and out of its mother's body. Then, totally unaided, it makes the arduous climb from the vaginal opening up the mother's abdomen to the lip of the pouch. It then climbs over the lip and into the pouch, where it finds a nipple, grasps it in its mouth, and settles in for the balance of the fetal development period. Throughout this truly incredible journey, the mother provides no assistance, but merely sits quietly while licking her vaginal area, presumably clearing it of amniotic fluid and so forth. At this stage, the fetus is about one inch long, weighs less than one ounce, is blind, and has no use of its rear limbs. Of relevance to this discussion is the fact that the kangaroo fetus succeeds in its essential journey using the same reflexes present in the newborn human— that is, grasping, rooting, and coordinated limb and sucking reflexes. In the kangaroo, these reflexes function in an impressively orchestrated manner. In the human, they all operate, but in almost total isolation from one another. In place of this miraculous instinctive pattern, the human infant gets its nourishment and other needs mostly via the activities of the parent.

The wonderful work on the kangaroo surely helps us understand why the newborn human is endowed with certain reflexes. It also helps us understand something about the differences in applicability of the concept of instinctive behavior to humans as opposed to other animals. In general, full-fledged instinctive patterns such as those seen in the movements of the red kangaroo fetus, as well as in the web-spinning of spiders and nest-building of birds, and so forth, simply do not exist in humans at any stage of life. What does remain is what we call vestigial remnants and other contributions, especially in connection with the early attachment process. In this process the human infant forms its first social relationships to older people during the first two years of life. These evolutionary leftovers are also reminders that though human beings are unique both as a species and as individuals, we are clearly not totally different from other mammals.

Lack of Mobility

When on her back, a baby in Phase I cannot turn her torso so that she is lying on her side, nor can she otherwise move her body about, except under one condition. Some babies, when angry, manage to propel themselves the full length of the crib by repeatedly digging their heels into the mattress surface and thrusting out their legs. A soft bumper placed around the interior walls of the crib or bassinet is therefore mandatory. It should also be noted that even a newborn, when placed on a blanket on a floor or on some other surface without confining walls, may move quite a distance. Parents are well advised, because of this little-known capacity, to be watchful.

By four weeks of age the characteristic posture of a baby, when on his back, has become the tonic neck reflex (TNR) position, or the "fencer's pose," with both hands fisted. About 90 percent of all babies spend about 85 percent of the time with their head turned to the far right. During the other 15 percent of the time the baby's head is turned to the left. If you gently move her head from one position to the other, you will find that the arms and legs will move to the corresponding fencer's pose. This automatic quality is typical of much of the infant's behavior during the first three months of life. At birth, the TNR is not as obvious or well established. It becomes most noticeable during the four- to ten-week period, then recedes and disappears by four months of age.

Ordinarily, when a Phase I baby is placed on his stomach, he is only capable of barely clearing the mattress surface with his nose for a moment or two. Again, however, when angry he may do considerably better. It will be several months before a baby can cope well with his disproportionately large head. When he is propped up in a sitting position, his head will slump

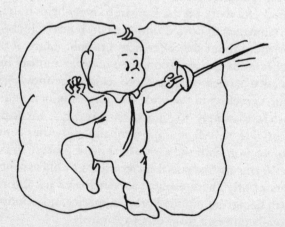

The tonic neck reflex ("fencer's pose")

alarmingly. It is best *always to provide head support for a Phase I baby, especially when lifting or holding him*. Limited head control is one of several indications of weakness and fragility that all normal Phase I and Phase II babies show. All that changes with Phase III.

Hypersensitivity

In addition to being weak, sleepy, and irritable, the Phase I baby is likely to be unusually sensitive. This normal sensitivity can make a jumpy parent even more nervous, but it is perfectly natural for an infant to startle and cry at any abrupt change in stimulation during her first weeks of life. Sharp nearby noises, a jolt to the crib or infant seat, or a sudden change of position may trigger startling and crying, especially if the baby has been inactive. A second, less dramatic indication of sensitivity at this age is the infant's avoidance of bright light. A Phase I infant will keep his eyes shut tightly in a brightly lit room or when exposed to direct sunlight. He is much more likely to open his eyes and look about when in a dimly lit environment. Another curious behavior during this stage is the "doll's-eye" effect. At times, a baby's eyes will open when he is moved from a horizontal to a vertical position.

Smiling

You shouldn't expect frequent full smiles during Phase I. New parents often report that they are a common occurrence. With reluctance I have to report that this is not usually the case. At times, a Phase I baby may show a clear smile, but that will happen just as often during sleep as when he is looking at another person. Vision skills and social awareness are simply too limited during the first weeks of life to enable an infant to examine nearby details and relate to people. We all would like to think that our children feel an immediate and deep love for us, but I don't believe this is so. Toward the end of your baby's first month, however, you may begin to see episodes of serious interest in your face. As babies move into the second month of life, the region of the face between the hairline and the nose becomes increasingly attractive to them.

The Visual Discovery of the Hand

The six-week-old baby, when placed on his back, will usually adopt the TNR position. Although he is now able to turn his head more freely than before, he rarely looks directly overhead. His hands, though still usually fisted, are now frequently held aloft. The hand on the side to which his head is turned is, from time to time, directly in his line of sight; but whether the hand is still or moving, *the child does not seem to notice it*. This situation can be quite disconcerting to a parent, because the baby appears to be blind. That is rarely the case. The Phase I baby is simply not yet able to see small nearby objects very well. His eyes do not yet converge or focus on such objects, and he is still not capable of clear three-dimensional vision.

Sometime after five or six weeks, if you look closely, you might notice your baby casting a brief glance at her hand as it moves through her line of sight. She may even do a double take, indicating that she has noticed something. Each day the tendency to look at her hand will become more stable, changing gradually into sustained hand regard. If she has a nearby object to touch—for example, something dangling from a crib or from a floor gym—you may notice her growing absorption with that toy rather than with her hand alone. Regular episodes of staring at the hand, either by itself or as it touches objects, is one common indication that your baby's near vision is developing normally and that she is entering Phase II.

While hand-to-mouth activity is very common from the first days of life, regular episodes of eye-hand activity will emerge between six and ten weeks of age. This development represents the beginning of the process that will lead to the mastery of the hand as a tool for reaching out and grasping objects to be brought close for examination. Hand-eye behavior will challenge and absorb your child from its emergence on through at least his second birthday. Learning about the process step by step will be fascinating and very helpful to you in providing interesting activities for your child. It will also guide you in choosing appropriate toys. In addition, early visual activity is the way all babies begin to show their innate curiosity, a quality of great importance and one that should be nourished consistently throughout the first years of life.

APPARENT INTERESTS OF THE PHASE I INFANT

A rattle is probably the most common toy purchase for a newborn baby. Unfortunately, very young infants have no interest whatsoever in rattles. Nor do they pay any attention to stuffed animals—or to baseball gloves. During the first weeks of life babies are not interested in *any* aspect of the external environment. If you manage to get a Phase I baby to grasp a rattle, he will neither look at it nor transfer it to his other hand. After a few seconds he will drop it and show no sign that he has lost anything. In fact, don't be surprised if, as he moves his arms about in a mostly uncontrolled manner, he hits himself on the nose or cheek with the rattle before he loses it. So if a rattle doesn't interest a new baby, what does?

Simple Comfort

Any extensive observation of newborns leads one to the conclusion that what they seek is comfort, or at least the absence of discomfort. The newborn baby is easily and regularly discomforted. There is no way to prevent many such episodes. She is very likely to be restless and unhappy just before feedings. Normal babies often cry during and after feedings. They cry when their diapers are wet and cold, but interestingly they don't seem to mind a wet and warm diaper. Any sudden change in stimulation that brings on a startle reaction is usually followed by crying. Put simply, newborns cry a lot. When they aren't crying, they are usually sleeping. The message of the crying seems to be "Please relieve my discomfort. I need my rest." Note: the message is not "I want to explore the world." That comes later but, happily, not *much* later.

Being Handled and Moved Gently Through Space

People have known for years that one way to soothe the easily disgruntled newborn baby is to pick him up, hold him close, and rock him or walk with him. An automobile ride can work wonders for an infant when he seems inconsolable. Such experiences seem somehow to be so overpowerfully comforting or pleasurable to the Phase I infant that these activities can at least temporarily mask discomfort from many sources.

Sucking

As the Phase I child develops, she will have an increased capacity to get her fist to her mouth and keep it there. Whenever her fist or any similar object is at her mouth while she is awake, the baby is likely to suck. If you are patient you can get your baby to suck on a pacifier, especially in times of moderate distress. (A raging baby seems less interested and less able to suck a pacifier). Since sucking her hand is a very common activity in an infant of this age, we must assume it is very satisfying. In fact, at least throughout the first eight or nine months of life, all babies are very likely to put everything they can into their mouths and either gum it or bite down on it for a while. (This habit can be hazardous to a nursing mother, especially once her child acquires some teeth).

Looking

Toward the end of his first month of life, your baby will occasionally reveal some interest in looking at his environment. That interest will usually be brief and principally oriented toward the area one or two feet from his eyes. His incompletely developed vision will limit the show of interest. Nevertheless, curiosity, as indicated by visual exploration, will have made its appearance.

Three sights will absorb the baby's budding visual interest: a mirror placed against the side of the crib at head level; a properly designed and located mobile featuring the top half of a face; and the general scene confronting him, viewed from an infant seat or when he is on his back. More details on providing what's needed will follow.

Learning Developments During Phase I

During the first weeks of life, learning consists primarily of a stabilization of the unsteady, somewhat fragile pieces of behavior present at birth. These pieces of behavior were cited earlier in this chapter. For example, you will find that during the first weeks of life your baby becomes more skillful at finding and sucking the nipple, bringing her fist to her mouth and holding it there, and locating and tracking a slowly moving nearby object. In essence, the modest collection of simple reflexlike acts present at birth undergoes a gradual finishing process during the next six weeks.

Though Phase I is not characterized by dramatic learning, some discussion of the major areas of development may be useful, partly to indicate what a baby should *not* be expected to do.

Intelligence

Students of human development generally agree that babies do not begin life with any extensive intelligence and do not acquire any for several months at least. Definitions of intelligence vary widely, and judgments about when babies first reveal any such capacity will depend on the particular definition one chooses to use. One common definition of the earliest kind of intelligent behavior focuses on a simple problem-solving behavior. According to this view, well expressed by J. McVicker Hunt of the University of Illinois, the first sign of intelligence is evidenced when the baby intentionally pushes aside obstacles in order to get at desired objects. Such behavior is not often seen before a baby is six months old. Hunt's interest in this kind of behavior came from his studies of Piaget's research, which identified the aforementioned behavior as the first "means-end," or intentional, act of babies.

Most adults think of intelligence as involving the perception and manipulation of ideas in the mind. Alfred Binet, the father of intelligence testing, defined the core of intelligence as good judgment. Good judgment presupposes the comparison of options. As far as anyone can tell, that form of intelligence does not make its appearance in any substantial form until late in the second year of life. There is little reason to think that Phase I babies do very much thinking, in the ordinary sense of the term. Throughout the first eighteen months of life, most of whatever intelligence a baby possesses is revealed in a trial-and-error style of problem-solving that features hand-eye behavior. In other words, you can witness problem-solving in the behavior of your baby between six and twenty-two months of age.

The initial collection of reflexlike behavior patterns that newborns show is not, however, irrelevant to intelligence. According to Piaget, it is from these simple isolated acts, like grasping and glancing, that mature intelligence develops.

Emotionality

The Phase I infant has few mood states. Her favorite condition, day and night, is sleep. When awake, she will present one of several emotional-behavior sets: groggy, sober, inactive, and quiet; or alert, sober, inactive, and quiet; or alert, sober, and active with an occasional noise or two; or alert, active, and in mild distress, with occasional squalls; or obviously very unhappy (active and raging). Throughout the first year of life, babies shift moods with surprising speed.

Motor and Sensory Skills

During Phase I an infant's motor abilities increase noticeably. By four months of age he will be routinely holding his head in an upright position for many minutes at a time, and even at six weeks of age his head control will be noticeably better than at birth. He should then be able to hold his head just clear of the surface he is lying on for a few seconds at a time. It will be obvious, however, that the Phase I baby much prefers lying on his stomach or back over any other position.

Similarly, the newborn's initial tendency to turn her head and grasp with her mouth an object touching her at or near her lips will be more regular and efficient by six weeks. Some progress, too, will be made in tracking slowly moving objects with her eyes. To test for this ability, hold a large (more than five inches in diameter) brightly colored object about a foot from the baby's eyes, shake it to get her attention, and move it rather slowly to one side. You may have to recapture her attention several times. The difference in performance between the newborn and the six-week-old in this activity is ordinarily substantial.

Another easily observed improvement in motor ability is the increase in facility at getting the fist to the mouth and keeping it there. The newborn seems to be only partially in control of the movements of her arms and hands. By six weeks of age, however, she manages much more often to hold her fist at her mouth. Her purpose, of course, is to have something to suck. By six weeks of age some babies get so skillful at hand-to-mouth behavior that they can pacify themselves. Don't count on such good fortune, however.

The surprising strength of grasp of the newborn is well known. Especially when alert, the newborn usually has about two pounds of holding power in each hand. This automatic "holding on" persists throughout the first six weeks and gradually disappears shortly thereafter. Perhaps the earlier description of the usefulness of this behavior in fetal kangaroos helps to explain its presence.

An accompaniment to the act of holding on by the newborn is the typical fisted position of the fingers. It appears that the Phase I baby has no control over this situation, which prevents tactile exploration during the first six weeks of life. By three months of age this restriction disappears, as does the tendency to grasp with the toes as well as with the fingers.

Sociability

Newborns are not sociable in any ordinary sense of the term. However, two simple signs of sociability do emerge routinely during the first six weeks of life. The first is a tendency, which may begin as early as the first week, for the baby to look toward the eyes of the person holding her. The second is the aforementioned appearance of the first modest "smiles" while doing so. These behavior patterns have a mechanical, almost impersonal quality to them. They are rare during Phase I.

Language

The Phase I infant is far too young to understand words and won't be able to do so for another six months or so. However, he is not deaf. Although his hearing is not quite as acute as that of normal young adults, he can discriminate between an impressive range of sounds, even during the first weeks of life. As I have already remarked, loud noises of all kinds—particularly when he is resting in deep sleep—are likely to startle him. This special sensitivity is most pronounced in the weeks after birth, and startling may be followed by a good deal of crying. A baby who does not startle readily under those conditions may have a congenital hearing loss and should be seen by a pediatric audiologist fairly promptly.

Phase I babies make noises. They not only cry and shriek but may also produce simple sounds when not in distress, although they show little interest in listening to any sounds in the first weeks of life. By three or four months of age, they will be babbling during play.

RECOMMENDED CHILD-REARING PRACTICES: PHASE I

Child-rearing practices in Phase I should be guided by the goals described in Chapter 1, keeping in mind the infant's specific skills and interests. It is also important to remember what an infant cannot do and is not interested in.

Giving the Infant a Feeling of Being Loved and Cared For

You can begin to give your baby a sense of being loved and cared for in the first postnatal weeks by doing your best to relieve her inevitable frequent bouts of discomfort. I recommend you handle your new infant frequently and that you *respond promptly to her cries as often as you can.* You should get into the habit of checking to see whether there is any obvious reason for the distress, but do not be surprised if you cannot always find one. Take care to look for underlying causes of distress routinely and check with a medical professional if the symptoms are persistent or severe.

Giving your baby a feeling of being loved and cared for is by far the single most important goal of the first years of life. Few students of human development would dispute that statement.

How to Comfort a Phase I Baby

It usually takes first-time parents three months or so to become really good at this job, so try not to despair if you have trouble during the first weeks. That's normal. There are only a few typical causes of discomfort in this early stage, and they are all physical rather than psychological, as far as I can tell. The baby may be unhappy because she is hungry, sleepy, cold, or gassy, because her diaper is wet and cold, or because she's sick. She may also be uncomfortable for other reasons that no one can identify. If that happens often, we say the baby is "colicky."

If you have fed your baby recently and you think she had a good feeding, clearly the problem is likely to lie elsewhere, although at times the baby may still be hungry. If it has been over two hours since the last feeding, hunger is a good bet, because a newborn's stomach empties out in slightly less than three hours.

If the problem is not hunger, and if she has been fed recently, the problem may be gas. Try burping her. If that doesn't work, check her diaper. Of course, these recommendations all assume that the baby is not sick. If she is, you should consult your medical person.

You should move through these procedures fairly rapidly. If none of them works, distraction (of the baby, not you) is your next step. Fortunately, Phase I babies are usually easily distracted and comforted in several ways.

Perhaps the most common method of distracting and thereby comforting a very young infant is through the use of a pacifier. Throughout the first six months of life the urge to suck vigorously is so strong in most babies that sucking a pacifier or a fist or finger (his own, or yours in a pinch) will often calm an uncomfortable infant. Having discussed pacifier use with pediatric dentists and found absolutely no objections, and having seen the benefits, I strongly support the practice. Some parents can't stand the sight of a pacifier in their baby's mouth. Such people will have to make do with one less option. By the way, although there are exceptions, the typical baby will give up pacifier use spontaneously toward the end of his first year.

Introducing a pacifier can sometimes baffle new parents. You shouldn't wait until the baby is frantic. He may not even notice it under such circumstances. If your baby is raging and doesn't seem to notice the pacifier you are trying to get him to suck, try the "elevator move."

THE ELEVATOR MOVE

The "elevator move," a tactic popularized by my wife, Janet Hodgson-White, works like this: Hold the baby firmly at your chest, being careful to support her head, and jounce her gently and repeatedly by bending your knees and lowering her a few inches, then stopping abruptly. Try to duplicate the effect of an elevator stopping a bit too quickly. This experience will almost always calm an unhappy baby enough so that she will notice the pacifier, grasp it, and suck it.

Many kinds of distress can be relieved by gentle handling and rocking. A particularly useful item during this stage is a rocking chair or a rocking cradle. Such old standbys will not only soothe a cranky newborn but will offer you many pleasant moments as well. Rocking a baby is an age-old comforting tactic that often works. A battery-operated swing can also be very helpful during the first three to four months.

More exotic tactics sometimes work. The sound of a vacuum cleaner operating nearby is one. Running water is another. Gadgets that feature the recorded sounds of the womb may work. Loud static from a radio is worth trying. Placing your baby on top of an operating clothes dryer (with you close by, of course) is yet another option. Many parents have resorted to an automobile ride as a last resort. If you want to save effort and gasoline, for under

$100 you can purchase a device that can be fastened to the underside of the mattress and which will shake the bed gently to simulate the sensations of a car ride. It includes an audiocassette of the sounds heard during a ride in a car.

Armed with all of this information, you are likely to be able to comfort your baby effectively most of the time. You are not likely, however, to have 100 percent success. At times—I hope not often—you may have to let your baby "cry it out." If you resolve never to let her cry it out, you may wear yourself out, to no one's benefit.

Helping the Infant Develop Specific Skills

I don't think it makes much sense to try to encourage the development of abilities during the first few weeks of a baby's life. Babies are just not ready yet. What they appear to want above all else in the early postnatal period is rest and comfort.

A BASIC PRINCIPLE OF EFFECTIVE CHILD-REARING

Virtually all of the important specific skills that can develop during the first seven or eight months of life will develop well, provided that the baby is surrounded by love and adequate care. Good eyesight, growing mastery of the body, and the ability to reach accurately for nearby objects are so important that we have evolved in such a way that only severe deprivation will prevent adequate development in these vital areas. Yet I still recommend that you provide your baby with certain kinds of toys and other objects during the early months. Why? While I cannot prove it, I am thoroughly convinced that a baby whose environment contains options for activities that relate well to his rapidly evolving interests and abilities is more likely to enjoy life and become increasingly enthusiastic about new learning than he otherwise would. Because of that strongly held view, this book will be as specific as I can make it about what babies are engaged by and enjoy as they move through these fascinating and formative early years.

Placing a baby on her stomach several times each day, unless she won't tolerate the position, will elicit head-rearing. If the infant is always on her back, she cannot practice this behavior. (Parenthetically, it should be noted that some medical practitioners advise against routinely placing a baby on her back, especially for sleeping, for fear that spitting up may cause choking.)

Since the new baby is mostly a sleepy individual and since his visual powers are limited, providing interesting things to look at is probably of limited use at this time, although it certainly won't hurt.

When he is being held, he is presumably exercising various bodily responses to his changed position. Beyond these simple fragmentary notions, however, I do not see much point in being concerned with specific skill development in the first few weeks of life. Gradually, toward the end of his first month he will begin to show more interest in the world around him. We have found that many three- and four-week-old babies will look at suitably designed mobiles. Since very few good ones are commercially available,★ you may prefer to make your own.

How to Make a Mobile for a Three- to Nine-Week-Old Infant

A mobile should be placed where the infant tends to look. Typically, a baby of this age living on her back will look to her far right 80 to 90 percent of the time, and to her far left for the remainder. About 10 percent of all babies will favor their left side. (Whether or not this early preference is predictive of later handedness is not yet known.) A mobile for a baby this age should therefore not be placed directly over the baby's midline but rather off to her far right or far left or, if you choose, on both sides.

Place it at a distance the infant is comfortable with. At this stage of development, three to nine weeks, most babies avoid looking at objects closer than five inches and pay little attention to anything farther than eighteen inches from their eyes. I would recommend a distance of between ten and twelve inches.

A mobile should be designed with a view toward what the baby sees while living on his back in the crib. Most commercially available mobiles are designed to look attractive to an adult consumer looking for a gift rather than to a baby lying in a crib. Since babies are especially interested in looking at that area of the human face that lies between the tip of the nose and the top of the head, the mobile should feature such shapes. It should also be drawn with bold contrasting colors, since such young infants pay more attention to them than to pastels and other subtle color differences. The target should face the baby rather than the adult standing over the crib. One typical example can be seen on page 58.

With very little effort, you can make good mobiles at home, particu-

---

★ The Stimobile, featuring small black-and-white circular targets (faces, checkerboard, and bull's-eye patterns), has become popular recently. Its high contrast is a plus, but the individual targets are too small, and the placement—above the baby—is not the best. Furthermore, I am not happy with the company's marketing approach, which would have you believe that there is something especially "educational" about their toys. The checkerboard and bull's-eye targets were chosen because they were featured in the work of Robert Fantz of Case Western Reserve University back in the 1950s, but Fantz's work did not indicate that there was anything educational about such patterns. Face targets, on the other hand, are obviously more relevant to the interests of the newborn human. In any event, for about fifteen cents, and in about fifteen minutes, you can make a better mobile.

larly since the Phase I infant for whom they are designed will not try to reach for them. For this reason, you need not worry about a strong support for a first mobile. Any method by which you can suspend facelike patterns into the proper locations will do just fine. You can use simple sheet cardboard as the basic material on which to paint or paste patterns. By the way, though an infant of this age cannot perceive fine detail, it will do no harm to incorporate some in your design. So feel free to express your artistic impulses.

Although I recommend the use of mobiles, don't look for any striking gains in development from the use of such devices. Nevertheless, since a baby's earliest interest in the outside world involves visual examination of the nearby surroundings, you might as well begin the important basic task of designing the world of your baby so that it relates effectively to her current interests. Very few objects meet those requirements during Phase I except for the face of whoever feeds the baby, a mirror, and a suitably designed mobile.

Another useful device for this purpose is a mirror fastened to the side of the crib. Use a good-quality unbreakable mirror five or six inches in diameter. Fasten it to the crib rails so that when she looks far right or left she will be looking at herself. The mirror should not be vertical but rather tilted in at the top some 10 degrees or so in order for the baby to look straight at her face. Fisher-Price and Mattel both sell mirrors with the angle built into them. (Their designers have read earlier editions of this book.)

Beyond trying to hold his head up off the surface he is lying on, and staring at face patterns, there are no other specific skills to be encouraged in Phase I. Some people advocate other ideas, but I know of no substantial basis for any of them.

An Important Note on Language Development

Although it may not seem entirely natural to you, it is unquestionably a good idea to begin "talking" to your baby right from the beginning of Phase I. If you are the kind of person who spontaneously talks a lot to your baby from the beginning, so much the better. We have found in our studies, however, that many parents are not inclined to talk to their infants very much, not only in the first weeks of life, but throughout the first year and a half, at which time most babies begin to use words regularly. The best language teaching occurs when the talking habit is well established by the time the baby first becomes capable of understanding the meaning of words. This happens by about six months of age.

Try to develop the habit of identifying and talking about what your baby is attending to at the moment. For their first two years of life, babies are predominantly oriented toward the here and now. They are simply not capable of understanding references to objects they are not looking at or events in the past or future. Talking about a trip you are going to take in a week or two, for example, is much less likely to register with an infant than are comments about your face or the baby's hand, if that is what she is looking at.

The most effective talking, then, consists of trying to identify what your baby is attending to at that moment and then talking in simple, normal language about that topic. Diaper-changing, bathing, and playing lend themselves nicely to this type of teaching.

Encouraging Interest in the Outside World

Until the baby reaches the next phase of development, there is no point in trying to encourage curiosity. The baby's interest in exploration will really blossom in the next phase. You can, of course, provide a good mobile, a mirror, and, by shifting your baby's location several times a day, perhaps an occasional change of scenery, but that's about it. You should also know that an unhappy baby, when calmed by sucking on a pacifier, is likely to show some interest in looking around. A screaming baby will not.

Sleep

Lack of sleep is a classic source of trouble for parents, especially during the first year of life. In our experience, most bottle-fed babies settle into a civilized sleep pattern by the end of the sixth month of life. This pattern consists of going to sleep between seven and eight in the evening and sleeping through for about ten hours. In addition, the baby will usually take two naps during the day, totaling about three hours. Parents of breast-fed babies do not reach this promised land until about two months later.

Those are the most common patterns but the variations are numerous. Some lucky parents are out of the woods by the time their baby is four months old while others, sadly, do not reach that point until eight months or even later. Unfortunately, it is very common for parents to have a great deal of trouble with this issue throughout the first two years of their baby's life. Books and seminars on the subject are common because of the widespread existence of stress resulting from a lack of sleep. We have pretty good success with our recommendations. They will be dealt with in detail in succeeding chapters.

You will lose a lot of sleep during Phase I. Because of your baby's small stomach, she can only take in, at most, a three-hour supply of food. Although there are exceptions, you have to be prepared during the first ten weeks of your baby's life for no more than three hours of sleep at a stretch at night.

It is very important that you do the best you can to comfort your baby whenever she wakes and cries throughout this and the next two phases. Don't let anyone convince you that comforting your infant will "spoil" her. That simply is impossible until the intentional cry comes in at about six months of age.

CHILD-REARING PRACTICES NOT RECOMMENDED

In addition to recommended child-rearing practices, I believe some comment on inadvisable practices is necessary to counteract existing misinformation about child-rearing.

Providing an Infant with an Elaborately "Enriched" Environment

If someone urges you to stimulate all your newborn infant's senses by purchasing and using a set of "educational" materials, be skeptical. The concept of an enriched environment, which has come into vogue in recent years, has merit, but only when used with care. Some commercial firms and some child development personnel have misused the concept.

The Phase I infant is a poor candidate for an enriched environment, especially during the first half of the period (the first three weeks of life), when he is rarely alert. It is not very likely that enrichment benefits a sleeping infant. Then again, when a Phase I baby is alert, his limited sensory capacities, combined with primitive intellectual status, severely restrict learning. In short, it is too soon to be seriously concerned with extensive enrichment of the environment.

Letting a Baby "Cry It Out"

Infants brought up in institutions cry less and less as their first year of life proceeds. They seem to learn, at some primitive level, that crying usually produces nothing but fatigue. Home-reared infants whose cries are ordinarily responded to quickly do continue to cry more than institutionally reared infants, but not as much as home-reared babies whose cries are responded to inconsistently. According to research by M. Ainsworth at Johns Hopkins University, regular prompt response to an infant's crying leads to a better quality of attachment between caretaker and baby and is to be preferred to either deliberate or inadvertent ignoring of crying. It is important to note that occasionally you will not be able to make a Phase I baby comfortable. Some "crying it out" will have to happen, but it should not be a regular practice.

Neglecting to Handle Your Infant for Fear of Harming or Overstimulating Her

A substantial amount of evidence exists to indicate that newborns are beautifully designed to be handled, caressed, and moved gently through space. The parts of the nervous system that are activated by handling are much better developed at birth than those involving the mind, the eyes, and the ears. In addition, handling a baby is often very comforting to an unhappy infant.

As for overstimulation from gentle handling, as far as I can tell, there need be little concern at this age that this will occur. If for some strange reason someone should insist on trying to keep a groggy infant from falling into a deep sleep, "overstimulation" might be an appropriate label, but such behavior seems unlikely.

RECOMMENDED MATERIALS FOR PHASE I BABIES

You should obtain the following materials for use during your baby's first six weeks of life.

PACIFIERS
Finding the right pacifier is a matter of trial and error. Of course you should buy only well-made brands. One of the most popular currently is the Nuk, which comes in different sizes. Other brands have different shapes. Pacifiers are inexpensive. Try three or four kinds to find the one your baby prefers, and then buy at least a half dozen of them. It is also a good idea to buy a few Velcro pacifier straps with clips that can be fastened at one end to the pacifier and at the other end to the baby's clothing. Few creatures get as panicky as a new parent trying to cope with a screaming baby but unable to find a pacifier.

MOBILES
Create two or three for the crib and the changing table. You needn't buy one. Your homemade version will probably be better.

A MIRROR
Obtain one or more of the four- to six-inch mirrors described above.
That's all you need for now. The list will lengthen later.

BEHAVIORS THAT SIGNAL THE ONSET OF PHASE II

Look for several rather dramatic changes as your infant passes from Phase I to Phase II. Keep in mind, however, that these will not occur overnight, nor will they appear precisely at a specific age. Development is a gradual process, and the rate varies widely among babies, although less so in the first months of life than later.

Reliable Social Smiling

Reliable social smiling cannot be expected at any precise age. Nevertheless, most home-reared babies do begin to smile regularly at the sight of nearby faces during their third month, and you may begin to see signs of such behavior as early as six or seven weeks of age. You may also see such babies smiling at their own hands and other familiar objects at about this time. What does that suggest about the social meaning of the first smiles? More about that subject later.

Hand Regard

Though your baby's fist will be in his line of sight increasingly often during the second month of life, you can expect him to stare right through it as it moves on by. He is not blind; he is just not yet very skillful at looking at nearby objects. By the third month of life, however, the infant's visual abilities will have developed to the point where he can see a fairly clear single three-dimensional image of his own hand, particularly if it is five to nine inches from his eyes. From that time forward, he will begin to spend increasingly longer periods of time studying his hands and their movements. If you use a floor gym or a crib gym, you may first notice your baby watching his hand as he touches and explores objects. Signs of such activity may be present as early as seven or eight weeks of age, but often they do not appear until a few weeks later. The first instances of hand regard may be in the form of brief double takes. After the hand has passed by where he is looking, the baby may abruptly look after it. Gradually, in the weeks that follow, the looking will become more sustained and the baby will seem to make regular attempts to keep the hand within view.

A Substantial Increase in Wakefulness

Soon after the sixth week, and especially as hand-eye activity becomes common, you are likely to observe a rather sharp increase in the number of hours each day a baby spends awake and alert. From about five minutes an hour at one month of age, the average infant of two months of age will move to fifteen to twenty minutes of wakefulness an hour during the daylight hours. Again I must remind you that babies vary greatly in the pace of their development. Suffice it to say that most two- or three-month-old infants seem to be visually alert very often during the day, whereas Phase I infants are characteristically sleepy beings. At the same time, your baby will begin to sleep for correspondingly longer periods during the night.

3

PHASE II: SIX TO FOURTEEN WEEKS

GENERAL REMARKS

Unlike the newborn infant, the Phase II infant appears to have a genuine interest in what is going on around her. This interest is most strikingly apparent in longer and longer periods of wakefulness. This is also the stage when social responsiveness really begins to surface. Thank goodness it is also the stage when sleeping through the night usually begins.

One of the most dramatic landmarks of this second phase is the appearance of genuine and frequent social smiling. Another highlight of Phase II is the infant's visual discovery of her own hand, which will be followed by many hours of staring at the hand, either by itself or while she feels for or strikes at nearby objects, and, as the weeks go by, at her fingers as they move overhead. These two dramatic events, social smiling and studying her hands and their examination of nearby objects, appear against the back-

ground of increased wakefulness and seem together to represent the beginning of serious interest in exploration.

Learning during Phase II, however, will be modest in total amount and
type because at this age babies still have very limited skills, along with significant obstacles to cope with. After all, this baby cannot move about in any
real way, and for the most part she has poor control of her head, which is
still disproportionately large. Indeed, even her eyesight, which is so necessary for learning, is only partly developed throughout the major part of this
particular phase. Nevertheless, adaptation to and mastery of the environment
has begun.

GENERAL BEHAVIOR DURING PHASE II

Body and Head Control

Although the Phase II baby is very limited in many ways, this special
period of life is a time of perhaps the most rapid rate of development you
will see during the first years of life. The Phase II baby cannot yet turn over,
reach for objects, or even turn her torso very much from side to side, yet her
behavior is much more coordinated than it was in Phase I, and very different in many ways.

In the six-week-old, the position of the arms is dictated by the head
position. To demonstrate this, if you gently turn your baby's head from one
side to the other you will find that her arms will shift their position ac-
cordingly. The baby has no control over this linkage during Phase I and
early in Phase II.

Between six and fourteen weeks, your baby's favorite resting posture
shifts gradually from the asymmetrical side orientation (with his head resting on his cheek) to a position where his cheek will be held off the surface
of the crib mattress, at first just a few degrees, then gradually more, and then,
by his fourth month, to the point where he is capable of holding his head at
the midline for long periods of time.

In your fourteen-week-old, head position no longer determines the
position of the arms. Furthermore, each arm and hand seems to be able to
act more or less independently of the other. Unlike the child at six weeks of
age, when the child of fourteen weeks comes to favor the midline symmet-
rical orientation, she is not restricted to this preferred position. Whereas the
six-week-old has very little fine control over his head movements, the
fourteen-week-old, when lying on his back, can move his head freely
throughout the full 180-degree range. If you look at a fourteen-week-old

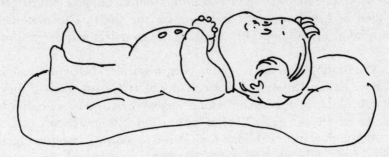

Midline position of a late Phase II baby

baby lying on her back, you will very often find her with her head in the midline position, with both arms and legs flexed, and with her legs held slightly off the crib surface.

Sociability

Another rather dramatic change occurs in the area of sociability. The six-week-old baby is a pretty sober individual. Except for an occasional fleeting smile, at times not oriented toward a human face or voice, the baby generally does little smiling. Not so the fourteen-week-old. These babies usually smile a lot, and what a wonderful gift this is to parents. There will frequently be exceptions to these general statements, of course, and you need not be alarmed if your child is not regularly euphoric. By and large, however, this is the time when children seem to be chronically high. Easy and frequent social smiling seems to begin at between eight and ten weeks of age, along with a very strong interest in looking at the human face, particularly, as noted earlier, that area between the tip of the nose and the top of the head.

Motor Behavior

A more subtle but also important change your baby will show as he moves through Phase II is in the quality of his motor behavior. The six-week-old baby is in many ways like a small machine. If you gently turn his head from one side to the other, his hands and legs will slavishly follow. If you touch his lip lightly with your finger, particularly when he is alert, you will find that he turns his head abruptly toward the stimulating finger to grasp and suck it. This rooting behavior is as mechanical as the knee jerk elicited by your pediatrician. By fourteen weeks of age, however, a touch of your baby's lip will be followed not by an abrupt rooting response but by a pause and then perhaps a cautious searching for the finger. The machinelike, automatic quality is gone. This change seems to reflect neurological maturation.

The rooting response is not the only mechanical behavior Phase I babies show. Earlier I remarked that certain objects—particularly if they are large and colored in intense contrasting hues—when held over a resting baby would be effective in getting her to look at and to follow them.

Although getting a child to look at and to follow a target in Phase I is usually a fairly difficult chore, babies in the six- to ten-week age range follow that same kind of target with great skill and impressive reliability. Again, though, the performance has a machinelike quality. I have seen early Phase II babies follow a seven-inch bright red circle overhead back and forth several dozen times in a row. It seems clear that they really do not have control over their own behavior at that stage of development. At six weeks of age if a large target is held twelve to eighteen inches from the child and slightly off to the side of the line of sight, and then shaken lightly, it will elicit his attention. If the target is then moved slowly, the child will often track it.

By the time he gets to be fourteen weeks of age, however, your baby will be perfectly capable of—and interested in—tracking small irregularly shaped multicolored objects. At this age you will notice that his tracking behavior no longer seems as obligatory, or automatic, as it was earlier. This shift in style of looking has to do with the dramatic improvements in vision skills that happen during this particular phase.

Another area in which machinelike automatic responding can be seen has been studied in research laboratories. A three-inch black felt disk, started at thirty-six inches away from the baby's eyes and then slowly brought closer, will attract a six- to eight-week-old baby's attention, under ideal conditions, as it reaches about eighteen inches from her eyes. The baby seems to be obliged to watch this target until it comes as close as eight to ten inches, at which point she stops looking. Gradually over the next few weeks, the range over which a baby will maintain focus on the same target extends to its maximum, which may be from twenty-four to thirty inches all the way down to four inches. As the baby approaches fourteen weeks of age, her behavior changes. Instead of what looks like obligatory staring, you will now usually see a brief glance at the target when it is about two feet away, and then a total lack of interest.

These and other types of behavior have convinced students of early human development that the two-month-old baby does not actively seek contact with the environment but rather seems to be forced to respond to stimulation. In contrast, the baby of three and a half months (the end of Phase

II) no longer seems "stimulus-bound." She seems to be much more in control of her own behavior.

Increasing Strength

Another rather dramatic change in babies during Phase II is the shift from weakness to strength. Although the six-week-old baby is considerably stronger than the newborn, he is still a relatively weak creature. To prove this, all you have to do is put him on his stomach and note that he can usually manage to lift his head only a few inches off the surface on which he is lying. By fourteen weeks, however, that same baby can ordinarily lift and hold his head up so that it is vertical to the floor. Furthermore, he will be able to continue to hold it up and look around for ten to twenty seconds or even longer.

A baby's arms and legs are also considerably stronger at fourteen weeks than they were earlier. You will find that at this stage your baby takes great delight in exercising his newly acquired muscles, especially when you stand him on your thighs. Phase II muscle development is accompanied by a marked weight increase resulting in a rounder-looking, sturdier infant.

Visual Development

Still another dramatic change in Phase II involves vision, an area at the heart of the learning process. The Phase I infant has essentially no flexibility in his visual focusing system. An infant at this stage of development can focus clearly on a target only within a very restricted range. For most Phase I babies, seven to nine inches from the eyes is the ideal focusing range. Clarity of vision is, however, limited even in that optimal focusing range by other immaturities in the vision system.

By the end of Phase I, however, most babies are able to focus clearly at any distance between six and twelve inches and to perceive fine details fairly well. During Phase II the full development of flexibility of the focusing system takes place in most babies. The fourteen-week-old baby can adjust the focus of his eyes for objects at all distances.

Another major visual ability is also undergoing its principal development during Phase II. This is the convergence of the eyes that allows us to see a single three-dimensional object when we are looking at small targets less than one meter (39.37 inches) away. The capacity to turn both eyes in as a target approaches the face is not present in the newborn and does not appear until the child approaches ten weeks of age, at which time it seems to come into the baby's repertoire rather abruptly. A child under two months of age, when looking at an object five to seven inches away, not only has inadequate focusing ability but also cannot keep both eyes on the target. He sees double. A baby of three and one half months, on the other hand, has near mature visual capacities.

Observe the way your baby looks at small, detailed nearby objects during the first three and one half months. You will find that if he attends to such objects at all before he is seven or eight weeks of age, he is likely to give them no more than a brief glance. In contrast, thereafter he will be much more inclined to look at small nearby objects, and as he looks at them, you will find that he is examining their features with skill and speed. He has become a sophisticated visual creature.

Hand Position and Hand Regard

Another development of consequence, and one that is easily observable, has to do with the baby's hands. The six-week-old baby generally rests with her hands in a fisted position, and she does not actually look at the hand toward which her head is turned. Sometime during Phase II, however, she will start to stare at her hand, either by itself or as she uses it to feel nearby objects. By three months of age she may be gazing at her hands for five to ten minutes at a time and repeatedly throughout the day. This new habit of prolonged hand and finger regard appears at about the time the child acquires the capacity to focus clearly on and perceive a single three-dimensional image of a nearby object.

Another interesting development accompanies the onset of the hand-eye connection. Sometime during Phase II the fisted posture of your baby's hands will gradually be replaced by fingers held loosely clenched and occasionally totally unflexed. What this does, most conveniently, is to provide the baby with an even more interesting visual spectacle, because the four fingers and thumb are much more variable and interesting to look at than the fist. Therefore, during the third month of life you will see a good many finger movements accompanied by fascinated staring.

An additional emerging universal behavior of normal infants at the end of Phase II is what we call "hands to the midline and clasped." The six-week-old baby lying in the tonic neck reflex position was unable to put his hands together except on rare occasions, but as he gets to be three months of age or so, you should be on the watch for the tendency when lying on his back for your baby to bring both of his hands over his chest, where they will begin to explore each other. This behavior will soon be followed by the visual study of what must be a fascinating set of mutual tactile sensations.

In the weeks to follow, during the day, you can expect to see your child repeatedly bringing his hands to the midline where they touch and feel each other. He will raise them together to his mouth for gumming and then move them away and look at them intently while they simply clasp each other or touch each other in varied ways.

Leg Position

Another in the long list of striking changes in Phase II involves leg position. Sometime during the fourth month—usually by the end of Phase II— your baby's legs will have reached such a degree of strength and musculature that he can very often hold them an inch or two above the surface of the crib. Furthermore, they seemed primed to thrust out, and if any resistant surface happens to be available that provides pressure to the soles of his feet, those flexed legs will push against the surface powerfully and repeatedly. Evidence of increased strength in the legs and the tendency to extend them when pressure is applied to the soles of the feet can also be seen in the surprising ability of the baby by the end of Phase II to support much of his own weight when you hold him upright with his feet against your thighs or some other firm surface.

Curiosity

While you could characterize the younger Phase I baby as a seeker of peace and quiet and the older Phase I baby as a beginning "looker," the Phase II baby is a very different kind of person. Increasingly, between six and fourteen weeks of age, your baby's hands will begin to play a prominent role in her explorations. This interest in her hands will be a central feature in your baby's daily life from about two months of age on through to at least two years of age and should not be underestimated. We have found that if you present a small, attractive object such as a rattle five or six inches from a child's eyes and off to her right when she is eight to ten weeks of age, she will look at the target, and in many cases her right fist will abruptly rise, approach the target, and strike it. This "batting" or "swiping" behavior is likely to appear a week or two after the first episodes of sustained hand regard. From here on, babies are no longer content to just look. They want to use their hands as well as their eyes as they explore. Bear in mind, however, that in spite of their curiosity, Phase II babies are extremely limited in their explorations by their physical immaturity. The world has to be brought to them. Imagine for a moment that you are in a fascinating environment, have a lively curiosity, but are unable to move about to learn more about the features of your surroundings. By doing so, you may, to some extent, come to understand the situation of a normal three-month-old baby.

The three-month-old shows her curiosity in many ways. You will see that she is very much interested in studying your face and also her own hands, either by themselves or when they are exploring objects. She will also show you that she is interested in feeling clothing and crib sheets and in bringing objects to her mouth. One consequence of this desire to get her hands on everything within reach is that mobiles for the Phase II baby should not be suspended from the same sort of flimsy support devices that were perfectly adequate for the child under six or seven weeks of age. In Phase II the baby is ready for a crib gym or floor gym, and it must be sturdy enough to stand up to extensive abuse.

Coordination of Behavior

The newborn baby comes equipped with a small number of reflexlike behaviors that function separately from each other. For example, the newborn will hold on to a rattle placed in the palm of his hand but he won't look at it. The Phase II baby, on the other hand, is considerably more mature in this regard. A ten-week-old may take a swipe at an object placed within his reach. A slightly older child, twelve to fourteen weeks of age, is likely to show other hand and arm behaviors at the sight of a nearby object. When an object is placed in his hand, particularly after ten weeks of age, he is very likely to look at it and bring it to his mouth to be gummed. According to Piaget, these combinations of activities that occur in response to the presentation of a small object show that several action systems—grasping, looking, and sucking—are to some extent now coordinated.

Another interesting indicator of the coordination of behaviors will surface when the baby is twelve to fourteen weeks of age. When shown a small, reachable object, the fourteen-week-old baby commonly responds by bringing both hands over her lower chest and clasping them. In addition, an object placed in either of the baby's hands at this age will often be incorporated into the hands-to-midline pattern. The other hand will join the one holding the object and engage in some fingering of the target or the object. This fingering is a form of tactile exploration and again illustrates how an object being grasped has become something to be examined by the other hand as well as by the eyes and the mouth.

THE APPARENT INTERESTS OF PHASE II

Exploration

If there is one label that characterizes a baby's major interest during Phase II, it would have to be "exploration." Unlike the sleepy Phase I baby, the Phase II baby, particularly from the middle of this period on, impresses the observer with the brightness of his eyes and with his increasing alertness and responsiveness. He goes about his exploration in several interesting ways.

LOOKING

Your baby at this age is first of all a looker—he is all eyes. He is particularly interested in looking at faces or pictures of faces. He is very much intrigued by small, detailed objects about five to twelve inches from his eyes, and he is attracted especially by slowly moving objects. He is still not very much interested in looking at anything across the room, but his interest in more distant objects is gradually evolving.

TOUCHING

While looking means a lot to your Phase II baby, she shows that using her hands has become a strong interest as well. Whether she is in your arms, looking up at your face, holding a small object, or looking at anything within reach, after two and one half months of age she is likely to try to use her hands to explore all surfaces and shapes.

GUMMING

A third means of exploration for your baby at this age is to put objects to his mouth. Gumming is a favorite occupation. At first the most common small object he will gum will be his own fist. As the weeks go by, he will gum and suck his fingers. As a matter of fact, he will gum just about anything that he can bring to his mouth. He does this for two apparent reasons: (1) his mouth is an exploring organ, and (2) in advance of the eruption of teeth, his gums may be tender and somewhat painful. He can often relieve this discomfort by gumming objects.

LISTENING

Toward the end of Phase II another more subtle sign of exploration and interest in the world becomes noticeable. Your baby now displays interest in listening to the sounds he can make with the saliva in his mouth. From this point onward, his interest in sounds will grow steadily.

Motor Exercise

Yet another emerging interest during Phase II is motor exercise. Your baby is considerably more active now, and her arm, leg, and neck muscles are much bigger and more powerful than they were a few weeks earlier. If you place your baby on her stomach from time to time during this period, you will find that her ability to lift her head will steadily increase from about 30 degrees off the horizontal to a full 90 degrees. This ability, combined with much more advanced visual abilities, enables the three-and-one-half-month-old baby to begin to study a much broader range of her surroundings. In any event, her tendency to practice head-rearing at this stage will be pronounced. She will also show much more arm and leg activity when awake than she did during her first postnatal weeks.

EDUCATIONAL DEVELOPMENTS DURING PHASE II

Unlike the Phase I baby who is getting used to living outside the womb, the Phase II baby is beginning to familiarize himself with his environment. In a sense, his education can be properly said to have begun. Between six and fourteen weeks of age the rate of development is dramatic. Such milestones as the release from the constraints of the tonic neck and grasp reflexes, the maturation of visual motor capacities, and the emergence of sociability all help free the Phase II baby for further learning.

Phase II also marks the beginning of the coordination of various simple action systems. Your baby is much better at bringing his hand to his mouth for sucking, and he now spends a fair amount of time watching his hands as well. When he is three months of age he will routinely bring his hand to his mouth to suck just after having spent some time staring at it. His hand has become something to be seen, moved about, brought to his mouth, and sucked. Shortly after he begins to stare steadily at his hand, he will grasp any object that you place in his hand, and then he will routinely bring it to his mouth for sucking. In this way, objects seen become objects to be sucked, and two major action systems become intertwined.

Another type of coordination also begins to occur in Phase II—a link between hearing and looking. Things heard begin to be things to look at as well as to listen to. In Phase I most nearby sounds will regularly produce at most an alerting response or some other sign of listening, but will not usually link up with his looking tendencies. While a newborn will occasionally turn toward the source of a sound, by the end of Phase II, your baby will do so frequently.

Another Sign of Learning: Quieting at Your Approach

When a newborn is crying because of discomfort, she will usually continue crying as you approach her. Only after you pick her up and try to make her feel better or get her to accept a pacifier will the crying lessen or cease. Toward the end of Phase II, however, you will probably see an interesting change in this situation. When your baby is crying but not raging, you will now find that she will occasionally stop crying when she sees or hears you approach. As time passes, this behavior will become more common. There are two possible explanations for this: the cessation in crying may be a form of anticipation, similar to the increased sucking commonly seen at about this age when she first catches sight of the bottle or the nipple; or this behavior may be the result of the distracting effect of hearing your voice or seeing you. Both reasons reflect the growth of adaptive abilities. Anticipation is clear evidence of learning, and distractibility reflects your baby's increasing awareness of her environment.

A Very Special Cycle of Experience

From birth, all babies repeatedly undergo an absolutely vital learning sequence. No matter how healthy they are, they become uncomfortable many times every day, and they show their discomfort by crying. Their cries are usually followed by the arrival of an older person who tries to make them feel better. Because of the way babies are designed, and because most of their needs are simple, comforting usually succeeds. During the first months of life babies routinely go through hundreds of such sequences. By the time the baby is well into Phase II, she has learned to associate relief from her distress with the arrival of a person who looks, feels, sounds, and smells a certain way. This type of learning by association, which goes on throughout life, is extremely important, even though it doesn't involve conscious awareness or thinking on the part of the very young infant. Repeated experiences of this sort are vital to the establishment of a solid basis for all later development.

Specialists in mental health unanimously agree that what a baby learns through these experiences plays a major indispensable role in establishing a sound emotional foundation in a new baby. At the same time, these experiences begin to build a uniquely important bond between the baby and whoever is nurturing him. This bond will develop whether the nurturing person is the baby's biological parent, an adoptive parent, or someone unrelated to the baby. By three and one half months of age there is evidence that the baby, at a primitive level, has identified or "learned" who has been his primary caregiver.

There is other evidence that a modest amount of learning is taking place during this time. For example, you can expect a Phase II baby to begin to show signs that he has learned something about feeding. When a baby of twelve to fourteen weeks of age becomes less active or stops crying when his mother appears to feed him, he is showing anticipatory behavior. Furthermore, if you watch the sucking movements of your baby, you will notice that at about the same age, in advance of feeding, a child may begin to suck more rapidly at the sight of the bottle, of the breast, or even of his mother beginning to undo her bra as she prepares for nursing. In these modest ways a child is behaving differently from the way he did in the first weeks of life.

Emotionality

By the end of Phase II most babies are smiling at everyone quickly and frequently. In fact, they have become smile machines. What the smile means about sociability and the baby's emotional state is less clear than the fact of regular smiling at a human face. It has been shown in research that with a black-and-white sketch of that part of the human face between the tip of the nose and the top of the head (see sketch), you can rather easily get most babies of about ten weeks of age to smile repeatedly. In fact, if you are very clever at designing this target, you may get them to smile more reliably in response to that target than to their mother's face! It seems that one of the universally inherited human behaviors is the tendency, from six or seven weeks on, to smile at human faces, or at things that look like them, especially when such a face is between eight and twelve inches away.

That fact, coupled with another—that most people are able to get a twelve-week-old baby to smile at them—suggests a rather interesting notion in terms of the survival of the species. It would appear that babies in these very earliest stages are designed to smile at just about anything that resembles a face. When you think about it, this behavior makes sense. Every baby has to have some guarantee of a positive response from another creature who can help ensure its survival. The smile of the typical three-month-old baby is a very powerful force in winning over an older human. Therefore,

*Phase II babies will smile at this
kind of pattern*

the question of the relationship of smiling to sociability is a bit more complicated than it might seem.

It is further complicated by the research of Piaget. He observed that his children not only smiled at any person's face at this age, but also, at times, at their own hands, at familiar toys in their crib, and even at a strand of thread that dangled overhead as they rested! From these and other indications, he concluded that a baby's first smiles were a sign of cognitive or mental growth, recognition of the familiar, rather than love, friendliness, happiness, or sociability!

As far as the relationship of the smile to the baby's true emotional state is concerned, again the picture is not as clear as it might seem on the surface. When adults smile, it is usually because they are feeling comfortable or happy or showing affection toward another person. In the case of a two-month-old, however, the most we can safely conclude is that when she is wearing a smile she is at least comfortable and, at most, experiencing a feeling of physical well-being. You will not see either laughter or high hilarity in the Phase II infant. That comes next.

The other obvious emotional state the Phase II baby shows at times is rage. But as in the case of the first smiles, the anger has nothing personal about it. At this stage of life, rage seems to be simply a response to significant physical discomfort rather than an expression of anger toward another person. Toward the end of the first year, your child will begin occasionally to express rage that is clearly directed toward you.

Studiousness

Phase II, then, is a time when only a limited number of emotional states are likely to be seen: the feeling of well-being, signified by the presence of a full smile; a feeling of neutral emotions, manifested by a sober and alert expression; feelings of gross discomfort, revealed by fussy or outraged behavior; and finally, a very interesting emotional indicator that might best be labeled "intense concern," which seems to be present when the three-month-old is staring steadily at his own hand or finger movements. We regularly see such behavior in children in Phase II. The concern expressed during this prolonged staring seems to reflect serious inquiry rather than worry.

MOTOR AND SENSORIMOTOR SKILLS

The Phase II infant accumulates an impressive collection of motor abilities in the period from six to fourteen weeks of age. Motor abilities in this phase can be discussed under two headings: those the baby brought with him at birth, which are fading out; and those which are emerging.

Inborn Motor Abilities

ROOTING

One of the inborn motor abilities is rooting ability, the skill that helps the baby find the nipple in order to suck. This kind of behavior seems to be mechanical, yet it becomes increasingly efficient in the first six weeks of life and remains efficient and mechanical in the early stages of Phase II. By the time a baby is three months of age, however, searching with his mouth is accomplished in a multi-step, deliberate manner.

VISUAL TRACKING

Another interesting behavior that bridges the first two phases of life is visual tracking. The Phase I baby has a built-in tendency to notice rather large, highly contrasting objects that move slowly from slightly off his line of sight. When the very young baby looks toward such an object, he tries to center it in his visual field. He brings the target into his line of sight, where his eyes are best suited to fine visual examination. Unfortunately for the very young baby, his eyesight is not yet developed enough for fine visual inspection, so once the object is centered in his line of sight he cannot see it clearly and he therefore quickly loses interest in it. You can usually get a baby to track an object over a couple of feet, even though he is less than six weeks of age, by repeatedly recapturing and "dragging his attention along" (by his eyes) a few inches at a time.

Like rooting behavior, visual tracking or pursuit remains a dependable behavior during Phase II. Indeed, it reaches a peak of efficiency for a few weeks at about six to eight weeks, then gradually drops out, to be replaced by what looks like a more mature type of behavior. The ten-week-old baby tracks objects very smoothly as they move slowly overhead. If you watch your baby's eyes very closely, you may notice she actually leads the target slightly, just the way an older child or a young adult does. One reason for this smoothness is that she has acquired considerably more control over her head motions; the other reason has to do with the aforementioned shift from apparently involuntary tracking of targets to a more controlled type of activity.

FINGER POSITION

Still another kind of motor development that spans Phase I and Phase II has to do with the fingers. The grasp reflex and fisted hand, both characteristic of Phase I, gradually drop out as the child moves through Phase II. By the time she nears three months of age she can put a single finger in her mouth and suck it, whereas before, she was largely limited to sucking her fist.

STARTLES

The startle response common to the Phase I baby gradually drops out during Phase II. Both spontaneous startles, most common during deep, inactive sleep, and elicited startles occur less and less frequently as the child moves through Phase II.

EMERGING PHASE II SKILLS

With the decrease in influence of his inborn motor reflexes, we find a much more able Phase II baby. You can expect, for example, that your six- to eight-week-old baby will hold his head, at best, only about 45 degrees off the horizontal and for a few minutes at a time. Subsequently, improvement will be steady, and by fourteen weeks of age he will be able to hold his head 90 degrees off the horizontal (totally upright) for several minutes at a time.

By the end of this phase, your baby will have acquired almost fully developed eyesight; adequate hearing ability, provided that he has avoided chronic respiratory distress and allergies; and greater hand and body control. He will have developed impressive arm and leg strength, which he will need in the months that follow in order to assume and maintain an upright sitting posture, to pull himself to a standing position, and ultimately to walk.

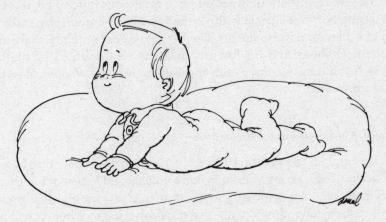

Three and one half months: head at 90-degree position

Vision Skills

Three basic vision skills undergo their major development during this phase. They are flexible focusing, convergence, and mature tracking. Flexible focusing allows a person to maintain a focused image as she looks at a target between three or four inches and 39.37 inches (one meter) from her eyes. This ability is very limited during Phase I, but reaches full maturity by the end of Phase II. "Convergence" is the turning in of the eyes to keep both eyes focused on a small target as it comes close—most conspicuously within a foot or less. Convergence is required for a three-dimensional view. Mature convergence develops rather abruptly between eight and ten weeks of age. Tracking refers to the ability to keep a target in view as it moves in various directions and at different speeds. By the end of Phase II, with the improvement of head control, most babies can track targets quite well.

Social Development

Living with and caring for a Phase I baby is usually very exciting but also exhausting. There is so much to do, and you don't get anywhere near enough sleep. Just when you may be getting down to your last ounce of reserve strength, two major changes will usually, but not always, appear. During the eight- to twelve-week period, most babies begin to sleep for stretches of five and six hours during the night, and they start to produce large numbers of quick, glorious smiles! If they have suffered from a modest level of colic, this too very often subsides dramatically at about the same time.

The smiles of a Phase II baby have enormous power. Parents—or any adult, for that matter—are invariably totally enthralled. What a survival tactic!

The fourth month of life is simply a marvelous time to be, and to be with, a baby. Not coincidentally, this is the age when photographers take pictures of babies for advertisements. The baby is not only smiling all the time, but she is chubbier and has lost any unattractiveness caused by the birth process. It is a very rare three-and-one-half-month-old who is not responsive and beautiful.

Special Relationship with Parents

Research at the Tavistock Clinic in England has shown that by fourteen weeks of age, a baby will smile more quickly and longer at her parents, if they have been her principal caretakers, than at anyone else. It is assumed that the baby would show such special responsiveness to whoever had been caring most for her, parent or not. Though the baby favors the primary caregiver, she will continue to smile readily at everyone for several more months.

That responsiveness appears to be a form of insurance, guaranteeing that any older person who spends a lot of time in the presence of a baby during the first months of life will fall in love with her. After all, at least one person has to, or the baby wouldn't survive.

Language Development

One of the many charming experiences you will have is to hear your baby, when she is alone and comfortable, making saliva sounds in an apparently experimental fashion. This behavior often occurs in the morning after the baby first wakes up, but when she is not yet uncomfortable. For a baby to fully enjoy play with the sounds she can produce, she has to be able to hear well. True language learning (understanding the meaning of words) will begin during the six- to eight-month period. We want babies to hear perfectly throughout their first three years, and the auditory orienting reflex is a useful development to help us monitor that ability.

Should a significant hearing problem be suspected, accurate diagnostic testing of hearing can be done, by qualified people, from the middle of the fourth month on. Pediatric audiologists can now perform audiometric examinations using conditioning techniques—procedures that are insufficiently reliable up until this age.

The Phase II baby gets noisier every day. Not only is he increasingly interested in the sounds he makes, but he is also entering into a euphoric stage that usually lasts for at least the next few months and often much longer. Babies vary in their characteristic mood states, of course, but if yours is free from physical discomfort from digestive problems, early teething, or other problems, he will show that he is very excited much of the time from late Phase II on. This excitement is especially noticeable in play with you and when he has had a lot of opportunity to look at himself in a mirror.

RECOMMENDED CHILD-REARING PRACTICES: PHASE II

Giving a Baby a Feeling of Being Loved and Cared For

As always, recommendations for child-rearing practices should be considered within the context of your goals. During Phase I, the repeated episodes of discomfort, followed by your efforts to ease the situation, are all you need to do to begin to build a feeling of being loved and cared for in your baby. That requirement will continue during Phase II, but your job will get easier as your baby gradually adapts to living outside of the womb, and as you become better at nurturing him. Once he begins to smile, you will be obliged to build his growing sense of being loved and cared for by providing a second ingredient: having fun with him. As you can see, your baby is not at risk when it comes to this goal, the single most important one of the first years of life.

Having fun with your baby is made considerably easier by his growing sturdiness. By the end of Phase II, he will look far stronger and more ready to be handled and bounced on your thighs than he appeared to be earlier. Of course you still have to be careful, but in addition to the changes in him, you will be justifiably more sure of yourself and confident than you had been. You will have learned so much about your baby's behavioral signs that indicate hunger, sleepiness, and other sources of discomfort that, in a real sense, you will have become the expert when it comes to your baby.

Helping the Infant Develop Specific Skills

Let us consider the skills that are developing during this phase—with the understanding that whatever you do, your baby is going to acquire them anyway. In other words these skills are not at risk.

HEAD CONTROL

By the end of Phase II we expect most normal babies to be able to hold their heads upright and steady for at least a few seconds at a time. A baby who lies on his back most of the time is less likely to achieve head control as early as one who has had a lot of experience lying on his stomach. Placing him on his stomach for a few minutes regularly, if he doesn't object, will trigger head-rearing. Placing him six to eight inches in front of a vertical mirror will make the experience more interesting for him.

An infant's own face has a special quality of attractiveness for her because, unlike the face of someone else, the image of her own face, as seen in a mirror, will move in a manner determined by her own movements. For this reason a properly placed mirror is very appealing to the Phase II baby— and to older infants as well.

The mirror should be placed approximately seven inches from your baby's eyes. A mirror placed more than seven inches or so away will be less effective because the target the baby sees in a mirror is twice as far away from his eyes as the distance to the mirror. In other words, if you place the mirror seven inches from the baby's eyes, he will see the reflection of his face apparently fourteen inches away. Objects more than a foot and a half away from your baby are less likely than closer ones to attract and hold his interest during Phase II. Suitably placed, a mirror can also be a useful device for you at diaper time.

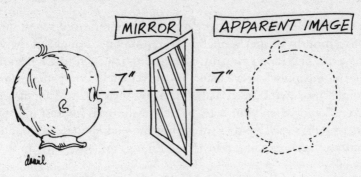

Locating a mirror for a Phase II baby

VISION SKILLS

Unless you rear your baby in the dark, all three basic skills—flexible focusing, convergence, and tracking—will develop quite nicely. Beware of toy companies that promise you "encouragement" or "enhancement" of such developments. Such statements are pure horsefeathers.

HAND-EYE SKILLS

Hand-eye skills undergo substantial development during this phase also. Probably because these and vision skills are so fundamental to every baby, no risk exists in this area either. Without a single toy, I can assure you hand-eye skills will develop just as well in your baby as they will if you offer her every toy made to "stimulate" these developments.

Does that mean there is no point to buying toys for this age? Not at all. But I want you to be able to make the distinction between developments that are at risk and those that are not. I want you to know, from the beginning, what you ought to be concerned about and what you need not be concerned about, especially because you will be assaulted repeatedly by claims with little or no basis throughout your baby's first years.

I recommended mobiles and a mirror for the Phase I baby. Both continue to interest babies into Phase II and, in the case of mirrors, for many months to come. Once your baby reaches the point where the development of vision skills has led to observations of hand activities, your baby is ready for objects that will encourage hand-eye play.

CRIB GYMS AND FLOOR GYMS

Until about the early 1980s the best toy for a baby to begin to practice hand-eye skills on was a crib gym. In fact, during the late 1960s I designed such products for a major toy company. The two-and-a-half to five-month-old baby loves crib gyms! Sadly, there were a few reported cases of older babies getting entangled and hurt as they used the gyms to pull themselves to a sitting position. At first, the response of toy companies was to put warnings on the package that the crib gym should be removed when the baby turned five months of age. Soon, however, someone thought of the idea of the floor gym. The Illco company offered the first such toy, and soon several other companies followed suit. Today very few companies offer crib gyms, while floor gyms are available in many forms. A well-designed crib gym, taken down when your baby begins to show an interest in using the crib bars to pull herself up to a sitting posture—rarely before five and one half months of age—is a useful toy. Most floor gyms, however, can fit in the crib as well.

While none of the currently available versions is ideally designed, most are excellent toys. Choose one that is made so that the suspended objects are not overly elusive. Links are less useful than plastic hangers or even straps. Your baby will handle the objects, feel their contours and surfaces, and try to get them to her mouth for chewing and gumming. These activities will become more frequent from two and one half months on. By the way, don't expect your eighteen-month-old to play with this toy as some manufacturers would have you believe.

Also, one of these toys, the original, has a useless mirror. It is much too small, and because of the way it is mounted, your baby is not likely to be able to see herself in it. A tip: Place your baby in an infant seat in front of the floor gym rather than on her back under it. When sitting, she will not have to contend with gravity when using her arms.

Toys for infants under six months of age should not produce sharp or very loud sounds or any alarmingly abrupt changes in stimulation, such as bright flashing lights. We have noted that children, especially during the first half of Phase II, are still susceptible to startling as a consequence of abrupt

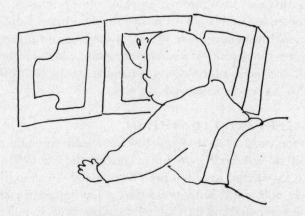

Locating a mirror for a Phase III baby

changes in stimulation. Therefore, toys with the above features should be reserved until your child gets a bit older.

Crib gyms must be removed from the crib when the baby seems nearly able to pull herself to a sitting posture. For reasons of safety, it is extremely important to follow this advice.

Encouraging Interest in the Outside World: Curiosity

If you encourage specific skill development using appropriate mobiles, floor or crib gyms, mirrors, an infant seat, and changes of scenery, you'll find that your child will show a great deal of curiosity. Even if you do none of these things, she will display increasing curiosity as she examines her own hands and fingers, and in her visual inspection of the mutual fingering done by one hand on the other. In other words, it's hard to get in the way of the growth of curiosity. If you provide some of the additional experiences I suggest, however, I'm confident you'll see even greater growth accompanied by many signs of enthusiasm and glee in your child.

Sleep

For the majority of parents, a wonderful development takes place during Phase II: their babies begin to sleep for much longer periods during the night. Notice I said for the *majority* of parents, not *all* parents. From ten weeks on, more and more babies begin to "sleep through." That means about five or six hours at first, leading to as many as seven or eight hours by the middle of the fourth month of life. One tip: as Phase II evolves, you will become increasingly knowledgeable about your baby's "sleep signs." It is very important that you be guided by them when it comes to both naps and bedtime. The sleepier your baby is when you put him down, the easier it will be to guide him into a civilized pattern with a minimum of fuss. It is especially important for you to have your baby sleeping in his crib as soon as possible. You should have him sleeping in another room, with one closed door between you and him and without the use of a nursery monitor. New parents, especially mothers, are supersensitive to their baby's sounds. If your baby sleeps in the same room with you or across the hall, or next to an active monitor, everyone will suffer.

Because intentional behavior has not developed yet, you can be confident that if your baby awakens, crying insistently, in the middle of the night, there is a physical cause. Respond promptly, and do your best to comfort him. After you have worked at comforting for thirty minutes or so, it may be best to let him cry. But that will probably happen only rarely.

Should you allow your baby to sleep in your bed? If you want to go this route, you will need to get your guidance on sleep from someone else. It's not that I object to the practice. Indeed, I am very sympathetic to the motives involved. It is just that in my experience it has very often led to difficulties when parents want to make the transition to a bed for the child. You can certainly do it, but I can't help you with the complications the practice usually leads to.

CHILD-REARING PRACTICES NOT RECOMMENDED

In the discussion of the Phase I child I suggested that you beware of the abundant misinformation available about child-rearing. I suggested that you need not feel guilty if you have not provided an expensive and elaborately "enriched" environment for your new baby. This still holds true. Although there is more that you can do in Phase II, if you still do little, in my opinion you will not have done a terrible disservice to your young child. Indeed, most of the basic learning processes will proceed quite nicely.

The second point I made during the earlier discussion was that the idea of spoiling your child during Phase I made no sense. This applies as well to the Phase II baby. I strongly urge you to respond naturally and promptly to any sign of distress in your baby; try to find out what is wrong, make certain there is no serious problem, and do the best you can to alleviate the discomfort. Let a young infant "cry it out" only as a last resort. Crying it out will in all probability be necessary at times. I've had quite a number of parents report attempting to prevent all episodes of crying, an effort that totally wore them out. Accept the fact that at times you simply won't be able to make her comfortable. Let's hope that such episodes are rare.

A third point I made was that babies are designed to be handled, caressed, and loved, and there is no reason at all why you should not indulge yourself in this regard. That statement remains true during Phase II.

RECOMMENDED MATERIALS FOR PHASE II BABIES

Crib Gyms and Floor Gyms

You won't find many crib gyms to choose from. They have been supplanted by floor gyms, some of which will fit in the crib. Ambi makes many good toys, one of which is the crib gym, but you are not likely to find it in large toy stores. If you get one, you should use masking tape to prevent the parts from swinging away from your baby.

Many floor gyms are available with few differences among them. Most

A floor gym

are adequate. None is without flaws. Using masking tape, you should try to minimize their elusiveness. Those that fold for easy transport, for trips for example, may be a bit more convenient than others. It is best that your baby be seated in front of the toy rather than lying on her back. That way she won't get tired of holding her arms overhead.

A Large Mirror for the Head of the Crib

Because your baby's ability to lift her head when she is placed on her stomach is improving steadily, she will now show some interest in a mirror placed vertically six to eight inches in front of her. You should fasten it to the head of the crib. Your baby, on her stomach, will rear her head and at times catch a glimpse of herself in the mirror. This will induce her to repeat the behavior and rear higher to get a better view. By the time she is three and one half months or a bit older, you will find her laughing and squealing with delight at her mirror image.

BEHAVIORS THAT SIGNAL THE ONSET OF PHASE III

HEAD CONTROL

When your baby, lying on her stomach, can lift her head so that it is vertical to the floor and hold it in that position steadily for fifteen to thirty seconds or longer, she is showing one reliable sign that she is leaving Phase II.

TORSO CONTROL

Prior to about fourteen weeks, few babies have much control over their upper bodies. Unlike the control they have acquired over their head and eyes, hands, fingers, and legs, the torso remains too much for most babies to deal with until the end of Phase II. At around fourteen weeks your baby, when on his back, will begin turning his body up onto one side or the other. During Phase III he may acquire the ability to turn over at will.

KICKING OUT

Another emerging sign of growing control over the body as Phase III begins is a tendency for your baby, when on her back, to hold her feet a few inches above the surface she is lying on and thrust them out vigorously, particularly if she feels some pressure against the soles of her feet. This tendency to exercise her newfound leg strength leads ultimately to the ability to use her legs for support when standing and walking.

SPECIAL RESPONSE TO A FAMILIAR PERSON'S FACE AND VOICE

Though somewhat less obvious, it should become clear that along with the growth of sociability, the fourteen-week-old baby is now especially oriented toward the appearance of his primary caregiver's face and voice.

THE TICKLE, THE GIGGLE, AND THE LAUGH, OR THE EMERGENCE OF HILARITY

This phenomenon is part of a rapidly growing tendency toward euphoria and enjoyment that characterizes the Phase III baby. Although the Phase II baby moves into a period of high spirits, it is in Phase III that a baby is most impressive in this regard.

4

PHASE III: THREE AND A HALF TO FIVE AND A HALF MONTHS

GENERAL REMARKS

This period is not only a time when an interesting style of life and set of be-haviors fade out, it is also a time when a remarkable quality of mood prevails.

In many cultures very young babies are carried and therefore held upright for large periods of the day, but in our society the infant spends most of the first three and a half months of his life lying either on his back or on his stomach. Starting from about fourteen weeks, however, your child will spend increasing amounts of time in a vertical or near vertical position, but throughout Phase III he will need help to do so. Sitting without assistance is a shaky proposition for most babies until they are well into their eighth month.

During Phase II your baby discovered and began to learn to control his hands. Sometime during Phase III, he will discover and begin to play with his feet.

Phase II is also the last phase when babies are predominantly oriented toward their near world. They pay little attention to anything or anybody more than a few feet away from their eyes. Babies under three and a half months of age do not spend much time looking across the room or at the scene outside the window, but during Phase III interest in their surroundings expands. Now your baby's attention will include entire rooms and even broader vistas when he is outdoors, in a supermarket, or in some other new place.

The final point worth remarking about is the tremendous geniality of the Phase III baby. The only things likely to disturb his marvelous mood are the appearance of teeth and occasional illness or indigestion.

GENERAL BEHAVIOR DURING PHASE III

The Phase III baby is likely to be awake at least half of the daytime hours. This is fortunate because he has a great deal to do. While he is doing the various things we will be talking about, he will seem very happy most of the time. Although he will show this happiness most dramatically in the presence of other people, especially his parents, he will also exhibit it while playing with toys or simply exercising. For example, if you make use of mirrors and other appropriate toys, you'll find the Phase III baby occasionally having a delightful time interacting with these devices even when alone.

Babies become much more active in Phase III than they were before. You can expect such high levels of activity to continue throughout the balance of the first three years. During this phase babies also become rather noisy, what with the emergence of laughter, squeals of delight, and several other new kinds of noises.

Large Muscle Activity

You will surely be impressed by how much vigorous arm and leg activity your baby engages in now. It is as if he is simply delighted to be alive and gets a great deal of pleasure out of sheer exercise of the large muscles which, after all, have only recently been endowed with substantial strength. With the emergence of each new motor skill, you'll find your baby practicing it. Turning his torso from side to side, once begun, will become a regular feature of his daily waking life; he will work very hard at his newly gained skill of turning over and will enjoy practicing turning from back to stomach and from stomach to back. When he's on his stomach, he will repeatedly lift his head and hold it up for longer periods of time as he scans the world around him.

Small Muscle Activity

During Phase III, hand-eye activity comes into its own and will remain a central focus of the day throughout the first years of life. This activity will provide valuable cues to you as you try to provide interesting toys and activities for your baby over the coming months.

Also during Phase III you will see the gradual emergence of your baby's capacity to use his hands as reaching tools under the guidance of vision. Your child will engage in many kinds of hand activities that lead to this important skill. While he is engaged in bringing his hands together over his midline, in mutual fingering, or in exploring his clothing, the sheet, or the crib bumper, you'll notice that his concentration is remarkable. He will thoroughly and intensively examine the fine details of everything he looks at. For him this kind of behavior has become possible only recently, with the nearly complete maturation of basic vision skills.

Interest in Exploration

Another general characteristic of Phase III is a dramatic increase in interest in exploration. As your baby learns to use his hands to reach, he is, of course, exploring. He also explores visually when he is placed prone and rears his head up to peer about, or when someone approaches him while he is lying supine or sitting in an infant seat. In addition to visual exploration, you'll find evidence of a strong exploratory drive in his experimentation with his own sounds, especially when he has saliva in his mouth. (This behavior is best observed when a baby is unaware that you are nearby.)

Another principal form of exploration involves the sense of touch. If you look closely, you'll find your baby spending a good deal of time exploring how things feel—at times, oddly enough, while looking elsewhere. She will explore through feeling both with her fingers and with her mouth, after raising an object to her mouth and gumming it.

In summary, the baby of this age spends a great deal of time exercising, practicing motor skills, responding to people when they are near, listening to sounds, especially those that she herself can make, and actively exploring anything that is nearby, especially her own body and hands.

THE APPARENT INTERESTS OF THE PHASE III BABY

The Phase III baby can best be described as a doer, a socializer, and a bon vivant with an absolutely irresistible smile. She is a doer in the sense that she is far more active in all ways than she was earlier. She is a socializer in the sense that she is marvelously responsive. She is a bon vivant in the sense of seeming to get more out of life than human beings do at just about any other age.

Visual Exploration

During Phase III, the baby continues to show an intense interest in the nearby visual world. He will be very much involved in looking at and actively exploring everything within reach of his hands and feet and also everything within view, especially if such objects are only a yard or so away.

Mastering New Skills

Another major interest is mastering new skills. We've remarked about emerging gross motor skills in the areas of torso control, head control, and turning over; the very important sensory motor ability of visually directed reaching is also a focal point for activities. The Phase III child is interested not only in exploring the nearby world but also in the process of mastering the skill of reaching per se, an effort that has a very special power for him. After all, no other animal achieves quite the level and variety of hand-eye skill as the human.

Socializing

The third major area of obvious interest is in people and socializing in general. It is extraordinarily important for the human infant to firmly establish a relationship with a caring adult. The social events of this period of life almost guarantee that the baby will learn to like the nurturing adults and that the nurturing adults will come to feel an extremely powerful affection and sense of responsibility for the baby.

Interest in Body Functions

The fourth area of interest is an apparent sheer delight in physical strength or simple body function. This is a time of life when an interest in gymnastic activities begins.

EDUCATIONAL DEVELOPMENTS DURING PHASE III

In the preceding chapter I stressed that parents and other child-rearers should not be shamed into feeling guilty if they do not take elaborate and expensive steps to stimulate the educational development of a baby in the first months of life. This advice remains true for Phase III. I believe that the average environment contains most of what children need in order to move ahead properly as learners. My remarks about educational practices should be taken in that light.

It is undoubtedly true, however, that the more you know about the details of development, the better job you can do in designing an interesting environment and enjoyable activities for your baby. My research experience has led me to believe that a baby ought to be provided with an interesting set of options on a regular basis throughout her early years. While I can't prove it, my guess is that such a baby will enjoy life more, maintain a high level of curiosity, and be less inclined to become overdemanding.

The Origins of Intelligent Behavior

A baby in Phase III is not yet intelligent according to the common definition of the word: she does not solve problems. She is, however, moving toward being able to solve problems and becoming an intelligent being. The steps she is taking have been outlined in a masterful fashion by Piaget, whose name will appear throughout this text as the leading expert on the growth of intelligence.

In Chapter 3, I described how the isolated, reflexlike behaviors of early infancy began to become coordinated during Phase II. This interrelating process continues during Phase III, and is highlighted by the gradual mastery of the use of the hand under the guidance of the eyes, a behavior focused on extensively by Piaget. This ability ordinarily emerges sometime during the sixth month of life, although recent research has demonstrated that a baby who plays with suitably designed toys can learn to reach as early as three and a half months of age. Taken by itself, early reaching ability probably has little significance.

When your baby is finally reaching for objects routinely, usually at about five and one half to six months of age, he is demonstrating the coordination of several systems of behavior. First of all, before he reaches, he has to find the object with his eyes. Then he'll move his hand out rather quickly and accurately to where the object is; in a mature reach, just before the child contacts the object, he will either open his fingers or close them slightly to grasp the object. Once he grasps it, he may do any number of things with it. Most commonly he will stare at the object for a while. He may also move it back and forth and twist it about to get different views of it and to see what it feels like in different positions. Another typical behavior is to bring the object to his mouth and gum it.

An additional kind of behavior the child is likely to engage in after she has grasped an object is to bring it closer to her, where her other hand may join the scene and either take or feel the object while she holds it with her first hand. While this tactile exploration continues, she may transfer the object back and forth from hand to hand.

In Phase III the child engages in more complicated and more focused hand-eye behavior than he did in the first two stages. While he is engaging in other behaviors he will begin to show increasing interest in the object itself, in contrast to younger infants who show very little interest in the object. From Phase III forward, exploration of objects—particularly small ones that can be grabbed, chewed, swung, and batted—becomes an increasingly important occupation for infants.

EMOTIONALITY

The four-month-old child is a delighted and a delightful creature. The smiling that began at anywhere from two to three months of age is now fully established, and unless the child is ill or uncomfortable, smiling lights up her and your time for many hours every day. This is an age that firmly solidifies the baby's hold on a parent's affections. Now, in addition to a broad and irresistible smile and a chronically good mood, babies show two other interesting emotional changes. For the first time, you will hear your baby laugh and giggle.

Response to Tickling

Babies first become ticklish during Phase III. The fact that you cannot elicit a tickle response from a child before she is about fourteen weeks of age has always intrigued me. Perhaps it is related to the fact that adults cannot tickle themselves. (Try it if you have never attempted it before.) The effectiveness of the tickle is dependent upon the "ticklee" perceiving that another person is producing the stimulation. You cannot tickle yourself because you know that you are not another person applying the stimulation. The child younger than about fourteen weeks of age is not well enough developed socially to have reached whatever awareness of another person is necessary to make the tickle functional.

DEVELOPING MOTOR SKILLS

Rolling Over

Sometime during the fourth or fifth month of life your child will acquire the ability to turn his body onto his side. This capacity to turn the torso from side to side is often followed toward the end of Phase III by a second significant motor achievement: the capacity to turn from the back to the stomach position. Once this ability begins to surface, babies practice it repeatedly.

Most children can turn from back to stomach by the time they are five and a half months old. Within a few weeks they will master the ability to turn from lying on their stomach to their back. (Some babies learn to turn over from their stomach to their back first.) Although they will become increasingly capable of turning over, and may even be able to balance themselves a bit when in a sitting position, it will be some weeks before they are capable of pulling themselves up to a sitting posture and maintaining that position on their own.

Kicking

The third motor development worth noting at this point is kicking behavior. By Phase III the baby's leg muscles have become considerably more substantial than they were earlier, and this is only one of many ways in which your baby will impress you with her sturdiness. She will usually hold her feet off the crib surface when she is on her back. In addition, whenever she senses pressure against the soles of her feet, she will get huge enjoyment from pushing out powerfully against that pressure. Day by day your baby will be able to support more and more of her weight as you stand her on your thighs. By nine or ten months of age, she will use those muscles to pull herself to a standing position, and soon thereafter she will begin to move about while upright. Not long after that, she will be walking.

Using the Arm Muscles

The Phase III baby's increasing interest in using the large muscles of his legs is paralleled by an interest in using the large muscles of his arms. You'll note that they too will have become considerably more substantial. If you provide an opportunity for him to exercise them, he will do so and have a great deal of fun in the process.

DEVELOPING SENSORIMOTOR SKILLS

While the distinction between sensorimotor and motor skills is somewhat technical, it is worth noting. Sensorimotor skills involve the sensory systems such as vision, hearing, and touch as well as associated muscular activity. Typical motor skills are crawling, climbing, and walking. Though they involve the senses, their principal component is muscle control.

Visually Directed Reaching

One of the most vital achievements of Phase III is the mastery of the use of the hand as a reaching tool under the guidance of the eyes. This particular skill is very basic for the baby, and it is through this skill that a baby will acquire much of his familiarity with his environment over the next year or so. Visually directed reaching also plays an important role in the development of intelligence. The remarkable levels to which adult human beings develop their facility to use their hands under the guidance of their eyes sets humankind off from all other animals in the same sense that language and culture do.

Eye-Ear Coordination

Another interesting and important sensorimotor change in the third phase is the considerable improvement in eye-ear coordination. At birth babies have some very limited skill in localization of sounds, but during Phase III they routinely become very accurate and reliable in turning their eyes and body toward the source of a nearby sound. Like most of the earlier skills they have shown, localizing a nearby sound is a reflexlike behavior. You can expect a child in Phase III, unless preoccupied or very sleepy, to turn quickly and accurately to the source of any nearby sound, even those that aren't loud.

Because this new behavior enables us to screen for mild to moderate hearing losses beginning at about age 18 to 20 weeks, its importance is surprisingly great. Being able to identify this very common threat to good hearing (from routine respiratory ailments and allergic reactions) has turned out to be a development of extraordinary significance. This subject will be discussed in more detail in the section on recommended child-rearing practices.

Touch

A third major area of sensorimotor skill involves touch. You'll remember that during Phases I and II your baby's hands were fisted most of the time. Fisted hands prevent exploration of the surfaces of objects. Once the baby gets into Phase III he acquires the use of his fingers for such exploration, and from then on, he will use his fingers as well as his mouth and eyes to explore the different textures, hardnesses, and shapes of materials and objects within reach.

Sociability

The marvelous mood state of the Phase III baby guarantees that life will often be very pleasant for parents, especially parents of firstborn children. Your baby's spectacular smile plays a large role in cementing the close affectional tie with you. If you respond often and promptly to her cries of discomfort or delight, she will learn to expect such a reaction to her cries. If on the other hand she is left to cry in discomfort repeatedly and for long periods of time, she will get used to that state of affairs as well.

Babies are remarkably adaptable in this regard. Infants I worked with in a state institution began to cry less and less during Phase III to the point where by the time they were six or seven months of age, they cried rarely. On the surface that situation would seem a desirable state of affairs. In fact, however, those children had learned that the only payoff for crying was fatigue. For me there are few sadder stories to be told.

CAPTURING ADULT ATTENTION: THE EMERGENCE OF INTENTIONAL CRYING

One set of fundamental social skills that we've found to be a sign of very good development in three- to six-year-old children is a collection of socially acceptable behaviors for getting and holding the attention of another person, particularly an adult. In respect to the capacity to get attention and, perhaps more important, in respect to the early signs of spoiling in young children, a fascinating development becomes observable near the end of Phase III.

Earlier we described an inevitable cycle of experience that infants undergo. That cycle started with feelings of distress from any of several causes. That distress is followed routinely by the baby's cry, which in most situations is heard sooner or later by an older person who will often respond by attempting to make the baby more comfortable. Since such episodes of distress are very numerous during the first months of life, and since babies, for some reason not fully understood, are usually comforted by being picked up and handled and moved gently through space—even when the cause of the distress has not been identified or removed—infants build up large quantities of experience that begin with distress and fairly soon thereafter are followed by the reduction of that distress. Although clearly not yet able to understand what is happening, babies do learn, at some primitive level, from these experiences. They learn to associate the sight, smell, sound, and feel of people who regularly comfort them with the experience of feeling better. As a result, a remarkable and very important shift takes place during Phase III in respect to crying. Initially and throughout Phases I and II babies cried solely as a response to discomfort, but toward the end of Phase III a second important reason for crying will surface. That second reason is to bring an adult to them with the hope of being picked up and cuddled by that adult. This second use of the cry is the first sign of *intentional behavior* in babies. Put another way, babies younger than five and one half months of age cry when they are uncomfortable; babies late in Phase III begin also to cry for attention.

This new tool, the intentional cry for company, which soon will develop into a demand, comes in very handy when your baby is bored and frustrated, a condition that begins to become common during Phase III.

From about four and one half months on, your baby will, for the first time, be able to sit up comfortably, with support, and see across the entire room. Although he is full of curiosity about the world, he is still unable to move about on his own to get close to those intriguing things out there. Day after day, he will spend increasing amounts of time, alert, looking around, dropping small toys without being able to retrieve them, and, in general, becoming frustrated and then bored. What to do? The cry is the only tool he can use to find something to do.

Babies who have little to do during Phase III frequently develop into seven-month-olds who cry regularly to be picked up and held. Such behavior is annoying and indicates that a baby is on the way toward becoming difficult to live with. Nonetheless, most professionals would rather see a seven-month-old infant cry too much for attention than cry too little because her cries have been habitually ignored.

Understanding the process of early socialization and, in particular, the development of the intentional cry, can save you and your baby much unnecessary stress, particularly in regard to sleep problems, which are a common source of grief during the first two years of life.

Language

When your baby is about four and a half months of age, you may be delighted to see him responding when you call him by name. If you call his name a few times from out of sight, about six to eight feet away, there is a very good chance that he will pause, turn to you, and give you a big smile. However, if you wait a few minutes and, when he is looking away, call him Rover or Fido or Snow White or Sneezy, he will pause, turn to you, and smile. It is not his name he is responding to, but rather any fairly abrupt and loud nearby noise. A knock on the door from a television program will produce a similar orienting action but without the smile, of course.

This kind of behavior, known as the *auditory orienting response,* is parallel to the visual orienting response that is so striking in the young Phase II baby. The auditory orienting response is present in a limited way from birth, but becomes conspicuous and reliable only during the fifth month of life. We use this behavior to screen babies for the common mild to moderate hearing losses of the first two years of life. Such screening becomes important from four and one half months on.

Understanding the meaning of the first words will surface fairly soon, usually between six and eight months of age. These understandings are routinely tested in babies of that age by offering them a variety of familiar objects and then asking them to orient toward one or another, thereby giving them the chance to make a mistake. There is no understanding of language in the mind of a Phase III baby. There is progress, however, in related areas.

During the fourth month of life a baby will begin to play with sounds, especially the sounds he makes with saliva. You may notice when passing his crib that he is repeating small sounds to himself in what seems like experimental fashion. These delightful episodes are common in the fourth month of life, and will persist. From this point on, healthy babies usually get noisier and noisier.

RECOMMENDED CHILD-REARING PRACTICES

During the first eight months of your baby's life, you have three principal goals: to give your baby a solid sense that she is loved and cared for; to encourage simple skill development, and to sustain innate curiosity. During Phase III, two hazards will surface that warrant your special attention: potential hearing loss and the overdevelopment of the demand cry. The demand cry evolves from the intentional cry for company and is a normal result of healthy social experiences of the first months of life. It is a sign of good mental development, but the demand cry is also the beginning of a process that is more likely to cause your family grief than anything else that occurs during the early years, because its appearance ushers in the time of preventable spoiling.

Giving the Baby a Feeling of Being Loved and Cared For

As in Phases I and II, I suggest you let a child cry for a long period of time only if you simply cannot avoid it. If crying persists, try to determine what is wrong and remedy the situation, comforting the baby as well as you can. By all means use a pacifier if it helps.

The baby swing, which I suggested would be useful during Phases I and II, will have begun to be less effective by the beginning of Phase III. In part this is so because the angle of the seat is too shallow. Four- and five-month-olds have acquired a righting reflex (an urge to be vertical) that makes them uncomfortable when they are lying at angles that are between about 30 and 60 degrees.

In addition to giving prompt attention to your baby's distress, I strongly urge you to spend a lot of time having fun with your baby. While you are doing so, be affectionate and talk a lot, especially about what the baby seems to be paying attention to at the moment.

Advising parents to have fun with their own baby may seem unnecessary, but some people have conflicting ideas about this subject, often supported by the fear of spoiling him. I am convinced there is no way to spoil a baby less than six months old. Certainly engaging him in frequent periods of play will not do so.

Helping Your Baby Develop Specific Skills

To repeat an important point: even if a parent pays little or no attention to specific skill development in the first six months of life, all of the skills of early infancy will develop anyway, and pretty much on time. Nevertheless, I do feel that the most suitable early experiences for a child are those that are relevant to his naturally emerging skills. If you learn what those are, and if you provide opportunities for them to function, I firmly believe that your baby's educational development will proceed better and his zest for life will increase. Bear in mind, however, that if, for example, visually directed reaching (a major specific skill) does not appear exactly on schedule, there is no reason to become concerned. Furthermore, if your baby begins to reach for objects one or two months before most babies do, no great significance should be attached to that event either. The story of early learning is more complex than that.

HAND-EYE SKILLS

Floor and crib gyms and lots of safe gummable small objects are all you will need to encourage the continued development of hand-eye skills. And, as I have indicated, if you don't provide them, your baby will have less to do, but her skills will improve anyway.

MASTERY OF THE BODY

Your baby will need a lot of practice in learning to deal with her body. Once again, this is not a risk situation, but if she is placed on a blanket on the floor for several hours a day, you will find her practicing torso control, turning up on her side repeatedly at first, and working at turning over.

Giving her opportunities to exercise her leg muscles is also a good idea. From about four and one half months on, your baby will have enough neck and back muscle strength to be able to enjoy a jumper toy, the kind that is suspended in a doorway. Fisher-Price makes a very good one. Used for about an hour a day, this toy, combined with supervised use of a walker from the same age will be very useful in helping to hold down the overdevelopment of the demand cry. More about that topic later.

LANGUAGE

Try to maintain the habit of talking a lot to your baby, particularly about what he is oriented to at the moment. This behavior on your part will reinforce his naturally growing interest in any kind of sound, including language, and it is a very desirable practice which increases the likelihood that when true language learning begins, you will be able to play your role as effectively as possible.

SOCIAL SKILLS

Whenever your young baby, at any time during infancy, begins to cry at any level beyond a slight whimper, I urge you to respond as quickly as you can. Make it a habit to respond frequently to your baby's coos and gurgles as well. She will gradually learn to associate making noise with your arrival and your presence, and with pleasure—or at least with reduction of discomfort.

These experiences will feed into the emergence of the intentional cry for company, the first and only social skill your baby will acquire during her first nine months of life.

Encouraging Curiosity

While research-based evidence on the topic of curiosity is very limited, I am convinced that you can nourish it in your baby. I recommend that you try to see to it that your baby has something interesting to do most of the time. This job is easier to do than you might think. From this time in her life right on through to her third birthday, she is primed with numerous interests. All you have to do is identify them and then design her world so that she has lots of suitable options from which to choose.

WHAT IS A PHASE III BABY INTERESTED IN?

She's interested in exploring and gumming small objects, exercising new motor skills, looking around at anything and everything, socializing with people, especially you, and satisfying her curiosity. Provide her with many small safe objects. Retrieve them from time to time, when they fall out of her reach. Use a floor gym. Use a crib gym, if you can find one. Using an infant seat, move her frequently during the day so that there is variety in what she can see.★ She will especially enjoy watching you. Give her a chance to look in a mirror once in a while. Take her out for a stroll. Take her out in the yard. Take her to a mall or a park.

Let your baby spend time on a blanket on the floor. Also give him an hour a day, broken up into three or four short sessions, in a jumper toy, a seat suspended from above in a doorway by straps and a heavy-duty spring about a foot long. As soon as your baby can sit comfortably in this gadget (usually by four and one half months of age), it becomes a great toy. I am rarely enthusiastic about toys, but this one, used correctly, is a winner. I recommend the kind that has a padded plastic-framed seat rather than one made entirely of fabric. Fisher-Price makes an excellent one called the Sure-Grip Jumper. (Note, however, that companies from time to time change the names of their products.) The height of the seat from the floor is important. The baby must be able to feel some of her weight against the soles of her feet to trigger her leg extension reflex and thereby start the bouncing action. It is also important that her feet be bare, winter and summer. This device works best when suspended over a wooden or tiled floor rather than a rug with a thick pile.

If your baby doesn't like her first experience in the jumper, take her out of it promptly. You don't want her to be turned off by the experience. Most babies like the jumper right away, however, particularly if they are closer to five than four months old. Each version of the toy has a weight limit, generally marked on the seat. The weight range is from 23 to 25 pounds. Most babies, therefore, can use them until they are between eight and nine months old.

★ An important warning about infant seats: Many different types of infant seats are commercially available, some considerably better than others. The growing strength of babies during Phase III is impressive, as is their dedication to mastering their bodies. You must make sure of two things in connection with the use of an infant seat. First, the seat should be well made—that is, it must have a low center of gravity, be sturdy, and be unlikely to tip over easily. Second, never leave a Phase III baby alone in an infant seat that is placed on any surface higher than a few inches above the floor. More information about materials for this age will be presented later in this chapter.

After your baby becomes an accomplished jumper, her pleasure will be enhanced by your enjoyment of her actions and also by music with a strong beat. Many a six- or seven-month-old baby will dance excitedly to the music, and everyone will have a delightful time.

Give your baby similar experience, *but always under close supervision,* in a walker each day. In 1992 alone, 28,000 accidents involving baby walkers were reported. In spite of that fact, I still enthusiastically recommend the use of the walker under careful supervision, for important reasons. It will usually take about three months for your baby to progress from first becoming comfortable supported in a vertical position to being able to crawl across a room. This process takes place from about four and one half to about seven and one half or eight months of age. By four months of age babies can see accurately across a room. They are deeply interested in most of what they see, but they can't get to anything on their own, and so they spend more and more time every day feeling increasingly bored and frustrated. A walker, once they learn to move it about, relieves frustration and boredom, feeds their curiosity, and provides exercise as well.

As with the jumper toy, I recommend a total of about one hour a day in a walker, broken up into three or four segments, and *only when you have nothing to do but watch!* If you are watching, there will be no danger.

If you follow this advice, you will have to be concerned about accident prevention earlier than usual. We used to tell parents that accident prevention had to start when their children were six months of age, in anticipation of early crawling. As your baby becomes able to propel her walker across a room, however, you will have to worry about accidents that would not happen if she remained in one place. This problem, though important, is not difficult to cope with, provided that you follow my strong recommendation to always supervise your baby whenever she uses the walker. As you watch her move about (rarely before she is five and one half months old), she will move toward potential dangers and, in effect, begin to teach you how to make your home accident-proof. She may move near a doorjamb, for example, or a dangling cord, but as long as you are watching, you will be able to prevent accidents.

You should obtain a small, well-made walker. An example of an excellent one is the Graco Totwheels II. The first thing you should do is remove the bar that features several small objects. This bar ordinarily snaps off with very little effort. A walker should be used to encourage a baby's interest in distant targets. A few boring objects in front of your baby's face will only be in her way.

Babies, when first placed in such a walker, if the soles of their feet are bare and if the height is adjusted correctly, will soon feel pressure on the soles of their feet and will extend their legs. For the first week or two your four-to five-month-old baby may just sit there, or more likely, she may push herself backwards. It will take her anywhere from a few days to a few weeks to add sideways movement to her repertoire. Within another few weeks she will learn to lean forward before she extends her legs, and the result will be forward motion. From then on, she will become increasingly skilled at zooming around the house.

Follow these practices and I guarantee that your Phase III baby will remain full of curiosity.

Avoiding Two Major Hazards

AVOIDING THE OVERDEVELOPMENT OF THE DEMAND CRY

The intentional cry for company first surfaces between five and one half and six months of age. Once present it soon acquires an insistent, demanding quality. Over succeeding months, few of your baby's behaviors will become as annoying as an overdeveloped demand cry. I cannot emphasize enough the importance of guiding your baby's right to get your attention and services into a socially desirable form. The alternatives can get to be grim for all concerned. The time to begin the guidance process is during Phase III. If you do a good job of keeping your baby routinely engaged in interesting and enjoyable activities from this stage on, you will go a long way to avoiding a whiny, chronically discontented fourteen-month-old, and you will prevent even worse consequences later on.

How can you accomplish this task? Much of the answer to this question lies in the preceding section on nourishing curiosity. The five-and-a-half-month-old who has been chronically bored for a month may begin to overdevelop the intentional cry once it emerges. Keep your baby busily involved with small objects, interesting things to look at, play in a jumper, exploring in a walker, and play with you. This will do the trick.

I should add one other bit of advice. During Phase III, three and a half to five and a half months, and continuing on through until your baby starts to crawl (usually between seven and a half and eight months of age), make a special effort to initiate play frequently instead of waiting until your baby calls out to you. Each time you start an interchange is one less time she will use the cry for company.

PREVENTING UNDETECTED HEARING LOSS

It is important for parents to understand the special importance of monitoring hearing ability. Only within the last few decades has it become clear that a surprisingly large number of otherwise normal infants suffer a significant delay in development because of repeated episodes of mild to moderate hearing loss during infancy—episodes that go untreated. The problem seems to stem primarily from two sources: the infant's limited capacity to resist infections, and the susceptibility of some infants to allergies. It has been reliably estimated that repeated episodes of otitis media with associated fluid in the middle ear are suffered by anywhere from a quarter to a third of all infants in the United States. That percentage is markedly higher in areas where the pollen count is very high at certain times of the year.

Several recent reports have indicated that infants who spend many hours a day in group day care are likely to have middle ear problems three to four times more frequently than are home-reared babies. This ratio is true regardless of how good the day care facility is, because the disease is transmitted through the air and is, as of this date, not preventable. During the first two years of life, the capacity to resist infection is low. Sadly, such repeated minor threats to the baby's physical health often constitute a substantial threat to the learning process.

From the third month of life on, babies begin to exhibit substantial interest in sounds, and this interest gradually leads to their ability to acquire language. That ability in turn underlies not only learning success later in life but also early development in language, intelligence, and, interestingly, social skills. We do, after all, teach our babies about relating to other people largely through spoken words.

Unfortunately, the problem of temporary hearing losses due to infections and fluid in the hearing system is not always dealt with adequately by the medical profession. If a child is born with a profound impairment, that situation is rather quickly noticed, if not by the physician then certainly by lay people who spend time with such a baby. Children with losses above 50 to 60 decibels are considered seriously impaired, and the impairment very rarely goes unnoticed for more than a few weeks. Early identification and treatment take place even in families with minimally adequate health care. Unfortunately, however, children with mild to moderate hearing losses are far more numerous and are much less likely to be identified and treated during the first years of life.

Many parents have told me with anguish about their children who, in spite of regular medical attention from birth, were not diagnosed as hearing impaired until they were six or seven years of age. Most commonly one or both parents suspected a hearing problem and brought their suspicions to the attention of their pediatrician or general practitioner, who advised them not to worry about it. Usually the explanation went like this: "Infants behave rather strangely in a wide variety of ways, and in most cases the behavior means nothing at all. There's no need to be unduly alarmed. Pay no attention to it; the child will grow out of it."

Such situations are anathema to pediatric speech and hearing specialists, but they are not rare. Do not be surprised if you run into the same sort of response yourself. It happens every day. Even in our model program in Missouri, which had the support of the head of the state pediatric association, we still had trouble getting full cooperation from some of the pediatricians who worked with our families.

The innate tendency of the normal hearing child, from about eighteen weeks on, to turn accurately toward any nearby source of sound (the auditory orienting reflex) offers us a valuable tool for early screening. Just about anyone can perform these screening procedures.

How to Screen for Mild to Moderate Hearing Loss in Babies Eighteen Weeks and Up

When your baby is awake, comfortable, and not intensely engaged in an activity, call to her in a normal voice from out of sight, six to ten feet away. The baby should, within a few seconds, pause and turn accurately toward you and usually smile. A few moments later repeat the activity from a different position, again from six to ten feet away and out of sight. The baby should respond in the same fashion. If you call to your baby three times in this manner from different positions and the baby responds reliably each time, you will have set up a simple game orientation in the baby's mind.

Next, repeat the entire procedure, but this time in a whisper rather than in a normal voice. The infant over eighteen weeks old should respond in the same manner. If she doesn't, you should not run off to a hearing specialist or get alarmed. The behavior of babies is variable enough that, on any given occasion, they may not perform the way you expect them to even though they can. Repeat the procedure later in the day and again on the following day. If on three or four occasions over two or three days your baby doesn't react appropriately, refer the whole situation to your medical practitioner.

If your medical practitioner refers you to a pediatric audiologist for an audiometric examination, you're in good shape. All major hospitals either have such a person on staff or can refer you to one. Your medical practitioner may, however, not respond this way. He may instead try to reassure you that there is nothing worth being concerned about. He may tell you that middle ear problems are very common during infancy, that they are not life-threatening, and that they are likely to disappear in a matter of days, especially if not accompanied by a high fever.

One reason medical practitioners respond this way is that healthy babies sometimes behave during the first six months of life in ways that are alarming and yet have no significance. Startling worries parents, for example. Spiking a fever of 105 degrees worries parents. Some normal young infants actually have minor seizures. Small wonder that parents are often a bundle of nerves.

The problem seems to be that babies are born about six months too early. Brain waves—as seen in EEG records, for example—don't stabilize until the baby is about six months old. With the common occurrence of so many false alarms, along with the persistent failure to prepare parents for raising a baby, it is easy to understand why so many caring pediatricians try to calm first-time parents. Unfortunately, hearing difficulties should not be regarded as inconsequential. They are not.

It is true that fluid in the middle ear, especially if not accompanied by infection, is rarely an indicator of a damaging illness. Indeed disagreement is ongoing among medical practitioners on whether to actively attack such conditions, using antibiotics and the familiar small pressure-equalizer tubes surgically inserted into the eardrum, or to just let them run their course. That controversy remains unresolved, but the fact of the matter is that repeated middle ear problems very often are accompanied by a diminished capacity to hear.

A child who has repeated middle ear infections or allergic reactions and associated congestion is living with a learning obstacle that could become serious. We strongly urge all parents to insist that their medical practitioner treat this condition the same way she would treat a fever. Medical practitioners don't tell anxious parents that their baby will outgrow a fever. From an educational standpoint, we don't think they should tell parents not to be concerned about repeated middle ear problems.

I urge you to do everything you can to make sure your baby hears perfectly throughout her first three years of life. Few things you can do are more important in ensuring that your child will get off to a good start in life.

RECOMMENDED MATERIALS FOR PHASE III BABIES

Gummable Objects

Starting in Phase III and throughout the balance of the first year of life, your baby will try to put everything she can reach into her mouth. One reason is that, especially for the first six months, she has a strong sucking drive. As the weeks go by, perhaps in anticipation of teething, her gums will become tender, and chewing on hard objects apparently relieves the discomfort. Finally, there is reason to believe that babies use their mouths to explore objects, though I'm not sure that is the case.

In addition to the urge to suck and gum small objects, Phase III babies are working hard on such hand–eye skills as handling, feeling shapes and surfaces, transferring objects from hand to hand, and getting them to the mouth. For all of these reasons, a Phase III baby's environment should include as many safe, small objects as possible. They don't have to be store-bought. Babies at this age do quite well with plastic measuring spoons, egg-shaped containers for panty hose, and just about anything else that is unbreakable and small enough for them to handle but not so small that they might choke on it. To guard against the latter problem, you can buy a no-choke tube (a simple device to check the size of small objects) for about a dollar from the Toys to Grow On catalog company (800-542-8338).

This is the age when babies will finally show some interest in rattles, especially metal ones, and most especially sterling silver ones. The reason is that metal, and particularly sterling silver, will conduct heat away from the baby's gums and thereby help relieve the discomfort. Interestingly, Phase III babies also like plastic keys on a ring, probably because the keys slide around the ring, producing a small challenge that appeals to them.

The Jumper

Fisher-Price makes a very good version of the jumper toy. Remember, though: bare feet, a hard surface, and your baby's legs slightly bent and his feet planted on the floor.

Leading pediatric orthopedists have assured us that this kind of toy is perfectly safe for physically normal infants. If you are still apprehensive, check with your health practitioner.

Rock Music

Once your baby becomes a "jolly jumper," put on some rock music— she will love it. You might try "Baby Rock," a video that is widely available from the company that produces Baby Songs videos.

A Small, Well-Made Walker

Do not obtain a large, heavy walker. They are too difficult for a young infant to manage. A good example of a well-made, light walker is the Graco Totwheels II, which sells for about $40. Since you will use it for only a few months, a used or borrowed walker is the way to go.

SLEEP

Typically, by the end of this phase or shortly thereafter, babies go to sleep at seven-thirty or eight o'clock at night and sleep for about ten hours. They also take about two naps a day, totaling about three hours. Some babies do not nap. About one in thirty still suffers from colic and just can't seem to sleep through the night. My heart goes out to you if that is your situation. Rest assured that your baby is not crying in a deliberate attempt to keep you near her. It is almost certain that she just hurts. In two to three more months, your baby may acquire the unpleasant habit of demanding your company at obscene nighttime hours, but that isn't the case yet. At the end of Phase III the intentional cry for company has hardly surfaced, although it will soon. In the meantime, if your baby should awaken after having fallen asleep, and if her cry is more than a whimper, I urge you to continue to respond promptly and do your best to comfort her. My advice will shift after your baby leaves Phase III.

MATERIALS NOT RECOMMENDED FOR PHASE III BABIES

I advise parents to be extremely suspicious of so-called educational infant toys. This warning applies even to playthings produced by major manufacturers and endorsed by leading authorities in child development. To date, there is no such thing as an educational toy with proven benefits. Even the toys that I designed were in no way vital. The most you can say about the value of any toy is that if it is well designed and presented at the appropriate developmental level, it can help you create an interesting environment for your baby. This usefulness is not trivial, but it should not be mistaken for significant educational power.

One symptom of the widespread lack of professionalism in the toy industry is the marketing of a toy for one age group when it is really appropriate for another; manufacturers are often unaware of the play value of their toys. Another is the practice of indicating that a toy will be interesting to a baby for a much longer period of time than is true. Naturally if a toy is marked as appropriate for birth to eighteen months, it will seem like a better buy than one that is recommended for just a few months. In all these years, I have never seen a toy recommended for less time than it actually appealed to a baby.

It is fair to say, however, that over the last twenty years the quality of toys available for infants and toddlers has improved substantially. The Fisher-Price Company, for example, has been upgrading its materials, which have always been sturdy but many are now more appropriately designed from an educational perspective.

Hard sell and oversell are natural by-products of the increased interest in early learning, especially among literate parents, and are a continuing problem in the field.

BEHAVIORS THAT SIGNAL THE ONSET OF PHASE IV

Visually Directed Reaching

One of the more obvious landmarks signaling the emergence of Phase IV is the mastery of the use of the hand to reach for seen objects. This fundamental skill typically appears at five and one half months, give or take a few weeks. In our research on this topic we found that reaching ability can emerge as early as age fifteen weeks if a baby is given experience with appropriate playthings, such as a floor or crib gym. There is, however, no reason to be concerned—educationally or for any other reason—if reaching does not appear before six months.

Turning Over

The second landmark ability to look for is facility in turning the body from supine (on the back) to prone (on the stomach) and vice versa. Babies will occasionally manage to turn over much earlier in the game, especially when they are very angry. The powerful leg thrusts that accompany rage in the very young infant will sometimes result in a flip from back to stomach.

5

PHASE IV: FIVE AND A HALF TO EIGHT MONTHS

GENERAL REMARKS

Phase IV is the final prelocomotive period of life. Your baby is in many ways much abler than he was at birth. He has greater command of his body, and his eyes and ears function on a par with those of a typical young adult. In addition, like many babies at this stage, he can turn his body from back to stomach and vice versa at will. Your baby now has significant control over his head movements, and he can use his hands to reach for objects under the guidance of his eyes. He can also localize sounds and turn his body back and forth. But he still cannot do one very important thing: he cannot move about on his own. If left on a rug in the middle of a room, for example, he is not able to propel his body any distance through space. There are exceptions to this statement, of course. Some babies acquire a precocious ability to get from place to place by rolling over and over; and of course when they are extremely angry, some Phase IV babies, while lying on their backs, are able to propel themselves by digging their heels into the surface they are lying on and thrusting out powerfully with their legs. Since your baby spends more and more time in an upright position, in an infant seat or some substitute, his field of view is now far more extensive than it was. And of course his interest in exploring everything he sees is keen.

If you have followed the advice given in the last chapter about how to feed the interests of your Phase III baby, she will very probably be happy most of the time and will not have begun to overdevelop the demand cry. Now you will have to continue to keep her engaged in interesting activities until she can move about on her own.

The normal baby at this age has a very deep and powerful desire to learn about the world around her, much the way a puppy or a kitten does. With her newly expanded capacity to see and to hear things at a distance, she would love to get up close to the many interesting-looking objects around her, but she can't do so on her own.

Toward the end of Phase IV she will probably overcome two major handicaps. She will be able to sit up and maintain her balance all on her own, and she will acquire the ability to move about by crawling or scooting, or by dragging herself forward with her arms. These new talents will make a very substantial difference in her life and in yours.

Parents generally find this phase a troublesome one if they are unfamiliar with how to keep a baby of this age interested. Because they don't know what to do with the baby, and because she cries more and more often to be picked up, such parents often find they spend a good deal of time each day carrying an increasingly heavy baby.

My colleagues and I have characterized Phase IV as the lull before the storm. We regularly remind the parents we work with that life will change dramatically as soon as the baby acquires the ability to move about on his own. Phase IV, then, is an excellent time for parents to pause in their child-rearing and prepare for what is coming in the balance of the first three years. During this period they can start to get ready for the exciting events that will happen soon.

Also worthy of note at this point is the fact that some normal children will not begin to move about on their own at the most common age of seven and one half to eight months, but will do so several months later. Should you be in that situation, you'll find living with your baby more of a strain. Avoiding overattachment and the development of an overly demanding style by a baby who is a late crawler is more difficult than it otherwise would be, but it's certainly doable.

GENERAL BEHAVIOR DURING PHASE IV

The first weeks of Phase IV are usually comparatively easy for parents. The baby's generally chronic good humor continues, unless some physical discomfort is present—from early teething, for example. My advice to you: enjoy it while you can, because once your baby acquires the ability to move across the room with ease, the situation is going to change. You will find considerably more stress associated with rearing a baby in the months to follow and, indeed, in the fourteen months that follow.

Small Object Play

What kind of baby will you have during Phase IV? Hands and eyes will still be a principal focus of your baby's behavior. Bear in mind that she is still physically handicapped in that she cannot move about on her own. Yet she does have a great interest in exploring her world.

If you watch your Phase IV baby closely, you'll observe all sorts of things going on in connection with her hands and eyes. She will spend most of her waking time in an upright position. Occasionally while she waits for you—as you prepare food, for example—you may provide her with small toys or other objects to play with. This is the age when children start showing a strong interest in dropping or throwing small objects to the floor as soon as they are placed within reach. It is also the age when infants begin to study the consequences of banging objects against different surfaces. We will talk more about this particular collection of behaviors in the section on intellectual development. For now suffice it to say that small object play is a key activity at this stage.

Fascination with Small Particles

A related activity that is common toward the end of this phase is a special interest in very small particles. Sometime around seven months of age you should start looking for special staring behavior, directed at crumbs and other very small objects on the surface before your baby. This rather peculiar behavior lasts for only a few weeks. It seems to indicate the final stage of development of fine vision.

This interest in small particles has been explored in some unusual research studies. In one test, ball bearings of various sizes ranging from one-sixteenth of an inch in diameter up to one-quarter inch were used in an ingenious way to attract the attention of seven- and eight-month-old babies. Since these objects could easily be swallowed by infants, the experimenter placed one of them in a box with a clear glass top. He held a powerful magnet beneath the box so that he could move the ball by moving the magnet beneath the box. If the ball was a quarter inch in size, most babies, because of their special interest in small particles, watched closely as it was moved about. As the size of the ball used was reduced, the point was eventually reached at which the baby did not follow the target visually or attempt to reach for it with his fingers. At that point the examiner concluded that the limits of the child's visual discrimination had been reached.

Your Baby as a Gymnast

Another general characteristic of the Phase IV child is his devotion to motor activities, especially those that use newly emerging motor skills. Throughout the first two years of life this determination to practice such emerging skill until he gets it right is striking. I will examine the educational implications of this interest in later chapters. This deep, universal, natural tendency underlies the success of the infant exercise programs that have become so popular around the country. Many such programs promise a great deal to parents. Indeed, they promise too much, in our judgment. Nevertheless, those operated by reasonable, caring people can provide hours of genuine and appropriate pleasure to parents and infants.

ARM AND LEG EXERCISE

During Phase IV the infant's pleasure in exercising her leg muscles continues. This behavior underlies the effectiveness of a properly designed walker and is also responsible for the enjoyment babies derive from a doorway jumper.

In addition to leg thrusts, you will find that your Phase IV baby tends to use her newly developed arm muscles for hard physical activity whenever she has an opportunity to do so.

TURNING OVER

Another emerging motor ability in Phase IV is the capacity to turn from back to stomach and onto the back again. Children practice this skill repeatedly during this ten-week period. Also remember that an occasional infant in Phase IV will use this newfound torso control to move quite some distance by rolling his body over and over in one direction.

SITTING UNAIDED

The next motor skill to emerge during this period is the maintenance of the sitting posture. You can expect your baby to begin practicing this skill soon after he reaches six months of age. By the time they are seven months old, most babies can sit rather well, without falling, but cannot yet get up to a sitting position without help. By the end of Phase IV, at eight months or so, the majority of normal babies, but certainly not all of them, can do both.

Interest in Sounds

Another characteristic of children of this age is a growing interest in the world of sound. The interest shown by the Phase III baby in the sounds he produces, especially the ones using his own saliva, continues to grow in Phase IV. This involvement with sound is a prelude to the beginning of true language learning, which will occur during this phase.

An Important Warning

Although we expect children to begin to crawl sometime from seven and a half and eight months of age, you may find your Phase IV baby starting to move about on the floor even sooner. Indeed, it is not unheard of for babies to be able to crawl across a room by six months and to walk by eight months of age. Fortunately, this is not at all common.

THE APPARENT INTERESTS OF THE PHASE IV CHILD

New Motor Skills: Testing Their Effect on Objects

Babies go through a four-step process with respect to the amount of interest they show in small objects. The first step is characterized by no interest whatsoever in such objects; this is the condition of the baby during her first five or six weeks of life. If you succeed in prying open her fisted hand, you may be successful in getting your baby to grasp a rattle, but she won't look at it. After a few moments she will very likely drop it, and she won't look for it. All that has happened is that you have elicited the innate grasp reflex. The baby at this stage may glance briefly at some targets offered to her, provided she is comfortable and alert and they are more than three or four inches in diameter and contrast markedly with their background. By and large, however, that interest is short-lived.

The second step of the process begins when the infant is about eight to ten weeks old. He is now capable of more sustained visual examinations, made possible by the dramatic improvements in vision that occur early in the third month of life. The Phase II baby will look at his own fist or his hand as it touches an object on a floor gym. When he is around ten weeks of age, you will see evidence of progress in vision skills as the baby begins to examine the details of a target. You will notice small, rapid movements of his eyes as he scans the target.

The third step of the process is a transitional phase during which the child tries out his newly acquired motor skills on objects. Now his focus begins to shift from the motor act itself—for example, reaching for an object and batting it—to the effect of that motor act on the object. A good example of this kind of divided interest between the motor act and the object in question occurs when a six-month-old baby repeatedly drops things from his high chair and watches what happens to them as they begin to fall.

The fourth step of the process, starting at about eight months and continuing for several months, is one in which the motor act—reaching, batting, banging, releasing, and so forth—is now well within the ability of the child and is therefore accomplished rather quickly and indeed taken for granted. (This development process has been beautifully described by Piaget.) Now the concentration is on the characteristics of the object and its movements. More about this fourth step in our discussion of Phase V.

The Phase IV baby is in step three. He is especially interested in the effect that his newly acquired motor skills have on objects, hence the dropping, throwing, and banging as well as the mouthing, of course. Also at this time you'll find that your baby will occasionally become interested in the effect he can create by using his feet under visual control. Of course opportunities for coordinated eye-foot play are much less common than those for eye-hand control.

During the early stages of this transitional interest in objects, your baby's interest in the patterns of movement of objects will be limited to the beginnings of the movements. If your child drops an object off the highchair tray, she is not likely to look over the edge and follow the movement of the object all the way to the floor and through a bounce. She is much more likely simply to study the releasing act and the beginning of the fall of the object. As the weeks go by, however, if you look closely, you will notice her direction of gaze gradually moves to watch the complete path of fall of the object.

People and Affectionate Interchanges

During the first weeks of Phase IV you can expect the euphoria of Phase III to continue. Barring physical pain from teething, which can start at about this time, or from other physical sources such as a high fever, extreme fatigue, or hunger, your baby will continue to be very happy, agreeable, and sociable. He will bestow glorious smiles, laughter, and squeals of delight on almost everyone, but especially on the people he lives with. Anyone who spends time with him will fall in love. From a biological standpoint, this almost indescribable appeal makes very good sense. After Phase IV, babies become, at times, far more troublesome and difficult to live with. Since they continue to need a great deal of help to survive, it is of fundamental importance that some older person fall intensely in love with that baby before he begins to crawl.

Toward the end of Phase IV, however, a dramatic change often takes place. That previously incredibly agreeable, smiling, ticklish, giggly, and beautiful creature may very well abruptly reject any person he does not see on a daily basis who tries to get close to him. More about that a bit later.

Over and above the delightful responsiveness when somebody tries to elicit a smile from the early Phase IV child is the genuine pleasure she seems to get from playing with adults. Babies of this age really enjoy exchanging smiles and sounds with their parents. These behaviors are indicative of the tremendous importance of a solid relationship with an adult figure in the first years of life.

Stranger Anxiety

It is very possible that as early as six months of age you will see a dramatic shift in your baby's social behavior. Instead of offering an immediate broad smile to everyone, some babies begin to show a certain wariness to everyone but those they live with. Sadly, this wariness may include even visiting grandparents. At first you can expect to see a sober stare. That may last for just a few seconds or for several minutes. During the early stages of the process, the stare is usually followed by smiles. The delay before smiling begins seems to be a kind of warm-up period. If, however, someone not of the intimate circle, approaches your baby quickly or while making loud noises, don't be surprised if your baby shows a dramatic fear reaction.

As the weeks go by you should expect the warm-up period to lengthen and the number of fear responses to increase. This pattern will generally last about two months. Some babies, however—perhaps one in twenty—will skip it altogether.

Sounds

Phase IV is a time when babies become increasingly interested in sounds, those made by the people with whom they interact and those they produce themselves. Because this interest is soon followed by the beginning of true language learning, it is particularly important that you continue to pay close attention to your baby's ability to hear. As often as possible she should be attending to sounds as a prelude to learning language.

At the beginning of Phase IV your baby will respond to sounds but will not understand the meaning of any words. Toward the end of Phase IV, however, she will truly begin to respond selectively to a few simple words. For babies who have English as a first language, the first words in their vocabulary are almost always the same. Those first words are usually "Mother" (or some variation of it), "Daddy," "bye-bye," and "baby." At this stage of life, the words your baby uses do not have to be in the dictionary. If she consistently says "Ba-ba" when she sees her bottle approaching, and she does not use "Ba-ba" for any other object, person, or pet, then she has a word.

In the first half of Phase IV, there is no significant evidence of any special interest in words per se. A good deal of activity takes place, however, on the part of the baby in regard to her own noisemaking and the simple sounds that you make when you play with her. You will notice in particular that when your baby has saliva in her mouth she can make sounds that are different from her ordinary sounds. She is very likely to enjoy playing with such sounds, making them and varying their characteristics, when she is alone or with another person. One of the most pleasant experiences new parents have with their first child is listening in on their baby playing by herself with these sounds.

PRACTICING MOTOR SKILLS

Reaching

Most babies have mastered the use of the hand for reaching by the beginning of Phase IV. Once that skill comes in, and at least for the first half of Phase IV, you can expect your baby to attempt to grasp repeatedly for anything within reach. Babies of this age do not reach out for objects that are five feet away, even if the objects are large and attractive. But when your baby is lying on his back or sitting in an infant seat, he will usually reach for anything graspable if it is less than eight inches away.

Reaching is important to a baby for many reasons. Not only is the use of the hand as a reaching tool better developed in humans than in almost any other animal, but in Piaget's theory of the development of intelligence, reaching is seen as one of the major ways babies begin to explore the object world and build the foundations of intelligence.

When your Phase IV baby grasps an object, he is likely either to gum it or to hold it at a comfortable distance from his eyes—usually six to eight inches—and simply look at it. He may also transfer it from hand to hand or move it about while watching it.

Another common activity related to reaching involves bringing both hands into play. At least four out of five babies of this age favor the right hand, and if an object is offered on the left side, your baby may reach over with his right hand to grasp it. If he should take it with his left hand, or if you place it in his left hand, he is likely either to explore the object with his right hand while holding it in his left hand, or to transfer the object to his right hand. This pattern of using both hands for tactile exploration under visual guidance is very common at this stage.

Interestingly, if your baby drops the object at this point, he will react as if he knows that he has lost something, whereas such was not the case when he was two months old. Nevertheless, early in Phase IV he is not yet adept at following the path of the dropped object or at retrieving it.

Turning Over and Sitting Up

In addition to practicing reaching, babies of this age are very much into the business of practicing turning their bodies from stomach to back and from back to stomach. By now they should be reasonably skillful at this behavior. Toward the middle of Phase IV, you will begin to see your baby working on the problem of bringing herself to a sitting posture. By the end of this phase she will probably have acquired this ability. She will practice each new skill repeatedly for many hours.

Crawling

The culminating motor skill of this phase is crawling. When babies start to crawl, they sometimes do so in classical fashion, getting up on their hands and knees and moving in a coordinated manner using all four limbs. Many babies, however, begin by pulling themselves forward with their forearms and dragging their legs along behind them. An occasional baby manages to move about by rolling. The important point is not the style of locomotion chosen but the fact that most children attempt to move from place to place as soon as possible. They want to move partly because of their desire to exercise new motor skills; but the motion is due even more to their burning curiosity to conduct a firsthand investigation of the many things they have been able to see from a distance for several months.

THE DEVELOPMENT OF INTELLIGENCE: LEARNING DURING PHASE IV

Experiences of this age play a basic role in the formation of the roots of intelligence in the same sense that they have since birth. Again, the main source of this information is Piaget's work on the development of the mind.

Interest in Objects

In Phase IV the baby seems to be gradually shifting the focus of her interest from her own motor skills to the objects she handles. The dropping, banging, and throwing of Phase IV reveal the beginning of a serious interest in the characteristics and movements of objects. The classic example of this interest occurs when a seven-month-old drops a spoon or other small object from a high chair and then looks to see where it went. This interest in the effects of hand-eye interaction on objects is part of a surprisingly intense and long-lasting interest in such effects. This pattern, which began with the observation of hand movements at about ten weeks of age, will continue to be a primary focus for the healthy child right on through to the second half of the second year. Understanding how fascinating this kind of activity is to a young child is an important key to selecting toys for children during the first two years of life.

Interest in Cause and Effect

A second aspect of the development of intelligence in Phase IV is the child's beginning interest in causality—cause-and-effect relationships. Crib and floor gyms that offer an immediate effect to the child's eye-hand activity stimulate a child's growing interest in making things happen. Toys that contain sound-producing devices and those that feature a simple mechanical connection, so that pulling on one part produces an effect on another, especially when that effect is accompanied by moderate noise, will engage the baby's interest. It is this universal interest that underlies the fascination with pop-up toys that emerges toward the end of this phase.

This interest in making simple things happen is yet another developmental theme that will begin to gather momentum during Phase IV and will grow throughout the balance of the first three years of life. From Phase IV on through the second year of life your child will spend much time getting to know the effects of the many actions he becomes able to perform. In a few months he will begin to explore what happens when he pushes a large ball or full-sized door. He will also play the "researcher" by repeatedly flipping a light switch and looking up to see the consequences. This kind of curiosity will also be revealed in his deep interest in your loud protest when he strikes your glasses, pulls your hair, or engages in other innocent but sometimes painful behaviors toward the end of this phase.

Another closely related theme, also described by Piaget, is the appreciation of time and of the sequence of events. Every cause-and-effect relationship involves some sort of temporal order or sequence of events in time. The baby pushes on one part of a toy and another part makes a noise or continues to move about. The baby drops an object from his high chair and then watches the consequences. There is no reason to assume that a newborn child has any understanding of either cause-and-effect relations or the time relationships between events. Yet it is clear that during infancy he learns the fundamentals of such relationships in the course of innumerable simple activities that all babies experience, especially while handling or observing small objects.

Memory

Another topic of special interest in examining the growth of intelligence is memory. The most common approach to studying human memory involves asking subjects to tell you about events they have experienced in the past. This procedure obviously cannot be used with infants. But the topic of memory is ingeniously explored in some of the films of Professor J. McVicker Hunt illustrating Piaget's views of the early growth of intelligence. Hunt and Ina Uzgiris have produced a film called *Object Permanence,* in which the task of the baby is to find a small toy that has been hidden under a scarf, some other piece of fabric, or a pillow. The year-old baby usually has no trouble removing the scarf and finding the toy; but if there are three scarves on top of the toy, the year-old baby very often whips off the first scarf and then seems confused and gives up. The two-year-old baby, on the other hand, will continue to remove scarves until she finds the toy. The persistence of the image of the missing toy in the baby's mind is greater in the two-year-old than it is in the one-year-old or younger child.

One of the most dramatic examples of a baby's limited notions about small objects is what happens in the Piagetian test when you hide a toy in front of an eight-month-old baby. If you hide the toy under a pillow or a scarf on the baby's right side, most eight-month-old babies will find the object quite quickly. If you hide such an object in that manner four or five times in a row, the baby will routinely succeed in finding it. If, however, you immediately afterward hide the same toy directly in front of her but on her left side, while retaining a pillow or scarf on her right side as well, typically the baby will, after a slight delay, try to find the object on her right, where she previously found it, rather than on her left side, where she just watched you hide it. This behavior can be mildly startling when first viewed, but Piaget uses it to illustrate the fact that at first the existence of a small object is tied to the activities the baby has been involved in with that object rather than to any general set of rules about the existence of objects. This, by the way, is just one of many remarkable "little experiments" performed by Piaget in his attempts to learn how the mind of a baby functions.

In my judgment, Piaget was a genius, and he was the only genius ever to study infant behavior. As of this date, his research, performed only on his own three children, remains the only comprehensive study of the week-to-week development of intelligence during the first years of life. Interestingly, he was not even remotely interested in helping a baby develop her intelligence but only in understanding its evolution.

Following up on his work, researchers at Rockefeller University have examined the growth of short-term memory in the period between six months and two years of age. That research has shown that short-term memory begins to stretch at seven or eight months of age. It does so steadily in the months that follow until, by the time a child is a year and a half old, short-term memory will last for at least twenty-four hours. Desirable objects hidden one day in an unusual location will immediately be located when a child is given an opportunity to find them the next day.

This information, combined with what we know about the insatiable and all-encompassing curiosity of the infant, has great practical value. This understanding comes into play with the important issue of controlling babies when they are handling objects that we would rather they didn't touch. Then, too, to be able to look beneath the surface of your baby's activity and understand something about the wonderful world of the development of the mind makes raising a child even more exciting than it might be otherwise.

Emotionality

The usual emotional tone of most babies, especially during the first half of Phase IV, is one of contentment or delight. This is especially true in terms of interpersonal relationships. This is also a time when infants exhibit rather abrupt mood changes. A baby who is crying can often easily be induced to stop crying and to start smiling, even laughing, quite abruptly. This remarkable tendency to move quickly from one mood state to another is probably somewhat related to the baby's lack of memory.

Motor and Sensory Skills

Motor development plays an important instrumental role in early education. As a child acquires new abilities, he gains additional freedom to learn, because he is gradually shedding limitations he was saddled with at birth. The activities of dropping and throwing objects, and what these activities teach about object qualities and the physics of objects, are much easier and better entered into, for example, once the child can sit unaided, at about seven and one half months of age. After all, lying on his back or even his stomach does not allow him to drop objects very far, to throw them very well, or to monitor their movements. Also, once the baby starts crawling, the opportunities for learning become considerably greater than they were.

Sociability

We have already remarked that it is during times when the baby is interacting with others that she most often reveals her capacity for hilarity and pleasure at this stage. We have also noticed that as Phase IV draws to a close, the baby will begin to stop showing affection indiscriminately. She will start to focus on her nuclear family as preferred people and is likely to become shy or apprehensive with others. Her disposition may also be marred at times by the pending eruption of teeth.

Language

Somewhere toward the end of Phase IV the baby's first words will begin to have true meaning for him. By this I mean that the word "bottle" may begin to signify a bottle, or something that looks like a bottle, and nothing else. Also the baby's own name means him rather than anything or anyone else; and "Mommy" or some reasonable facsimile means only mother rather than mother or father. By referring back to page 92, you can see what these first words are likely to be.

The Phase IV baby is not likely to understand even the simplest instructions, but very soon he will. Once he starts to learn language, you will begin to witness a remarkably interesting process. The rate at which he will acquire language is slow at first and then accelerates dramatically during his second year.

One caution: although he will surely acquire substantial language skill over the next year, he may very well not say anything at all during that time. It is not unusual for well-developing children not to say very much until they are eighteen months or even a bit older. (The word "infancy" actually means "without words" and is conventionally used to denote the first eighteen months of life.) You should watch for the rate at which the child is learning to understand words, phrases, and grammatical structures.

RECOMMENDED CHILD-REARING PRACTICES FOR PHASE IV

General Remarks

I have characterized Phase IV as the last period of infancy during which you will be living with an essentially stationary creature. You should enjoy the lull before the storm.

Prior to eight months of age there are, of course, difficulties of one sort or another. Some infants go through periods of physical discomfort during their first months that are lumped under the term "colic." Other infants may not sleep through the night until long after the typical up-every-three-hour routine of the first six weeks. Some infants experience discomfort associated with precocious teething. But from eight months on, the difficulties you will experience in child-rearing are of a different order. Once your baby starts to crawl about the home, you are going to have much more to cope with, both in terms of the very real dangers she exposes herself to and the possibility of missing the boat on one important educational process or another.

Giving Your Baby a Feeling of Being Loved and Cared For

Assuring the Phase IV child that he is cared for should be pursued in ways similar to those that I have recommended for the preceding three phases. The only difference of consequence in this particular phase is that playing with your baby is now even more rewarding than it was before, thanks to his greater responsiveness and his usual cheerful mood. Furthermore, you can use play to focus your baby's interest.

A Major Hazard Surfaces: Preventing the Emergence of an Overly Demanding Style (Spoiling)

As we proceed with this book it will become clear that raising a bright three-year-old is much easier than raising a pleasant, unspoiled three-year-old. During the past six years, as we have worked very closely with families in our model program, we have learned considerably more than we ever knew about the details of the process by which some children turn into delightful three-year-old human beings whereas others don't. Interestingly, the roots of overindulgence and later selfish behavior lie in the first six months of life, and Phase IV is a very special time to begin influencing the process.

By the time your baby is five and one half months old, he will have had thousands of experiences where an older person has approached him and he has felt better, usually within a few moments, either because a discomfort had been lessened or removed or because he was treated to some kind of fun episode. These experiences build the foundations of emotional security in your baby. I cannot overemphasize their importance.

During the first months of life babies are responders to stimulation. Contrary to some popular views, a good deal of evidence indicates that babies don't intentionally initiate interaction with adults. Put another way, in the first four to five months of life, babies cry because they feel pain or discomfort. Almost every student of human development agrees that you cannot spoil a baby during his first months and that attempting to make him more comfortable is extremely important.

From five and one half to six months on, however, there is a new and very important change. From about the end of her sixth month, your baby will sometimes cry because she is uncomfortable, and at other times she will cry in order to get somebody to come to her. She will have begun to deliberately use the cry as a method of getting attention and company. This new ability is an important sign of normal mental development. It is also the point at which preventable spoiling usually begins.

By the end of the seventh month of life, the typical baby has developed a habit of crying frequently throughout the day to be picked up and held. In addition, the cry has usually taken on a demanding quality. As I mentioned earlier, this does not happen with institutionally reared babies. By this age, the frequency of their daily crying usually has begun to lessen substantially. When crying produces only fatigue and hoarseness, it is used less.

At thirteen and fourteen months of age, babies reveal routinely that they are able to skillfully control adults by using a whine or a demand cry to overcome resistance. Many of them fight diapering as if their lives depended on it. It is very common for eight- or nine-month-old babies to get into the habit of using the demand cry at two or three in the morning. By two years of age unpleasant, selfish children who whine and complain incessantly are common.

I believe the beginning of this nasty process occurs when, toward the end of the sixth month of life, the baby acquires the intentional cry. In recent years, through the operations of our model New Parents as Teachers program, we have become increasingly convinced of the validity of this pattern of development, and we have also learned how to cope with it.

As with most of these early formative processes, the later you get into the process, the more difficulty you will have in shaping it the way you would like. We suggest that the easiest way to avoid an overly self-centered three-year-old is to begin in Phase IV to be sensitive to the increased rate at which babies can call to be picked up and held and to learn how to avoid the overdevelopment of the use of the demand cry. Handling this really important part of the parenting job requires that you be aware of what is happening and also that you provide opportunities for your baby to be happily involved in interesting activities most of the time. In other words, you should become knowledgeable about the developmental process and especially about the rapid evolution of your baby's interests and abilities.

Providing Interesting Options for Your Phase IV Baby

Here is a list of things that Phase IV babies find interesting:

- Looking around at different people, places, and things
- Playing with the key people in their lives
- Gumming anything that is fairly hard and can be brought to the mouth
- Studying the paths of movements of objects
- Investigating cause-and-effect phenomena
- Exercising their hands, arms, torso, and legs
- Satisfying their curiosity
- Practicing hand-eye skills

If you give your baby a chance to pursue these interests for most of her waking hours, she will be involved in challenging, intriguing, and pleasurable activities. She will be chronically jolly and will not overdevelop the demand cry. From the emergence of the demand cry until your baby can easily crawl across a room, you should also go out of your way to initiate play with her regularly. Every time you start an encounter is one less time she will have to call you to her.

How to Do the Job

The following important recommendations are similar to those I suggested you follow during the second half of Phase III. I repeat them here because they are of special importance and to save you from having to flip pages.

To provide interesting situations to look at, move your baby regularly during the day to different places for variety. Take her on outings frequently. Play with her often, and don't always wait for her to call you. Surround her with safe gummables—the more the better—but make sure you use a no-choke tube to check your judgment. Give her plenty of floor time so she can practice turning over, reaching for objects, and pulling herself up to a sitting position.

At this stage it's a good idea to use devices that will help support your baby while he is sitting. A support seat for the tub enables your baby to have much more fun during bath time. You can also purchase a horseshoe-shaped cushion for support (one is called a Boppi) when he is sitting on a dry surface. Be sure to have a pillow behind him, at the very least, when he is not yet able to sit securely. Tipping forward or sideways won't result in a hard fall, but falling backwards can produce a painful blow to the back of his head.

Use a doorway jumper for no more than an hour a day, perhaps fifteen minutes at a time. Make sure your baby's feet are bare (indoors), winter and summer, and that the height of the jumper is adjusted correctly so that she feels some of her weight on the soles of her feet.

And last but far from least, *when you have nothing else to do and can watch your baby,* put her in a well-made walker for no more than one hour a day. As with the jumper, her feet should be bare and the height of the walker should allow her to feel some pressure on the soles of her feet. Most babies get to love walkers. Do not be put off by physicians who tell you not to use them. Accidents can happen in walkers, but they occur when babies are not watched, and they usually happen to much older babies. Once your baby can crawl across a room, I recommend that you stop using the walker. The device is quite valuable during the four-and-one-half-month-to-crawling stage, because it relieves the boredom and frustration of the baby while it simultaneously allows her to use her legs and satisfy her curiosity. Used properly, walkers and jumpers are dynamite toys that babies hugely enjoy, and they can help to hold down the overdevelopment of the demand cry.

HELPING YOUR BABY TO DEVELOP SPECIFIC SKILLS

Language

It is toward the end of this phase that true language learning begins. For the balance of the first year, however, progress will be slow and will occur mainly in the area of understanding rather than speech. You will inevitably hear of other, younger infants who use more words than yours. This is a common source of needless anxiety for parents. If your baby uses words very early, he is doing well. If not, it almost never means that there is a problem. Throughout the first two and one half years of life, what a baby understands is a much more reliable indicator of developmental status than what he says. Trust me.

For the best possible language development, there are two requirements at this stage of development: good hearing ability and effective language fed to your baby. If you have a feeling that your baby isn't hearing everything he should, he probably isn't. If either parent is concerned, then use the screening procedure I described earlier. If your baby fails the test several times over a few days, get him to a pediatric audiologist promptly. From here on, over the next two years, you should actively seek any needed professional assistance in order to ensure that he hears at his very best all the time.

TALKING TO YOUR CHILD

During Phase IV you should continue to talk a lot to your child. Try to determine what your baby is attending to at the moment and talk about that. Talk about the here and now, not next week or next door. Throughout your baby's first two years, he will be able to process only simple, concrete information. Abstract thinking ability will not emerge much before his second birthday. There is nothing "bad" about any kind of talk, but unless it is concrete and specific, most of it will go over the baby's head. Talk about the sock that you are putting on, the toy that you are holding before him, some feature of your face, or his fingers, if he is looking at them.

Motor Skills

Motor development is dramatic in Phase IV and will proceed pretty much on its own. You can, however, help things along a bit, and you should at least know what is happening so that you do not inadvertently get in the way. Also, if you know the details of motor development you can deal with safety considerations more effectively. Finally, the emergence of each new skill is a natural opportunity for you to begin to build a sense of pride in your baby for his achievements.

The main skills that are appearing are torso control (turning over), the ability to sit unaided, crawling or some other form of mobility, the ability to get up to a sitting position, and continued leg and arm development in the form of increasingly frequent and powerful movements.

You need do little to encourage the development of torso control or the ability to sit up. As long as you allow your baby freedom of movement, which you can prevent only with difficulty, she will practice every newly emerging skill until she gets it right. Some books and programs claim that they can help with mastery of motor skills, but in my judgment, such help is not needed. This is not a risk area. On the other hand, healthy babies love to exercise and practice new skills. They also very much enjoy watching how excited their parents get when they are engaged in energetic activities of this kind. A case in point is the baby who has become pretty good at using a doorway jumper. When you put him into the gadget, your baby will begin to bounce immediately. In fact, he may start to bounce *before* he is in the seat. Once he notices that you are having fun watching him, he will usually smile at you and jump even more vigorously. It is hard to exaggerate how much fun you can have with this situation.

There is no question at all that babies get great pleasure from mastering their bodies and exercising in appropriate ways. Furthermore, anything that they enjoy a good deal and that brings them into delightful activities with other people, especially their parents, obviously is recommendable. No one has established that any collection of exercises will make a substantial difference in the acquisition of these early motor skills, but I do recommend group programs that give babies a chance to practice their motor skills on good equipment. Many 45-minute programs are now available that feature music and a little play for babies grouped according to age. Babies enjoy such activities. These programs ordinarily are scheduled once a week, and they should be inexpensive.

I believe that in addition to the baby's pleasure in such programs there is a more subtle but equally important second benefit. This second benefit is to the parent of the baby, provided that the baby is a first child. It can be very reassuring to first-time parents to see that twelve other babies are not that much different from theirs and, for that matter, that the other babies' parents seem about equally competent with their babies. These and other group programs can help a parent build perspective. It helps.

A warning: If a program claims that it will provide "important" educational experiences, move on. There is no proof, and no reason to believe, that such programs teach "self-confidence, learning-to-learn skills," or any other vital lessons. At their best, they are great fun for all, and they're comforting for new parents, and that's not bad.

From an educational point of view, the most important motor ability that surfaces during Phase IV is the ability to move about on one's own. This capacity will usher in a time of tremendous importance for early learning, and it is central to the process, provided that you allow your baby maximum access to your living area.

MAKING YOUR HOME SAFE FOR YOUR BABY

In order for babies to be safely turned loose to roam, it is essential that the home be modified for two principal purposes. The first is to make it a safe place for a baby to explore; the second is to make it safe *from* the baby.

The Kitchen and Living Area

Making a home safe for a baby who can move about the home starts with making the kitchen safe, because that is where she will ordinarily spend much of her waking time. Look for any substances that might be hazardous to your baby if she managed to put them into her mouth, and move them out of reach. Many cleaning fluids and abrasives are toxic. Fragile glass or other breakable kitchen material should be stored out of your baby's reach. Objects that can cut, such as knives and sharpening utensils, also must be moved away.

You should examine all areas of your home within three feet of the floor for potential danger. Electric cords and outlets could be dangerous. Wherever there is an outlet not in use, you should purchase the kind of plastic cover that fits into the outlet. It is advisable to move all appliance cords out of reach of the baby. It is particularly important to see that all electric insulation is intact.

A less obvious but important problem to cope with is that of unstable physical objects. If you have an ironing board that folds down from the wall, for example, you should make sure that it is very difficult for the child to release it. If you have a chair or a floor lamp that is easy to tip over, remove it. In addition, you should check any wood furniture for splinters. You'll also want to make certain that all paint within reach of the child is lead-free.

Plants can be a double source of difficulty. If they are within reach, they and the sometimes heavy pots in which they are contained can be pulled down onto a baby. Furthermore, many common houseplants are poisonous. The best source of information about accidental poisoning is your local poison control center. Keep their telephone number handy.

You should be sure that any television or stereo controls within reach of the child constitute no shock hazard, and that any removable knobs do not come off readily. Also be sure that the knobs cannot be easily swallowed—in other words, that they are no smaller than an inch and a half in any dimension.

Stairs

Falls are another principal source of danger to the infant. All healthy and newly crawling infants love to climb stairs. Furthermore, they'll climb as many as they can find—one or two, or one hundred, given the chance. Why they have this urge to move up in space no one knows, but the urge is there. What to do? You could put a gate at the bottom and top of every staircase. I don't think this is the best idea, however. Instead, I suggest one gate at the top of the stairs and a second on the lip of the third step from the bottom, along with some kind of padding at the foot of the stairs. With only two steps to climb, babies can't hurt themselves, and therefore don't require a great deal of supervision. More important, and in the spirit of this book, is the notion that babies normally want very much to climb and to learn how to do it well. The gymnastic interest of the healthy Phase IV child is perfectly natural and probably very important. Putting a gate on the third step allows your baby to practice climbing safely, an activity that clearly gives her a great deal of pleasure.

Interestingly, we've learned something else about stairs that was not obvious to us at first: babies are fascinated by "stepness" rather than by one or another flight of stairs. The typical step is between seven and nine inches high. We have found that babies get just as much pleasure from climbing a two-inch step as they do from climbing a regular step. For those so inclined, you might consider building a special set of shallow steps for your Phase IV baby.

The Bathroom

The third important area to concern yourself with is the bathroom. Phase IV children have a universal interest in playing with water. But they also have a tendency to pull themselves over the edge of the tub or the toilet, and unfortunately they can fall in. The only way to cope with the danger of accidental drowning and the damage that can come from banging a head against a hard surface is to declare the bathroom off limits to your baby unless you are in there with him. The door should be kept latched, perhaps with a simple hook and eye that is fastened too high for your baby to reach until he gets old enough to understand instructions and be trustworthy; but this won't happen until he is at least two years old. Of special importance is seeing to it that all medicines are kept out of reach of the child. For just a few dollars you can buy a small strongbox that can be kept locked, in which to store all medicines. It is well worth the inconvenience and the modest expense.

Outdoors

You would be well advised not to leave a child of this age outdoors unsupervised. Even if she is in the company of a slightly older child, you should keep a close eye on your Phase IV child whenever she is outdoors. You should of course be certain that there are no sharp objects around on which she can cut herself, and you should be especially careful of backyard pools. A child can drown in as little as an inch of water.

You should also inform yourself about the subject of "water intoxication." During the first two years of life, babies can suffer severe physical distress from swallowing too much water. You should avoid aquatic programs that involve forced submersion of infants, and in general, when your baby is near fresh water, perhaps at poolside, you should be certain that she doesn't swallow very much water.

Common sense should get you through the business of accident-proofing an outdoor area. The cardinal rule is that it is unwise to expect your baby to use good sense when it comes to safety during the first three years of life. You are going to have to be his good sense.

Protecting Your Home from Your Baby

It is important not only to protect the baby from the typical adult-oriented home but also to remember that a baby can be hazardous to your home. Any fragile possessions that you treasure should be placed beyond the reach of the baby at this stage of development. Even those possessions that you simply like having around are clearly in jeopardy—like that plant you spent three years growing from seed. Be forewarned: I remember a time when a baby found a five-pound paper sack of flour in a cabinet. He then proceeded to decorate several rooms of his home with flour. There is no question that newly crawling children create far more housework than those who have not yet learned how to move about on their own or those who are kept confined to a small space.

Several good books are available on the subject of baby-proofing the home. (See the Recommended Readings.)

INTELLIGENCE

You can encourage your baby's intellectual growth at this stage in several ways, but don't expect to see any major development for a while.

Providing Suitable Small Objects

Phase IV babies enjoy dropping, banging, and throwing small objects. In order to pursue these naturally interesting processes, babies need access to many droppable, throwable, bangable things. Bear in mind that these objects should not be too small. Anything that is less than an inch and a half in any dimension might very well get stuck in the child's throat. Beware as well of very small parts that could break off larger objects.

Exposure to Simple Mechanisms

The Phase IV child shows a special interest in how things work, or cause-and-effect mechanisms. You probably will begin to see some interest in the working of light switches when your baby approaches eight months of age. If you operate a light switch, directing the baby's attention to what happens to the lights in the room, you will begin to see a dawning of interest. At the same time, the operation of instant-on television and radio sets will begin to interest him.

He will also begin to show interest in pop-up toys. When I wrote the first edition of this book in 1974, there was only one pop-up toy on the market, and it was recommended for two- to five-year-old children. Today you can find at least two dozen, although few are recommended for the correct age range or designed so that the eight- to fourteen-month-old baby can operate them. Later in this chapter, I shall indicate which ones are appropriate for young infants.

Setting Up Simple Problems

The Phase IV baby shows increasing interest in solving simple problems. One of the first problems he is likely to be able to cope with will involve moving one object out of his way when he is trying to grasp another. The baby, on his stomach, at six or seven months of age, is usually capable of reaching out with one hand while supporting his upper torso with the other arm or elbow. If objects are in his way, he will become increasingly sophisticated about moving them aside in order to get at whatever he is after. Until he is about seven months of age out of sight will still be out of mind, but you can begin to play hide-and-seek with him, using your own face or any small object in which he shows interest.

By providing many small objects and allowing your child to indulge himself in gumming, dropping, banging, and throwing them, you will be feeding one dimension of mental growth. By giving him some exposure to the way simple mechanisms work, you will be nourishing another. And by setting up simple problems for him—by placing an occasional easy-to-surmount obstacle in the way of his procuring some desirable object, for example, or by playing hide-and-seek with him—you will be providing a third kind of encouragement to mental growth.

Curiosity: Encouraging Interest in the Outside World

By using language with your baby, by providing small objects and related materials for her, and most especially by giving her access to your home,

Hide-and-seek

you will be simultaneously encouraging and broadening the growth of her curiosity. A very effective way to encourage both intellectual growth and curiosity at this stage of development is to use a walker several times a day, but continue to keep the total time limited to an hour. And remember, *always supervise a baby every moment she is in a walker.*

RECOMMENDED MATERIALS FOR PHASE IV

A DOORWAY JUMPER

Use this device as described in Chapter 4: Phase III.

A WALKER

Continue to supervise your baby's playtime in the walker. Once she can easily move across a room, discontinue the use of the walker.

SMALL GUMMABLE OBJECTS AND A LARGE PLASTIC CONTAINER

Many materials that will keep your child interested for a relatively long time at this age are free. If you allow a child from the time she is five or six months of age to spend a good deal of time on a blanket on the floor with a variety of small objects and a few gallon-size or larger plastic containers to put them in, you will find she will spend a remarkable amount of time exploring those objects and practicing simple skills with them. The objects should be two to five inches in size. Some should have fine details to be fingered and looked at. They should be of many sizes, shapes, and textures. Objects that are slightly difficult to handle and those suitable for hard gumming are the best.

Also provide the baby with a very large plastic container or two into which she can put these objects and out of which she can pour them. This collection will entertain your baby far longer than you would expect—well into the second year of life. The interest in exploring small objects and practicing simple skills is at the center of the educational process at this age and will remain there on through your baby's second birthday. You might just as well begin to encourage it at this point.

SUPPORTS FOR SITTING

During this phase, most babies live through a period of two months or so when they improve at maintaining their balance while sitting but they can't remain upright for long. The resultant insecurity limits their enjoyment of bathing and playing with small objects. For the bath you can get a support seat that will help your baby sit securely; many good ones are available for less than $20. For sitting on the floor you can obtain a horseshoe-shaped cushion called a Boppi. Unfortunately this product costs between $25 and $40, but perhaps you can create something similar on your own.

POP-UP TOYS

Toward the end of this phase your baby may learn to use the simplest pop-up toys. Fisher-Price makes one, currently called the Pop-up Bunny, which is unique in its simplicity. It sells for about $16. The top is activated by turning a horizontal roller on the front of the toy. The typical baby can learn to open it sometime between seven and nine months of age, and within another few weeks she will learn to close the top. A baby will stay with this toy for several weeks once she gets the knack.

THE GERTIE BALL

The Gertie ball costs less than $4. It is soft, inflatable, and squeezable, a quality that enables even a Phase IV baby to pick it up easily. It is a great first ball whose appeal is heightened by the fact that it wobbles when it rolls. Be aware, however, that it will not stand up to pets, as it is easily punctured.

MIRRORS

The Phase IV child continues to show interest in mirrors, and their use above the changing table or the crib is still advisable. You may be able to find safe mirrored-plastic sheets that you can mount low on a wall. Newly mobile babies get a kick out of encountering their image as they perambulate. The appeal of such mirrors will last indefinitely.

BATH TOYS

Hardly a bath toy is made that isn't enjoyed by babies between seven and twenty months of age. Water, and what happens to it in play, has universal appeal. The best of the bath toys do more than just float or allow your baby to pour. Those that feature water wheels and squirters, for example, are more entertaining. Bubble-makers are available, and they are great, but to date most have failed to produce bubbles reliably.

MATERIALS NOT RECOMMENDED FOR PHASE IV

BUSY BOXES

Busy boxes have been available commercially for some time, and they have enjoyed a good deal of popularity. But they are not very interesting to infants. By this I mean that if you watch a fair number of infants repeatedly, you will find that beyond the initial exploratory interest they show in any new object, they rarely spend much time with the busy box in the weeks that follow its introduction.

Busy boxes do have a few cause-and-effect mechanisms, usually including a small squeaky horn; a spring-loaded device that makes a sharp sound when an object is pushed along a track; colored balls or wheels that show alternating colors when they are turned; and the ever-present telephone dial. But the fact is that none of these objects is very appealing to an infant at any stage of his development.

A mirror will provide twenty times more enjoyment than any commercially made busy box. Infants seem to demand more variety in terms of feedback than they get as a result of the actions of busy box items. One of the reasons a mirror is so interesting to a baby is that he never sees exactly the same scene twice. When an infant pushes a little button that produces a horn squeak, all he ever gets is the same old horn squeak. It just is not enough variation.

Busy boxes have sold well in the past because they look as if they should be interesting; because they seem to offer you a lot for your money; and because until recently they have not had much competition.

Over the last twenty years, as interest in infant learning and development has grown, many companies have moved into the field of infant toys. Often one of the first toys they develop is yet another form of the busy box.

We now have nicer looking, more smoothly working busy boxes, including a Walt Disney busy box, a Sesame Street busy box, and even a Barney busy box. Fisher-Price changed the name of its toy to "activity box." Now you will find hundreds of toys that feature the same "activities" found in the original thirty-year-old busy box. These toys bored babies then. They bore babies now. None of them has very much play value. None of them is worth buying.

PLAYPENS

Playpens have been sold in huge quantities in this country for some time now. They certainly play a valuable role in preventing accidents, but I strongly urge you to consider other ways of dealing with danger during your child's infancy. Babies develop best when they are given the chance to explore their surroundings as a regular feature of their lives from the time they can move about on their own. The very word "play*pen*" implies that you are confining your baby to a small space. You *pen* him, either to stop him from moving about or to protect him from other children or from hazards in the home. We have watched hundreds of babies in playpens for hours at a time, and we have come to the conclusion that there is no way of keeping most children from being bored in a playpen after a very brief period of time, perhaps ten to twenty minutes.

I believe that allowing a baby to be bored on a daily basis is a very poor child-rearing practice. I will discuss this situation in greater detail in the next chapter when we move fully into the phenomenon of exploration of the home by the crawling baby. Basically, I believe that though it may be effective to cage your baby as a way of saving work and aggravation, as well as preventing accidents, it is the wrong way to solve such problems. By the way, though manufacturers now call the product a playyard it is much more a pen than a yard.

BEHAVIORS THAT SIGNAL THE ONSET OF PHASE V

Locomobility

The ability to move the entire body through space, usually by crawling, is one of the most dramatic and consequential emerging abilities of infancy. It usually surfaces at about eight months of age, although it can happen several weeks earlier or even months later, and it plays a large role in the education of an infant.

Locomobility and its repercussions will be discussed in detail in the next chapter. If you leave your Phase IV baby, especially in the early stages of the phase, on a blanket on the floor, he will very probably be in the same place, give or take a few inches, when you return five minutes later. But the Phase V baby, who can crawl or scoot about, definitely will not be in the same place after five minutes. There is no mistaking this new behavior. When your baby learns to crawl or move about in any manner beyond a few inches or so, you will know it.

Some babies do not begin to move any distance of consequence immediately. For others there is a period of a few days when they may begin to move back and forth a few inches, perhaps even a foot or two, before they can move across the room. At any rate, once locomobility has begun, you have entered Phase V, so brace yourself.

Understanding of First Words

As babies enter Phase V, words begin to have meaning for them. We have noted that the first words likely to cause unmistakable signs of recognition on the part of the baby are "mommy," "daddy," "bye-bye," and "baby." You can tell if the word "mommy" means "mother" by having someone else, usually the father, ask the baby where Mommy is. If you ask, "Where's Mommy?" when she is nearby, and one or two other people are present, and if your baby turns toward her mother and smiles, you have a reasonably reliable indication that the word might be linked to mother. In the early stage, however, the word may not be exclusively linked to her, it might be used for anyone or anything that generally resembles her.

Soon thereafter, babies begin to understand simple instructions. One of the first is commonly to wave bye-bye. This is generally easily identified. When babies begin to wave bye-bye with some regularity, it is reasonable to assume that they have linked those words to a particular behavior pattern. If you want to be sure that your son knows the words "wave bye-bye," you should use only the words. Do not yield to the temptation to wave to him as you ask him to wave. Other typical simple instructions that are part of the early repertoire of a child are: "No," "give me a kiss," "sit down," and "come here."

A Potential Change in Behavior Toward Non–Family Members

Eight months has traditionally been considered the age at which babies for the first time exhibit rather dramatic fear of non–family members. Closer inspection of this phenomenon, however, indicates that this so-called stranger anxiety is not universal, nor is it always intense, nor does it happen regularly at eight months of age. Nevertheless, from this point on, the baby's social sophistication increases steadily and is fascinating to observe. During the second year, for example, the child's entire world will revolve around his primary caretaker, usually his mother. He will then gradually move off during the third year toward true socializing with children of his own age.

The first eight months of life can be characterized as a period when the baby is attracted to all people, and for a very good reason—survival. That "I love everyone" style sadly exits for most babies between seven and eight months of age, sometimes a bit sooner. You will begin to notice a slight wariness in your baby when anyone he doesn't live with comes close to his face. Do not be surprised if that wariness escalates into outright screaming. These changes in social behavior, starting at about seven or eight months of age, are also signs that mark the emergence of Phase V.

6

PHASE V: EIGHT TO FOURTEEN MONTHS

GENERAL REMARKS

The Special Importance of Phase V

With the onset of Phase V, raising a baby becomes a dramatically differ-ent proposition. Whereas today most families in this country get their babies through the first six to eight months of life reasonably well developed, I have come to the conclusion that relatively few families—perhaps no more than one in ten—manage to get their children through the period from eight to thirty-six months as well educated and developed as they can and should be.

Not all professionals agree with me. There are child psychiatrists, for example, who think that the first weeks of life are the most important and that prospective parents must be educated in the best way to establish a healthy parent-child relationship. My response is that I am just as much an advocate of love and of close emotional relationships as anyone, but I believe that very few parents fail to establish a solid relationship with their baby in the first months of life, and this minority probably won't read books of this kind anyway.

There are, of course, exceptions. Tragically, some small fraction of American families are doing an apparently abominable job with young children. Some children are abused physically or emotionally, some are born into families so burdened with problems that neglect takes a heavy toll, and of course some children are afflicted with diseases or physical anomalies. But my remarks are not addressed to these extreme cases. They are addressed to the majority of families, who do not have to cope with such extraordinary difficulties.

By the time a baby reaches fourteen months of age, if she is developing especially well in respect to language, we can identify such precocious ability reliably. Furthermore, exceptional language at fourteen months usually is a reliable early indicator of first-rate intellectual progress and later advancement as well. In fact, it is the earliest reliable indicator of an outstanding intellectual start in life. This statement does not apply in the case of giftedness, however.

Giftedness is occasionally seen in babies as young as one year of age, but it is very rare. If your baby is using two-word sentences and has an expressive vocabulary of fifty words before his first birthday, he is probably gifted. Students of giftedness say that unless your baby's behavior makes you gasp, he may be advanced, but it is unlikely that he is truly gifted.

Throughout the first year of life, a child's scores on tests of intelligence, motor skills, language, and social skills do not seem to bear any meaningful relationship to what she will score on similar tests when she is two or three years of age. The only exception to this concerns the 15 percent of children who look seriously weak from birth or who, in tests during the first year of life, consistently score very much below most of the population.

The fact that test scores in the first year of life generally have no predictive power is very well established. I believe that the reason we do not see dramatic evidence of poor development in the first year of the lives of most children who will do poorly later is simply that they have not yet developed the deficits in academically relevant areas such as language and intelligence. Groups of children who underachieve in the elementary grades almost never look particularly weak in terms of achievement when tested at one year of age. On standardized language and intelligence tests, for example, such children will pretty clearly reveal where they are headed educationally by the time they are three years of age. In report after report—whether from low-income urban American children or from children in low-income homes in Africa, India, or other parts of the world—the pattern of findings is pretty much the same. During the first year of life such disadvantaged children make a fairly good showing on standard baby tests like the Bayley mental scales.

This result holds true even if they have not had the best of nutrition and even if their parents have had little or no education. It is not until they reach the middle of the second year of life that their scores begin to decline. Subsequently, it is all downhill. That is, it is all downhill for such groups of children, not necessarily for every individual child within those groups.

It is very important to point out that many children from low-income families are not underachievers. Large numbers of such children, both in this and other countries, develop as well as any children, from the first two years on through to graduate school. To be born into a poor family is far from a guarantee of academic underachievement.

This subject is complicated, emotionally charged, and confusing. Perhaps it is best to summarize the situation with a graph.

Curve A on this graph represents development for most children. In this figure, we indicate overall ability, excluding motor and sensory skills—not just performance on an IQ test but all the other major abilities of the young human, including social and language skills. Curve A indicates the progress of the average child from birth through five and a half years. You will note that curve B starts and stays lower than curve A. Curve B represents the 15 percent of the population who for one reason or another are in substantial trouble. Starting at about eight months of age, two additional curves, C and D, are sketched in. Curve C moves up more rapidly than the average; Curve D, however, falls below the average. Curves A, C, and D begin to diverge at about eight months of age.

Phase V is a time of critical importance not only for the development of language and intelligence but also, along with Phase VI, for social development. The experiences of the eight- to twenty-four-month period determine to a large extent the shape of each child's personality, social habits, and everyday level of happiness.

While there is no doubt that some portion of what a child is like in these areas at two years of age is determined genetically, I am totally convinced that parents, through their child-rearing practices during the next sixteen months, make a far bigger impact on the shaping of children. Put another way, from this point on, until your child's second birthday, you will have the opportunity to help her become either a wonderful companion who relates well to people and enjoys life to the fullest or one who is difficult to get along with and not so happy about life. I realize that is a somewhat frightening statement, but I am totally convinced it is true.

When your child moves into her third year her interest in age-mates will grow at the expense of her previous concentration on you as her social focus. Your capacity to influence her habits, attitudes, and social style will diminish dramatically.

Furthermore, I believe the social structures you see in your two-year-

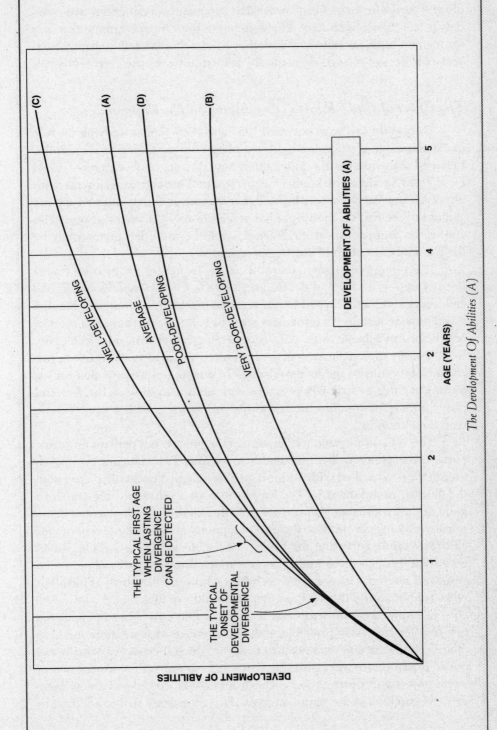

The Development Of Abilities (A)

DEVELOPMENT OF ABILITIES (A)

AGE (YEARS)

DEVELOPMENT OF ABILITIES

(C) WELL-DEVELOPING

(A) AVERAGE

(D) POOR-DEVELOPING

(B) VERY POOR-DEVELOPING

THE TYPICAL FIRST AGE WHEN LASTING DIVERGENCE CAN BE DETECTED

THE TYPICAL ONSET OF DEVELOPMENTAL DIVERGENCE

old will persist for years. I can't prove that statement, but delightful two-year-olds (except those who have a new sibling in their lives) continue that way for many months, at least. On the other hand, self-centered, unhappy two-year-olds do not change dramatically, at least not over the next few years.

The Effect of Child-Rearing Conditions on Development

During the ten years between 1957 and 1967 I spent studying the role of experience in the development of children during their first six months, I learned many interesting things about how the rate of development could be affected by different kinds of experiences. Through experiments with physically normal children, I learned that the rate at which children acquire abilities in the first six months of life, at least in regard to visual motor skills and to the foundations of intelligence, could be modified dramatically by the manipulation of child-rearing circumstances.

It has long been known that you can easily prevent a baby from reaching any significant level of development in the first six months of life. My colleagues and I also learned in our research on the first months of life that if you provide certain circumstances for your baby during those first months of life, she can achieve some skills considerably earlier than most babies do.

Visually directed reaching, for example, is acquired at about five to five and a half months of age by most babies. In our studies we provided babies, starting at three or four weeks of age, with objects to look at, bat, feel, and play with. This resulted in the acquisition of mature reaching at a bit more than three months.

This is a considerable acceleration of the process, but perhaps more important, the children involved had a marvelous time. During the fourth month they were filled with enthusiasm. They giggled excitedly, played with the objects around them, looked happily into an overhead mirror, and did a good deal of vocalizing. You can see how this kind of pleasurable and occasionally exciting play leads to the goal of supporting the development of specific skills while nurturing the baby's zest for life and curiosity. The babies who went through those studies became much more spirited and interested at six and seven months of age than babies who were like them at birth but who had little to do during their first six months of life.

We now have information at hand that could enable us to provide future children, at least in principle, with circumstances that are more suited to their earlier needs and interests than those to which they were normally exposed. It also means, very probably, that what we now call a normal rate of development will, thirty or forty years from now, be considered a slow pace.

As you look at the figure on page 120, you will see that in addition to the same curves that appear in the preceding figure, there is an additional curve, labeled E, that describes the course of accelerated development of babies in our research studies in the first six months of life.

In the research during the intervening years we soon arrived at another conclusion of practical significance in addition to the notion that somewhere between their first and third birthday children begin to reveal where they are headed in later years: we also concluded that two years of age is already much too late to begin to look at a child's educational development, particularly in the area of social skills and attitudes.

In fact, in our current parent education work, we do not enroll families whose babies are over ten months old. We have found that by fourteen months a baby can have developed a pattern of social behavior that is painful for all concerned and surprisingly difficult to modify. I believe that part of the problem is that parents have already adopted a style of responding to their baby's demands that has led to the unhappy social behavior of their baby and that is somewhat resistant to modification.

I do not mean to say it is all over by fourteen months of age. Of course not, but we have often seen well-entrenched, unpleasant learned behaviors in fourteen-month-olds, and we have experienced a surprising amount of difficulty in helping in such cases. By contrast, when we start with a family before their baby is ten months old, preferably much earlier, we usually succeed in avoiding poor results during the first fourteen months.

A two-year-old is a much more complicated, firmly established social being than an eight- or fourteen-month-old. We have found that it is not uncommon for a two-year-old already to be severely spoiled and very difficult to live with. In more tragic situations the child may even be somewhat alienated from people, including his own family. We have seen these phenomena repeatedly, but we have never seen a six-month-old who was spoiled.

By fourteen months, however, poor social development has clearly become a substantial problem in many families. For these reasons we attach very special significance to the process of social development between eight and twenty-four months of age. As you observe your child's evolution as a person as she goes from eight to twenty-four months of age, you will be amazed at the difference in complexity these sixteen months bring. You will not find any such dramatic changes in your child's development after age two.

The period that starts at eight months and ends at three years is a period of primary importance in the development of a human being. The period from eight to fourteen months of age is the first major phase of that exciting time span.

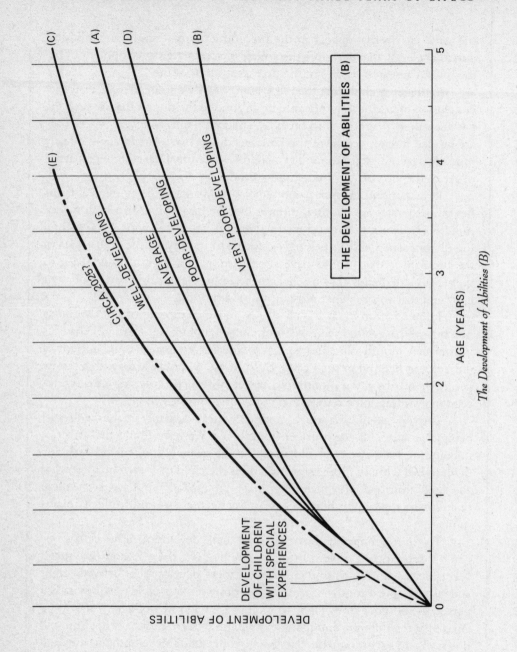

THE DEVELOPMENT OF ABILITIES (B)

The Development of Abilities (B)

EDUCATIONAL GOALS

Over the years, three useful ways of describing educational goals for the period from eight months through three years have emerged in our work. First, we have found that all healthy eight-month-old children seem motivated by three major interests aside from physiological needs such as hunger, thirst, and freedom from pain. These three major interests are *socializing,* especially with key people; *satisfying curiosity;* and *mastering and enjoying new motor abilities.* These interests, which have obvious survival value, are vigorous and in balance in all healthy eight-month-old babies. When development goes well, each grows steadily and the balance is maintained. Too often, however, these interests develop unevenly between eight and twenty-four months of age, and the result is mildly or severely debilitating. For you, with your obvious deep concern for your baby, the only difficulty you are likely to face is the threat of overdevelopment of your baby's social interest. The most common consequence is what we call overattachment. Guiding the balanced, solid growth of these primary interests will be discussed in later sections.

A second way of discussing educational goals is to talk of the emergence of the pattern of intellectual, linguistic, perceptual, and social competencies our research has found typical of beautifully developed three- to six-year-old children. Four important social competencies emerge in Phase V. Between nine and a half and eleven months of age, babies begin to realize older people can be helpful, and they begin to deliberately seek assistance from them (use of an adult as a resource). At roughly the same time, the seeking of approval for simple achievements and cute behavior surfaces as an indication of a baby's first feelings of pride in accomplishment. Also at this time, babies begin to express their feelings toward their key people. They may snuggle up or hug or even kiss you without being asked. They will also look you in the eye and make it clear to you that they are angry with you. Finally, shortly after the first birthday, children begin to engage in simple make-believe or fantasy behavior. Common examples are "talking" on a toy telephone or pretending to drive a toy truck, car, or airplane.

The third way we characterize the educational goals of this special period of life is to describe four fundamental processes that undergo their primary development during the first thirty-six months of life. These processes are language, curiosity, intelligence, and social development.

Language Development

Although children may respond to words during the first six or seven months of life, there is no reason to believe that they understand the meaning of those words. A five-month-old will respond when her name is called. However, you can call her by virtually any name and she will respond in exactly the same way. From seven or eight months of age on, however, babies clearly reveal that they have begun to understand the meaning of their first words. The average one-year-old will understand between five and ten words and a few simple instructions such as "sit down," "no," and "wave bye-bye."

By three years of age, children understand most (about 70 percent) of the language that they will use in ordinary conversation for the rest of their lives. Progress in the ability to understand language is different in important ways from progress in learning to use language (talking). In all physically normal babies the ability to understand language begins to develop at about the same age, between six and eight months. It then grows steadily and at an increasingly rapid pace over the next two years. Speech, on the other hand, is a notoriously poor indication of language development during the first two years of life. If a baby says nothing at fourteen months of age but is otherwise developing normally, it is very unlikely there is anything wrong. If she doesn't understand at least twenty-four words, however, it is very likely she is developmentally delayed. Many a bright child talks very little before eighteen or nineteen months of age. But just before the second birthday, we expect an explosion of speech from most babies.

Language, like so many of the issues we will talk about, is interrelated during the first year of life with other major developments. No child can do well on an intelligence test at three or four years of age, for example, unless his language development is good. Indeed, you can usually predict with reasonable accuracy a child's IQ from any reliable assessment of his language skills once he gets to be three or four years of age.

Over and above its fundamental role in the development of intelligence, language plays an equally important part in the development of social skills. Much of what transpires between any two people involves either listening to or using language. So, in a very significant way, good language development underlies good social development.

The Development of Curiosity

Just about everyone knows that kittens go through a stage during which they are incredibly curious. We also know that monkeys and puppies are similar in this regard. Indeed, it appears that many young mammals, including horses, go through an early period when they are consumed by the need to explore. We have never really pinpointed such a stage with human beings before, perhaps because those charged with the responsibility of researching early human development have left much of that research undone even to this date. I believe, however, that research over the last three decades—especially our own in the homes of many kinds of children—has helped to fill this gap in our knowledge.

We have never come across a healthy eight-month-old child who is not incredibly curious. We have never known an eight-month-old child who, once she learned to crawl, needed to be encouraged to explore the home. Bear in mind that a very strong exploratory drive is of central importance to humans. Unlike most other animals, humans go through a very long developmental period and come equipped with fewer coping instincts than do other animals. Nothing is more fundamental to solid educational development than pure, uncontaminated curiosity.

The Development of Intelligence

According to Piaget, a child at eight months of age has turned a developmental corner. He has received his early introduction to the world and to his own basic motor skills, and has started to focus on small objects. The year or so that follows features active exploration of simple cause-and-effect mechanisms, of the movement patterns of objects, and of their textures, shapes, and forms. This is an incredibly rich time during which the child is acquiring the foundations of higher mental abilities. Surely as far as education is concerned, few things are more central than the substructure of sensorimotor explorations upon which higher levels of intelligence are built. It is perhaps worth pointing out that the bulk of these acquisitions that underlie later thinking ability come about through thousands of simple explorations of small objects and without the benefit of any special input by other people. These sensorimotor foundations of higher learning do not appear to be at risk.

Social Development

The two-year-old child is an extremely complicated and sophisticated social creature. His social world, for the most part, revolves around his primary caretaker (usually, though not always, his mother), and ordinarily he has worked out with her an extraordinary contract full of ifs, ands, and buts that constitute to a great extent the rules that govern his behavior. He has learned whether or not she is a gentle, friendly person. He has learned all the subtle cues that help him to identify her mood state at any given moment. He has usually learned a whole different body of information about his father and about his siblings, particularly those close in age to him. He may have, at age two, developed into a delightful human being who is a pleasure to live with, a minicompanion good for all sorts of extraordinarily delightful experiences; or, sadly, he may have developed into an overindulged child who constantly badgers his mother, particularly if there is a younger child in the home. He may have become, in other words, either a total joy to be with or an extraordinarily difficult and unpleasant child. Even sadder is the child who at two has been consistently rejected by people, who has learned to isolate himself, who has never had the pleasure of a free and easy rewarding relationship with another human being.

Yet another not uncommon pattern is that of the child who has learned a good deal about fear during the period between eight and twenty-four months of age. Not infrequently a young child learns to stay away from his own mother unless she gives clear signals that an approach is okay. Far more common is the two-year-old whose slightly older sibling has made it clear through hundreds of small encounters that he doesn't care for her very much.

Each of the four educational foundations—the development of language, curiosity, intelligence, and social makeup—is at risk during the period from eight months to two years. What do I mean by "at risk?" I mean that unlike the achievements of the first six or eight months of life, which I propose are more or less ensured by virtue of their simple requirements and the characteristics of the average environment, the full achievement of the educational goals of the eight- to twenty-four-month period is by no means ensured. It is not at all inevitable that the child will learn language as well as he might. It is not at all inevitable that he will have his curiosity deepened and broadened as well as he might. It is not at all inevitable that his social development will take place in a solid and fruitful manner. Finally, the higher mental abilities that begin to surface toward the end of the second year share with the other three foundation processes a similar susceptibility toward less than optimal development. This susceptibility exists even though it would appear that the substructures for intelligence—that is, the sensorimotor foundations—are not particularly sensitive to common environmental variations. Indeed, I must repeat that, in my opinion, no more than one child in ten achieves the level of ability in these four fundamental areas that he could achieve.

OBSTACLES TO OPTIMAL DEVELOPMENT BETWEEN EIGHT AND THIRTY-SIX MONTHS

There are three common and significant obstacles to successful educational development in the period from eight to thirty-six months of age. They are ignorance, stress, and lack of assistance.

Ignorance

Typical young parents are quite unprepared for the responsibility of educating their first child. We do next to nothing in this country to educate parents for the responsibility of raising young children. With the apparent success in 1985 of the New Parents as Teachers program, which I designed and supervised for the state of Missouri, I had high hopes for parent education for all families starting to raise children. Although that program, now called Parents as First Teachers (PAT), currently operates in varying degrees in some forty-two states, I am not at all happy with its quality. It is a rare parent educator who is receiving more than a woefully inadequate amount of training for the job. Here in Newton, Massachusetts, we operate a model program based in our nonprofit Center for Parent Education, but that is no substitute for a well-run national effort.

It is also worth noting that until the 1970s, the amount of useful, accurate information about day-to-day development and child-rearing was remarkably limited. Until that time, the period between five days of age and three years was hardly looked at by students of human development. The consequence was that up until very recently we simply have not had enough useful information to teach.

We have known for some time, of course, when the typical baby starts to walk, to sit unaided, to wave bye-bye, and so forth. But sophisticated, extensive, and detailed information about the growth of the young human, and especially about the causes of good or poor development, has been in remarkably short supply in spite of all the opinions and all the words that have been written on the subject. Psychological and educational research people have agreed unanimously on the importance of the processes that are developing in the first three years of life, but until very recently, those researchers have not developed the necessary knowledge. Because of long-standing styles of raising children, until the late 1970s doing research on a child younger than two and a half years of age required going to his home or making an appointment for him to come to your office or your laboratory. Going out to the home is an inconvenient activity for a child development researcher. It is also an extremely inefficient way to do research. Studying a child in his own environment not only requires transportation to and from the home but, more important, does not provide ideal conditions for this kind of research. How much easier it is to have a group of college sophomores come to your laboratory, where they can be studied for thirty minutes at a time. The college sophomore coming into a psychology laboratory to be a subject doesn't bring his parents along. He is not overly apprehensive about what might happen to him, and he has been conditioned for years to do what he is told, particularly when he is told to do something by someone with prestige or someone who is going to give him a grade in a course.

To complicate matters, there are many different kinds of children. It is useless to make general statements about children on the basis of one middle-class child. Samples must be drawn from all major categories, depending upon the particular topic under study. Moreover, on any given day a child of two years of age may do one thing in a test situation or in his spontaneous behavior; the next day, or even an hour later, he may do something else. Even if you have gone to a home five times, you cannot assume that you have acquired a fair sampling of a very young child's behavior.

All in all, it is not surprising that the actual basic building of the science of early human development made so little progress until the late 1970s in spite of the hundreds of millions of dollars that have been poured into the enterprise by the federal government and private foundations.

All sorts of misinformation on child development, and especially on parenting, has been offered to the public. Scratch the surface of these materials, however, looking for the basis on which the recommendations about child-rearing made, and you'll generally find that the basis is very shallow. With few exceptions, until the last twenty years or so if you wanted legitimate information about raising a very young child, you would probably have been better off asking an intelligent mother of several children than seeking help from any professional. To some extent, that situation still prevails.

During the last two decades, as awareness of the special importance of learning during the first few years of life has grown, there have been serious attempts to make up for the lack of solid information. We have in our files at the Center for Parent Education, for example, information on more than eight hundred programs designed to help people raise their young children effectively. The sponsorship of these programs is extremely diverse. Some of them are based in public school systems, others in preventive mental health programs, still others out of church groups, and so on. This diversity reflects the immaturity of this new field. Many of these programs do wonderful work. Most of them, however, suffer from the history of the field and its neglect of the informational needs of society. Most of the people operating the programs for young parents have very little training, and the weaknesses in their background are passed on to parents. The subject of early learning is a complicated one. Thus it remains difficult to identify reliable information and to translate it into a realistic program for both professional staff and families.

Stress

Not only are families much less aware than they ought to be of the details of early learning, but they also have to do their job, from time to time, under a fair degree of stress. I am referring here, for the most part, to the mother, because she is the one who is most likely to have the major responsibility for a baby's upbringing. This stress occurs routinely from pregnancy through the first years of life. During the first two months of the infant's life, the common practice of infants to awake repeatedly during the night leads to chronic fatigue. In addition to the standard sleeplessness, there is also the baby's initial digestive problems, which add to the anxiety of new parents. And if that isn't enough, add to it the fact that babies in the first two months of life are neither as good-looking nor as responsive as our mythology has led parents to believe.

From the middle of the third month until the baby is about seven and one half months old, stress on parents is usually, but not always, much lower, and parenting becomes enormously enjoyable for perhaps five out of six families. Then, when the baby starts to crawl about the home at seven to eight months of age, the stress level rises again. If you have a first child, the principal sources of stress will come from your fear of physical danger to the baby, and damage to the home as well, along with the extra work that is a consequence. Newly crawling babies are incredibly curious about everything they can see and reach; they use their mouths to explore, they don't know very much about the characteristics of objects, and they are inadequate masters of their own bodies. Certainly they don't know how fragile or how valuable objects might be. The life expectancy of the newly sprouted avocado seed in the hands of a typical ten-month-old, for example, is about ten seconds.

All this adds up to a worried parent, and rightly so. The period from eight to twenty months of age is the time when the vast majority of accidental poisonings take place. A baby crawling about the home will find everything new. She has seen many of these things from a distance, but she has never before been able to come up close to such intriguing objects as those bits of beautiful shiny glass from a broken jar that happened to fall in an out-of-the-way place, or that interestingly frayed spot on the lamp cord.

And nothing, of course, is more appealing to a ten-month-old than a flight of stairs. Put her at the bottom and you can bet with confidence that she will attempt to climb to the top, although even in this there are exceptions. Some ten-month-olds are pretty good at climbing stairs. At times, however, they will pause after climbing three or four steps and, in the moments that follow, be distracted, perhaps by a mark on the banister that captures their attention or by a small toy left there by another child. This distraction may cause them to forget where they are, and they may turn around and fall. No wonder anybody who's reasonable and loving worries about the safety and well-being of a baby who is crawling about the home for the first time.

There is also stress from the extra work that a baby of this age produces. If you give a baby a chance to roam about the home, you'll find yourself spending more time straightening up the house, particularly if either parent insists on keeping the household neat. Babies create clutter; it is as natural as breathing. And a cluttered house with a ten-month-old baby is, all other things being equal, a good sign. In fact, an immaculate house and a ten-month-old baby who is developing well are, in my opinion, usually incompatible. If more adults were aware of this contradiction, they would probably endure a lot less grief.

By far the greatest stress, once a baby can crawl, occurs if there is a slightly older sibling in the home, particularly if that sibling is a first child. You have to expect deeply rooted feelings of anger based in jealousy on the part of the slightly older child. Sibling rivalry, though reasonably well known, is usually not fully understood by young parents. People are inclined to think that any such problem will begin as soon as the new child is brought home from the hospital. But sibling rivalry is rarely a major problem at that stage of the game. After all, the new baby is likely to weigh about six pounds, have a relatively soft cry, and live mostly in a box in another room, showing up only occasionally during the day. The newborn makes a comparatively small dent in the life of the one-and-a-half-year-old. The problems begin to surface when the new baby becomes mobile. For all of the reasons just listed, such a child has to have more attention from whoever is caring for her, and that attention, from the point of view of a two-year-old, is very difficult to deal with.

Because of the importance of this subject, we will discuss it in detail in later sections. For now it is sufficient to note that according to studies of average families of various kinds, the biggest single source of stress is usually the presence of closely spaced siblings.

The final form of stress worth noting in this brief summary is the negativistic behavior that emerges with most children in the second half of the second year. Although the eight- to fourteen-month-old baby creates a good deal of stress for the previously mentioned reasons, there is nothing personal in the child's behavior: he is simply acting in accordance with his nature. After he has destroyed a cherished plant, for example, he will move on to the next interesting situation. His mother, coming upon the remains, may very naturally make a loud noise in expressing her displeasure. The typical response of a normal ten-month-old is to pause in his new exploration, turn reflexively and promptly toward the noise made by his mother, and upon seeing her face, regardless of her expression, smile.

That same child at fifteen or sixteen months of age is an altogether different person. From the time he began to crawl, he has been collecting experiences in which he has been forbidden to do A or B or to play with objects C or D. From fifteen to sixteen months on, as his self-awareness becomes more substantial, something in his nature we don't fully understand will lead him to deliberately try each of these forbidden activities, specifically to see what will be allowed and what won't. In other words, he will begin systematically to challenge the authority of the adult he lives with. Resistance to simple requests becomes very common at this time, and if there is more than one child around, this can be a low point in the parenting experience. Dealing with both a fifteen-month-old and a thirty-month-old day in and day out is usually extremely stressful. We will go into more detail on this topic in the next chapter.

Lack of Assistance

The last major obstacle to optimal educational development during this period relates to the fact that many young parents must go through this experience alone. Indeed, often the mother lacks even the benefit of a sympathetic husband and has to cope with his dissatisfaction on top of everything else. This constitutes cruel and inhuman punishment in my judgment. Pediatricians vary in the degree to which they provide support; the ones who do help are often revered. Very often, however, pediatricians have no extensive background in child development and parenting and are ill-equipped to help inexperienced parents. Quite a number of parent support programs exist today, but while they do wonderful work it is usually nowhere near sufficient to meet the need. In some instances, of course, a young mother is on good terms with her mother or mother-in-law, and with luck, she can profit from their wisdom, experience, and good sense. By and large, however, the typical young family, and particularly the mother, has to go it alone.

GENERAL BEHAVIOR DURING PHASE V

A unique and invaluable feature of our research has been our extensive monthly observations (for up to two years) of many children as they go about their ordinary activities at home. We have done a lot of "fly on the wall" data-gathering. Using a category system we devised that covers all types of experience, we sampled the behavior of babies using stopwatches and tape recorders. Some of the results are presented in this book in the form of charts of typical experiences of babies between twelve and thirty-six months of age.

As you can see from the chart on page 130, twelve- to fifteen-month-old babies spend much more time in nonsocial pursuits than they do relating to people. Most parents find this very surprising. You probably feel as if you are interacting with your baby much more than 11 percent of the time. To be fair, this chart includes first, second, and third babies, and first babies do spend somewhat more time than subsequent ones in social interactions, but not a great deal more. Even first babies rarely spend more than 15 to 20 percent of their time socializing. Your year-old baby is much more of an explorer than a socializer.

The single most common daily focus of the twelve- to fifteen-month-old child involves various activities with small objects. Babies stare at them; explore their qualities by banging, mouthing, and throwing them; and practice simple hand-eye skills on them. Small objects mean a lot to infants. The second most common experience is steady staring at objects or people. This activity takes up more than 17 percent of the day, some part of which includes staring at small objects. Also notable is the fact that the typical one-year-old spends a fair amount of time just hanging around, doing very little. Nontask behavior occupies about 13 percent of the time.

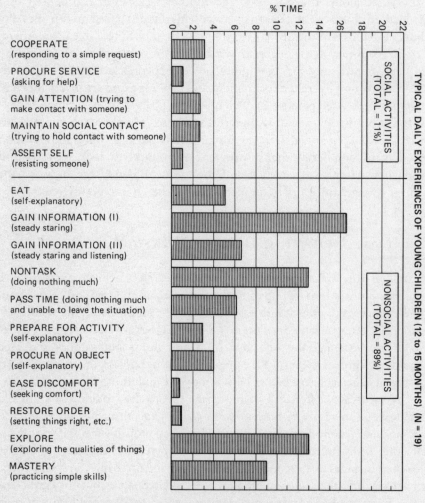

Typical Daily Experience of Young Children (12–15 Months) (N = 19)

The Remarkable Curiosity of Phase V Children

At about eight months of age babies enter into a period that closely parallels the peak period of curiosity in the young of other mammals. One cannot help but be impressed by this curiosity, which shows itself in the baby's dedication to physical exploration as soon as he can move his body through space. Except in children who are ill or seriously damaged, this behavior is highly predictable.

It seems logical that in the course of the hundreds of hours prelocomotive children spend looking about at distant, unreachable objects, they will build up great anticipation with respect to exploring their environment. Remember that from the time your baby was approximately four months of age she has had enough back and neck muscle strength to be comfortable sitting up, and she has also had the capacity to see and hear clear across the room.

These new abilities are combined with an intense need to explore the world. As a result, you can expect your crawling infant to explore whenever she's given the chance. If you have an eight-month-old who can move about on her own but who shows no interest in exploring her environment, I urge you to see your pediatrician or other health specialist promptly to find out if she is ill or has a handicap of some kind.

Situations that most adults would find uninteresting often fascinate a baby. Don't be surprised if you find your baby swinging a kitchen cabinet door back and forth several dozen times a day for several consecutive days. Don't be surprised if he is intrigued by small pieces of dust that he has picked up from the floor. Don't be surprised if he is fascinated by the cellophane wrapper from a package. This means, of course, that razor blades will interest him, too, as will anything else he can inspect closely, particularly if he can handle the object and bring it to his mouth. You can therefore see the mixed blessing of curiosity: it is the motivational force underlying most learning and achievement, but at the same time it is the cause of many childhood accidents—and of a great deal of anxiety for parents.

Motor Skills

The incredible curiosity of Phase V is accompanied by an equally intense interest on the part of all healthy babies in mastering the use of their bodies. From eight to fourteen months of age especially, your baby will develop new motor skills of a very important kind. It is the nature of the baby to practice each of those skills over and over again until she gets them right. In addition and more subtly, in practicing these skills, children begin to learn a good deal about people—their usefulness and their reactions. Babies are now registering others' reactions to their efforts and their achievements. Al-

"Why? Because it's there."

though the acquisition of motor abilities is reasonably assured under a wide variety of child-rearing circumstances, the social consequences of those abilities are more likely to be at risk, especially given today's family lifestyles. No one gets as excited about a baby's achievements as parents and grandparents.

CRAWLING AND CLIMBING
The first motor skill of Phase V is some form of crawling. This initial crawling is followed by the ability to get higher in space, a skill that takes two forms: the ability to pull oneself up to a standing posture, and the first ability to climb.

STANDING AND CRUISING
At about nine to ten months your baby will acquire the ability to pull himself up to a standing posture. It could happen a few weeks earlier or as much as a few months later. The later it happens, the fewer gray hairs you will acquire. This is not a risk area.

She will pull herself up to stand against a piece of furniture or perhaps against your leg, using your slacks, skirt, or any other article of clothing that is handy for support. Some babies become apprehensive about getting back down to the floor, even though the floor is not far away. Most babies carefully flop. If yours doesn't, you can easily teach her to do so by guiding her through the motions. If she is afraid and you don't teach her how, she will repeatedly pull herself up and then cry out for you to help her down.

This new skill is followed fairly soon by cruising, which consists of moving about on two legs while holding on to supporting objects. Usually, just before one year of age, but sometimes several weeks sooner, cruising is followed by unaided walking. Walking is followed by running and, at about thirteen or fourteen months of age, by the ability to straddle small four-wheeled objects and drag them about.

These are the primary motor acquisitions having to do with the large muscles of the body during Phase V. The new freedom made possible by these skills means a great deal to a child, and he will spend a great deal of time practicing them, given the opportunity.

CLIMBING

The ability to climb is an extraordinarily interesting and momentous affair to infants. It appears in two stages. The first stage emerges at somewhere between eight and twelve months, when children begin to climb relatively modest heights of eight or nine inches. This height is coincidentally just right for typical stair climbing. You may find your baby managing to climb a low footstool when he is eight to ten months of age. He finds this capacity to get up off the floor very exciting and will practice it again and again. This practice is slightly dangerous to him in that his ability to maintain his balance is only marginal and his judgment as to where his behind will land if he turns to sit is not particularly good. In addition, his memory leaves something to be desired. Thus there is now a strong likelihood of a daily fall or two.

Sometime around eleven or twelve months of age babies acquire a second climbing skill: the ability to climb as much as 16 inches at a time. This improved ability allows the baby to get up on the living room sofa, and from there she will generally be able to climb onto the arm of the sofa, and then onto the back of the sofa, and so on. Likewise, she will climb onto a kitchen chair, from the chair onto the table, and from the table onto the counter. This two-step process seems to be universal with all infants; you can see its important safety consequences as well as its payoffs in the excitement of new places that she can now reach and explore. Obviously, now that your baby is capable of climbing sixteen-inch heights, you have to take special precautions with poisons and other hazardous substances and objects.

Staring

During our extensive observations of many kinds of Phase V children, we have been struck by the surprising frequency of a behavior we call "staring," whereby the baby gains information by simply looking steadily at something. In our observations of hundreds of children the single most frequent activity found in this phase, other than sleeping, was simply looking at an object or scene. If you watch your child for any length of time, you will see for yourself that your Phase V baby is a "looker." She will stare a lot. My colleagues who study other primates tell me that young apes and monkeys also spend a good deal of time staring at objects and at other monkeys. All human babies spend a substantial amount of time looking at their mothers or other primary caretakers. They'll stare at objects before or just after exploring them more actively. They also like to look out the window and will watch other children playing at a distance. We have found that children spend about 17 percent of their waking time staring at one thing or another during this phase.

The First Responses to Words

The Phase V baby, week by week, will reveal greater and greater interest in and understanding of words and phrases. Now the development of the understanding of language is slowly beginning. This first understanding of words will reveal itself in the compliant behavior of this period. Increasingly, children will tend to respond when you call their names, will look toward other family members whom you are addressing, and will go along with simple requests—to throw a kiss, wave bye-bye, or retrieve an object. But don't expect your child to do a great deal of talking yet. A few children do indeed begin to talk before their first birthday, but not many. Normal children begin to say their first words between eight and 20 months of age.

Increasing Interest in Mother

In addition to satisfying curiosity and trying out new motor skills, the third principal interest of Phase V babies is in the person around whom the day revolves. From eight to fourteen months of age you will notice a steadily increasing orientation toward the primary caretaker. At about ten or eleven months, this increase will feature the first clear requests for assistance from that person and the first expressions of affection and also of anger directed at that person, hopefully on rare occasions. The first requests for assistance are most often for things like more milk or cookies, or sometimes for help when the child can't do something for herself.

Interest in Small Objects

Your eight-month-old may show a striking interest in tiny particles. While sitting in her high chair or on the floor, she may scrunch up her forehead and stare intensely at small objects, some of which you cannot even see from a distance. Looking closer, you may find the child concentrating on cracker crumbs or perhaps a small bug. You are seeing the result of two processes reaching maturation: the capacity to see very fine detail, and the capacity to explore that fine detail in new ways because of the newfound ability to sit up and move about. This interest is linked to the more general but equally deep interest in exploring the qualities of small objects. From eight months until two years or so, and increasingly during Phase V, children spend roughly 25 percent of their waking time actively exploring small objects. That interest takes three principal forms. One is simply staring at the object. The second is what we call exploratory behavior: the child explores all the attributes of any new object she comes across. That exploration includes bringing the object to her mouth for gumming, banging it, striking it, throwing it, turning it around, and then staring at it from different angles, rubbing it against things, and so forth. She will try out a wide variety of actions on the object. The third type of small object exploration is what we call mastery experiences—practicing simple skills on objects. If the object has a base so that it can be stood up and then knocked down again, you may find the child engaged in doing this. If it is a crayon, you may find her rolling it back and forth and watching the motion.

Phase V children also have a peculiar fascination with collections of items, particularly if they are irregularly shaped and have fine detail. One of the simple skills they practice at this time is the emptying of objects out of containers one at a time. Once she has emptied out all of the objects, the child may very well return them to the container one at a time, pausing to examine each as she does.

Mouthing Objects and Other Materials

At this stage of life, the mouth continues to be a prominent tool for exploration. You can also expect, with most babies, that new teeth will be erupting. Because of both factors the child will bring most objects to his mouth, at times with unfortunate consequences for his safety.

Clumsiness

Although motor abilities are emerging rapidly, you must not forget that babies of this age are not terribly skillful. You'll notice that by and large your baby will be surprisingly careful about herself. It is our estimate that at least four out of five babies of this age are careful climbers. Nevertheless, there is that one baby in five or six who seems to be bent on self-destruction. I've seen them too often not to warn you to watch closely.

Friendliness

The eight- to fourteen-month-old, particularly during the early stages of this phase, is very friendly when he is among people with whom he interacts every day. He may be causing you all sorts of grief, extra work, and anxiety, but he is not doing this in order to upset you. The difficulties he creates are simply a natural accompaniment to this particular stage of his development. Furthermore, you'll be rewarded over and over again with gestures of affection and wide, totally irresistible smiles. If you are lucky, you may be spontaneously hugged and kissed often, as well as on request. Enjoy this friendliness while it lasts; with the onset of Phase VI, things will take a turn for the worse.

Anxiety and Shyness with Strangers

Especially during the first months of this phase, your baby's friendliness is chiefly reserved for her primary caretaker and other people whom she sees every day. Soon after Phase V begins, you will realize that she has become a serious student of your reactions to her behavior, especially her various types of cries. At the same time, the hail-fellow-well-met quality of your baby during Phase IV is gradually receding, indicating that she has made her social choices. She has learned that her security lies with her parents or other principal caretakers. Outsiders, even those as close as grandparents living elsewhere, are likely to be treated during Phase V with apprehension and shyness. These qualities will likely be more pronounced when your baby is in a strange environment. Put her in her grandparents' home and, more often than not, your baby will want to stay close to one of her key people. This kind of behavior, normal at this age, persists with an occasional child until the child reaches two years. For most, however, it becomes less pronounced after the first birthday.

Behavior with Siblings

INTERACTION WITH A SIBLING THREE OR MORE YEARS OLDER

We have seen repeatedly that siblings four years old or older usually treat the Phase V baby with affection and interest. Siblings more than three years older than an infant do not spend a great deal of time with babies. They have entered into a period of life where they are much more oriented to children their own age, and as a result, they are much more inclined to play with peers than with an infant brother or sister. A baby's most common experience with such older siblings therefore involves watching them either when they are alone or while they're playing with their friends.

INTERACTION WITH A SIBLING LESS THAN THREE YEARS OLDER

When the baby has a sibling not much older than he is, the situation differs in very important ways. The older child, especially if she's a first child, and especially if she has been somewhat overindulged—two circumstances that occur together rather commonly—can be expected to gradually come to feel and to show genuine resentment and dislike toward the baby. This behavior, while very unpleasant to witness and to live with, is so common that it must be considered normal. Parents should anticipate this, because they will have to cope with it, just as the infant will. Because of the normal resentment and occasional anger that the older sibling feels toward the younger child, from time to time she will act aggressive and selfish toward the baby.

Notice that I did not introduce this topic of sibling rivalry until the baby has reached eight months of age. A newly crawling baby is much more likely to get hurt than a younger infant, and she is also more likely to break things and create extra work in the home as a result of her explorations. Both developments inevitably require parents to pay more attention to the baby now than they did in the preceding months. Attention, in the mind of an older sibling only eighteen to thirty months of age, means love. A five-day-old sibling newly arrived from the hospital doesn't trouble a toddler very much. After all, newborns sleep most of the day and tend, therefore, not to be a constant object of attention. Even when a baby gets to be four or five months of age and is awake much of the time, she still does not intrude a great deal on the moment-to-moment experiences of the slightly older sibling. The picture changes dramatically, however, from the moment the baby begins to crawl about, especially if parents allow her to explore the home rather than confine her to a playpen for most of the day.

Because of these realities it is totally natural for slightly older children to begin to behave aggressively and selfishly toward the baby. The older child may even hit the baby now and again, may knock him down or take toys away from him. At first the baby is likely to be bewildered by this behavior, but sooner or later the older child will cause him pain. That pain will be followed by a cry, bringing a parent, who is likely to size up the situation and conclude that the older child was the cause of the pain that the baby is experiencing. A harsh word or a punishment of some kind is natural under such circumstances, but it certainly doesn't make the older child feel less unhappy.

As Phase V continues, this emotionally intense process will evolve. We expect to see an escalation of jealousy, hard feelings, and aggression on the part of the older child, and a tendency on the part of the baby to cry sooner and sooner and louder and louder. The result very often is that by the eleventh to twelfth month, the baby may flinch and cry even before the older child touches him. The older child, having gone through dozens of learning experiences in respect to the effectiveness of the baby's cry, enters gradually into a period of frustration. He has clearly learned that aggression toward the baby leads to crying and, in turn, punishment by the central person in his life. As a result, by the time the baby is about a year of age, or midway through Phase V, a standoff often has developed. This temporary armistice is likely to persist through the balance of Phase V and to take a surprising turn once the younger child enters Phase VI.

The severity of this problem is directly related to the age gap between the children. The closer they are in age, the more frequent and intense is the hostile behavior the older child directs to the baby during Phase V. This hostile behavior comes as quite a shock to many young parents. After all, they've had approximately a year and a half of experience during which that first child brought them an incredible amount of pleasure and pride, and now, try as they might, they cannot avoid concluding that their older child is capable of active dislike of their equally precious baby. Parents are ill prepared to cope with this unhappy situation. One of the benefits of the new knowledge in child development is that we now understand the origins of this kind of behavior. We have found that when parents are informed before the fact, things can go much better.

Younger babies in this situation do learn during Phase V how to cope with older siblings, how to defend themselves, how to avoid getting into difficulty, and—sad but true—how to behave in a like manner toward the aggressor.

We will talk more about interactions between siblings in later sections. To be sure, there will be times when the older child will treat the baby with genuine affection, but don't be surprised if such occasions become fewer and fewer in number as Phase V progresses. Suffice it to say that spacing children at least three years apart is an extremely good idea.

THE APPARENT INTERESTS OF PHASE V

Aside from physical needs such as the satisfaction of hunger and freedom from pain, the Phase V baby has three central interests: (1) the primary caregiver, (2) exploring the world, and (3) practicing and enjoying new motor skills.

Interest in the Primary Caregiver

How children progress from eight months to about two years of age in respect to their interest in their primary caregiver is very exciting and extraordinarily important. The topic of attachment to another person has been a popular one in child development research in recent times and, by other labels, has been popular for many years. Popularity does not always produce wisdom, but we have learned a great deal about the details of the attachment process.

We know for certain that the newborn baby simply cannot survive without a deep commitment from a more mature and capable human. A newborn baby is helpless, and survival is impossible for him unless someone provides for him. I have described the various assets babies are born with that heighten the probability that someone will come to love them dearly, to care for them, to nurture them, and to protect them. A new phase of that ongoing development begins in earnest at about eight months of age.

Between eight and twenty-four months a good many of the child's waking activities will revolve around her primary caretaker, usually her mother. She will watch her mother's actions for substantial portions of each day. She will use her mother as a haven whenever she is feeling threatened. She will use her mother for assistance whenever she can, increasingly from about ten to eleven months of age on. She will learn a great deal from her mother. She will learn, for example, whether she is allowed to pull on the curtains, climb on furniture, climb on her own or her parents' bed, touch the plants in the living room, and go out onto the porch. She will learn thousands of specific answers to questions that will arise as she goes about her explorations.

She will learn many fine details about her mother's disciplinary style, and by the time she is thirteen or fourteen months of age, she will have become quite sophisticated in all these areas. If her parent is a talker rather than a doer, she will learn that threats are only words and will not be followed by actions. She will learn how to determine whether or not a parent means business. She will learn, albeit imperfectly, whether a parent gives her undivided attention or is often distracted. She will learn whether an instruction or an admonition requires immediate compliance or after a brief pause can safely be disregarded.

I have been using the word "mother." However, if the father is the principal caregiver, your baby will learn exactly the same way from him. The sex of the key person is, as far as I can tell, quite irrelevant.

By the time a child is two years of age, and often much earlier, she will have established an elaborate and detailed social contract with her primary caretaker. That contract is relatively hard to alter or modify subsequently. What children acquire in those first two years is the first set of social skills and attitudes they will begin to use with other family members, and with other children as they enter into peer relations.

Between eight and twenty-four months you have remarkable power to influence the shape of your child's personality and, at the same time, her day-to-day happiness. Having closely observed the process of development during these special months in the lives of many children, I am totally convinced of the validity of these slightly scary statements.

Your reaction to his social explorations during these sixteen months can result in a two-year-old who is either a chronically happy person and a delight to live with or a self-centered, chronically unhappy child.

If a child of this age is prevented from having a free and easy exchange with his parents or some other primary caretaker in these months, and if, for example, he is provided with all sorts of toys and areas to explore, you may find him showing less and less interest in people and more interest in objects. Given most circumstances, however, the interest in people will not only remain strong throughout this period but may very well overpower his interest in objects.

Interest in Exploring the World

The child at eight months of age is an explorer. He wants to see everything, touch everything, and bring everything that he can to his mouth. This interest is shown in the active exploration of any area to which he is allowed access. You'll find absolutely no need to induce him to explore and to learn; he'll do so for the sheer joy of it. He will explore any small, portable object for its novelty or to practice simple hand-eye skills. Your baby will show interest in the controls on the TV, the radio, the stereo. He will become interested in doorknobs. He will become interested in the contents of kitchen cabinets. He will be interested in particles of dust, leaves—just about anything he can get close to.

The Phase V baby's keen interest in the object world has several important consequences. One is the role that interest plays in deepening and broadening his curiosity and in promoting the development of the foundations of intelligence. Another is the role it plays as a balancing agent against the possible overdevelopment of his interest in social relations with you. The Phase V baby starts out with his three main interests in balance, but there is no guarantee they will remain that way in the year or so that follows. Furthermore, when that balance is distorted, the educational progress of the baby is affected negatively and life becomes more difficult for all concerned. This balance is most commonly thrown off when the normal focus on the mother expands at the expense of the other two interests.

The final point to be made concerning the Phase V baby's interest in exploration is the apparently universal appeal of water play. Unless you inadvertently frighten them, most babies love bath time from here on. The fact that they can sit upright with security helps.

Interest in Practicing and Enjoying New Motor Skills

In an earlier section I discussed the sequence of emerging motor skills, from crawling to standing to climbing. Phase V children spend many hours practicing their new ability to move through space in all directions, provided of course they are given the opportunity. One of the most common interests at this stage is in climbing stairs. Steps have an amazingly hypnotic power for the very young child.

LEARNING DEVELOPMENTS DURING PHASE V

Let me preface this discussion by reemphasizing an earlier declaration. It is my belief that the educational developments that take place between age eight and twenty months are the most important and most in need of attention of any that occur in human life. Absolutely basic educational foundations begin to develop in very important and fundamental ways as soon as a child starts to crawl about the home and simultaneously begins to take shape as a social being.

First-rate development of those educational foundations is by no means ensured. The responsibility for the quality of the educational outcome, for most children, rests with their parents and, more specifically, with the primary caretaker. Parents are not routinely prepared for the job, nor are they given very much assistance. I am convinced that not more than two-thirds of our children currently get adequate development in the areas dealt with here, and no more than 10 percent do as well as they could during the first three years of their lives. This state of affairs may be a tragedy, but it is by no means a twentieth-century tragedy. In the history of Western education there has never been a society that recognized the educational importance of the earliest years or sponsored any systematic preparation and assistance to families or institutions in guiding the early development of children.

Language Development

Language development was dealt with extensively on pages 121 and 122. Let me stress again that language is absolutely central to the development of intelligence and social skills.

/

The Development of Curiosity

The importance of curiosity for the Phase V child was discussed on pages 122 and 123. Curiosity can be broadened and deepened by intelligent child-rearing procedures during this period.

Social Development

Children two years of age can evolve into delightful companions who have free and easy social relationships and who, at the same time, are profoundly curious about the world at large. Unfortunately, they can also develop into human beings whose world revolves excessively around one adult, usually the mother. Often the mother is badgered from morning to night by a two-year-old who has a consuming desire to monopolize her time and attention. This type of child very often loses intrinsic interest in exploring objects and motor skills and now sees a new toy primarily as a tool for manipulating his mother.

It is even sadder, of course, to see a child who by age two has learned that his mother is not an approachable person unless she is in a good mood and indicates that she would like him to come closer. We have seen children systematically turned off from their primary caretaker by repeated rejection during Phases V and VI. This is tragic to see, and when it is accompanied by a lack of interesting physical materials and opportunities to explore the home, you get the saddest situation of all—a child who seems somewhat empty at two years of age. Poor social development can be avoided. More about how to achieve the desired patterns will follow.

Phase V is a particularly rich period in respect to social development. Four of the five special social competencies emerge; the three critical social lessons are learned; and stranger and separation behaviors make their appearance. By fourteen months of age, your baby will give clear indications of how well you are succeeding in this vital area of development.

Nurturing the Roots of Intelligence

I have described a powerful and universal urge in healthy eight-month-old children to explore the world. This urge is the principal motivating power underlying the acquisition of intelligence. That force can be deepened and broadened, or it can be kept shallow or narrow by child-rearing practices.

The Growth of Learning-to-Learn Skills

The underlying motivation to learn is as important as any other factor in regard to a child's educational well-being. In addition to developing that urge, children are collecting learning skills—that is, they are learning how to learn—during Phases V and VI. Piaget has described the exciting and fundamental events of this age. Our own research on many children as we have watched them develop during this period adds many details to the story.

Learning-to-learn skills come easily to the baby who is given the chance to explore the world along with a healthy dose of encouragement and assistance by adults. Babies do not produce products of any consequence in this particular phase, nor will they until they are at least two years of age; but throughout Phase V they are learning prerequisite skills. You won't find Phase V children drawing pictures, for example, but you will find them learning to handle small devices like those they will later use to write and draw. Signs of an interest in scribbling will begin to appear toward the end of Phase V. The innumerable efforts directed at getting to know the characteristics of objects, whether they bounce or roll, plop or slide, will later be used in the construction of products such as towers, ships, trucks, and scenes that feature dolls, animals, and buildings.

The retrieval skills that children are learning when they roll or throw a ball and then seek and reclaim it are also prerequisite elements in the more complicated and elaborate activities that come a year or two later. At this time they are also learning their first lessons in how to put things together and take them apart. You'll find that Phase V and VI children are very much interested in putting objects into each other. For example, putting lids on containers is a common interest seen at this point; sliding one gadget into and out of another is another activity of particular interest at this stage. These simple skills are interesting to a child in and of themselves, but they are also preparing the child for more complicated experiences later on.

HINGES AND HINGED OBJECTS

A curious related interest of Phase V is in hinges and hinged objects. Early in our observations of Phase V children we noticed their fascination with the activity of swinging doors back and forth. The most common door we have seen used in this manner is a kitchen cabinet door.

Interest in hinged objects is also revealed in the Phase V child's fascination with pop-up toys with lids that swing open. After they have caused the lid to open, they very often will swing it back and forth repeatedly.

The first toy that worked well in this respect was introduced about twenty-five years ago. It was called the Busy Surprise Box, from the makers of the original Busy Box. It had five small jack-in-the-boxes lined up next to each other in a single plastic box. In order to get a lid to swing up to reveal a small animal figure, the baby had to perform one of five simple motor activities, which included pushing a lever one way or the other, rotating a telephone dial, or pushing a button. Of the five required acts, the only one a Phase V baby could manage was pushing the lever one way or the other. We found that most Phase V babies enjoyed this particular toy. They played with it for as long as five to ten minutes at a time and came back to it repeatedly over a period of several months. This relatively prolonged use of a commercial toy was, and remains, most unusual, especially at this age. Over the last ten years or so, numerous similar toys have become available.

A more subtle manifestation of the apparently universal interest in hinged objects is the Phase V baby's interest in books. She is particularly intrigued by those that have stiff cardboard pages. Her interest is based not so much on what is printed on the pages as on what is required in hand-eye skill to separate the pages, turn the book upside down, and so forth. In other words, the small book with cardboard pages is an object on which she can practice simple motor skills. One of the skills she is particularly interested in involves treating any single page like one-half of a hinge and swinging it back and forth. Small board books are also great for gumming.

It is relatively easy to see how some of the simple skills that are practiced by babies in Phase V will play a role later in more complicated activities. It is not quite that easy to see how an interest in swinging kitchen cabinet doors fits into the larger scheme of things but, whether or not we can understand the reason for this interest, it is indeed there.

In addition to their value as materials to feed the Phase V baby's interest in perfecting hand-eye skills, books begin to be of some use at this stage in the acquisition of language.* The rate of language acquisition during Phase V is quite slow in comparison with what will come in the balance of the first three years; nevertheless, language learning is taking place. Books without stories—that is, books which simply illustrate familiar objects—are the most suitable for language teaching at this stage. The language teaching should be principally in the form of labeling. If you can manage to get the Phase V baby to sit still long enough to actually attend once in a while to what's on the page, naming the particular picture can be a pleasurable and profitable activity. You shouldn't be discouraged if you have a particularly active Phase V baby who simply refuses to sit still for quiet activities like reading and storytelling. If on the other hand you have the kind of child who will listen to you talk about the pictures, especially at bedtime, so much the better. Bear in mind, however, that the typical fourteen-month-old can understand only about three dozen words and a few simple expressions. As a

---

* Surprisingly, research on the possible benefits of reading to an infant has never been done. Common sense suggests that the practice has to be beneficial, but I try to make a distinction between recommendations that are backed up by evidence and those that are not.

result, stories are not likely to make much of an impression on him. Labeling, of course, shouldn't be restricted to books. It is the most natural thing in the world for parents to put a name on anything a baby of this age is interacting with, and this makes good sense. Indeed, the more often you do this kind of labeling, the better.

The Growth of Short-Term Memory

During this phase, the infant begins to retain for a longer time some sort of mental image of objects. By placing more and more obstacles between a baby and a desired object, by making it take longer and longer to get the hidden object, students of child development have learned to plot with some precision the actual limits of Phase V object permanence and short-term memory. The baby of about one year of age, for example, will easily find an object hidden under one pillow, but if you place three or four coverings on top of an object, requiring that the baby persist for ten to fifteen seconds, he is very likely to abandon the search before he succeeds in getting the object. Even by the end of Phase V the child's capacity to remember an object is not quite fully developed. It will be by seventeen months of age, however.

There are valuable practical consequences of this knowledge. When you combine the limited memory of a Phase V child with his intense curiosity about everything, you have the basis for distracting a child once he gets involved with something you'd rather he did not have. If, for example, your nine-month-old has found a cigarette butt, you could offer her a set of plastic spoons. This will usually result in the baby turning her attention away from the cigarette and toward the spoons. After four or five seconds of play with the spoons, your baby is not at all likely to seek the cigarette butt again; she will have forgotten about it. Once a baby reaches twelve to fourteen months of age, however, given the same circumstances, she will continue to look for the first item even after an interruption. But move this same child to another room and provide her with three new objects, and her preoccupation with them for a few minutes is usually long enough so that she will forget about the first object.

RECOMMENDED CHILD-REARING PRACTICES FOR PHASE V

As your child's primary caregiver, you have three major functions during Phase V, which will persist throughout the balance of the first three years. They are (1) architect or designer of your baby's world and daily experiences; (2) consultant, providing assistance and encouragement to the child; and (3) authority, the source of discipline and limit-setting. Let us examine each of these roles in turn.

The Primary Caregiver's Role as Designer

PROVIDING ACCESS TO THE HOME

Once you have made the home safe for and from your baby, your next step in designing her world is to give her maximum access to the home.★ Even the smallest, simplest home is a rich environment for a Phase V baby. At this age everything is new and fascinating. Simply allowing your Phase V baby to explore to her heart's content will nourish her curiosity in a natural and powerful way. At the same time, you are giving her the opportunity to encounter and work on physical challenges. Finally, you are giving her innumerable opportunities to confront social circumstances that will ultimately teach her about people and their reactions.

By providing maximum access to a safe home, you will also go a long way toward preserving the balance of the baby's major interests. Think for a moment of the contrasting situation in which, to avoid danger, extra housework, and stress, you routinely confine your baby to a playpen, a small gated room, or a crib. In the short run you will undoubtedly have an easier time of it, but in the long run the negative effects of such confinement on a child's curiosity and on the growth of his capacity to play alone will far outweigh the short-term returns.

SUPPLYING PLAYTHINGS

I recommend you have available certain toys and other materials for special times. Occasionally even children who are allowed maximum access to the home appear bored during Phase V, although boredom is not nearly as common now as it will be later in life. More about this topic in the section on recommended materials. Bear in mind that few toys will hold the new crawler's attention for long. He has so much to do and see during these months.

The Primary Caregiver's Role as Consultant

If you've provided your Phase V baby with a safe home and a few stimulating materials, you can be sure he will explore and find things that interest and often excite him. In addition, he'll sometimes find himself in situations

---

★ Bathrooms, however, cannot be made safe for a Phase V baby. I recommend that you install a simple hook-and-eye latch high on each bathroom door and keep it fastened except when the bathroom is in use. Toilet seat latches are not enough. Far too many serious accidents befall infants who are left unsupervised in bathrooms.

that are frustrating or that cause him modest pain, and he will increasingly turn to you for assistance, shared enthusiasm, or comforting. When your baby approaches you, you have another primary opportunity to be effective as your child's educator. Most of the time, a baby's interests during this stage of life are easy to identify. When your baby comes to you excited by some discovery or achievement or frustrated by something difficult, you have a motivated child. If you know what he is focusing on, you have an ideal teaching circumstance and an opportunity to use a powerful *responsive style*.

AN EFFECTIVE RESPONSIVE STYLE

First of all, be available for such experiences. If you are rarely around, you can't do this really important job. Quality time in this respect can't take the place of quantity. In the course of a typical day, you can expect your eleven- to fourteen-month-old baby to make about ten overtures to you each hour. Respond promptly to these overtures. Try to determine what is on your baby's mind. You will rarely have trouble doing so at this stage of development.

When appropriate, instead of dropping whatever you are doing, if your need is more pressing than your baby's, tell him he will have to wait. This is a very important part of the socializing job. Your baby will begin to get the message that most of the time he will promptly get what he wants, but that occasionally someone else's needs are more important than his.

Why is this approach more effective than others? Consider someone who has been told that language learning is vital at this stage and who routinely tries to get a child to pay attention to a book or to flash cards. Here the parent begins with a need to direct the attention of the baby to something the adult is attending to. But when the baby comes to you, all you have to do is to identify the object of his attention and deal directly with it.

The next step, of course, is to provide whatever your baby needs, whether it be a kiss on a hurt finger, the separation of two stuck objects, or some enthusiasm about a discarded box. Respond with ordinary language. Use full phrases or sentences rather than single words, and include a related idea or two. It really makes no difference what that idea is as long as it is linked to the subject at hand. Once your baby seems satisfied with the interchange and shows an interest in moving on, let him go. This entire process takes on the average about twenty-five seconds, and we have encouraged this kind of parenting with consistent success for many years.

In this response pattern we have a beautiful mechanism for the effective education of a young child. First of all, the child is learning to use another person as a resource in situations that she cannot handle herself. This social skill will serve her well in the years to come. Second, she is beginning to learn a bit more about the nature of other people, an understanding that will stand her in good stead when she begins to interact with people outside her own nuclear family. Third, she is learning that someone values her excitement and is willing to satisfy her curiosity. Fourth, she is getting language instruction, since someone is providing language that is relevant. Fifth, her intellectual world is being broadened by the content of the information she is receiving. Sixth, when she asks for assistance, she is learning about completing tasks. Seventh, when she is attempting something that will not work, she is being taught realistic task limitations as well. Finally, in those instances when she is made briefly to wait, she is beginning to learn a fundamental lesson—that though she is very important and precious, her needs are no more important than anyone else's.

HEALTHY SELFISHNESS

I believe the wisest attitude for parents to take with their eight- to thirty-six-month-old child is what we call healthy selfishness. As one mother puts it, "I love my child's curiosity, but she doesn't have to play with my makeup." Few parenting behaviors are more important. As you can see, the issue of how to respond to overtures from the Phase V child is a topic of substantial importance.

In the role of consultant you'll find it both natural and very enjoyable to nourish your baby's emerging social competencies. Some of your baby's overtures will be requests for assistance, and your natural inclination will be to help. By all means do so. But as your baby passes his first birthday, be careful not to let yourself become his all-purpose tool. Watch for the subtle differences between the three ways in which he makes use of you: (1) when he has determined that he can't handle a task himself; (2) when you are simply the easiest way to achieve a goal; and (3) when he appears simply to want to monopolize your attention. The first use is fine, but the second and third lead to an overindulged child.

As your baby turns fourteen or fifteen months of age, some of her overtures toward you will be attempts to gain praise or exclamations of delight for remarkable achievements like climbing down a single step safely. Encouraging healthy growth in this area is a real pleasure.

Another pleasure involves your baby's first make-believe play. Often this behavior is hugely entertaining, especially when your baby seems very serious and grown up in her involvement, for example, in nurturing dolls. Increasingly during the second year she will call upon you to participate in such episodes. Lucky you.

The Primary Caregiver's Role as Authority

In homes where children are developing well, we've always seen parents run the home with a loving but firm hand. The babies in these situations clearly don't have any question about who is the final authority. Conversely, in homes where children don't do very well ambiguity often prevails with respect to the setting and maintaining of limits and the question of who is going to have the final say on disagreements. If you are firm with your infant, if you deny him things from time to time on a realistic basis, or even occasionally on an irrational basis, you need not fear that he will love you less than if you were lenient. Children in the first two years of life do not become detached from their primary caretakers very easily. Even if you were to spank your child regularly, *which I do not recommend*, his attachment would remain constant.

Be firm. You do your child no favor by routinely yielding to her desires in situations where your good judgment suggests that you shouldn't. If she is your first child, this can be difficult. In our work with many delightful families trying their best to produce a wonderful child, unquestionably the biggest source of difficulty they have is overindulgence. It's not hard to see how overindulgence develops. After all, the first child is a unique blessing, a source of love, pride, and excitement unlike anything the parents have ever experienced previously. To deny such a child anything is often very difficult for parents. Babies learn the rules of interpersonal relationships primarily through interactions with the primary caregiver. A parent does the child no long-term favor by routinely letting him impose upon her to the point where the baby learns that his needs are more important than anyone else's. We recommend a guiding principle for our parents: teach the child during Phase V that his needs are very important and that he is a very special person, but his needs are no more important than those of anyone else.

Discipline During Phase V

It is very important to begin to establish a pattern of solid and effective discipline during Phase V in order to prepare for more difficult challenges when the child is a bit older.

We have very rarely seen effective parents repeat themselves more than once in attempting to control Phase V babies. If a child does not respond in the desired way after a message is repeated once, the parents act, either moving the child to another situation or removing a forbidden object. Distraction is also a perfectly adequate technique throughout most of Phase V. You should try to avoid inconsistent attempts at discipline, as for example, when you insist that the child stop doing something and do not follow up when he doesn't stop. Such inconsistent behavior is extraordinarily common, and it lays the foundation for later problems.

THE IMMOBILIZATION TECHNIQUE

All normal babies between nine and fourteen months hate to be held perfectly still for more than two or three seconds. This is why diapering invariably becomes a struggle. This is why a medical person will have trouble examining the baby's ears. This is why you will have trouble dressing your child, and this is why he will resist having his nose wiped. We do not know why babies are like this, but just about all of them are. You can use this characteristic as a control when you are coping with the common attempts of Phase V babies to persist in the kind of unacceptable behavior that often begins to surface at about eight or nine months of age.

If your child is doing something that might damage a telephone or a television set, that behavior should be stopped. Stopping antisocial behavior is even more important. If your baby is causing pain to anyone—by biting or hair pulling, for instance—then you have to use a procedure that will make the price of such actions too high.

The procedure we recommend is based upon the earlier description of what to expect when you try to diaper a baby of nine or ten months of age. At that age babies routinely object vigorously when you try to hold them still. There are exceptions but not many. Even those who will hold still for diapering are not at all happy about the restriction of their movements.

If your baby insists upon biting you and you have said no twice, it is time to raise the price of her behavior. Pick her up and move her at least across the room or into another room. Sit down and hold her in front of you, facing you, getting a firm grip on her shoulders and upper arms. Don't squeeze her shoulders, but hold her firmly enough so that she cannot move so much as a sixty-fourth of an inch. Don't be surprised if she looks at you and smiles or laughs. Your job is to not respond in kind. If she simply stays in place for two, three, or four minutes and doesn't complain, you're allowing too much movement. If you're holding her firmly enough, after a minute or two she will start to show you that she doesn't like what's happening. At that point take a look at your watch, but continue to hold her for fifteen seconds. She should complain more and more. At the end of fifteen seconds, make a very brief speech. Say something like: "We're going to go back into the other room now and I'm going to let you play, but if you bite me again, I'm going to do this again." That's all. No warnings about infections, or damage to the epidermis, just a short, sweet setting of a limit from which you do not budge.

Our experience has demonstrated repeatedly that with a nine-, ten-, or eleven-month-old child, this kind of control, used properly and consistently, will get rid of a bad habit within seven to ten days.

If you have to use this procedure, I suggest that on the day you start you record the date and the behavior you want to get rid of, and post it somewhere. If the habit is still a part of the baby's behavior after seven to ten days, you are either not restricting the movement enough or not using the technique for a long enough time. I suggest that you lengthen the time to thirty or even sixty seconds. More commonly, the problem lies in the fact that parents are understandably reluctant to hold a baby firmly enough because the baby soon begins to cry.

At this point I have to mention one of the more difficult aspects of raising a secure, unspoiled child. I have never seen the job done well without the baby becoming unhappy from time to time because of some restriction put on his behavior by adults. This is especially true during Phase V, when the child first begins to learn the rules of his family. There may be a way to raise a wonderful three-year-old without having to bear up to a baby's crying at times, but I have never seen it, either in our own parent training programs or in the many families we have simply observed. Therefore, in all of my writings since the late 1960s, I have advocated firm, loving control by parents even though, in the short term, a baby will be made unhappy by what his parents do at times.

The really excellent new information we have acquired in recent years is that a firm hand never needs to mean striking a baby. Unfortunately, however, it does mean that parents will occasionally be responsible for their baby's unhappiness as she goes about learning how to live with people. As I introduce this first recommended form of punishment, however, I should also point out that a baby raised from eight months on with this kind of firm control will invariably become a much happier child as the months go by than another baby whose parents do not exert control from this time of life and on through the balance of the first three years.

Parents often wonder whether I advocate physical means of punishment, such as spanking. Let me begin to deal with that subject here, with the Phase V child.

Fortunately, because of the relatively short attention span and the generally compliant nature of the Phase V child, spanking is not even an issue during this stage of life. The key to good limit-setting is a clear understanding that the child has to learn limits at this stage, not later, and that it is the parent's day-by-day responsibility to follow through properly when a limit has been set. These and other principles described in this section constitute the basic guidelines for functioning as an authority with a child during Phase V.

The next stage of life, Phase VI, is the time when parents very often begin to spank their children, because the provocation becomes much greater. But we have learned how you can effectively set limits without resorting to spanking even then. Read on.

SLEEP PROBLEMS

By six months of age most bottle-fed babies are sleeping through the night (for about nine hours) and taking two naps a day totaling about three hours.

In other words, a civilized pattern has usually been established. Breast-fed babies, however, do not get to this point much before eight months of age.

Unfortunately, sleep problems are common throughout the first two years of life. Some authors, most notably Richard Ferber, focus on sleep disorders more or less in isolation. He is usually consulted when the disturbance is fairly severe. My approach is different. First of all, I deal with sleep problems of the common type, which are only of mild to moderate severity. Second, and most important, I consider sleep difficulties in the total context of social development. It is one thing to deal with a baby who can't sleep because she has an illness of some sort. It is quite different and far more common to have to deal with a perfectly healthy baby who insists on gaining and holding on to your attention at three in the morning. Once the demand cry emerges at six months or so, I am especially concerned with the use of that cry in two situations: (1) when a parent tries to put his baby to sleep, and (2) when the baby awakens late at night and resists going back to sleep. Phase V unfortunately is often the time when parents begin to have difficulty with children who awaken long after they have been put to sleep for the evening and then insist on staying awake.

How to Get Your Baby to Go to Sleep During the Day and During the Evening

At this age, everyone will be better off if your baby sleeps in a crib in her own room and with one closed door between her room and you and if you do not use a monitor. You don't need a monitor at this stage, unless you sleep so far away from your baby that you won't hear a hard cry. Remember, most first-time mothers hear every little sound their babies make when they are supposed to be asleep.

In avoiding or curing sleep problems in the eight- to twenty-four-month age range you should be guided primarily by signs of sleepiness rather than by the clock. By this age, you know your baby's sleep signs better than anyone else in the world. The classic signs that a baby is sleepy are as follows:

- The baby will rub her eyes.
- Her eyelids will begin to droop.
- She will be excessively cranky. Even when you know your baby is in good health, her behavior will start to deteriorate after she has been up longer than usual.
- Her frustration tolerance will be unusually low, and her impatience will be considerably more obvious than usual, especially if she has been up a bit too long.
- She is likely to cry excessively after small falls and bumps, and even a minor pain that she usually takes in stride may produce lots of tears.

When you notice such signs, whether during the day or around bedtime, wait a few minutes to confirm your judgment. The closer your baby is to exhaustion, the less trouble you will have putting her to sleep. Next, check her diaper and change it if necessary. Then put her in her crib, tell her you love her, and leave. Close the door. Look at your watch. Give her five minutes. She will probably go to sleep within that time. She may not. She may not have been sleepy enough, or she may already have developed a habit of resisting you in a variety of situations. Remember, she has had a demand cry since she was six months old, and she has been learning how you react to it. If, after five minutes, she is still crying, go in and get her. Take her back to her toys and sit her down. Do not hold her in your arms. Wait for the signs of sleepiness to reappear, then repeat the procedure. Put her down in her crib. Tell her you love her. Leave the room, and close the door. Look at your watch. Give her five minutes. If she is still crying, repeat the procedure again. Within a few days, if you are consistent, she will become accustomed to going to sleep in her crib when you put her there, when she is tired.

How to Get Your Baby to Sleep Through the Night

If your baby wakes up and cries after he has gone to sleep for the evening, you should listen to see whether it is a minor affair that will blow over by itself in a minute or two. If the crying becomes intense, go quickly and see if anything is wrong. Throughout the first years of your baby's life I urge you always to respond promptly when your baby, from out of sight, begins to express genuine distress. When you enter his room, say something as you approach, but don't pick him up. See if there is anything wrong. Check his diaper. Change it if necessary. Do not talk much. Get the job done quickly, and then leave the room. Close the door. Glance at your watch. Give him thirty minutes. If he is still crying, go to him, check him again briefly, and then tell him you love him, but that it is sleep time and everyone needs to sleep. Leave the room. Close the door. Do not go back in. In four to ten days, depending on how deeply entrenched his use of the demand cry is, he will sleep through the night.

Will you make him feel unloved? No one can know or say for sure, but I have been offering this advice for a long time. In our parent education work, we usually find the babies treated this way are more consistently happy, once they accept this practice, than those who are brought into their parents' bed or given special attention in other ways at three in the morning.

A NOTE: If your baby is ill, forget about teaching him to go to sleep. Give him all the comfort you can, and save the learning for later.

SIBLING RIVALRY

Earlier in this section I explained that problems with sibling rivalry are very likely to become very substantial when the age difference between children is less than three years, and that such problems will begin to develop from the point when the younger child begins to move about the home—that is, from the beginning of Phase V. I said that jealousy and aggression are to be expected from the slightly older baby. The younger baby now becomes much more a part of daily activities and tends to receive attention in much greater quantities than before, often at the expense of the older sibling. If you understand what's going on in the mind of your slightly older child, you've taken the first step toward dealing with the situation. But of course, you must do more than merely understand why your previously angelic older child has started to behave in a most reprehensible manner. Is there anything you can do, or are you locked into two years, or perhaps considerably more, of civil war?

You can take steps that will help. The first is to protect the baby from aggression. It makes no sense to try to make the older child feel guilty—after all, his dislike of his sibling is totally natural—but it must be made clear to him that aggression of any sort, while understandable, will not be permitted.

Your second task is to make life more bearable for the older child. The happier she is, the easier life will be for the baby and you. Many parents have asked me if there is a way to prepare a two-year-old for the arrival of a new sister or brother. Do stories help? What about support sessions for expectant parents? Unfortunately, rational explanations of complicated future situations are useless when the listener is less than three years old. So, too, are the usual parent discussions. Once the baby is home, however, you can reduce the upset in a variety of ways.

First of all, avoid lavish praise of the younger baby in the presence of the older one. Second, as soon as possible, provide more out-of-home experience for the older child. These help relieve the pressure in the family situation. If the older child, for example, is two and a half or older, regular sessions with a friend would be an excellent idea. The use of a baby-sitter to take the older child on trips to the park, the zoo, or the mall will also help.

Although out-of-home experiences can help to reduce the older sibling's exposure to the new jealousy-producing situation in the family, they shouldn't be allowed to make the older child feel he's being shunted aside. An essential way to avoid the development of that feeling is to spend some private time with the older child every day. In our judgment it is terribly important that the older child have the undivided attention of at least one parent each day, to reassure him in the only language he can fully understand that he is loved just as much as ever.

Unfortunately, instead of trying to help the older sibling, many parents place extra demands on her. The older child, who is developing rapidly and is obviously much more mature than the baby, is expected to act with restraint and wisdom. Far from getting sympathy for the unhappy predicament she faces, she's asked to be extra grown up and not to be a bother. Most parents don't mean to be unfair to the older child; they simply overestimate her abilities.

Hard as it is on parents, the fact is that when there are two very young children in the home, both need special attention, and the parents' job is therefore going to be more than twice as demanding as it was before. Let me once again repeat my caveat: there is simply no way of making life with two closely spaced children as easy as dealing with a first child only or with widely spaced children. We have worked with many very talented parents who were raising two closely spaced children. I can't think of one family that didn't have substantial and continuing problems. There is no point in pussyfooting around this issue: the job gets to be very hard.

We urge anyone in such a situation to avoid full-time at-home parenting. It is very important that both parents understand just how normal it is to be overwhelmed by day-to-day life with two closely spaced babies, once the younger child becomes a crawler. The principal child-rearer in such a situation should be away from the children for at least a few hours every day. Part-time work outside the home or just indulging oneself is essential.

RECOMMENDED MATERIALS FOR PHASE V CHILDREN

The Phase V baby may appear bored from time to time. A modest amount of time, perhaps 10 percent, is typical of well-developing babies. Frequent long stretches of inactivity, during Phases V and VI, however, should be avoided. With too little to do, your baby will be inclined to concentrate on you too much, making the socialization process and life in general more difficult.

Toys

The best way to avoid boredom is to allow your baby to explore as much of your living area as possible. Toys, while nowhere near as exciting as exploring the home or climbing stairs, can play a useful role. Effective parents occasionally provide babies in this phase with a new toy or a new set of materials to rekindle their interest. Although not foolproof, this approach often works. The number of important developments in a child's life during Phases V and VI is so great, however, and their significance is so fundamental that commercial toys rarely can compete successfully for baby's attention. Nevertheless, a small number of commercial toys for this age range are clearly worth buying.

In an earlier section I discussed the three basic interests of Phase V children: curiosity, motor-skill challenges, and the primary caregiver. Understanding specifically what interests your baby as those interests evolve rapidly during the first years of life is the key to choosing effective toys and other objects for play as well as activities.

The toy situation today is far better than it has ever been. The dramatically increased awareness of the significance of learning in the first years of life, which surfaced in the late 1960s, has led to much greater activity by the toy companies. Although the majority of the toys that are available today continue to have little play value and are therefore not worth buying, a fair number of new toys are of substantial interest to children.

TOYS TO FEED HAND-EYE INTEREST

I have described how, from age two months on through the second birthday, hand-eye activities are surprisingly interesting—in fact, compelling—to the typical baby. A Phase V baby is of course right in the middle of that developmental process, and some of the commercial toys available are eminently suitable for hand-eye practice. One such toy that I have been recommending for twenty years is Playskool's Poppin' Pals, formerly known as the Busy Surprise Box, described in an earlier section. The first part of the toy the Phase V baby begins to master resembles a standard light switch and requires only that the child move a lever in order to cause the cover to rise abruptly, revealing a Disney character inside. Unfortunately, many of the newer models are too difficult for the Phase V baby to operate. If you can, check to see whether the effort required by the baby is trivial. The operation should be hair-triggered, as it was in the earlier models. You shouldn't buy any pop-up toy that is not extremely easy to operate. A currently recommendable version is made by Shelcore. Sadly, most current Playskool versions are not.

Closely related to this kind of device are the simple plastic key sets that sell for under two dollars. Why should a simple set of plastic keys be appealing to a very young baby? It probably has something to do with the fact that there is just enough challenge in attempting to handle the keys to make it intriguing. Also, there are numerous contours to feel and gum that are interesting to this age baby.

Many bath toys also feature mechanisms that are interesting to babies.

Quite a number of the major companies have produced toys that can be attached to the side of the tub and used by the Phase V baby for water play. Containers that allow your baby to pour water back and forth will be very interesting. And if the toy has other features, like a water wheel that spins when water is poured into the top, or a squirting device, the child's level of interest will be substantially greater. Just about all of the bath toys that are available are highly recommendable.

Also under the heading of manipulable toys, I recommend nesting toys of various kinds. They are inexpensive and usually appealing.

TOYS TO FEED THE INTEREST IN THE PATHS OF MOVEMENTS OF OBJECTS

In addition to hand-eye challenges, a second toy category that begins to be extremely appealing for the Phase V baby is the ball. In our research, the most popular single toy throughout the second year of life is a ball of one sort or another. But even before the first birthday, babies enjoy and play with balls. The best first ball is the inflatable Gertie ball. It sells for less than $4. The Gertie ball is made of a soft material that allows a baby as young as six or seven months of age to pick it up with ease when it is inflated to five or six inches in diameter. One caution, if you have a dog or cat: this ball is easily punctured. It is, however, a best buy.

Another best buy for a baby between one and two years of age is an inflatable beach ball, which still sells for about two dollars, though it's not likely to be available in the dead of winter. These balls come in several sizes, ranging from twelve to more than twenty-four inches. Once your baby starts to walk, carrying a twenty-four-inch ball will become a source of enormous pleasure. Carrying it, throwing it, watching its movements, and then trying to retrieve it are all favorite activities.

Another note of caution: Some balls are made of a spongelike substance. They are not recommended for this age range. Once babies have teeth, they are capable of biting off a piece of this material and gagging on it.

TOYS THAT FEED MORE THAN ONE INTEREST

Books, of course, are desirable for this age range. They should have cardboard rather than cloth or paper pages. This type is called a board book. Books with pages that turn easily are best for the Phase V child. At first, books serve three purposes. Your ten-month-old will gum them about 40 percent of the time, especially if she is cutting a tooth. She will spend another 40 percent of the time practicing hand-eye skills by separating and turning the pages. For the remaining 20 percent of the time she may look at the pages while you talk about what is pictured. For the ten- to twelve-month-old baby, I recommend books with one or just a few familiar objects on a page. In the Recommended Readings section of this book, under "Play and Toys," you will find help in identifying books that are particularly well suited to the developmental level of your baby.

TOYS THAT FEED THE INTEREST IN MAKE-BELIEVE PLAY

Telephones and cleaning equipment such as small brooms and vacuum cleaners are recommended to encourage the fantasy play that emerges shortly after the first birthday. Toy telephones with a dial or wheels and a pull cord do not have any special appeal. Pull toys are never particularly popular with babies, and the dial feature is also uninteresting, as are squeeze-type squeakers. It is the opportunity to imitate you making a telephone call that makes telephones appealing for your Phase V baby. The same can be said about brooms and vacuum cleaners: it is the fantasies that are interesting, not "activities."

The best toys for Phase V babies are those that challenge hand-eye skills; that give a child a chance to produce a dramatic physical change, like instant sound from a television set; that feed a child's interest in movement and variations in materials; and that support imaginative play.

In this section I have been trying to combine an understanding of developments at this stage with our observations of which toys children actually spend time with and those that are well made. If you understand where a child is developmentally, you will be better able to choose wisely from the occasionally bewildering displays and claims found in any sizable toy store.

TOYS YOU DON'T HAVE TO BUY

Phase V babies love collections of small objects. Save large rigid plastic containers, or use a small plastic laundry basket and accumulate several dozen small but safe objects that can be placed inside such a container. Plastic measuring spoons, empty spools from thread, egg-shaped containers from hosiery—just about anything is usable if it's not so small that it could be swallowed (at least an inch and a half in every dimension), if it's not coated with a potentially hazardous substance, and if it has no small parts that could become disengaged. It is perfectly all right to mix parts from various toys. Safety, diversity, and quantity are what count. Offer this container of objects to your Phase V baby when she seems bored. You'll be pleasantly surprised by how much time she spends taking each item out, examining it, gumming it, then setting it aside and reaching for another, or perhaps even pouring the whole batch out all at once. This interest in collections of objects will last for many months, and the price is right.

Babies of this age also find pots and pans very appealing. My only reservation about pots and pans is that the resulting racket can be unpleasant.

Nothing is more interesting to a Phase V baby than your kitchen. Give her access to as many cabinets and drawers as you can. Then stand back and watch the "play value."

TOYS TO AVOID

For a variety of interesting reasons, some toys have become popular even though they don't deserve it. Other toys have been marketed very heavily when they aren't worth very much. Toy companies furthermore routinely put recommended age ranges on toy boxes that are inaccurate, and they always overstate the period of time during which a toy is appropriate for a baby. Perhaps the most blatant examples of this are the various forms of busy boxes and activity boards that you'll find in any toy store. These usually feature some eight to twelve "activities" that are supposed to fascinate infants from roughly six months to the second birthday. In reality, however, they have no more appeal than any other small toy or object that is handed to an infant for the first time: usually about ten minutes' worth. The baby may explore the toy later in the day for a few more minutes and perhaps on one or two other occasions, but compared to a beach ball, a water toy, or the surprise busy box, these products have negligible play value.

Other traditional offerings with little appeal to the Phase V baby are the xylophone pull toy, form-sorting toys, (though the baby will enjoy putting the forms into the container, taking them out, and spilling the contents), and—believe it or not—stuffed animals and hand puppets.

I would also suggest you not purchase any of the expensive electronic toys that are being offered for infants. Those that talk to the baby have language that is too difficult for babies to deal with, and their sound quality doesn't catch and hold the baby's attention. I should also mention that they are quite expensive.

Remember, as of this date, no toy company has developed a single toy with proven educational benefits for any age baby.

CHILD-REARING PRACTICES NOT RECOMMENDED

Forced Teaching

Over the last two decades a trend has grown toward forced teaching, or attempts to have children acquire specialized skills such as reading and identifying the names of artists much earlier than they ordinarily would. For a time a good deal of attention was focused on the so-called super baby. There isn't any question in my mind that babies, even in Phase V, are capable of learning some things that would otherwise come later in their lives.

Programs to teach so-called prereading skills have been in existence for some time now. People have claimed to be able to help parents teach premathematical knowledge, gymnastic skills, swimming, and even musical skills. I will discuss this issue more extensively in later chapters, but for the time being I'd like to comment in an abbreviated fashion on the general trend.

All healthy Phase V babies learn naturally. They are incredibly curious. They have an intense desire to master their bodies and an equally intense interest in learning about the people around whom their day revolves. They have a full, natural agenda. Much basic learning of lifelong importance is taking place during these first years of life. A pattern of forced teaching is, in my opinion, inadvisable. I cannot recommend, for example, the commercially available reading kits that claim to start babies on the road to reading at nine months of age. Strong statements to the effect that you must read stories to your child or that you must buy educational toys only exploit the insecurities of new parents and prey upon their feelings of guilt about whether they are doing enough for their children. Such statements also reflect an overemphasis on the value of the bright child at the expense of whether or not he is a decent, likable, secure child.

I have listed four educational foundations undergoing development during the age period of eight to twenty-four months. You should examine the possible negative consequences of any proposed educational program on each of those processes. It is very possible, for example, that in attempting to teach a baby to read at one or two years of age, you may use procedures that are costly in time, energy, and money, or that affect your baby's natural learning processes. Any program that requires a baby to spend fifteen to thirty minutes or more on a regular basis, concentrating on adult-imposed material or activities, runs the risk of negative side effects, such as a reduction of natural curiosity, or disappointment in parents' minds if their baby doesn't achieve at the promised rate. To date, no research is available on this topic.

Restrictive Devices

Another child-rearing practice I discourage is the use of restrictive devices like playpens, jump seats, and gates for lengthy periods every day. It is clear that such devices cut down on the work for the parent, on hostilities between siblings, on breakage in the home, and on danger to the baby. These are four very good reasons that might tempt a parent to prevent the newly mobile baby from moving freely about the home. Nevertheless, in families where children are developing very well, we have found that such restrictive practices are rarely used. In contrast, restrictive practices play a prominent role where children are developing relatively poorly.

Very rarely can a nine- or ten-month-old be confined in a playpen for more than a few minutes without lapsing into boredom. Because the baby is confined and can't find anything interesting to do, we refer to this sort of experience as "passing time." There should be very little passing time in the life of a child in Phase V. Given the chance to explore their home, Phase V babies find many interesting things to do. If they are placed for long periods of time in a playpen, however, or in a jump seat in front of the television set, or if they are given long naps morning and afternoon, they will end up passing a good deal of time.

Boring the Baby

The routine practice of keeping a baby in a playpen or a crib for most of the day is a common way to guarantee that a baby will experience a good deal of boredom. Other ways include trying to read a story to him when he is not interested and trying to teach him something or otherwise force his attention when he is obviously not responding. Effective parents we have observed do not bore their children or force activities on them. Instead, they provide a variety of developmentally suitable options for the baby, then stand back and marvel at their baby's endless curiosity and enthusiasm.

Substitute Child Care

I have examined in some detail how babies at this age enter into social experiences that are critical to the basic shaping of the human being. During Phase V all of the major social skills that are involved in effective relationships with older people are being learned. They include (1) refining the innate ability to get and hold the attention of another, (2) using an adult as a resource when the child can't do something for himself, (3) beginning to express emotions to another person, (4) showing pride in achievement, and (5) engaging in make-believe or fantasy play.

Several related acquisitions in the social realm include the baby's first perception of herself and the beginning of the process of learning the rules of living in her home. All of these are best guided by a baby's parents. If both parents are working full-time during this period, they obviously will have much less to do with these formative, once-in-a-lifetime learning processes. If parents leave someone in the home whose primary job is to take care of the house, then the child is going to be shortchanged. If, on the other hand, they leave someone whose job is defined so as to emphasize interaction with the baby, the baby has a better chance. But in my opinion, except in rare cases, babies do best when they are raised by someone who is passionately in love with them, and that usually means parents and grandparents.

Parents who are aware of the importance of a baby's development at this point will be more likely to try to retain their role as principal child-rearers. However, since most babies of this age nap in the morning, I see relatively little loss to the baby from some substitute care that includes their nap time. I know of nothing that argues against up to four hours or so a day of first-rate substitute care, even for seven days a week. Indeed, a few hours away from the baby on a regular basis will make the full-time parent's job much easier.

I don't recommend full-time parenting for anyone raising even one baby between eight and twenty-four months of age. If you have two closely spaced children, with one or both passing through those stages, it becomes imperative to avoid full-time parenting. Believe me, this is so.

The stress caused by twenty-four-hour, seven-day-a-week responsibility for a precious baby is something very few parents handle with ease. Note I use the word "parents." It is clear that men can do this job as well as women in every respect except breast-feeding. Recent research clearly indicates that breast-feeding for six months or longer is highly recommendable during the first year or so of life. In all other ways, however, fathers can—and, in my opinion, should—participate equally in this very special responsibility.

What do I mean by "first-rate" substitute care? I certainly do not mean group care. Setting aside the fact that high-quality group care is hard to find, there is the problem of infectious disease. During their first two years of life, babies do not resist infections well. When they spend a good deal of time in group care, the frequency of colds and other infectious diseases multiplies three to four times. When one baby catches something, they all do. While ear infections are not life-threatening, I hate to see a baby, just beginning to learn language, have repeated middle ear problems with the usual resultant diminished hearing ability.

Your best choice, if you decide to use child care, is to have someone, chosen with great care, come to your home to provide the service. Second best would be a carefully selected person who would care for your baby, and only your baby, in her home. Family day care is next best, but frankly, I would not use it or group care for my own baby during her first two years of life, so how can I recommend it for yours?

Overindulgence

Parents very frequently feel that they are showing deepest love for a baby when they do everything they can for him. A corollary of this principle is the notion that you must give in to a baby's demands when he is being stubborn and especially when tears are streaming down his face, even though it is against your better judgment. For the baby, for any younger siblings, and for other children he may deal with later, parents do their child no favor if they overindulge him or give in routinely to his occasionally unreasonable demands. Your baby is, after all, going to have to live in a world with other people, and it is much easier to begin to teach him how to do so when he is between eight and twenty-four months of age than it will be later on. This is certainly one of the most important notions I can give you about raising a baby. The successful parents we have studied have always been loving but firm with their children from about eight months on.

The principal problem that average families run into in this area is allowing the baby to infringe on their own rights too much. It is best if the baby is taught to respect the rights of other people, usually his parents, early in life and consistently. When parents are successful in this respect in the eight- to twenty-four-month period, the benefits are truly wonderful.

Overfeeding

The Phase V baby rarely expresses her wishes clearly. Although her needs of the moment are usually obvious, from time to time they are not. Furthermore, if you have not provided suitable conditions to keep the baby interested, she can get bored. In many homes we have studied, parents have taken to offering the child snacks of juice, milk, cookies, or other foods throughout the day. Offering a small treat is thought to show that you care, especially in certain of our subcultures. It also seems to be effective in subduing a child's minor discomforts and her occasional badgering. And of course supplying treats is easy. But please don't do it very often. In our studies, Phase V children who are developing very well do nearly all of their eating and drinking at mealtime. Frequent between-meal snacks more often than not accompany comparatively poor development. Furthermore, there are indications that some cases of lifelong obesity have their roots in this rather common child-rearing practice.

BEHAVIOR THAT SIGNALS THE ONSET OF PHASE VI

Negativism

Far and away the most significant behavior that signals the onset of Phase VI is what we call negativism, or challenging the authority of parents.

Negativism is a perfectly normal but often very trying form of behavior that occurs regularly, for a minimum of six months during the second year of life. In a sense, this period represents a preview of adolescence. For the first time in their brief lives, babies begin to be aware that they are separate beings. When you ask your baby to return something to you and she holds it away from you and says, "No, mine," or "No, Annie's," you will know she has acquired self-awareness. As her spoken vocabulary grows, she will begin to use her own name, start to be possessive about her toys, become choosy about what to wear, and begin resisting simple requests from you. She will start testing her will against yours. The word "no" will become fascinating to her. Negativism is the first and most compelling sign of the onset of Phase VI.

Hostility Toward Older Siblings

A second sign of the onset of Phase VI is present only when the infant has a slightly older sibling. But it deserves special mention because it is regularly associated with the onset of negativism. In Phase VI the worm turns with respect to sibling rivalry, and this change in dynamics is routinely a source of substantial discomfort to parents in homes where there is a sibling who is less than three years older.

Early in Phase V a closely spaced older child is likely to express his jealousy and hostility toward the baby with increasing intensity. The younger child in such a situation becomes accustomed to abuse and intimidation. During the intermediate stage between eleven and thirteen months, the baby adapts to the situation, learns how to complain—that is, to cry more and more quickly and loudly—and thereby begins to use a parent as a defense. Starting between fourteen and sixteen months of age, however, the baby will usually begin to initiate hostile activities with the older child as part of his new individualism and sense of personal power.

In addition to the important day-to-day increase in stress caused by close spacing of siblings, there is reason to believe that the long-term intellectual consequences of very close spacing should be of some concern to parents. This topic is discussed in detail in Chapter 7 under "Life with a Slightly Older Sibling."

Onset of Expressive Language

A third sign of the new phase is the onset of expressive language. Although many normal children do not speak much before their second birthday, most generally begin to speak their first words between twelve and fourteen months of age. This particular phenomenon has a powerful effect on adults in that it is often the stimulus for adults to start talking to their babies much more than they had in previous months. Even though it can easily be shown that babies understand some language when they are one year old, the fact that most do not speak much seems to keep even knowledgeable and perceptive parents from using language extensively with them. There are exceptions, of course—for example, parents who talk a great deal regardless of whether anybody is listening. But by and large parents characteristically begin to talk far more to their babies once they enter Phase VI and themselves become talkative. A special bonus that accompanies this development is the very exciting opportunity to begin to understand the mind of a child in a way that simply was not possible before. Indeed, parents who are professionals in child development report regularly that the dramatic impact on them of the onset of speech by their children took them by surprise. No amount of reading in books prepared these parents for the delightful experiences that came with this newfound skill.

7

PHASE VI: FOURTEEN TO TWENTY-FOUR MONTHS

GENERAL REMARKS

The Very Special Importance of Phase VI

The fourteen- to twenty-four-month period is, in my opinion, make-or-break time. The first eight months of life are, of course, of great significance as well. The difference is that for most families, good results are almost guaranteed during the earlier period, whereas from eight to twenty-four months the developments are almost as important, but good results are by no means ensured. Indeed, in my judgment, Phases V and VI are the periods when the government's neglect of the learning processes regularly results in remarkable damage to many children and their parents.

The fourteen- to twenty-four-month period is also perhaps the most interesting, difficult, and exciting phase during the first three years of life. By the end of Phase VI the fundamental learning processes have developed so far that my colleagues and I feel we have missed far too much of the story if we see a baby for the first time at two years of age. In fact, as a matter of policy, we do not accept a family into our new parents program if their baby is over ten months old. It has also been demonstrated in many studies that a poorly developed two-year-old is likely to continue to develop poorly, regardless of remedial efforts. Remarkably, a two-year-old is in many ways developmentally old!

The two-year-old is a child whose language development can be rather remarkable and extensive, including the capacity to understand and use hundreds of words and deal with all the major grammatical forms, or whose language skills can be quite limited. Either the child arrives at age two with a well-nourished, broad, and extremely healthy inquisitiveness or she can have lost quite a bit of her natural interest in learning. In some cases her curiosity may have been constricted and channeled into a specialized area: some two-year-olds are extraordinarily interested in physical materials and not much interested in people; others are deeply involved with their primary caretaker and show surprisingly little interest in any other person or in the physical world, in contrast to their behavior only one year earlier. Also, a child's social style seems to have become very well established by the time she is two years of age.

The Surprising Power of Parents at This Stage

It is vital that you be aware that Phase VI is the last period during which you have an enormous impact on the basic shape of your child's personality. After her second birthday that shape will be increasingly difficult to modify and your behavior won't have the moment-to-moment influence on her that it has during Phase VI. She will be spending increasing amounts of time with peers and out of your presence. You have a grand and sobering responsibility to put the finishing touches on your child's basic personality during these ten months. You have the power to help her become a chronically happy two-year-old who is a pleasure to live with or a chronically dissatisfied child who regularly engages in power struggles with you. Let me add that I believe this particular task is the only, as well as the most, difficult part of your job. Everything else is quite easy and enjoyable.

Socializing your child at this age is difficult because he will show increasing determination day by day, he will not yet be rational, and he will very probably remain quite limited in his ability to express his desires. Between seventeen and twenty months of age you can expect him to reach the depths of his limited ability to tolerate frustration and, at the same time, the peak of his willfulness.

Every two-year-old we have seen has been a complicated social creature in the sense that her behaviors are far more sensitive to the particulars of
a situation than they were when she was eight months of age. Along with the
many nuances of emotion that she exhibits in interactions with people, the
two-year-old is far less abrupt in her shifts of mood from euphoria to darkest
gloom or anger than is the younger child. In the best of circumstances she has
by now acquired most of the social skills for use with adults that a talented
six-year-old has. Those skills include getting and holding the attention of adults
in a wide variety of ways, using an adult as a resource, expressing affection and
moderate annoyance toward adults, and directing an adult in various activities. She also has an impressive collection of make-believe or fantasy behaviors. I will examine these abilities in greater detail later in this chapter.

All in all, socially, a child is a complicated, well-formed person at age
two. She has spent much of the preceding sixteen months working out an
unspoken social contract with the people with whom she interacts regularly.
This agreement is highly detailed. In it is contained what the child has learned
through thousands of interchanges with her caretakers since she began to
notice, at six months of age, that some of her behaviors had an effect on her
key people. To the extent that another sibling has been regularly involved in
her life, she has assimilated a whole set of behaviors with respect to interaction with him as well. Finally, in the realm of social development, there is
the emergence of individuality and personal power—a development that is
very exciting to watch.

The fourth major educational goal, nurturing the roots of intelligence,
is another area where a child may or may not have made tremendous progress
by twenty-four months of age. During the months that immediately pre-
cede his second birthday, he will have entered into a qualitatively new and
vitally important style of intellectual functioning. This new style features the
use of ideas and images rather than physical action when solving problems.
His short-term memory is now totally developed. His sense of time has also
expanded substantially to the point where he can recall and talk about the
events of the day and look forward to the next day.

Phases V and VI cover a period when the basic shaping of a young human can be influenced in powerful ways by whoever is responsible for the
child. It is not possible to overemphasize the importance of this sixteen-
month stage of life.

Difficult Features of Phase VI

This period inevitably will be very trying for parents from time to time.
Babies at this age are compelled to oppose the will of their primary care-

takers. All children we have observed go through this process, even those who are developing very well. During Phase VI, babies begin to be aware of themselves as separate entities with social power. To determine just how much power they have, all babies seem to be obliged to test the resolve of their key people. Living with a baby who is not yet fully reasonable and yet is chronically self-assertive and resistant is stressful. Some families do better than others at coping with negativism and testing.

In general, families with well-developing children get through this period more easily than those with poorly developing children. Nevertheless, all parents should be prepared for a fair amount of friction during this phase. It is, by any measure, the most stressful of the first three years of life.

Why a baby has to become ornery and stay that way for a minimum of six or seven months is one of the many mysteries that make the study of early human development so rich and fascinating. Every baby must some-how go from a condition of total dependence and lack of self-awareness to one in which he can face the world on his own. The second half of the second year represents a stage at which a major step in this process takes place.

Redeeming Features of Phase VI

As difficult as child-rearing is during the second half of the second year, a successful outcome is well worth the price. The achievements of this par-

Negativism

ticular period of life are so exciting that no description can do them justice. You have to experience them.

Between twenty-two and twenty-four months of age (when development has gone well), children stop testing you. Their behavior loses its defiant, subrational quality. The sun comes out. Language growth now enables your child to begin holding real conversations with you. Thinking ability and imagination have emerged, along with humor. You simply won't believe how blessed you are.

Toward the end of Phase VI, parents begin to realize that they no longer have a baby. He is now a small child. At this time babies' personalities are becoming clearer, more fixed, and more individualistic.

Throughout most of this phase, your baby will focus on you much more than ever before as she goes about the business of winding up her basic attachment to you. This concentration, which is essential, can become oppressive, but it will subside during the third year of life, ordinarily never again to be such a constant preoccupation. These developments, along with the grace with which your child can now use her body, will contribute to a general feeling that you are living with a very interesting young person rather than with a baby. Don't, however, be fooled by the impressive intellectual and motoric accomplishments of this phase. Lurking just beneath the veneer of maturity is a person who is not yet fully civilized or rational.

The Balance of Major Interests

As in Phase V, the three major interests of this age are the primary caretaker's behavior, exploration of the world, and practicing and enjoying motor skills. In the best of circumstances these three interests are pursued vigorously and will remain in balance throughout Phase VI.

In situations where a baby is developing nicely, much of the child's interest will focus on his parents in their role as people who can be relied on for assistance, counseling, nurturing, encouragement, and simple pleasantries. During the second year of life your child will seldom spend long periods of time without checking on your whereabouts. This orientation is essential for the completion of the social contract and the first reflected identity of your baby.

GENERAL BEHAVIOR DURING PHASE VI

Predominance of Nonsocial Activities

In spite of your baby's intense interest in you during Phase VI, if you watch your fourteen-month-old baby as she goes about her ordinary activities during the day, you will find that she spends no more than 10 to 15 percent of her time interacting with you, or with any other person for that matter. Most of her time is spent in nonsocial activities. The amount of time spent in social activities will increase during Phase VI, reaching about 20 percent by the second birthday.

STARING

The most common nonsocial behavior during Phase VI is simply staring—at objects, people, and events. Between ages twelve and fifteen months your baby will spend more than 17 percent of his waking time staring. Between eighteen and twenty-one months of age, this behavior will decrease to just under 12 percent, but it will remain one of your child's most common activities of the day.

EXPLORATORY AND MASTERY EXPERIENCES

Two other major nonsocial activities during the fourteen- to twenty-four-month period are exploration of and hand-eye practice with physical objects, usually small, portable ones. We call these two types of experience exploratory and mastery activities. In exploratory activities, which are more common at fourteen months than mastery experiences, the baby spends a good deal of time examining the various qualities of as many objects as he can in the course of the day. These objects will include anything small that he can manipulate with his hands or bring to his mouth for gumming. They will range from toys to the cellophane wrapping from packaged goods. Babies routinely try out a pattern of standard actions on these objects, apparently trying to get to know as much about them as they can. They will strike them against various surfaces, throw them, drop them, look at them, and feel their surfaces. They will use objects to load and unload containers. They will mouth them and chew on them, sometimes to relieve tenderness in the gums.

The second category—interaction with small physical objects to practice simple skills on them—is what we call fine motor mastery activity. Several skills are being practiced here: dropping and throwing objects; swinging hinged objects back and forth; opening and closing doors and drawers; repeatedly standing objects on end and then knocking them down; putting objects together and taking them apart; putting objects through openings; pouring materials into and out of containers; manipulating simple locking devices; and activating switches that produce light, darkness, sounds, changing visual patterns, or other interesting consequences.

Together exploratory and mastery activities take up about 20 percent of a baby's waking time early in Phase VI. Interest in perfecting numerous eye-hand skills is very strong at this stage, reflecting the continued fascination with hands and what they can do. A particularly interesting activity is the spinning of various sorts of wheels. Many times we have seen Phase VI babies spinning wheels and watching the consequences. They can be the wheels of very small toy cars and trucks or of a tipped-over bicycle. Children also seem to be especially interested in rotating the pedals on a tricycle. And Phase VI babies continue to practice finger skills on the pages of books and magazines, especially books with stiff pages. As time passes, however, interest in studying what is printed on the page grows steadily, and fine

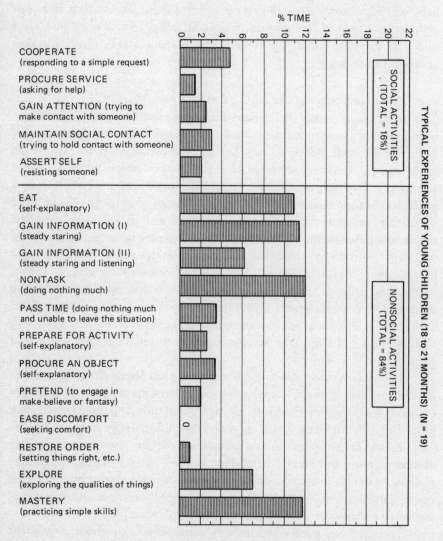

Typical Experience of Young Children (18–21 Months) (N = 19)

motor mastery behavior, as a focal activity, gradually declines. Redundancy, repetition of the same developing skills, is the defining quality of mastery experiences. If you have a piece of furniture that is relatively low and slightly difficult to climb, your toddler is likely to climb the object, carefully come down, and then start all over again. As Phase VI proceeds, you will see more and more interest in gymnastics; for example, climbing and descending small slides, running, and jumping. You will also notice that most toddlers are more careful than you might expect when they try something new that could result in an accident.

By two years of age ordinarily a reversal has occurred in the way children play with small objects. There has been a steady decrease in time spent in exploratory behavior and a corresponding increase in mastery or practice activities. We have also observed that children developing rather well have a steeper rate of increase of mastery experiences versus exploratory ones in regard to small objects.

NONTASK BEHAVIOR

By nontask behavior I mean activity that is apparently without purpose, in which the child seems to be just hanging around or idling. Such behavior is surprisingly common in the lives of young children. Phase VI children may spend up to 30 percent of their time in such a state on any given day, but most spend from 5 to 10 percent. The amount of nontask behavior can grow during Phase VI. We have seen two-year-old children who spend a great deal of time doing nothing, just standing in place. They may be thinking great thoughts, but such frequent nontask behavior in two-year-olds has been so routinely associated with poor development in our studies that we are more inclined to think that not much is going on in the child's mind. Boredom has become a routine part of her day. If we see a two-year-old who spends 5 to 10 percent of her time in this fashion, we conclude that she is clearly within the normal range. But when a child begins to approach the 15 to 20 percent range in this activity, we suspect that we are dealing with a child who, at least for the cultures we have studied, may very well be showing signs of a considerably poorer pattern of development than we would like to see.

PASSING TIME

A related type of behavior that is common in the lives of all young children is what we call passing time. A child who is passing time is not doing much of anything. In contrast to nontask behavior, however, he is not free to get out of the situation and find something to do. A good example of passing time occurs when a mother says to a two-year-old, "Wait here, please, while I get you a fresh diaper," or "Wait while I get a car seat; we're going for a ride." If the child does wait and cannot find anything to occupy himself with for more than a few seconds, we say that he is passing time. Probably the most common type of passing time in the life of a fourteen-month-old occurs when he is placed in a restrictive device such as a playpen, crib, jumper seat, or high chair for a long period of time. Another common passing-time experience takes place during an automobile ride in a car seat. Infants don't like car seats. They have to become accustomed to them, and most do, but they never seem to learn to like being in them.

If the child, while she is restricted psychologically or physically, can find something to engage her attention, we don't call the experience passing time. If, for example, a baby in a playpen plays with a fascinating toy or a small object for more than fifteen continuous seconds, we consider the experience a form of active play.

We have found it extremely difficult to keep a child engaged in any form of active play when he is a psychological or physical captive in a playpen, high chair, a crib, a small gated room, or a car seat. You might expect that a Phase VI child in a car seat would spend a great deal of time drinking in the scenery on driving trips, but that doesn't happen. We can't say why; but from our observations of children under three in such restrictive situations, we have concluded that they simply find themselves with nothing interesting to do most of the time.

LOOKING AND LISTENING TO LANGUAGE

Another category of special significance and one that takes up a substantial portion of a Phase VI child's day is what we call looking and listening to language. A typical example of this experience occurs when a child is looking at his mother and an older sibling as they talk at a level that he can understand. The two major classes of looking and listening experiences in Phase VI are (1) looking and listening to live language, and (2) looking and listening to mechanical language. By live language we mean spoken language that the child may overhear or spoken language directed toward the child by another person. Mechanical language is usually delivered by a television set, a record, or a radio. We have found that the amount of experience children have in these categories varies quite a bit in Phase VI. As you might expect, the more live language you direct to the child, especially about what he seems to be attending to at the moment, the better his language development will be.

Life Without a Slightly Older Sibling

EXPLORATION

When there is no slightly older sibling in the home, you will find that your Phase VI toddler will spend the bulk of her day exploring, if you allow her to do so. While you are occupied, most commonly in the kitchen, she'll be moving in and out of various parts of the home, returning frequently to the kitchen or wherever you are, to visit, to consult, or to seek help or comforting. If you have made the kitchen an attractive place for her, she will spend much of her time exploring there as well, indeed more than anywhere else in the home. The kitchen is already most interesting to her because of your presence; but it can be even more interesting if you have made the area safe for her and if most of the lower kitchen cabinets and drawers are accessible to her.

You will find as she moves through the other rooms that she will occasionally climb on a small chair in order to look out a window, a very common practice with children in Phase VI. At fourteen months, if there are ungated stairs in your home, she will spend a fair amount of time practicing climbing. Stair climbing is of universal appeal to fourteen-month-olds. Why? Who knows? It is part of what my wife calls "the urge to up." Once the ability to climb stairs emerges, a baby will climb as many steps as there are, one or fifty.

One place where she will ordinarily spend little time is in her own room with her own toys, at least during the beginning of Phase VI. There is just too much else to do and see.

THE NEED TO BE NEAR YOU

While most of your toddler's activities will be nonsocial, you will be very much a part of her world throughout this phase. Her interactions with you will feature more emotional intensity than any other activities. Toward the middle of Phase VI she may become quite clingy, wanting to be near you as she plays.

POSSESSIVENESS

As Phase VI continues, you will begin to see signs of possessiveness in your toddler, especially if there is another similarly aged child present. Your child will not want to share anything. He is incapable of sharing and will remain that way until he is at least twenty-two months of age.

I WANT TO CHOOSE

Another development you can expect to see during this phase is choosiness. Toddlers develop a need to decide which clothes they will wear, which foods they will eat, and, if you let them, who will feed them. This behavior reflects the normal growth of interest in personal power. The typical eighteen-month-old likes to be in charge of the parent-child situation as much as possible.

TELEVISION VIEWING

A fair number of myths surround the subject of the television viewing habits of young children. It has been claimed, for example, that by the time children reach five years of age they will have spent five thousand hours watching television. The article in question indicated that children watched television from birth (!) for several hours a day, seven days a week, twelve months a year. This assessment, of course, is nonsense. Newborns don't watch television at all, and we have learned from thousands of hours of observation in homes that very many children do not watch television for extended periods at any time during the first eighteen months of life.

The only reliable way to find out just how much television very young children watch is to have a professional observer spend many hours in the homes of large numbers of children, recording what they are looking at and apparently listening to. As far as I know, this expensive and laborious research has never been done, except as a part of our preschool project at Harvard. A rare child, one who is intellectually precocious may, toward the end of the second year of life, begin to spend a remarkable amount of time watching *Sesame Street*. Our observers found that one out of four precocious children at about eighteen months of age at times spent a full hour staring at that show. However, our data shows that the average time spent by Phase VI children in television viewing is approximately two minutes an hour for the waking hours.

During the first year of life, for the most part, television viewing is only momentary and sporadic. The activity seems to be the same sort of behavior that is first seen in children during the fifth month of life. All children who are healthy and hear well will respond automatically to any reasonably loud sound near them by turning promptly to locate the source of that sound. Such reflexive behavior persists at least until the second birthday and could be considered television viewing, but in almost all cases the baby, after turning toward the set, doesn't linger for more than a few seconds.

During Phase VI, a fair number of babies will show increasing interest in videos made especially for their age range. Several are now available that appeal to this age baby, including the Baby Songs series and Meet Your Animal Friends. Broadcast television, however, remains uninteresting for most toddlers during the bulk of this phase. Babies are more interested in operating the remote control than in watching what's on the screen. An exception to these statements is the programs featuring Barney the dinosaur. For reasons I don't understand, many Phase VI children become enamored of Barney.

Until a child is at least a year and a half old, his language and intellectual abilities are too limited to support prolonged interest in what he can see on the screen. Television commercials attract babies only because they generally feature frequent abrupt changes in sound. In fact, *Sesame Street* uses this device deliberately to regularly reattract the attention of young children.

Sustained viewing of television ordinarily doesn't begin much before the second year of life, and then only slowly.

At times during Phase VI a toddler will sit next to an older person who is watching television and will occasionally look at the set. But here the child's purpose is primarily social rather than an interest in viewing television.

OUTDOOR ACTIVITIES

Toddlers love to be outside. Don't be surprised if you have a hard time getting your Phase VI child to come back into the house. Given the opportunity, she will show the same profound curiosity in exploring a grassy yard, plants, dirt, picnic tables, and so on that she shows indoors.

Occasionally, toddlers behave strangely in their first encounters with the outdoors. A baby may resist being put down on the grass and may not want to crawl or walk on it; others will avoid asphalt surfaces. These are passing quirks and nothing to worry about.

A favorite of children of this age is swinging. A safe infant seat attached to an outdoor gym set will be huge fun for your toddler. Another favorite outdoor activity is water play. Miniature pools are inexpensive and widely available. Be careful, of course, not to let a child play unattended in or near such a pool; serious accidents can occur in relatively small quantities of water. Sandboxes have always been a source of great pleasure to children in this age range. They particularly like the texture of the sand, and they enjoy pouring it from one container into another. Sand is also appreciated by neighborhood cats, however, and you are strongly advised to keep the sandbox covered when it's not in use and to check it from time to time for unwanted contents.

Life with a Slightly Older Sibling

A Phase VI baby's life is significantly different when there is a slightly older sibling in the house. So is the life of the parents. Pity the poor full-time at-home parent of two closely spaced children when the younger one is in Phase VI.

From eight months on through the second year of life, the baby will be involved in thousands of interchanges with the slightly older sibling with whom he shares both his home and his parents. Throughout the eight- to twelve-month period the slightly younger sibling will be on the receiving end of increasing manifestations of jealousy. From about twelve to fourteen months, a stalemate will often develop because of the younger child's increased ability to use the cry more promptly to avoid getting hurt. During that period the older child may become increasingly frustrated as his jealousy continues to grow while his ability to act on it has been severely curtailed.

For the older child the situation gets substantially worse once the younger child enters Phase VI, especially after he reaches age fifteen or sixteen months or so. This worsened situation arises because the younger child, now beginning to sense his own interpersonal power for the first time, very often will become aggressive toward the older child. It is very common for a Phase VI toddler to begin to bite, hit, and pull the hair of his older sister. Since the older child has had considerably more experience in life, including the experiences of pain and parental punishment, it is not uncommon to find the younger one becoming dominant during this time of life. This situation is no fun for the older child. The impact on a full-time parent is also likely to be unpleasant (to put it mildly). During Phase V, when a parent heard crying from another room, the commotion was very likely being caused by the older sibling venting his hostility toward the baby. Now it gradually dawns upon the parent that the older child is no longer always the guilty party.

As the weeks go by, a new feeling ordinarily creeps into the parent's state of mind: impotence. Now the parent doesn't know who started the trouble. This condition doesn't go away quickly; it usually lasts for a minimum of six or eight months and sometimes for years. This condition is the single most common source of stress that parents have reported to us in study after study. The stressful atmosphere created by closely spaced siblings is one of the major reasons for our heartfelt recommendation that parents space their children at least three years apart if at all possible.

No one has yet adequately studied the long-term consequences of the normal chronic hostility between closely spaced siblings during their early years. It is quite possible that once such siblings reach their teens they end up being close companions with no long-term price paid for these early experiences. It is also equally possible that deeply rooted lifelong negative attitudes are created that prevent some closely spaced siblings from ever feeling fully comfortable with each other.

Although we have no substantial evidence of the long-term impact of close spacing on the emotional ties between siblings, some data is available with respect to intellectual development, and from our own research and other studies we have a good deal of evidence of the immediate impact on day-to-day living.

The long-term evidence is based largely on a study of 1,379,000 children from four Western countries performed by R. Zajonc of the University of Michigan. He compared IQ scores of teenage children who were closely spaced versus those who were only children or children with considerably older or younger siblings. He also studied the impact on test scores of the number of children in a family. His general conclusions: the closer in age the siblings were, and the more children there were in the family, the lower were their test scores. The only exception was the youngest child in families with many children; this last child sometimes achieved rather well, but only if there was a gap of several years between her and the next youngest child. The author suggested that the youngest child tended to benefit from the teaching of the older siblings. Such studies, of course, cannot tell us what is going to happen in any specific family situation. Many closely spaced siblings grow up to be very bright indeed, but as a matter of general policy, Zajonc's major conclusions seem to warrant consideration when planning a family.

In the short run the effects of sibling rivalry are quite clear in the day-to-day existence of closely spaced children and anybody who lives with them all day long. I feel most concerned for the older sibling in this situation, because she has to move over to make room for a younger competitor under conditions that substantially diminish her pleasure in day-to-day existence.

Think of how she must feel. It's as if she were twenty-five years old, married for a year or so, and very happy. Her husband treats her like a princess; she gets every consideration, huge amounts of attention, and plenty of love. Then one day her husband comes to her in a high state of excitement and says, "I have wonderful news for you: next week I'm going to bring someone else home to live with us. She's a full-grown woman a bit younger than you and somewhat better looking; she's going to be our second wife. Now, since she'll be new to the family I'm naturally going to spend more time with her than with you, but I want you to love her as I will. And here's a box of candy to commemorate this happy occasion." This would be a crushing development for any woman. For a three-year-old it is much more than she can handle emotionally. Small wonder that so many closely spaced older siblings turn sour during their third year of life. Later on, I will discuss how you can cope with this most difficult situation. If you are currently doing so, you may want to look ahead now.

Within the Phase VI baby's social experiences the effect of the slightly older sibling will be seen in two circumstances. First of all, there will be many more child-to-child encounters than would otherwise occur. And second, as noted earlier, these encounters, in marked contrast to most of the child's other social experiences, will be marked by jealousy and, at times, aggression. This is not to say that a kind word will never pass from the older sibling to the baby, but the baby will almost certainly get a good idea of unpleasant social interaction over a period that may last for several years.

THE APPARENT INTERESTS OF THE PHASE VI CHILD

The primary interests of the Phase VI child are the same as they were in the preceding phase: satisfying curiosity, practicing and enjoying motor skills, and socializing.

Interest in the Primary Caregiver

The Phase VI toddler's interest in her primary caregiver takes the form of a strong preference for proximity and frequent overtures to that person. These overtures can serve several basic purposes: to socialize or reestablish contact; to ask for help; and, less commonly, to express affection or seek approval. When a Phase VI child is out of sorts because of fatigue or minor illness, he is likely to be even more clingy than usual and more oriented toward his primary caregiver.

Interest in Age-Mates

Along with the recent rise in the use of substitute care for infants and toddlers have come claims of the benefits of play with age-mates during the first two years of life. This statement is not founded on any substantial study of the young child. On the contrary, the principal social interest of children during the first two years of life is the adults who care for them. When children seventeen and eighteen months of age have an opportunity to interact, more often than not they soon begin hitting and pushing each other and acting unhappy. In loosely supervised situations we have routinely observed a stronger or more aggressive child using intimidation and physical force on the other toddler in an attempt to establish dominance. In retrospect this behavior is not terribly surprising. It is exactly what we see when various monkey species are forced to live together in captivity. They seek to establish a dominant-submissive hierarchy. Most Phase VI children behave the same way. They show few social niceties in their interactions with each other; consideration for the feelings of others is simply not yet there.

The situation with children who are younger than Phase VI is quite different. They show nothing in the way of true social interest, but rather treat each other more like interesting objects than like people.

It is conceivable that group experience under close supervision during Phase VI may produce some social benefits, but at this point there is no evidence to support such a claim. I advise you not to believe any claim that play with age-mates—or, for that matter, with anyone other than you—is a necessity during your child's first two years of life. During that time, your baby's only social need is to establish a solid, healthy attachment to you.

If your toddler does spend time with others of the same age during this time of life, supervise them carefully. Treat this encounter as you did the use of the walker with the Phase VI child—as a situation that requires constant supervision. You can expect to see true social interest in age-mates as your child moves into his third year of life.

An exception: you will find that your toddler will play quite well with a three- or four-year-old. While your child doesn't need this experience, at least it won't ordinarily be hazardous and may provide some fun. Even here, however, you'd best keep your eye on the situation, especially if the older child has a closely spaced younger sibling at home.

Interest in Exploring the World

The second principal interest for a Phase VI child is in exploring her world. Phase VI children show a continuing interest in small objects, marked by a gradual shift in emphasis from exploring their qualities to practicing simple skills on them.

By fourteen and a half months of age a child can usually be introduced to puzzles. If you know how to do this (and I will show you), your toddler will demonstrate her determination and talent with them. Puzzles will become surprisingly useful over the next year or so.

Scribbling with crayons will also gradually become interesting to your Phase VI child, as will any hand-eye activity that is challenging but not too challenging.

Toward the end of Phase VI and especially as the third year of life begins, children begin to synthesize what they have learned about small objects and start to use objects for imaginative play, constructing scenes with dolls and animal figures, building towers, fortresses, and ranches. They may even begin representational drawing.

Beyond physical objects, which include toys and many common household objects, your child's physical surroundings will continue to intrigue him, but less and less so as he approaches his second birthday. It is as if he is gradually becoming so knowledgeable about what his home looks like, feels like, and contains that the novelty is wearing off. He is now becoming interested in new events within and outside the home.

He will spend more time looking at images on the television screen. His explorations will shift toward scenes that change more from day to day than do the static objects in the living areas that occupied him during his first explorations of the home.

WATER PLAY

Water play continues to be great fun for the Phase VI child; it seems to have more lasting appeal than many other kinds of play. Unlike most commercial toys, whose uses are restricted by their design and physical limitations, water can be used in an infinite number of ways. Because of the continuing possibility of water intoxication, however, it is important for you to continue to be watchful about how much water your toddler swallows at pools and other places where he plays with fresh water.

BALLS

In repeated observations of toddlers' use of toys and other physical materials, we have found balls at the top of the list in terms of frequency of use. This preference is especially noticeable in the first half of Phase VI. One of the best ways in which to engage the attention of a fourteen- or fifteen-month-old toddler is with a Ping-Pong ball, particularly when it's used on a hardwood floor. Just dropping a Ping-Pong ball creates a lot of movement that lasts for quite some time. The movement has an antic quality, a bouncing that is crisp and orderly in contrast, for example, to that of a tennis ball or a piece of Silly Putty. Then, too, the bouncing is accompanied by interesting sound patterns. And furthermore the Ping-Pong ball is small enough so that the child can manage it much better than a ball five or six inches or more in diameter. It is light enough so that the child can throw it some distance and—although this is of less significance from the child's point of view—throwing a Ping-Pong ball is not likely to elicit a scolding from the parent, as compared to a golf ball. In addition, playing with a Ping-Pong ball can feed a child's growing ability to chase and retrieve thrown items. This activity feeds the child's third principal interest, the mastery of newfound motor skills.

A precautionary note: your toddler may try to put a Ping-Pong ball into his mouth. Although it is too large for her to swallow, you should wait until she is at least fourteen months of age before you give her one. Also check once in a while to see that the ball is still intact, because the hard edges of a crushed Ping-Pong ball can constitute a hazard.

Probably the most appropriate ball for use during Phase VI is a plastic beach ball. The bigger the ball, the better, up to about twenty-four inches in diameter. Phase VI children, at least in the beginning, have usually only been walking for only a few months. They delight in trying to carry large light objects. The eighteen- to twenty-four-inch beach ball is perfect for this game. Carrying it is a delicious challenge. Dropping it and watching it move feeds their deep interest in the movement patterns of objects. Finally, in attempting to retrieve a beach ball, the young Phase VI child is very likely to kick it away with her foot as she bends down to pick it up. This experience is apparently just frustrating enough to give the child an extra charge when she is playing with such a toy. All and all, especially considering that these balls cost less than two dollars, you really can't find a better toy for your child during her second year of life.

ORAL EXPLORATION

Throughout Phase VI toddlers continue to use their mouths as exploratory organs. In studies that I performed for a major U.S. manufacturer, we found that the young Phase VI child is very likely to put any substance, solid or liquid, to his mouth. His next act is to gum the stuff and swallow some if he is hungry or thirsty. It is not surprising that this is the time of life when accidental poisonings reach a peak. You should be doubly cautious about such matters in Phase VI. Our research has consistently confirmed the impulsivity of children at this age. Phase VI children don't care what something smells or tastes like. Poison control centers report that Phase VI children swallow all sorts of foul-tasting substances, including gasoline, Drāno, and cleaning fluid. Indeed, our research found that odor has absolutely no effect on the tendency of a child to swallow a substance. We used odors ranging from pleasant foodlike smells, such as chocolate and flowers, to extraordinarily unpleasant, noxious ones like rotten eggs. The amount of swallowing was totally independent of the odor. Here is one place where the powerful curiosity of the child can have harsh consequences.

Interest in Practicing and Enjoying New Motor Skills

The third major area of interest in Phase VI is in motor activities. The fourteen-month-old generally is a fairly good walker, although she is still slightly unstable and inhibited by a good deal of body fat. She is also reasonably skillful at climbing and, as noted earlier, loves to do so. I would encourage you to let her climb, but always under close supervision until you are certain that she can handle a situation well. By eighteen months of age, you may find your baby wanting to climb up and down stairs while holding your hand rather than crawling. By the end of Phase VI she will walk up and down stairs safely by herself.

Beyond walking and climbing, the emerging motor activities of Phase VI include running, jumping, and playing with low four-wheeled wagons by straddling them and dragging them along. Although your Phase VI child will enjoy practicing her new ability to move four-wheeled objects, she is not likely to be able to do much with even the smallest tricycle until her second birthday.

EDUCATIONAL DEVELOPMENT DURING PHASE VI

THE FOUR EDUCATIONAL FOUNDATIONS

The four foundations of education—language, intelligence, curiosity, and social development—progress dramatically during Phase VI. Their develop-

ment is at risk, however. Whether development goes well during these crucial months depends much more on what babies learn than on their genetic
endowment. Furthermore, what they learn during this phase will depend
more on your behavior than on anything else.

Children develop best when parents know what they are doing and
provide effective guidance. Unlike the first eight months of life, Phase VI is
a period when doing what feels right can be counterproductive in important ways. And of course I believe that if you have someone else do most of
the job, your child won't develop as well as she could have. You also will miss
some of the most wonderful experiences you could ever have.

The Balance of the Principal Interests

It is of basic importance to keep nourishing each of your baby's major
interests: curiosity, motor activity, and sociability. By far the most common
way the balance across a child's principal interests is disturbed during Phase
VI is for his social interest to overdevelop at the expense of the other two.

Less frequently the child's interest in exploration and motor mastery
are adequately supported by the environment but the normal growth of the
interest in parents is interfered with. This kind of interference can happen if
both parents work outside the home for most of the daylight hours during
the week and employ someone who, for any number of reasons, spends little time interacting with the child. The saddest of all situations is when none
of the three dominant interests is nurtured by a child's environment. This is
most unlikely, however, except in rather unusual circumstances.

THE GROWTH OF SPECIAL ABILITIES IN YOUR CHILD

The third way we deal with what is going on educationally in Phase VI stems
directly from the early stages of our research on well-developing young children. From our extensive naturalistic observations of children we determined
in some detail which qualities distinguished a well-developing three- to six-
year-old child from another who was not developing so well. We came to
our conclusions through observations of such children in their homes, at
nursery schools, and in day care centers.

The well-developed three- to six-year-old child shows the following
abilities in more impressive ways than does the average or below-average child.

Social Abilities

- Getting and holding the attention of adults
- Using adults as resources after first determining that a job is too difficult

- Expressing affection and mild annoyance, when appropriate, to adults
- Showing pride in achievement
- Engaging in make-believe play
- Leading and following peers
- Expressing affection and mild annoyance, when appropriate, to peers
- Competing with peers

Nonsocial Abilities

- Demonstrating good language development
- Noticing small details or discrepancies
- Anticipating consequences
- Dealing with abstractions
- Taking the perspective of another person
- Making interesting associations
- Planning and carrying out complicated activities
- Using resources effectively
- Maintaining concentration on a task while simultaneously keeping track of what is going on around one in a fairly busy situation (dual focusing)

This list of abilities can serve as a guideline for you in your activities with your child during the second year of life. Although some of these abilities will not be observable until your child's third year—namely the social abilities used in relations with age-mates—you will want to be aware of them in advance of their emergence. Later in this chapter we will examine these abilities more closely and see how you can help them along during Phase VI.

Progress in Mental Ability During Phase VI

THE EMERGENCE OF THINKING ABILITY

In Piaget's system the first signs of intelligence (defined as problem-solving behavior) are seen in connection with the reaching behavior of a six- or seven-month-old baby. When the baby pushes an obstacle aside in order to grasp an object, solving his first simple problem, he is showing practical or sensorimotor intelligence. Piaget does not regard the act of reaching as an act of intelligence. But when a baby pushes an obstacle aside so as to be able to grasp an object, there is a means-end relationship between the two behaviors. Piaget considers the use of a behavior to overcome difficulty blocking a goal to be a form of problem-solving and, therefore, of intelligence.

A second less thoroughly studied form of early intentional behavior actually occurs slightly earlier. Between five and a half and six months of age children begin to use the cry intentionally in order to get an adult to come to them. In the weeks that follow it becomes increasingly clear that the baby is at times crying not from pain but rather to be picked up and held or to affect adult behavior in other ways. This particular form of elementary intentional behavior was not described by Piaget, but it seems to me to be another legitimate example of early problem-solving.

In Piaget's system children toward the end of their second year begin to use manipulation of ideas to solve problems. In other words, as they approach their second birthday, children change from trial-and-error problem-solving, featuring the use of their eyes and hands, to insightful, thoughtful problem-solving.

INITIAL INDICATORS OF THOUGHTFULNESS

Children under eighteen months of age do not reflect upon ideas in any obvious way. In Piaget's system, at least, it is not accurate to call the child under eighteen months a thoughtful creature, although mental events certainly take place. As children approach their second birthday, however, it becomes increasingly appropriate to talk about thoughtfulness in the behavior of children. Toward the end of Phase VI you can actually begin to see the mind working, the wheels turning. Interesting and pregnant delays appear in a child's behavior, and you can often predict her next act by observing the circumstances and her facial expressions. Her next behavior often confirms that she was actually thinking about alternatives and options, or at least she was dwelling on a particular move that she was going to make.

In the filming of our television series, *The First Three Years,* we captured a revealing event in the life of a dynamic twenty-three-month-old who was showing off at the kitchen table for her mother and father. In asserting her personal power, she playfully refused to give her father some spoons that he wanted to put into the sink. As she attempted to move them away from his reach, she spilled a cup of milk and then looked down somewhat guiltily at the consequences. Her father said, "Good show, kid. You're all right." Her mother began cleaning up the mess, and her father then said, with mock-seriousness, "Who did that? Did you do that?" The child listened and remained motionless with her head down for about ten seconds. She finally replied, "No, I didn't do it. Lisa [her older sister] did it." This piece of behavior illustrates what we mean by elementary thinking ability. There is no doubt that the child in those few moments was thinking as rapidly and skillfully as she could of a way to avoid punishment. She actually created an idea. Such an early lie is perhaps the first obvious indication of the ability to deal with ideas.

This child seriously thought that her answer would work. She thought this not because she was dull—on the contrary, she was quite bright—but because her early thinking was what Piaget called egocentric—that is, she was unable to take into account the point of view of other people. She couldn't, at that early stage of development, factor into her answer the reality that both parents were actually watching what had happened and obviously would know that her older sister had not been involved. Well-developing children overcome this limited understanding of the point of view of other people by the end of the third year of life. By that time they recognize that others' point of view may be different from theirs.

Children under eighteen months of age are much more impulsive than two-year-olds. They try possible solutions out in the open rather than in their heads. In Piaget's original writings on the development of intelligence in his own three children, he described in detail how each of his children, at one year of age, would experiment in similar situations by trying out different ways of getting something that was out of reach, for example, when they were confined to a crib. However, when the same sort of problem was provided for the children as they approached their second birthday, they would pause as they apparently thought about alternatives, and then the first act after the pause would be a correct or near-correct solution to the problem.

More elaborate descriptions of the changes in the quality of intelligent behavior are beyond the scope of this book. The best and indeed virtually the only place to find such materials is in the writings of Piaget himself, some of which you will find listed in Recommended Readings, at the end of this book. The possibilities in dealing with a child expand directly with the growth of their mental abilities. One important example is that from the time your child can deal with ideas, and therefore has acquired abstract thinking ability, you can, for the first time, use rational means for disciplinary purposes.

During Phase VI the child's capacity to understand explanations grows. Because of her increased mental capacities her ability to deal with phenomena that cover time also grows. During Phase VI her short-term memory develops to its completion. In contrast to the eight-month-old who could retain an image of an object in her mind for only a few seconds, the seventeen-month-old can remember where a desirable object is from day to day.

In spite of these remarkable developments, the Phase VI child still exhibits clear signs of being far from mentally mature.

PHASE VI AND THE RANDOM EVENT
An interesting example of the mental immaturity of the Phase VI child is the absence from his mind of the possibility of a random event. One of the

most common kinds of evidence of this is in misunderstandings between siblings. Your two-year-old who is accidentally hurt by his older sibling is totally unable to understand the concept of an accident. He assumes that if he was hurt, someone *intended* to hurt him. It is as simple as that. You can argue the point with him, or explain it until you are quite fatigued. It is not going to make a bit of difference. In his work, Piaget gives many fascinating examples of the peculiarities in the early thinking styles of children.

RECOMMENDED CHILD-REARING PRACTICES: PHASE VI

You won't have any trouble doing a fine job of child-rearing in Phase VI except in the case of social development. You will have a grand time guiding the growth of the child's language and curiosity, and you won't have to worry about his growing ability to gain new motor skills. The difficulty will lie in teaching him how to live in your family. But have faith, a wonderful outcome is very possible, and nothing is more exciting than a well-developed two-year-old. They are simply one of nature's miracles.

Encouraging Language Development

After a slow start during the second half of the first year of life, language growth accelerates steadily during Phase VI. In the preceding chapter I described the most effective ways to teach language to your baby. Babies begin to make frequent overtures to the primary caretaker at about ten months of age. When they approach you at that age, it is for one of three reasons: they need help, they seek comfort, or they want to share something thrilling with you. Usually the reason is easy to identify, and if you respond in the manner I described, good language learning will result. The way you react to your baby's overtures and your understanding of the level she is at in language development underlie effective language teaching.

In a later section you will find a chart describing in detail the total picture of language acquisition throughout the first three years of life.

Talking to a young child is most effective if it is at or slightly beyond his apparent level of understanding. We have found that parents usually underestimate what a child can understand during the second and third year of life. Language development, like any learning, occurs best when a child is paying attention. That's why I emphasize the teaching that occurs when the child comes to you with a particular interest in mind. If you correctly identify that interest, speak to it, and act on it, you will be assured of her attention. Trying to redirect your toddler's attention to your topic of interest is considerably more difficult than identifying what your child's interest is.

Reading Aloud to Your Phase VI Child

There is still no evidence that reading to a baby will enhance language development. But common sense suggests that it can't hurt, and babies and parents love it. Reading simple entertaining stories to your child, particularly at night before she goes to bed, is a good idea. But if you insist on story reading during the day when your toddler wants to be doing something else, I don't think the results will be as good.

Because language acquisition is accelerating dramatically during Phase VI, the teaching task becomes easier and easier as each month goes by. Extremely simple stories will start to hold your toddler's interest at the beginning of this phase. As the months go by, he will show interest in more complicated stories. You will know when his interest flags. When it does, don't push it. He's not ready, but he will be soon.

In the Recommended Readings section, you will find help in selecting books appropriate for your child's developmental level. By the middle of this phase, he will very probably have become very keen on being read to and looking at books on his own.

The Role of Television

Toward the end of Phase VI you can expect your child to begin to pay more attention to television. Exposure to programs like *Sesame Street* may, in a modest way, have an impact on the child's level of language development, but rest assured that if he never sees a single television program he can still learn language through you in an absolutely magnificent manner.

Grammar and Comprehension

Even though the child under eighteen months of age still is not likely to speak much, the rate at which he is learning to understand new words and linguistic elements like prepositions, negatives, and plurals is remarkable. The receptive vocabulary of a child in the second year of life, for example, is likely to increase from five to ten words at his first birthday to about three hundred. (Children in our parent education programs usually acquire well over four hundred words by their second birthday.) Moreover, by the time a child is two years old he will be able to cope with a substantial percentage of the grammatical structures that are the basis of communication. The fourteen-month-old toddler can understand about six simple instructions such as "Throw me a kiss" and "Wave bye-bye." This means that if you are feeling harried and want very much to leave him alone for a while, you now, for the first time, are able to say, "I do not want you to do A, B, or C," and have some confidence that he will understand the message. Toward the end of Phase VI the typical child will understand far more complicated instructions. You will be able, for example, to ask your two-year-old to take a shoe to his room and then bring back a particular toy, and have confidence that he will not only understand the sequence of instruction but will continue to keep it in mind as he completes the task.

Although the Phase VI baby has come a long way linguistically, he still has far to go. You should not use instructions and admonitions that involve delayed consequences of several hours or a day or two, because your baby's sense of time is still limited. If you tell a fourteen-month-old baby he'll be punished when Daddy comes home unless he does X or Y, for instance, you'll be badly overestimating his capacities.

Babies throughout most of the first three years of life live in the here and now. They are still responsive primarily to things they can see in front of them rather than to things that might happen sometime in the future. Therefore, while you should take advantage of each new level of ability, you do run the risk of expecting too much from your child. Expecting too much from an infant, especially when a new baby arrives, is a relatively common phenomenon.

First Attempts at Speech

During the fourteen- to twenty-four-month period most babies begin to speak. No one knows what determines when a baby will begin to speak. It is yet another mystery about early human development. While speech grows gradually, we have come to expect a dramatic increase during the last two or three months of the second year of life.

It is a most unusual child who says nothing for several months and then begins to speak in complete sentences. Your baby is more likely to use a few words singly in a sort of shorthand—like "some" intended to mean "I want some" or "more" meaning "I want more."

By twenty to twenty-two months of age you can expect two-word sentences. Soon after the onset of these brief expressions the child will begin to expand into the use of phrases, and it is quite possible that shortly before her second birthday she will be speaking in fairly complete sentences.

A phenomenon that is interesting and fun occurs when the Phase VI child uses long collections of sounds arranged in sentencelike form, complete with inflections and emphases, but with no recognizable meaning. I have no notion as to the significance of this gibberish.

The Importance of Conversation

Once your child begins to speak fairly regularly, conversation becomes a possibility. You will be positively delighted with the result. The ability to converse, after all, is another sign of increasing personhood. Adults are not used to creatures who cannot speak; the only nonverbal creatures in the typical home are pets. Obviously an infant is considerably more complicated and important than a goldfish, but at the same time, until he can speak he is different from older children and adults in this very important way.

In a good child-rearing situation, the baby naturally interacts conversationally, sometimes for very serious purposes, at other times for fun, and at other times primarily to maintain social contact. Comfortable, effective parents move naturally into responding to such language and into carrying on modest conversations.

Once conversational ability surfaces, experiences with children become richer and your chances to encourage growth in several dimensions of competence become greater. For example, you'll find it easier to encourage the talking child in his role play and fantasy experiences than you did before he learned to talk. Furthermore, it is very exciting to get a better look at a child's mind through his expanded capacity to communicate.

Encouraging the Development of Intelligence

The emergence of thinking ability during Phase VI is a remarkable phenomenon. One of the mysteries of the ages, it is one of the most dramatic and exciting experiences parents can have, particularly with their first children. I can't count the number of times that new parents have told me how bowled over they were by the new mental capacities of their eighteen- to twenty-four-month-old children. You can only understand these feelings when you go through them yourself.

It does not take great resources for a parent to do a great job of fostering a child's thinking ability during this phase. Once a child gets to be two and a half years old, the parent with a good educational background may have an advantage over other parents in nurturing intelligence. Specific information and ideas become increasingly important for mental growth, and the more extensive your education, the richer the reservoir of ideas and information you can pass on to your child. Prior to two and a half years, however, the child's language and intellectual capacities are so limited that most adults, even those with modest capacities, are fully capable of providing all the input their children need to develop well. Indeed, in the second year of life most facts and ideas about the world are beyond a baby's comprehension. The core level of intelligence that all normal adults possess is sufficient to promote learning during the first two and one half years.

I am all in favor of solid intellectual growth during the early years. I am not, however, an advocate of forced teaching in an effort to produce intellectual precocity. If you can teach your toddler to recognize letters and numbers without jeopardizing the other developmental goals of the first years, I have no objections. Some children show curiosity early on about such subjects. If your child takes the lead by asking you about letters and numbers, that's fine, but coercing her into attending to instructional materials makes no sense to me.

The children we observed early in our research who developed exceptionally well, did so without any special tuition during their first three years of life, however. The children of the families in our successful Missouri program also achieved very impressive levels of intellectual ability by their third birthday without forced teaching. And the children in our ongoing New Parents as Teachers program also routinely score far above national averages by their third birthday. They achieved these levels through child-rearing practices that were, for the most part, identified under common family circumstances, where the child's natural desire to learn was nourished in a rather easygoing fashion. Basically, if a child's world contains a large number of learning opportunities that are appropriate for her developmental level, an opportunity to choose from among those options, and an interested older person who uses language effectively, her intelligence will flourish.

Interestingly, the same parenting practices that lead to good language development simultaneously produce good intellectual development. In addition, a baby who is taught the rules of family life effectively spends little time mired in social hang-ups and, as a result, has more time and energy for learning.

Finally, when parents devote excessive effort toward encouraging precocious intelligence in their children they run the risk of diminishing the child's intrinsic pleasure in learning and of valuing their child to some extent because of what she achieves rather than who she is.

Nourishing Curiosity

Feeding a Phase VI toddler's curiosity is easy. If she is developing well, everything interests her. The same general guidelines set down for Phase V continue to apply: make certain she has maximum access to the home; make the kitchen as interesting, as accessible, and as safe as possible; keep a supply of special toys and other materials available but out of reach, and give them to her when she seems bored or in need of something to do.

Try to build on your toddler's natural enthusiasm for learning by responding as warmly and as supportively as you can when he makes an overture to you and wants to share an enthusiasm. Build on his interests by introducing related information and ideas whenever you can. If, for example, he brings you a piece of Play-Doh and indicates that he is proud of what he has made, you might agree that he has produced something wonderful and then suggest that he try to make a car like Daddy's. Or you can suggest that he make an apple or a banana. It is not terribly important that you come up with a brilliant observation; the major requirement is that you support and broaden his interest. Implicitly, such behavior on your part makes it clear to him that to be curious, to be learning, to be exploring, is something you strongly approve of. Your approval means a great deal to your child, especially at this particular phase of his life.

You can supplement the usual activities of home life by taking your child outside or to a shopping mall or anywhere at all, and you can be sure she will always find something that will interest her.

Here are two things you should avoid: (1) depriving her of lots of time with you, and (2) subjecting her regularly to long periods of boredom.

Nurturing Healthy Social Development During Phase VI

COPING WITH NEGATIVISM

Between fourteen and sixteen months of age, for the first time in his life, your baby will become aware of himself. The first faint signs that he knows he is somebody will appear during these months. You will know for sure when this has happened because you will ask him for something and he will say "No, mine!" or something else that clearly indicates an awareness of self. Once this happens, negativism has surfaced.

The emergence of negativism is inevitable. It may appear as early as thirteen or as late as eighteen months. Negativism is the clearest indication of the beginning of Phase VI, often occurring before a toddler uses his own name or a possessive. Negativism takes several forms, none of which are terribly pleasant to live with. The child may or may not say the word "no," but he certainly will express the concept in his behavior.

With the dawning of self-awareness, toddlers become excited about their newly sensed executive prerogatives, and so begins a minimum of six months of experimentation with power. Challenging your authority becomes a regular event, and any activity that gives your toddler a sense of power will have an intoxicating effect on him. He will want to call the shots. He will become stubborn and choosy about all sorts of things, including which clothes he'll wear and which foods he'll eat.

Once negativism begins to take hold, it, along with other developments in the child's life, such as his continued love of climbing and of putting things in his mouth, will result in more pressure on you as the primary caretaker. With this increase in pressure, the issue of discipline will become more pressing. We have seen that distraction is usually very effective in dealing with a Phase V baby. Unfortunately it ceases to work when Phase VI begins because at this point sustained stubbornness rears its head. During these months, your child's determination will grow steadily, but he will not yet be reasonable. That combination is potent. What to do?

Humane Discipline for Use in Dealing with the Phase VI Child

During Phase VI many parents, out of exasperation, first begin to spank their children. We saw this in our early observational work—on occasion in families where children were developing extremely well. As a result, in previous editions of this book, I did not feel that I could tell parents never to spank their babies. How else could a parent be firm with a subrational eighteen-month-old? I am happy to be able to tell you that we have found an effective, humane alternative that has a cumbersome name: prevention of proximity to the key person.

PREVENTION OF PROXIMITY TO THE KEY PERSON

You will recall that for Phase V, I recommended a disciplinary tactic based on the universal resistance to total immobilization shown by nine- and ten-month-olds. Such babies have a need to be able to move freely whenever they feel like it. Take away that ability, even for just a few seconds, and you learn just how important it is to your baby.

My suggestion for discipline for the Phase VI toddler is similarly rooted in the child's need to come close to her key people whenever she wants to. This is a universal, deeply felt need in children of this age. It is a necessary element in the completion of the process of attachment that is the focus of the toddler's social activities during Phase VI. We are not normally aware of the child's need to be able to approach his parent whenever he would like to, simply because we do not usually withhold such behavior from children.

If your sixteen-month-old begins to get out of hand in the course of his routine challenging of your authority, tell him that if he doesn't stop the offending behavior you are going to have to use the gate. If he persists, set up a gate in the doorway of the room you are in and put him on the other side of it. He can go anywhere he wants to except the most important place in the home, next to you. Wait until he starts to complain. Look at your watch. Let him cry for fifteen seconds, then approach him and say, "I'm going to let you in now, but if you do anything bad again, I'm going to use the gate again." Then remove the gate.

If you will behave this way consistently, after a few episodes, the word "gate" will acquire meaning and the threat of its use will probably work. This technique may not be effective at the outset of Phase VI; it may take a few weeks, but it will work, given time. Each time you set a limit effectively, you reinforce your authority. Each time you don't, you undermine your authority.

It is critical here that your toddler learn that you have the ultimate authority in your relationship. He needs to understand that no matter how much he is loved, whenever you say no firmly, he won't get his way, no matter what he does. Interestingly, babies who are raised this way become the happiest two-year-olds you will ever see. On the other hand, giving in to your toddler because tears are streaming down her face may produce immediate cessation of unhappiness, but over time, things will get much worse.

By setting limits firmly and effectively you teach your toddler the terms of the social contract. He will learn that most of the time he will get what he wants, and quickly, but whenever you make it clear that he won't, nothing he does will make any difference.

His expectations and his entitlements will develop in a realistic way. Before his second birthday, the message will get through, and one day the testing and the acts of defiance will stop, and he will have become the happiest two-year-old on the block. If you follow this advice, you will be the happiest parents on the block.

This setting of limits is the single most difficult part of raising a great child during the first three years of life.

Here is one other piece of advice for this important chore: when your Phase VI toddler does anything at all that disturbs you, ask yourself, "If he were eight years old would I let him do that?" If the answer is no, stop him.

Perhaps the most exciting thing I have learned over the last five years is that you can hold a child under two years of age to decent standards of behavior and that if you do, life is better for everyone, and the baby becomes much happier than if he had been overindulged.

The interpersonally directed orneriness of the Phase VI child can be hard to live with, but there are two consolations for you. First, this happens with just about every child, so your baby is not behaving this way because you are an inadequate parent or a disagreeable person. Second, the negativism will probably—though not certainly—go away. Whether and when it does depends directly on you. Under optimum conditions, by the time the baby reaches twenty-one or twenty-two months of age, the unpleasant behavior will subside. The clouds will break, the sun will come out, and living with your child will become delightful again. However, do not expect a perfect outcome, especially with a first child. It is more realistic to expect continued contentious behavior, at least until the second birthday. We tell the parents we work with that if testing and defiance are gone by twenty-two months, they have done a marvelous job. If they are gone by twenty-four months they have done very well. If they are still there at twenty-six months they are in for a struggle.

Children who are dealt with ineffectively in terms of limit setting during Phases V and VI routinely continue into the third year of life (Phase VII) with unresolved conflicts in connection with discipline and control. These are the children who during the third year exhibit temper tantrums. Given their increased strength, intelligence, and determination, they become considerably more difficult to live with than they might otherwise have been.

I want to emphasize that we have learned that temper tantrums in the third year, while common, are not inevitable. One of the more important benefits of setting firm and reasonable limits from the beginning of Phase V onward is that you won't have to deal with any temper tantrums of consequence during your child's third year.

Firm discipline is absolutely essential during Phase VI. However, because it is clear that there are very great pressures on the Phase VI child, especially during the fourteen- to twenty-one-month period, to persist and to win in this struggle with authority, wise parents are well advised to yield occasionally to their child in areas where the stakes are not high from the parent's point of view. This occasional yielding does not imply a general permissiveness or an abdication of responsibility for controlling the home. The parents we have watched doing an effective job with their children never abdicate their control in this regard; but they are wise enough and personally secure enough to let the child win an occasional minor struggle at this stage of life when it seems especially important for the child to flex muscles a bit.

USING RATIONAL MEANS TO DISCIPLINE YOUR CHILD

Quite a few parents try to use reason when dealing with their very young infants. This pattern becomes observable from the time their baby is seven or eight months old, when bad habits, like hair pulling, first appear. They try to explain why the child shouldn't. They also try to use explanations when their baby is crying because she is not being allowed to do something she wants, like end the diapering session or pull a toy away from another infant.

This behavior is ineffective for two reasons. First, the language used is usually far beyond the capacity of the infant to understand. Second, the concepts involved are also difficult for the infant to process. These limitations restrict disciplinary styles for the better part of the first two years at a minimum.

We tell our parents that once abstract thinking ability appears, they can shift from the use of the gate for control purposes to the use of reason. When development is proceeding well, this reasoning ability happens at about twenty-two months of age or soon thereafter. We suggest that you use the following procedure to test whether this new stage has arrived: Watch for your child to cause an insignificant accident, like spilling some juice, where someone is going to have to do a small cleanup job as a result. Without letting much time pass, ask with mock seriousness, "Who did that? Did you do that?" When your twenty-two- or twenty-three-month-old hesitates and then says, "I didn't do it. The cat [or someone else] did it," your child has clearly acquired the ability to create an idea. It is not just the denial that signals the new stage; it is rather the creation, after due consideration, of the related idea, the scapegoat.

You and your partner should create two lists—one, of the objects your child is most fond of that day; the other, of the activities he is keen on that day. These lists will have to be updated regularly for maximum effectiveness. Armed with these lists, when your child is misbehaving or being defiant, you can say, "If you throw something at your sister one more time, I won't let you play with your favorite truck for twenty minutes!" You should emphasize the "twenty minutes." Or you can say, "If you won't come in the house now, I won't let you watch Barney for one half hour!" You shouldn't threaten a very long deprivation. That doesn't work as well.

Every time you make a threat, you must follow through with it if your child disobeys you. Every time you do, you are strengthening your authority. Your child should know that your authority is absolute whenever you want it to be.

"USE YOUR WORDS"

Your child's frustration tolerance is at its lowest level when he is between seventeen and twenty months old. Often, at the same age, he is just beginning to expand his use of words. It will help if, when you see frustration building, you develop the habit of saying, "Use your words, please."

Guiding healthy social development will be easier if you can maintain the balance among your child's principal interests. If you are not mindful of the importance of this task, you may inadvertently encourage a child's natural tendency to gravitate around you too much. A twenty-four-month-old clinging vine is very difficult to live with. I have seen a fair number of parents get themselves into this situation and sorely regret it. In addition, such a situation can lay the groundwork for further grief if you are dealing with a first child and are soon to produce a second. A child who is excessively wrapped up in his primary caretaker and is relatively poorly developed in terms of his interest in the rest of the world is a child who is less likely to succeed in overcoming the difficulties brought about by the introduction of a second child into the family. He is also the child who is likely to have difficulty moving into the world of the nursery school.

You really should not, at this time, prolong your child's initial notion that the world was made exclusively for him and that it revolves solely around him. This prolongation is relatively easy to do, especially with a first child. But you are doing him a disservice if you fall into such a pattern.

Phase VI is a transitional period between early infancy and that time when the child is going to begin to move out of the home to play with agemates or to attend nursery school. You should, of course, teach your child that he is terribly important, that his needs and interests are very special, but that he is no more important than any other person in the world, especially you. This apparently contradictory message turns out to be very effective. Your goal, after all, is to turn out a delightful three-year-old as well as one whose skills you can admire.

Dealing with Sibling Issues

PREPARING A PHASE VI CHILD FOR THE ARRIVAL OF A YOUNGER SIBLING

You may have heard of programs or lectures or books that promise to help you prepare an older sibling for the arrival of a new child. These programs almost invariably advocate a good deal of talking to the older child, reading particular kinds of stories, and so forth. In my judgment, if the older child is less than three years old the best way to prepare him for the arrival of a younger sibling is to teach him during his first few years to respect your rights.

HELPING A PHASE VI TODDLER WHO HAS A SLIGHTLY OLDER SIBLING

A fourteen-month-old baby with a sibling less than three years of age can find the combination of stresses he has to cope with too much to handle at times: he has to deal simultaneously with the onset of self-awareness and negativism, plus repeated acts of aggression by his older brother or sister, plus his limited control of his emotions. Remember, too, that the older child is also still mentally and emotionally quite immature. Given such circumstances, you as the parent may find yourself in one of the more painful kinds of child-rearing situations.

If you do, it is very important that you continue to be firm but loving with the older child. Reassure him that you still love him, not just by telling him so, but by spending a small amount of time, perhaps an hour, alone with him daily. You should also encourage his out-of-the-home interests, so that if he has an unhappy experience at home from time to time it will not be so crushing.

HELPING A PHASE VI CHILD WHO HAS A YOUNGER SIBLING

Given the normal emotional turmoil of Phase VI, it is easy to see how difficult it is for an eighteen- to twenty-four-month-old child to make room in her life for a younger sibling. This accommodation is particularly difficult if the older baby is a first child. While sibling rivalry is very stressful for the baby and the parents, it is perhaps even more painful for the closely spaced older child. Her whole world has changed, and it hasn't gotten better. She needs understanding. You mustn't forget, however, that she must also be controlled. Many a normal first child has seriously injured a younger sibling.

HELPING A PHASE VI BABY WITH AN OLDER AND A YOUNGER CLOSELY SPACED SIBLING

To understand social development fully, consideration of each of these constellations is necessary. One saving factor for the child in the middle is that she has never known the exclusive attention of parents, as a firstborn child has. The displacement caused by the new baby therefore will not be anywhere near as great for her as it is for a first child. On the other hand, as a closely spaced second child, she will have developed a more aggressive style than an only child, and this will not bode well for her younger sibling. She will need the same sort of control and consideration as the oldest child, and she will especially need regular reassurance that she is still dearly loved.

FOSTERING COMPETENCE DURING PHASE VI

Social Abilities

GETTING AND HOLDING THE ATTENTION OF ADULTS IN SOCIALLY ACCEPTABLE WAYS

Gaining the attention of another person is the earliest social skill of babies. Because of their ability to cry, babies learn to capture the attention of adults very early in life. The Phase VI child is still very much involved in getting attention in pursuit of her fundamental social needs, which are especially powerful during the second year. Having lived for fourteen or more months, however, she now has a fairly wide variety of methods, beyond simply crying, for gaining attention. We believe some parents do a disservice to their children by hovering over them too much at this stage. If a parent routinely anticipates a baby's needs, the child is less likely to learn very much about different ways of getting someone else's attention. Second and third children are probably better off in this respect because parents don't usually spend as much time anticipating their needs.

USING ADULTS AS RESOURCES AFTER DETERMINING THAT A TASK IS TOO DIFFICULT

During Phase VI the handling of a child's appeals for help becomes somewhat delicate. This natural tendency to seek help, on the whole very healthy, is intertwined with the child's intense desire for the attention of the adult. The Phase VI child of course should understand that you'll be there to help him when he needs you, but be watchful for the child's tendency to ask for help not because he cannot do something on his own, but simply because he wants to monopolize your time. Especially with the first child, this latter tendency is often strong and can lead to overattachment by the second birthday.

EXPRESSING AFFECTION AND MILD ANNOYANCE TO ADULTS

The capacity to express both affection and annoyance reflects a feeling of comfort and confidence in interpersonal relations. This strong sense of security and trust is extremely relevant to the day-to-day life of the Phase VI child, whose tendency to express modest annoyance will increase as she flowers as an individual and becomes self-assertive. With a child of this age, you need to maintain a balance between overindulging her tendency toward testiness and suppressing that tendency. If not done carefully, suppression can stifle her capacity to relate naturally to people. A parent's own deeply rooted feelings about the expression of positive and negative emotions will probably influence a young child's capacities in this area. I suggest you try to help the child acquire as much spontaneity of emotional expressions as your own behavior patterns will allow.

LEADING AND FOLLOWING

Since social behavior with peers is not much seen before the second birthday, the behaviors of giving and accepting peer leadership do not become visible until the third year. Presumably, however, the behavior of a parent or sibling is an influence on the later behavior of the child in the dynamics of peer leadership. Your child should be given the chance to direct some of your shared activities, but of course there will continue to be many occasions during this early period when he will be asked to do what you say.

EXPRESSING AFFECTION AND MILD ANNOYANCE TO PEERS

The easy expression of feelings with peers parallels a similar ability with adults and older siblings. Expression of feelings with peers begins to undergo rapid development during the third year of life, as true social interest in peers emerges and grows.

COMPETING WITH PEERS

Some parents would rather not encourage competitiveness in their children. It is nevertheless found regularly in the behavior of the well-developed three-to six-year-old children we have studied. Since the value of competitiveness is viewed differently by different families, I would not try to persuade anyone to encourage this behavior in his child. Whether or not you foster its development, however, competitiveness will probably appear sometime during the third year of life, most likely in connection with rivalry with an older sibling.

SHOWING PRIDE IN PERSONAL ACCOMPLISHMENT

Pride in accomplishment continues to develop substantially during the second year as the child begins to master skills that she can crow about. Most Phase VI achievements are manifested in new skills rather than in the creation of products such as drawings or block towers. The child very often shows great pleasure in her first success at walking, and she is delighted with praise. Likewise, when she manages to move a four-wheeled toy about with some success she may look at you with a light in her eyes that suggests she is quite proud of what she has done. I strongly urge you to support these feelings of pride in achievement. The first puzzles provide other opportunities for toddlers to feel pride in achievement and to bask in the warmth of your praise.

ENGAGING IN ROLE PLAYING AND MAKE-BELIEVE ACTIVITIES

You should encourage your child's natural tendency to fantasize and to pretend, particularly as he looks forward to being grown up. Especially toward the end of Phase VI, this behavior will begin to flourish. Expect your child to begin to organize "mealtime" or "medical examination" sessions with his stuffed animals and you. He will be quite earnest as he goes about these activities.

Nonsocial Abilities

LANGUAGE DEVELOPMENT

At the core of effective language teaching is the continuation of the responsive style I described for the Phase V baby. That response style, emphasizing the identification of the baby's interest at the moment, is, in my judgment, the single most important means by which parents can assist language development during a child's first years. Providing books, encouraging their use, and holding regular storytelling sessions also make sense, but I must again point out that there has never been any research to demonstrate the effectiveness of these practices.

The first picture books to become interesting to children, at about nine months of age, are useful primarily in facilitating practice of hand-eye skills. Nevertheless, at times, your baby will sit still for a labeling session. As she moves through Phase VI, her interest in books will grow steadily. She will acquire favorites. She will choose one and back up into your lap to be read to. She will occasionally pick one up, sit down by herself, and concentrate on what's on the page.

Books become quite important during Phase VI partly because they become useful in assuring the child of your close presence. Enjoy it while you can. This absorption with you is a primary feature of Phase VI. After his second birthday, your child won't seek you out anywhere near as often. And when he is fourteen years old you will miss Phase VI, when there was nothing he'd rather do than climb into your lap.

With the accelerating rate of language growth in the second year of life, toddlers will begin to pay more attention to simple stories and appropriate videos. In the Recommended Readings section, you will find help in identifying books that are suitable for your child's developmental level.

THE ABILITY TO NOTICE SMALL DETAILS AND DISCREPANCIES

We have found that well-developed three- and four-year-olds are very accurate observers. They notice small differences and anomalies faster than most children. This talent is apparent when somebody makes an error in a drawing or sets the wrong objects on the table; it is also present in respect to temporal sequences and, interestingly, in areas of logic. Talented three- to six-year-old children quickly notice when somebody, while telling a story or explaining something, makes an error in logic. They are also able to keep track of the sequence of events in a story or a playtime activity, and they quickly notice when someone goes out of turn in a game. Keep this ability in mind in your interchanges with Phase VI children, and try to point out to them interesting peculiarities as well as similarities and differences in small details.

THE ABILITY TO ANTICIPATE CONSEQUENCES

The baby as young as nine or ten months may begin to complain when he notices his parents heading toward the front door with their coats on. Such behavior is a typical manifestation of the ability to anticipate consequences, a skill that in later life is reflected in such areas as effective automobile driving. The earliest signs of such behavior occur in connection with nursing, when the three- or four-month-old child begins to suck in anticipation of being fed. Stable differences among children in this ability are quite visible by three years of age. This ability can be encouraged in the ordinary course of a day's activities. Again, doing so is easier when the child brings a topic to your attention than when his attention is directed elsewhere.

THE ABILITY TO DEAL WITH ABSTRACTIONS

Probably the two most common kinds of abstraction that children learn to deal with in Phase VI are words and numbers. This does not mean that they can count, nor does it mean that they can write words or even use them particularly well. But Phase VI children are learning that certain words apply to classes of objects rather than merely to individual items. To an eight-month-old the word "bottle" may mean only his bottle, but "bottle" to the two-year-old usually means any number of objects that have bottle characteristics. In that sense the two-year-old has learned an abstraction. Toward the end of Phase VI, when children learn that "two cookies" means one cookie and one more cookie, they have learned an abstraction that they can apply to other things as well.

Always remember that a Phase VI child is a concrete thinker. He can communicate in a limited way about objects that he can see, feel, and touch, but he is not yet particularly adept at thinking or talking about other objects. Stay with the here and now. If you want to talk about a particular object or event that is not on the immediate scene, try to relate it to something in the current situation.

THE ABILITY TO PUT ONESELF IN THE PLACE OF ANOTHER PERSON

Understanding viewpoints other than the child's own is a particularly interesting dimension of competence and one that I don't know how to encourage in a young child. Piaget points out that the capacity to put oneself in someone else's place and see things from his viewpoint is generally not seen much before the seventh or eighth year of a child's life. In our research we found that children who are developing well during the preschool years exhibit the ability to put themselves in the place of another person well before seven or eight years of age. Indeed, we have seen primitive forms of this behavior as early as age three.

THE ABILITY TO MAKE INTERESTING ASSOCIATIONS

Talented three- to six-year-olds frequently make clever associations. If your natural style with your child features interrelated ideas, and if you occasionally develop these ideas in storytelling, you'll be providing a model for your child in this desirable area.

THE ABILITY TO PLAN AND CARRY OUT COMPLICATED ACTIVITIES

In nursery school only a few out of a group of fifteen to twenty children can bring several others together and organize proceedings. This function can be taught by example. You can also assist the Phase VI child in taking on and executing tasks that are a little more complex than the one- or two-step tasks common to the first year of life.

THE ABILITY TO USE RESOURCES EFFECTIVELY

Closely tied to managerial ability, effective use of resources can be taught in a natural style if you show imagination in the way you use objects. For example, if, in order to reach something on a high shelf, you stand on a chair one time and a stepladder another, or if you use several different utensils to stir food, you may teach your child a bit about the multiple uses of materials. If, without overdoing it, you show your ability to use resources effectively, and if you occasionally point out how you are doing it, your example will probably benefit your child.

DUAL FOCUSING

The child's growing capacity to maintain concentration on a task and simultaneously monitor or be aware of what is going on around her in a busy place is fascinating to observe. If you visit a nursery school or a day care center where children are doing puzzles or drawing pictures, you will note that some children will be better than others at resisting distractions. You will see this select group frequently looking around, as if to keep track of what is happening. This ability is something that we really don't know how to teach. Theoretically you could encourage a child to engage in more than one task at a time, but if you attempt to do this too soon, you'll only interfere with her developing capacity to concentrate.

RECOMMENDED MATERIALS FOR PHASE VI

The table on pages 207–8 is a summary of selected recommended materials for the Phase VI child. It has been compiled on the basis of the child's special interest in exploring appropriate objects and practicing motor skills, especially climbing.

No commercial toys are really necessary to the child's educational development. Phase VI children are too involved in interacting with their parents, in practicing skills that help them master their own bodies, and in exploring the living area and all its elements to spend much time with toys. Nevertheless there are a fair number of commercial toys for this age that children enjoy, and grandparents need an adequate supply of options for gift-giving.

The Surprising Usefulness of Puzzles

A puzzle that is slightly challenging but doable can be a great toy for a Phase VI child. Not only is it developmentally suitable, but it can help reinforce your child's growing sense of pride in achievement. It can also be an inexpensive way to get a little extra sleep in the morning and some peace when you are off on a trip.

The first puzzle a toddler can succeed at consists of a board with a circular opening into which one can insert a wooden circle with a knob on it. I call this a level one puzzle. With this version, unlike most one-piece puzzles, the child doesn't have to turn the circle at all, it will fall into the opening no matter how he orients it.

How you introduce the puzzle is important. You don't want to create frustration and a bad experience that may sour your child on puzzles. Place the circle so that it is 99.99 percent in the opening. Demonstrate several times how to move it so that it will drop into place. Don't be surprised if in his clumsiness, your child moves the piece in the wrong direction. If, after a few tries, he still doesn't succeed, put the puzzle away and bring it out another day. By fourteen and a half months, the majority of toddlers can master this challenge. The moment your baby succeeds for the first time, make a big fuss. Tell him how talented he is, and set the puzzle up again. Watch his efforts closely. As soon as he succeeds again, shower him with praise. Repeat frequently. He will, in time, become intrinsically motivated to succeed, but because this is Phase VI, your praise will grease the skids. The more people who praise him, the better.

Do not move quickly to the next level of difficulty. Wait a few days until he is totally reliable with the circle, then bring out a level two puzzle. These are available from many sources. Your best bet is to buy a puzzle with the circle and a few other geometric shapes, but in the introductory stage, take away all of the pieces except the circle. Choose one new piece that seems easy. An octagon or a square will do. Show your child how to move the second piece using the same technique. Lavish praise on his successes.

By eighteen or nineteen months of age, he will probably be ready for level three. The level three puzzle still has knobs on each piece but there are at least two pieces that fit into one opening.

By twenty-two months or so, he will be ready for level four, a puzzle without knobs. Such puzzles can be obtained at every conceivable level of difficulty. Some thirty-month-olds can do them faster than their parents.

Puzzles challenge a toddler's hand-eye skill. Once the piece falls in place, he feels the success, so the gratification is immediate and unambiguous. Any praise from his key people for his success is an important bonus that reinforces his pride in achievement.

Puzzles are inexpensive. Many knobbed ones cost less than ten dollars. Those without knobs are usually less than five dollars. They are portable and you can take them on trips. After your twenty-month-old has fallen asleep, you can place in his crib one or two new puzzles that he will be able to do, but not easily. When he awakens, he will find them, and you may get another half hour of sleep. How's that for five dollars?

CHILD-REARING PRACTICES NOT RECOMMENDED

Rewarding Tantrums

During Phase VI it is quite likely that your child will throw tantrums. This will be increasingly likely to happen as negativism becomes established. You can't prevent tantrums at this stage of development, but it is very important not to reward them. Head them off whenever you can, and if you cannot, then do not—I repeat: do not—reward them. Paying a lot of attention to the fits of the normal Phase VI toddler is natural but remarkably unwise. Your baby must not be taught that he will get rewarded in any way for throwing a tantrum, and during Phases V and VI, your attention, even when you are scolding or consoling your baby, is remarkably rewarding. It therefore reinforces and perpetuates the behavior.

LARGE TOYS

Small wagons and other stable four-wheeled toys on which the child can sit and move himself about

Four-wheel walkers with high handles, like a supermarket shopping cart, that a toddler can use for support as he pushes the toy around (Little Tikes makes a very good one)

Doll carriages

Safe swing sets

Small slides and climbing apparatus

Play kitchen (Little Tikes and Fisher-Price both make good ones—be sure to equip the kitchen with "food, groceries, and other necessities")

Scenario toys such as garages and farms (several companies make very good ones)

Low, small table and chairs suitable for serving to stuffed animals, dolls, and parents

Playhouse (available for less than $20 or more than $300)

Outdoor items such as a sandbox (with cover) and a small (five-foot diameter) wading pool

SMALL TOYS

Books with story themes that range from the simplest (*Goodnight, Moon* and *Where's Spot?*) to more complex (*The Little Engine that Could*)

Electronic books featuring buttons which, when pushed, produce impressive sound effects that relate to the story

Balls of all sizes and shapes

Dolls and toys that feature small human and animal figures along with trucks and cars

Props for make-believe play: a purse with keys and a mirror, a toy telephone, a tea set

Level one, two, and three puzzles

Materials for scribbling: a large pad of paper and nontoxic, washable crayons

Bath toys

LARGE MATERIALS

Big empty boxes

Large unbreakable mirrors

Stairs

Adult furniture

SMALLER MATERIALS

Pots and pans
Plastic containers (Tupperware is especially good)
The safe contents of kitchen cabinets and drawers
Water (especially recommended)

Loving parents have a natural tendency to console their miserably un-happy toddler, but their consolation increases the likelihood that she will have another tantrum the next time she doesn't get her way. Console her when she is suffering from physical pain, of course, but not when she is screaming at you in anger. At that point, your comfort will not make her understand your position. It will simply prolong the screaming.

When children first engage in tantrums, they are usually seeking a limit, asking you to stop them. I strongly urge you to ignore them, unless your toddler behaves in a way that could hurt other people. In that case, she simply has to be restrained and even punished if necessary. Tantrums can become common during the second year of life. If you handle the situation well, there won't be many and they will disappear almost completely by the time your child leaves Phase VI.

Yielding in a Contest of Wills

Sometime between fourteen and sixteen months of age, your baby will very likely start challenging your authority. She will use three methods: she will test you; she will attempt to do things you do not want her to do; and she will resist you when she doesn't want to do what you want her to do. You can count on this behavior.

In rare cases, this contest of the wills does not begin until several months later than sixteen months, but mark my words: it will begin. Once it starts, you can expect a minimum of six months of struggling with your formerly agreeable angel. Do not try to totally suppress this defiance; do not try to win all of the disputes. Small victories seem to have a special importance to a child in Phase VI, a significance that will not likely occur again until the adolescent years. Under no circumstances, however, should your toddler get the idea that he has more authority than you. Don't ever let him adopt such an attitude.

This kind of stern behavior is difficult for people who have especially gentle personalities. If you are that kind of a person, you are bound to have more difficulty in socializing your Phase VI child, especially if she is unusually feisty. Dealing with defiance will not be easy for you, but at the very least try to work out a plan with your partner, if you have one. Regardless of your temperament, your baby simply has to learn to respect your rules. The firmer you are, the happier your child will turn out to be.

Premature Toilet Training

It does not make any sense to try to force toilet training—or weaning from a pacifier or any other habit that can wait a while—during this time in a child's development. Once the child gets to be about two years of age, he will train himself in a relatively short time. Trying to toilet-train a child much before two years of age is generally very difficult. If you attempt the training between fourteen and twenty-four months of age, you will run headlong into negativism. That period is the worst possible time to try.

The natural tendency of the Phase VI child to imitate other members of the family usually leads to earlier toilet training with second and subsequent siblings as compared with the first child. If parents have a reasonably casual attitude toward toilet habits, children, in the absence of undue pressure from parents, will usually begin to initiate toilet training themselves during Stage VII. It helps to have a small potty available in the bathroom, and to let your child watch as you use the bathroom.

Overfeeding

My comments about between-meal snacks in Phase V continue to apply to Phase VI. In Phase V parents may overfeed their child to show that they care or because they don't know how to keep the child happily engaged, but in Phase VI the normal negativistic behavior of the child may be the root cause of overfeeding. The Phase VI child can become a chronic source of stress, and you are likely to consider almost anything that will give you some peace. By following the suggestions in this book, you should be in less trouble on this score. If for any reason, however, you find yourself feeding snacks or drinks several times a day to the Phase VI child, pause and review the situation. Something has gone wrong. It is also worth noting that a number of medical research studies indicate that the origins of long-term obesity seem to be in the first years of life.

MATERIALS NOT RECOMMENDED FOR PHASE VI

WIND-UP TOYS

Wind-up jack-in-the-box toys require that a child turn a small knob 380 degrees several times while pushing a doll under a cover. This task is simply too great for most Phase VI children. If you are willing to do all the winding with such toys, and if you and the child enjoy the activity, go right ahead.

XYLOPHONES WITH HAMMERS, BEADS ON WIRES, AND PULL TOYS

Phase VI babies hardly ever play with these toys.

POTENTIALLY DANGEROUS ITEMS

You must be on guard against items that are small enough to be swallowed, sharp enough to cut, or small and heavy enough to be used as dangerous missiles. Swallowable items include marbles, checkers, and anything else under an inch and a half in any dimension.

Choking on food is also very common within this range. The types of food most commonly involved are round, fairly hard chunks of food, such as a piece of hot dog.

You should also be especially careful of food items and toy parts that could cause suffocation.

Examples of items potentially sharp enough to cut would be Match Box or Hot Wheels cars, because once the wheels are pulled off, which is not too difficult to do, the pointed axle that is left exposed is capable of inflicting significant damage to a young child.

Potentially dangerous missiles include toy soldiers and golf balls. Both are small enough to be thrown by children of this age yet heavy enough to inflict damage on people and things.

BEHAVIORS THAT SIGNAL THE ONSET OF PHASE VII

Phase VII, the third year of life, is the final stage to be covered in this book. Several fascinating new developments appear during this stage in a child's development.

The Emergence of Rationality

If all has gone well, you will find a decline in negativism sometime around the second birthday, perhaps as early as twenty-two months. Not only will your child become less contentious, but you can expect an increase in sociability and a delightful improvement in the quality of experiences with her. Congratulations!

The Emergence of True Social Interest in Peers

From the second birthday on, interest in play with other children will gradually increase, and the exclusive, intense concentration on the nuclear family and the home will decline.

An Increase in Mental Power and Emotional Control

With the emergence of Phase VII, you will notice a dramatic increase in your child's sheer mental powers and in his ability to control his emotions. You will find that you are living with a much more mature human being than you were six months ago. Instead of a baby, you will have a small child. This rather impressive maturity is not, of course, going to appear suddenly, but you will be struck by the rate at which your child substitutes reasoning and impulse control for subrationally motivated actions.

An Increase in Conversation

Closely associated with the preceding phenomena is a general increase in talking and especially in the use of conversational language. Phase VII children can usually deal with sentences and with streams of thought to an extent that makes it possible for them to carry on simple, pleasant conversations. This is one of the most rewarding experiences that parents will undergo in the first years.

8

Phase VII: Twenty-four to Thirty-six Months

General Remarks

The two-year-old has a fairly stabilized personality. She has constructed with great effort and persistence, over long periods of time and through many interchanges, an elaborate social contract with her primary caretaker. She has become truly familiar with and involved with the object world. She has achieved substantial control over her own body. She is still in a state that can perhaps be characterized as babyhood, but to call her a baby by her third birthday would be misleading. You now live with a young child.

Some two-year-olds are not terribly pleasant to live with. There is no question that spoiling can be a well-entrenched reality by a child's second birthday. Furthermore, a two-year-old who has learned that his needs are more important than anyone else's and who is also given to tantrums and related unpleasant behavior is likely to persist in this type of behavior for some time to come.

Another less than ideal outcome in the area of personality by the time a child is two years of age is excessive fearfulness. In our research we have seen many a child who by two has simply had too much experience with hostility and fear in the period between eight months and two years. Most commonly, such experiences have come at the hands of closely spaced older siblings. Less commonly, but even more painful to watch, is fear that has been generated by a child's own parents. It is easy to ignore the fact that many children go through their first two years in conditions very much less desirable than we would like. Setting aside for the moment children of underdeveloped nations being reared in extraordinary poverty, unfortunately many children are born into families that have too many other children, or to parents with severe emotional problems. In such unhappy circumstances, children by two years of age often have learned that the world can be a hostile place and that they must approach their parents cautiously and selectively. Happily, in most situations such is not the case.

In the best of circumstances, a two-year-old can be an absolute delight, full of humor, originality, and self-confidence, and a remarkable source of pleasure for parents.

Another important shift that takes place at around the second birthday is the movement away from subrational behavior to reasonableness. The civil behavior that is often seen toward the end of the second year as the child becomes more sophisticated, more aware, and more practiced with people is, in actuality, only a thin veneer. Lurking just beneath the surface is a person who rather easily loses control of her own emotions and may under such circumstances show all kinds of unpleasant behavior. Under good circumstances babies tend to leave such behavior behind as they move into the third year of life. This is most obvious, of course, in the much greater capacity to communicate verbally that most children show during their third year, but it is more general than just language facility. The thinking ability of the child in Phase VII reinforces the notion of growing maturity and early childhood rather than babyhood.

In your child's third year you will also see a substantial and steady growth in her interest in other children and an increase in true social interactions between her and them. We usually see a rise in activities outside of the home, along with a lessening of the intense, exclusive focus on the nuclear family and the parents. We also find a substantial increase in the child's mental powers, which are growing at a really remarkable rate; he seems more aware of things, particularly in the social realm. Whereas the one-and-a-half-year-old can be overwhelmed rather easily by feelings of anger or hurt, the three-year-old is far more in control of his emotions.

Along with these dramatic developments comes the flowering of speech and the resultant inclination toward conversation. In addition, the newly developed ability to use the body with skill for climbing, running, and jumping adds to the feeling that we are now dealing with a relatively complete junior human being. Babyhood is over. The distance already traveled by a three-year-old in terms of human development is staggering.

GENERAL BEHAVIOR DURING PHASE VII

The Decline of Nonsocial Experience

Starting with a child's first birthday, experiences oriented toward people begin to increase at the expense of those not oriented toward people. Near the first birthday about 10 percent of all activity is people-oriented. For some six minutes out of the average hour the baby will try to create an effect on other people—to get their attention or to get them to perform an act. By about two years, the balance is about 20 percent social experience to about 80 percent nonsocial. By the time the child reaches three years of age the figure is closer to 30 percent for social experiences, and nonsocial experiences have dropped correspondingly.

The major nonsocial experiences of the Phase VII child are similar to those she engaged in during Phase VI. Exploring object qualities and practicing simple skills on objects remain a prominent part of the child's waking life, but their relative importance is lessening. Our research indicates that children eighteen to twenty-one months of age engage in those two major small-object activities about 18 percent of their waking time. By two and a half, however, such activities have decreased to about 14 percent. As the years go by, the child will move beyond these simple interactions with small objects to more complicated social interactions with other children. Active play with small objects, however, still occupies a substantial amount of time in Phase VII.

The third year of life is also marked by a sharp decrease in staring. As we have seen, at one year of age we routinely find such behavior accounting for slightly under 17 percent of all waking time; at two years staring has dropped to about 14 percent of waking time, and at three years it has dropped to 6 or 7 percent. As steady staring decreases, a related activity increases: staring while listening to language. This behavior occupies a little over

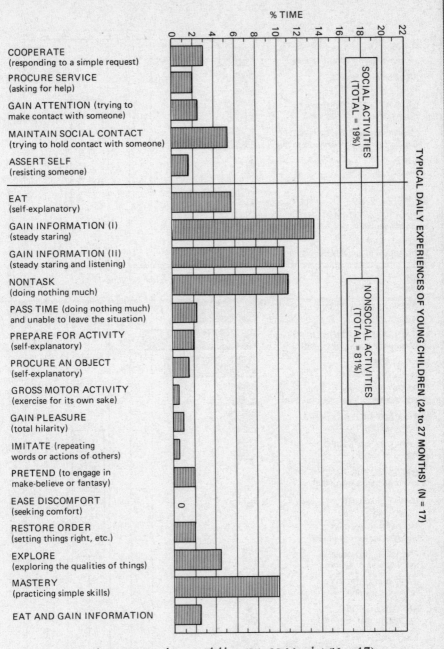

% TIME

COOPERATE
(responding to a simple request)

PROCURE SERVICE
(asking for help)

GAIN ATTENTION (trying to
make contact with someone)

MAINTAIN SOCIAL CONTACT
(trying to hold contact with someone)

ASSERT SELF
(resisting someone)

EAT
(self-explanatory)

GAIN INFORMATION (I)
(steady staring)

GAIN INFORMATION (II)
(steady staring and listening)

NONTASK
(doing nothing much)

PASS TIME (doing nothing much)
and unable to leave the situation)

PREPARE FOR ACTIVITY
(self-explanatory)

PROCURE AN OBJECT
(self-explanatory)

GROSS MOTOR ACTIVITY
(exercise for its own sake)

GAIN PLEASURE
(total hilarity)

IMITATE (repeating
words or actions of others)

PRETEND (to engage in
make-believe or fantasy)

EASE DISCOMFORT
(seeking comfort)

RESTORE ORDER
(setting things right, etc.)

EXPLORE
(exploring the qualities of things)

MASTERY
(practicing simple skills)

EAT AND GAIN INFORMATION

SOCIAL ACTIVITIES
(TOTAL = 19%)

NONSOCIAL ACTIVITIES
(TOTAL = 81%)

TYPICAL DAILY EXPERIENCES OF YOUNG CHILDREN (24 to 27 MONTHS) (N = 17)

Typical Experiences of Young Children (24–27 Months) (N = 17)

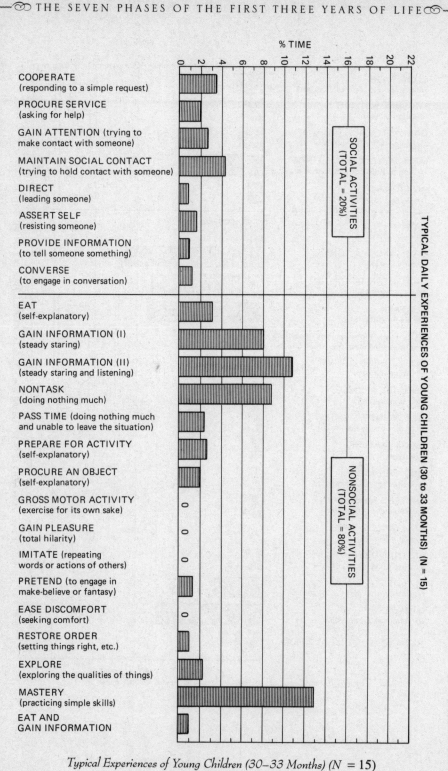

% TIME

COOPERATE
(responding to a simple request)

PROCURE SERVICE
(asking for help)

GAIN ATTENTION (trying to
make contact with someone)

MAINTAIN SOCIAL CONTACT
(trying to hold contact with someone)

DIRECT
(leading someone)

ASSERT SELF
(resisting someone)

PROVIDE INFORMATION
(to tell someone something)

CONVERSE
(to engage in conversation)

EAT
(self-explanatory)

GAIN INFORMATION (I)
(steady staring)

GAIN INFORMATION (II)
(steady staring and listening)

NONTASK
(doing nothing much)

PASS TIME (doing nothing much
and unable to leave the situation)

PREPARE FOR ACTIVITY
(self-explanatory)

PROCURE AN OBJECT
(self-explanatory)

GROSS MOTOR ACTIVITY
(exercise for its own sake)

GAIN PLEASURE
(total hilarity)

IMITATE (repeating
words or actions of others)

PRETEND (to engage in
make-believe or fantasy)

EASE DISCOMFORT
(seeking comfort)

RESTORE ORDER
(setting things right, etc.)

EXPLORE
(exploring the qualities of things)

MASTERY
(practicing simple skills)

EAT AND
GAIN INFORMATION

SOCIAL ACTIVITIES
(TOTAL = 20%)

NONSOCIAL ACTIVITIES
(TOTAL = 80%)

TYPICAL DAILY EXPERIENCES OF YOUNG CHILDREN (30 to 33 MONTHS) (N = 15)

Typical Experiences of Young Children (30–33 Months) (N = 15)

6 percent of the child's waking time at one year of age, and about 11 percent of his time at two and one half years. Since Phase VII is a time of tremendous growth in language ability, it is no surprise that children in this age group are very much interested in attending to language of one sort or another.

Language can come from a human being speaking in the child's presence (live) or from a television set, radio, or record player. A child can listen to live language as his mother talks with an older brother or sister or as she speaks to the child himself. We believe the latter is the most important with respect to learning.

Empty time, or nontask experience, generally declines during the third year of life, dropping from 10 to 12 percent of waking time during the second year to 7 or 8 percent during the third year. Its companion category, passing time, is also on the decline during this period. I think this trend reflects the fact that children are less prone to accidents after infancy and therefore are no longer often kept in confined areas or under close watch by their parents. Eating accounts for another 5 percent of a child's waking time during Phase VII.

You can see that relatively few types of nonsocial experiences account for the bulk of the child's activities during a typical day. In fact, the seven types of experience discussed above account for about 53 percent of the child's waking hours at three years of age. At two and a half years of age, the same seven account for about 47 percent of that time. This difference is significant in that with each passing month experience becomes more complex; children engage in more and more types of experience.

Social Experience

We find that the two-year-old, just beginning Phase VII, engages in very few kinds of social experience for any appreciable length of time and devotes considerably less time to these activities than to nonsocial experience. The most common social experience you find in Phase VII is the child attempting to hold on to another person's attention—that is, to maintain social contact. As might be expected, the child's mother is the person most often involved, about 90 percent of the time. At about two years of age maintaining social contact accounts for about 6 percent of all waking time. The two-and-a-half-year-old is considerably less clingy, with this type of experience accounting for only 4 percent of her time.

The second most common social experience, which occupies about 3 percent of waking time, is complying with simple requests that parents make. Attempting to get somebody's attention is the third common social experience, accounting for 2.5 to 3 percent of the child's time. Bear in mind that the child's skill at getting and maintaining attention has increased considerably and therefore takes less time now than it did in previous years.

Two additional important categories of social experience are attempting to get some help from an adult (about 2 percent of waking time) and resisting suggestions by an adult or another child (between 1 and 1.5 percent of the time). All five of these social experiences combined take less time daily than active exploration and the practicing of skills on small objects.

You will notice that the picture drawn of the life of a three-year-old does not suggest a child sitting from morning until night by his mother's side. Older literature on early child development was so concentrated on the importance of the mother-child relationship that people tended to assume that all a child did all day long was relate to his mother. The fact is that, for the vast majority of the child's waking hours throughout the first three years of life, he will be exploring the nonsocial world and practicing motor skills. From the perspective of a full-time parent, babies spend much more time in close contact with them, but there is a substantial difference between psychological time and objective time.

THE APPARENT INTERESTS OF PHASE VII

Continuing Interests

The three major interests of Phase V and VI children—the primary caretaker, exploring the world, and practicing new motor skills—continue to account for most behavior during the third year of life, but with some important changes. For example, in the area of social development, a decrease occurs in the child's almost total concentration of social interest on his parents, and especially on their reactions to his acts. During Phase VII a new and important element—true socializing with peers—emerges and grows steadily.

With respect to exploration of the world at large, you'll find that children in their third year have major interests on which you can capitalize. Especially noteworthy is the increasing interest in language, especially if the language is directed toward them. Concerning the practicing of new motor skills and the mastery of the body, the child is now adept at most of the fundamental motor skills that emerge during infancy. All children over two years of age can generally walk, run, jump, and climb with ease, and they immensely enjoy the last three activities, although they are not yet as skillful at climbing as they will be later on. Children can acquire new specialized skills during the third year of life, such as riding a small tricycle, and they continue to enjoy swing sets in the third year of life every bit as much as they did in the second. Many other fine motor challenges, like learning to use a nutcracker or a hole punch, will intrigue a Phase VII child. There are, however, no dramatic changes at this point.

Emerging Interests

CONSTRUCTING PRODUCTS

Toward the end of the third year children begin to combine the skills and information they have been gathering so busily for two years; using them together in what we call consummatory activity. During Phase VII you'll see the first representational drawings by children, especially if they are encouraged or if they have older siblings to imitate. You'll also find the first constructions. While playing with blocks, the child may now create forts or towers—again, especially if she's encouraged to do so or if she has a model to imitate. The creation of family, farm, or town scenes, facilitated by some of the first-rate commercial toys now available, is another sign of the newfound ability to coordinate and organize activities. These newly emerging interests will grow quite steadily in the months to come.

PRETEND ACTIVITIES

Another emerging activity of particular interest and importance is a newfound capacity to enter into more and more elaborate imaginative play, either alone or with others. A good deal of such behavior is a distinguishing characteristic of well-developed children.

TELEVISION

Yet another emerging interest of the third year is television viewing. This interest began with reflexive responses to commercials, particularly those with frequent abrupt changes in sound levels, when the child was about four months of age. Sustained television viewing doesn't begin until the end of the second or the beginning of the third year, because television viewing depends upon mental and linguistic developments that do not sufficiently surface until then. Don't expect your two-and-a-half-year-old to watch somebody give a televised lecture on how to sew an apron, but he will watch the changing sounds and moving forms on cartoon shows. He is also likely to show a good deal of interest in programs like *Sesame Street,* which are specifically designed to capture and recapture the attention of a very young child. In addition, his interest in videotapes will continue to grow, if you allow it to.

LEARNING DEVELOPMENTS DURING PHASE VII

The four educational goals listed earlier—language, curiosity, social development and intelligence—continue as objectives throughout the child's third year of life. Maintaining the balance among the three principal interests of Phases V and VI also continue to be of fundamental importance during Phase VII. Again, your desired goal is not only to encourage those interests but to keep them in balance.

Language Development

If all has gone well, your two-year-old should understand well over four hundred words, including the majority of those that you address to her in ordinary conversation. She should be speaking regularly, although she may not be saying very much yet. Some two-year-olds use short sentences and carry on simple conversations. Others are still only using simple words or sentence fragments. Many will amaze you with their regular use of seven- and eight-word sentences. Again, you need not worry too much about a two-year-old's speech, as long as her understanding of language is moving along well.

Development of Curiosity

I hope you have a two-year-old who can play alone well and who is genuinely interested in everything new. You should see the same intense curiosity that your child showed during her days of sustained hand regard when she was three months old.

Social Development

The third area, social development, is considerably more complicated. I hope your two-year-old has acquired all the basic social skills she needs to interact effectively with adults. She should be a joy to live with most if not all of the time. She should have left negativism and challenges to your authority behind her. She should like and be proud of herself. She should know that she is capable, and she should feel that she is valued by others. She should be able to get along well with almost everyone except a closely spaced sibling.

These social goals apply to the family with one child as well as to the family with several children spaced more than three years apart. But the picture changes in important ways if there are closely spaced children.

Sibling Rivalry—Again

THE PHASE VII CHILD WITH A CLOSELY SPACED YOUNGER SIBLING

I have cautioned you to expect dramatic changes in the behavior of a slightly older child when a younger sibling becomes a crawler. I described what we found in our extensive observations of families—that is, that older children found it most difficult sharing the attention of their parents with a newly crawling child.

The older Phase VI child was in a particularly difficult situation, because of the intensity of her social needs as she moved through the second half of the second year of life, and because of her intellectual and emotional immaturity during that time. Such a child moving into Phase VII is very likely to continue to put a good deal of stress on parents. Unfortunately, the hard feelings between older child and younger child don't go away during this phase of life. Two principal changes, however, warrant special attention. The first is that the younger child is no longer a pushover. The only defense an eight- or nine-month-old has against a twenty-month-old who is behaving aggressively is to cry. Physically and mentally the baby is no match for the Phase VII child. The cry, however, usually does the job: an older person will often hear the cry and protect the baby.

The Phase VII child may very well have gone through many months of intermittent discomfort as a result of the existence of the baby in the home. Once the baby reaches fifteen or sixteen months of age, however, she becomes a different kind of problem for the Phase VII child. The younger child is entering into a genuine awareness of herself as a person, and into negativism and self-assertiveness, and she may begin to behave toward the older child in a manner similar to the older child's behavior toward her in the preceding year. In addition, younger children in such circumstances will sometimes acquire two weapons that can become potent indeed: biting and hair pulling. The Phase VII child has by now had a fair amount of experience with pain, and the result of the baby's new aggressiveness sometimes is domination of the older child by the toddler. At the very least the children are more evenly matched at this stage.

Furthermore, a new problem surfaces for a full-time caretaker. In earlier months the parent could safely assume that any sounds of unhappiness from the children were caused by the older child, but that assumption is no longer always appropriate. The younger sibling may increasingly become the initiator of conflicts between the two. This particular situation is quite normal, but it is the single most common source of stress for full-time parents. The harsh feelings between closely spaced siblings often manifest themselves day in and day out.

Imagine the difficult situations that have erupted over the years as parent after parent has gone through this experience completely unprepared, each wondering what on earth was going on and why parenting was not what it was cracked up to be. I doubt that very many people, regardless of their talent, can handle the chronic stress that comes from closely spaced siblings when one is in Phase VI and the other in Phase VII, and for this reason I advocate part-time substitute care at this stage.

THE PHASE VII CHILD WITH A CLOSELY SPACED OLDER SIBLING

A second situation that warrants discussion at this point arises when the Phase VII child is the younger of two closely spaced siblings. In Chapter 7 I explained that Phase VI children often become aggressive with their slightly older siblings. That pattern usually continues as the child moves through Phase VII. In this situation, however, the circumstances are a bit better for the parents. The older sibling, now at least four years of age and perhaps five or more, spends much more of her time out of the home, in nursery school, in play groups, at friends' homes, and so forth, and has had a good year or two of growing interest in age-mates. These facts make life considerably easier for all concerned, especially the parents. Nevertheless, you should expect interchanges between the Phase VII child and the older sibling to continue to feature aggression and disagreements at times.

No one really knows how long this dimension will continue, but it certainly isn't going to go away quickly.

A PHASE VII CHILD IN THE MIDDLE OF THREE CLOSELY SPACED SIBLINGS

With no research available on this subject we must resort to speculation in discussing the Phase VII child who has both a sightly older and a slightly younger sibling. Probably the most important point to understand is that the middle child has never suffered the kind of displacement that the first child did. She never had the exclusive attention of inexperienced, anxious, and excited parents during her first eighteen to twenty-four months, and therefore moving over to make room for a younger sibling did not have quite so great an impact on her as it did on her older sibling. She may very well, however, have become more aggressive than the average child.

The starting point in coping with these interesting and important sibling combinations is a basic understanding of social development in young children. If parents understand the fundamentals of social development, they have at least a beginning with respect to coping with the problems that come from close spacing.

I hope that people who are expecting their first child or have only one child now will be persuaded, as a result of reading this book, to space their children three or more years apart. This assumes, of course, that the parents have a choice. We have worked with many couples who delayed having children until they were in their thirties and forties and who therefore felt pressure to have their children close together. Clearly, each family has to consider many factors in their planning. I can only help in a limited way. I am not a family counselor, but I do feel an obligation, given our consistent and extensive exposure to families with various combinations of children and adults, to be extremely clear about this one issue. If there is any way you can manage it, space your children three or more years apart.

If you end up with closely spaced siblings, this book will help you to minimize the problems. Unfortunately, as far as I know, there is no way you can raise closely spaced children without experiencing considerably more difficulty than you would with widely spaced children.

Suggestions for coping with the difficult problems of sibling rivalry will be found later in this chapter.

Interest in Age-Mates

Under good circumstances, as children move into Phase VII they begin to show a steadily increasing interest in true socializing with age-mates. The negativism and self-assertiveness of Phase VI are pretty much behind them; they know where they stand with respect to their parents, and now they turn their developing social interests to peers. But if your two-year-old is still struggling with you on a regular basis, if he still tests you, if he's defiant, or worst of all, if he has developed a tormenting style, true interest in age-mates will not emerge yet. Such a child, and I hope you don't have one, is often unhappy and has little use for anyone aside from his parents, especially his mother (or whoever has been the primary caregiver). He is also, obviously, not likely to be a good candidate for a first friend. However, he is not likely to show much interest in peers anyhow. His social energy will be focused exclusively on his mother.

Temper tantrums are not a part of the lives of well-adjusted Phase VII children. Unfortunately, however, quite a number of children move into Phase VII with unresolved issues in connection with their principal relationships. If a child has been dramatically overindulged during the first two years of life, that child may have developed certain persisting conflicts that will manifest themselves during the third year of life, and generally in ways that are not terribly pleasant. Many a twenty-eight-, thirty-, or thirty-two-month-old child will still be involved in a chronic tug-of-war with his parents, having learned that if he complains fiercely enough he can usually get what he wants. Such a child is also inclined to throw temper tantrums, especially during the first half of the third year. If parents have read this book and followed its advice faithfully, they won't have to put up with such difficulties, and their child will sail smoothly into his or her third year.

For well-developing children the third year will feature the emergence of the three remaining social competencies that are observable in the behavior of outstanding three- to six-year-olds: (1) the ability to express emotions easily to peers; (2) the ability to lead and to follow peers; and (3) an interest in competition and a willingness to compete.

We have already discussed the first of these competencies in respect to the expression of emotion with adults. Expressing emotions easily to peers reflects the same social confidence that well-developing children showed in their expressions of affection to parents in the preceding eighteen months or so.

As to the second competency, leading and following, some children in the three- to six-year age range are comfortable only when they are allowed to direct the activities of other children; they can't play the follower role. Others are comfortable when following but have little facility in leading; still others can't do either. The well-developed three- to six-year-old can both lead and follow effectively and comfortably. The emergence of this social ability can take place during the third year of life.

Finally, there is the competitive behavior of well-developed preschoolers. Three-year-olds who have developed well know that they're capable of competing, and they are eager to take on new challenges. "I can make a better one than that" is a typical Phase VII statement. I don't believe that means they have any intention of lording it over other children. When they say they can do something better, they are making a simple statement of fact. They know what constitutes a good job, and they know what they are capable of. They are not yet, however, tactful enough to realize that they may be hurting someone's feelings. You can look for this new competitiveness to surface as Phase VII develops.

We know that certain cultures in our society frown upon competitive behavior and disapprove of the tendency of children to express their annoyance with other people. Should you choose not to allow your child to exhibit such behaviors, that is, of course, your right. These characteristics, however, have been routinely found in the everyday behavior of well-developed three- to six-year-old children from many ethnic and socioeconomic backgrounds.

One last remark about social behavior of children in Phase VII: Phase

VII children tend to interact with only one other child at a time. This tendency will persist well into the preschool period.

The Development of Intelligence

By Phase VII I hope that your two-year-old will have entered a new level of intellectual functioning that increasingly features the use of mental problem-solving as well as trial-and-error problem-solving with his hands and eyes. Most intelligence shown in the first two years was of the trial-and-error kind, called sensorimotor intelligence. An infant trying to grasp a hard-to-reach object will usually try various physical methods of reaching the object, whereas the child over two years of age will very often consider alternatives in her mind, choose the one most likely to succeed, and then act. This shift from working problems out through actions to thinking them through takes place in late infancy. The child is now much more able to reflect upon events and situations than she was at age one. She has become a thinker. This new ability allows you to begin to use rational methods of controlling her. More about this subject under Recommended Child-Rearing Practices: Phase VII (page 226).

The Phase VII child is a considerably more mature mental creature than he was in the second year of life. He knows much more than he did previously about the world of objects and their permanent existence even when he is not there to observe them. He knows much more about the paths of moving things and about simple cause-and-effect sequences. He knows enough about how change occurs to anticipate the consequences in many situations. He has a fully developed short-term memory. He also lives in a longer slice of time than before. Finally you can talk about yesterday or even last week and your three-year-old will process the ideas well. The same, of course, is true of references to the future.

Now the Phase VII child is a thinker, or what Piaget has called an egocentric thinker. By "egocentric," Piaget means he tends to see things exclusively from his own point of view. Remember the incident involving the late Phase VI child who had spilled some milk on a kitchen table as she played with her parents. After a few moments of hard thinking, she announced that her older sister had spilled the milk, even though her parents had been with her throughout the episode. As a very early thinker, she was unable to take into account in her own thinking processes anything but her own need to escape punishment.

Piaget has described other peculiar mental qualities of the Phase VII child as well. One of particular interest has to do with the concept of life. For children in this phase, anything that moves is alive. It is therefore not safe to assume that a child will view a leaf being blown about the street by wind the way you will.

Let me illustrate this point with an anecdote involving my own family. I used an intact lobster shell to explore my three-year-old daughter's ideas about the concept of life. Her first view of the empty shell produced a small but real fear reaction until I assured her that the shell could not hurt her because the lobster was not alive. She did not fully believe me at first, but she was intrigued enough to make a cautious approach. Suddenly the shell, which was on a step, slipped slightly; she abruptly jumped backwards—for her that movement meant the object was alive.

In dealing with a two- or three-year-old child, it is important to remember that though his mind is active, it still works in very immature ways. Once your child reaches Phase VII, I urge you to study Piaget's findings. They are remarkable. In the Recommended Readings section, you will find some of his original writings and also some interpretations of his work that are easier to cope with. Piaget's research in this area, by the way, was done with Swiss children during the 1920s. In general his discoveries have been shown to be true, but the modern American child has often been found to reach new mental stages earlier than Piaget's subjects did.

A final approach to educational goals for the Phase VII child is in terms of the dimensions of competence discussed in Chapter 6. Our evaluation of the competent three- to six-year-old becomes increasingly relevant to this book as the child moves through Phase VII and approaches three years of age. During the third year of life, if things go well, you can expect to see all of the dimensions of competence become functional. In the following section we will examine how parents can foster the development of these competencies during Phase VII.

RECOMMENDED CHILD-REARING PRACTICES: PHASE VII

Fostering Competence: Social Abilities

GETTING AND HOLDING THE ATTENTION OF ADULTS

The child's techniques for getting and holding adult attention become increasingly sophisticated during Phase VII. It is important at this stage to be sure that the skills children use in holding your attention are socially acceptable and reasonable as well as effective and that the child knows when to stop. Earlier I pointed out the natural tendency of infants to concentrate on their primary caretaker at the expense of other kinds of experiences. Be alert to how (and how often) your child tries to hold on to your attention. This awareness will help you shape your child's ability in this particular area.

USING ADULTS AS RESOURCES AFTER DETERMINING THAT A TASK IS TOO DIFFICULT

Children have two ways of determining that a task is too difficult for them. The obvious way, which is especially common during the first two years of life, is to try it themselves. During the third year, as children develop more thinking ability, they resort to the second method of determining the difficulty of a task—by first trying solutions out in their minds. From the second birthday on, your child may make no observable attempt to solve a problem before asking for your assistance, but this does not necessarily mean that he has not thought it through and concluded that he cannot handle the problem. This shift in problem-solving style may lead you to the erroneous conclusion that your child is making too little effort before asking for your help.

When a Phase VII child seeks your assistance solely for the purpose of monopolizing your time, his motives are usually obvious. I recommend that you show a modest amount of indulgence regarding requests for help, but do not encourage children to mask their true purpose or to overconcentrate on close contact with you. This problem, like many other related ones, is generally more difficult to deal with in the case of a first child. Do not be surprised if you have to deal with it during the first half of Phase VII.

EXPRESSING AFFECTION AND MODERATE ANNOYANCE TO ADULTS

In reference to the Phase VI child, I spoke of the importance of spontaneous emotional expression. Again, my advice is to encourage a Phase VII child to express her feelings toward you whenever she is so inclined. By that I do not mean that you should repeatedly ask her whether she loves you. But when a child spontaneously shows affection, you should welcome and enjoy it. And correspondingly, if she shows mild displeasure toward you or someone else, pause to ask yourself if she is justified in doing so. If so, give her some leeway. This does not mean you should condone serious hostility or temper tantrums, which require understanding but very firm handling.

Parents often find it difficult to accept expressions of annoyance by their young child. But you should be prepared to deal with such situations, if they arise, by reminding yourself that the expression of negative feelings is a natural part of growing up. Be firm about setting limits, but be careful to explore possible causes of this behavior.

LEADING AND FOLLOWING PEERS

You can facilitate the development of your child's leadership ability by giving your child the chance to exercise leadership skills in her interactions with you. Although we do not know to what degree skills, attitudes, and behaviors that have to do with leading and following an adult or older sibling will transfer to interactions with peers, some transfer probably does occur.

To help your child develop leading and following skills with other children, arrange regular experiences with age-mates in pleasant and supervised circumstances. From the time your child is two and a half years old, such experiences can be arranged through play groups, nursery school, and even day care centers. We have found that unusually well developed two-year-olds can enjoy playing with age-mates in a preschool situation provided that the other children are equally mature and that the personnel are skillful with such very young children. We have recommended a gradual introduction to this experience, starting with a three-hour session one day a week, moving to three days a week over a period of a few months, and building up to a full five-day, three-hour nursery school routine by thirty months.

During the third year of life a child's natural peer-group size is two; there is no need for more than one playmate at a time in your Phase VII child's life. If there is another child or two nearby with whom yours can play regularly, she may have the opportunity for peer play at no cost to you. The problem here is that with only one or two other playmates the opportunities for diversity are limited, and Phase VII children can form unfortunate relationships in which one child becomes domineering. In such a small group, the opportunity to practice both leading skills and following skills is less available than it might be if more children were available.

EXPRESSING AFFECTION AND MILD ANNOYANCE TO PEERS

The capacity to express feelings, both positive and negative, to other people seems to be developed in the first three years of life, partly through nuclear family experience and partly through peer experience during the third year of life. It should be encouraged both at home and at nursery school.

COMPETING WITH PEERS

The notion of fostering a competitive spirit in children is distressing to some people. But if you have no strong objections to this behavior, let me urge you to encourage a reasonable spirit of competition in your child. Particularly in this country, with its orientation toward individual excellence, independence, and personal responsibility, a child who is reluctant to compete is probably at a disadvantage. Furthermore, many connotations of the word "competitive" are generally accepted as desirable. Implicit in the concept of competitive behavior is some perception of when a job is well done, some understanding of a beginning and an end to a task, and some interest in finding and using resources to do a job.

Competition is occasionally, in my opinion, misinterpreted when it comes to child-rearing practices. In the best sense of the term, a competitive person is very much interested in achieving, in doing things well, and in having his work compare favorably with others. She is also likely to have acquired a fair degree of self-confidence. It is in this healthy sense that the children we have studied have been competitive, and it is in this healthy spirit that I urge you to encourage your child. You can easily provide encouragement by paying attention to the child's achievements, offering appropriate expressions of pride, and providing assistance that might enable her to develop her skills further, produce better products, and, in general, become a more capable person.

SHOWING PRIDE IN ACCOMPLISHMENT

Along with the growth of sophistication and awareness in the third year of life comes a continued tendency to seek approval for activities or products successfully achieved. This tendency can be relatively well established by three years of age. Phase VII children will, from time to time, comment proudly on a new skill or a new creation of their own.

New abilities in the third year of life may include riding a tricycle, making a simple construction out of blocks, or producing a drawing or some writing that crudely resembles an older child's work. In numerous ways a child will show his interest in achievement and his pleasure in being praised for that achievement.

Of particular importance here is the reminder that you do the child no good if you praise him for things that are not really worthy of praise. This does not mean that you should set unrealistically high standards, but if you praise your child for an accomplishment considerably below his real ability level, he may develop invalid standards or inappropriate levels of aspiration. Keep your praise tied realistically to the level of achievement while remembering that achievement should be generously rated in the light of the child's relatively simple level of development, even in the third year of life.

ENGAGING IN ROLE PLAY AND MAKE-BELIEVE

In Lois Murphy's pioneering work, *Personality in Young Children,* one of the interesting qualities of behavior of her central figure, a well-developing boy named Colin, was that he frequently would come into the nursery school dressed up as one or another character and spend a good deal of the day acting as if he were that character. The role he selected was generally that of an adult.

Virtually all two- to four-year-old children engage in role playing to some extent. In our study, however, the role play of well-developed three- to six-year-old children differed in both amount and type from that of children who were not doing so well.

In general, the well-developed children selected adult roles. They routinely acted out such parts as doctor, lawyer, nurse, actress, truck driver, and pet store owner. In addition, these children would occasionally make believe they were fictional heroes like Batman or Superman. The children who were not developing particularly well were more inclined to participate in role play that looked backwards or involved more modest aspirations; the two most common forms of such role play were acting like a baby and pretending to be an animal.

Another type of behavior in this category is make-believe, or fantasizing—pretending, for example, to be baking a cake or interacting with imaginary playmates.

Role play is an enjoyable activity in which parents have an opportunity to interact constructively with their Phase VII children. Some parents may fear that a child's grasp on reality will be loosened if she is encouraged to engage in make-believe talk and play. Our observations suggest that such concerns are baseless. Most well-developed children seem to have received a good deal of encouragement from their parents to indulge in fantasy play. You probably would do well to give your Phase VII child similar encouragement.

Fostering Competence: Nonsocial Abilities

GOOD LANGUAGE DEVELOPMENT

We have repeatedly observed that well-developed three- to six-year-old children speak especially clearly, use a good deal of expressive language, and are, in general, strikingly advanced in all language skills. By the time a child reaches her third birthday, she should be able to understand most of the language she will use for the rest of her life in ordinary conversation. The more you use language effectively with her, the better off she will be in this regard. Remember the description of the ways in which apparently effective parents respond to overtures from their children. By now you will have had many thousands of opportunities to respond to such overtures, and you have undoubtedly developed a comfortable and effective style of interacting with your child.

By the time your child enters Phase VII, she should have achieved a higher than average level of language development. If you have been using the recommended techniques, especially the responsive style first suggested during Phase V, your two-year-old should understand more than four hundred words instead of the typical three hundred words, and she may even have become a chatterbox. And if your household is bilingual, your baby should by now have surpassed the national average levels of achievement in *both* languages.

Encouraging continued good language development requires very little of you. If your child's life is interesting, and if she continues to spend a lot of time with you daily, her language skills will expand dramatically during Phase VII. Once again, I advise the continued use of books and stories, with the reminder that no research proves their value, but that common sense supports the practice. Use the Kimmel and Segal book, *For Reading Out Loud* (see Recommended Readings), to help you choose appropriate titles.

Try not to underestimate your child's language ability, but don't speak at a level that is consistently beyond his capacity. I suggest you continue to talk to him at a level that is slightly above where he seems to be.

When it comes to television viewing, I recommend *Sesame Street* for the Phase VII child. Although it was originally designed for slowly developing three- and four-year-olds, a well-developing Phase VII child will generally enjoy the program. In my judgment, videos and good television, used sparingly, provide another interesting dimension for a young child. If you have strong negative feelings about TV viewing, however, don't allow it. There is absolutely no evidence that such television is either educationally powerful or necessary.

THE ABILITY TO NOTICE SMALL DETAILS AND DISCREPANCIES

Well-developed three- to six-year-old children are extremely accurate observers, quick to pick up inconsistencies and anomalies of all kinds. Helping your Phase VII child to refine his observational capacities is a simple and pleasurable job. If, for example, your child shows you something in a picture book, you have a natural opportunity to enhance his language development, heighten his curiosity, and sharpen his observational skills. Suppose he shows you a picture of a train. Instead of simply remarking "Oh, yes, that's a choo-choo," you can take another moment to say something like "Oh, yes, that is an interesting-looking train; it's got three wheels on this side and probably three on the other. Mommy's car has only two wheels on each side." The particular information provided is really not important, as long as it is logically related to the material or situation and stretches the child's mind a bit. You will have an infinite number of opportunities to point out similarities and differences, and all of them will be interesting to your Phase VII child. But let me remind you not to overextend these interchanges with your child. Keep them short and sweet unless he wants to prolong the event. You will find that his interest in these topics is real but usually limited.

THE ABILITY TO ANTICIPATE CONSEQUENCES

If you are filling the bathtub, and your child thinks ahead to what might happen if you fail to turn off the water, then she is anticipating consequences. Or if another child is trying to carry more than he can handle, your child may point out that he is going to drop something. A child with such a capacity to think through an opening sequence of events can head off trouble and, in general, meet her needs better than the average child.

Here too it is easy to help your child develop the habit of thinking ahead: just point out from time to time what is about to happen next. You can do this naturally whenever your child is hungry if you remind her that she must wait while you prepare her meal. She might not be very receptive to learning when she is extremely hungry, but a moderate degree of hunger is good for a learning situation in that the child is likely to pay attention to what you are saying.

THE ABILITY TO DEAL WITH ABSTRACTIONS

This is a very broad cognitive ability. A child who can count, one who can use words well and understand the names of classes of objects, one who knows letters and colors, is a child who is dealing effectively with simple abstractions. A child who can hold a conversation about things that are not physically present, or about events that took place earlier, is a child who deals well with abstractions.

Usually the conversations of three- to six-year-old children depend for their success on the actual physical presence of the person or object the children are talking about. Although abstract abilities have definitely emerged, children in the preschool years routinely do better when dealing with the here and now.

This is an area in which you must acknowledge certain limits in child-rearing practices, due to the mental immaturity of the child. For example, you can demonstrate to a Phase VII child how a key works, using several keys and locks in the home. You can then talk about keys as they relate to locks in general so that an abstract conception of a key and its unlocking function may be learned to some extent. But if you raise the stakes and introduce a topic such as truth, morality, or random events, you will quickly exceed the capacity of your child. I recommend that you be modest in your attempts to heighten the child's capacity to deal with abstractions, since such teaching will happen naturally as time passes.

THE ABILITY TO PUT ONESELF IN THE PLACE OF ANOTHER

Piaget created an interesting little test for this ability. He put doll figures at different points on a model of a mountain range. He then asked the child what the doll could see from the different spots where they were standing. The child who had not yet achieved the ability to take the perspective of another could describe only what he himself saw. But the child who had the ability could tell with a fair degree of accuracy what each doll saw from its own perspective. We have found this ability substantially developed in well-developed three- and four-year-olds, even though this is considerably younger than the average age at which Piaget pointed out the emergence of this behavior.

The ability to put oneself in another's place is a relatively difficult competency to encourage in the young child. Such behavior during the third year of life is contrary to a very powerful tendency not to take the perspective of another. The Phase VII child tends to see the world exclusively from the point of view of her own needs. This style of thinking is called egocentrism, a phenomenon that was extensively discussed and studied by Piaget.

If a two-year-old child approaches his parent wearing a bright, excited look on his face and a substantial amount of chocolate frosting on his clothes and hands, the response he gets will vary from adult to adult. The parent may perceive both elements of the situation—the frosting and what it may mean, plus the bright, excited look on the child's face—to an equal degree; or she may concentrate on the child's bright look, be pleased by it, and wonder why he is pleased; or she may barely notice the expression on his face because of an overriding concern for the chocolate frosting and what it signifies. Parents who focus on the chocolate frosting and the extra work it means for them are experiencing the situation from an egocentric point of view—in other words, with their own interests and needs uppermost in their minds. Parents who concentrate on the child's excitement are oriented toward the child's perspective. Egocentricity, then, is not exclusive to young children; we all engage in it throughout our lives. Ordinarily the degree to which we are egocentric varies as a function of the situation and its emotional importance to us.

Given a child's tendencies at this stage, we suggest you be modest in your attempts to influence your child's egocentrism. But whenever you get a chance to do so, point out to the child what the world looks like to someone else; you will find that the child will occasionally show some interest in such observations. Do not, however, try such teaching when she is feeling a good deal of anger or displeasure. If your Phase VII child comes to you furious because her older brother has reclaimed a favorite toy that she was

Test case: The chocolate child.

playing with, that is not the moment to teach her how to take the perspective of another. You will naturally want to point out that the toy is also one of her older brother's favorites. You probably will ask, "How would you feel if someone kept a toy of yours?" But do not be surprised if your remarks make surprisingly little impact on her. According another person his rights at the expense of your own is a very difficult notion at this stage.

It is fairly easy for most people to explain to children, even as young as two years old, how they feel about something, particularly when concrete clues are present to help such explanations. If you are talking about a pair of shoes that you are having trouble squeezing your feet into, you can make an example, pointing out that although the shoes seem too small for you and hurt your feet, they would not hurt her feet because they are obviously not too small for her.

THE ABILITY TO MAKE INTERESTING ASSOCIATIONS

In our observations in nursery schools and kindergartens we often watched teachers in storytelling sessions with children. The stories sometimes dealt with exotic topics such as prehistoric monsters or fairy-tale princes. We found that especially well-developed children introduced interesting and apparently original associations and trains of thought to story sessions often enough that our group agreed that creative imagination is a distinguishing characteristic and can be seen by the third birthday.

Listening to stories, whether they originate from a superior television show like *Sesame Street* or from some adult or older sibling, helps spark the imagination of a very young child. If you provide encouragement for any reasonable effort at original thinking, modest though it may be, you will help to stimulate the growth of a considerable talent.

THE ABILITY TO CARRY OUT COMPLICATED ACTIVITIES

We have characterized this competency as a "managerial ability." The three-year-old who is developing very well can bring another child and a collection of materials together and introduce, organize, and carry out complicated activities like playing store or house or lion hunting.

Here again is a talent that takes a certain degree of living and mental maturity to develop. In the first three years of life, you can help it along only modestly. For example, you can draw your child's attention to the way you organize activities. Without overdoing it, you can describe some of the steps you use when baking a cake, putting together a meal, or repairing an appliance. You can encourage the child to look over your shoulder while you assemble a toy and explain the steps in the process. Getting into the habit of talking out loud as you are doing things while the child is paying attention is probably the simplest way to be effective in this domain.

THE ABILITY TO USE RESOURCES EFFECTIVELY

Real lions along with cages to put them in and nets in which to trap them are ordinarily in short supply for children of this age. Using big cardboard boxes as cages is a way of using resources effectively. Here is another area in which your talking out loud can be helpful. If you do so as you decide how to organize a task, you can help your child to grasp the idea of multiple uses of resources. Tell him, for example, that if something needs a little force and a hammer is not available, force can be exerted by using substitute objects. Point out that using a heavy rock to pound in a stake can be as effective as a hammer, or that getting three or four people to help lift something rather than straining yourself is another good way to get a job done.

DUAL FOCUSING

Dual focusing is the ability to maintain focus on an immediate task while at the same time keeping track of what is going on around you in a busy situation. The well-developed three- to six-year-old children we have studied in group situations have this ability. The average child in this age range, on the other hand, has trouble splitting his attention in this way. Such a child, in the face of an overture by another, is likely either to yield to that overture and drop what he is doing or, at the very least, to lose his train of thought or his concentration. Some children in the three- to six-year range can never do concentrated work in a busy situation. Given the distractions typically present, they just cannot focus their attention. Again, we do not know how to foster the ability.

To sum up, each of the above types of competence can be used as a guide to effective child-rearing practices. It is not necessary, however, to concentrate on teaching them all of the time; few people can. The families that we have watched doing a fine job with their children do not put a tremendous amount of work into the process during the child's third year of life; nor do they give up all of their other interests, pleasures, and activities at any point during the child's first years of life in order to help the child acquire an excellent early education.

It is not unduly time-consuming to do a fine job of raising a child during the first three years of life, and I would be misleading you if I suggested or implied that it was. By actual count, parents with well-developing children spent about seventy minutes a day paying undivided attention to their one-year-old children. (First-time parents spent twice that much time, but then, first-time parents are a breed apart.) Even at later stages during the first three years, the amount of time that apparently effective parents spent in direct interactions with their children rarely exceeded ninety minutes.

Some parents wonder about the accuracy of these statistics. They certainly feel as if they are spending more time than that, particularly during Phase VI. But there is a substantial difference between psychological and real time. We have been consistently impressed with how many other things parents do in the course of their day at home, even in the most advantaged household.

COPING WITH SIBLING RIVALRY

By now it should be clear to you how impressed I have become over the years with the difficulties most parents have with sibling rivalry. If you have both a Phase VII child and a newborn, you are not, as yet, in substantial trouble on this issue. If you have a Phase VII child and a baby who is nine or ten months of age, you have already very probably learned that sibling rivalry is indeed troublesome·and that it requires special attention. If you have a Phase VII child and a Phase VI child, you may be looking forward to this section of the book because the chances are very high that you have been living through a chronically stressful situation for several months.

In discussing the Phase VI child, I briefly treated the subject of coping with sibling rivalry. At this point a more extensive treatment is clearly appropriate. The following advice works. We have used it over many years in our work with many families, and I feel comfortable passing it on to you.

Your first consideration has to be danger to the baby. At the risk of alarming you, let me emphasize that perfectly normal Phase VII children can and have inflicted serious damage on younger siblings. So be watchful. Make it as clear as possible to your older child that hurting the baby is something you will not tolerate. Furthermore, do not assume that because you have repeated this warning to your Phase VII child, your job is over. Vigilance is necessary.

Next, bear in mind the emotions that underlie the older child's unhappiness about his younger sibling. Understanding this is the first step toward coping effectively with the situation. It follows, therefore, that making a big fuss over the baby in the presence of the older child is going to make matters worse. Not only should parents be careful in this respect, but they should also warn others, especially grandparents, to avoid such behavior.

Next, reduce the pressure on the older child by giving him frequent opportunities to be out of the home. Play groups, nursery school, or a baby-sitter to take the child out of the home or on trips all help. The alternative—the older child constantly pressured by the unfair competition of the younger child in the home all day long, day after day—is not the best way to go.

The most important part of the plan, next to safety precautions, is to have one parent spend private time with your older child on a daily basis. A half hour or so of such time is strongly recommended, because undivided attention is what the older child needs more than anything else. No amount of verbal explanation about how much she is still loved will have any effect. No classes in sibling relations or books that assume an unrealistic capacity on the part of the older child for understanding and emotional control can substitute for undivided attention. During this private time, the younger sibling should not be on the scene.

As the months go by, the situation will gradually ease. During the third year of life the older sibling is very likely to show a combination of resignation and a reduced zest for life. Do not be too disheartened by these developments; they are a natural response to the situation. If both parents participate actively in coping with these problems, the older child will make her way through them. As she becomes more interested in age-mates and activities outside the home, the situation will become much less stressful for all concerned.

People routinely ask what the long-term outlook is for closely spaced children. Unfortunately, no substantial research is available on the subject,★ and therefore we cannot predict whether such children will ultimately be-

---

★ Although a small number of reports on sibling relations have been published in recent years, the information was invariably gathered through interviews. I believe observations of actual behavior under many different conditions is the only valid way to study such a subject.

come close friends or whether these early harsh feelings will persist for a long time. For every twenty-five-year-old who says, "My sister and I used to fight a lot, but now we get along very well," there is another who says, "I didn't like her when we were growing up, and I still don't."

CHILD-REARING PRACTICES NOT RECOMMENDED

Overemphasis on Intellectual Achievement

Perhaps the most common child-rearing problem seen during the third year of life among caring parents is a tendency to be too concerned about the intellectual achievements of their children. Because of inadequate information on early education, many people have come to the conclusion that it is extremely important for their two- to three-year-olds to be in an educationally effective nursery school. But there is no such thing as an educationally effective nursery school. This does not mean that I do not recommend nursery school. There are many reasons why nursery school might be a useful experience for the child and a help to his parents. In terms of solid intellectual growth, however, nursery school is not essential. This issue has been studied many times with many types of nursery schools. To date none has been found to provide any lasting benefits.

A two-year-old child is a complicated creature with many processes developing at the same time. To elevate intellectual growth to a position where it becomes the primary concern is, in my opinion, potentially harmful to a young child. In extensive observations of three- to six-year-old children, we have seen many who were intellectually precocious, able to converse fluently and to do simple arithmetic, equipped with all sorts of information far in excess of what most children of their age have, and yet they were quite awkward and uncomfortable in dealing with other children and adults, other than those of the nuclear family.

A child who is moving ahead in a balanced way—that is, both intellectually and socially—may not be able to achieve the same degree of precocity in any single direction as a specially taught child. If you work very hard to produce a musical prodigy, for example, the number of hours spent in teaching, in learning, and in practice may very well produce a child with extraordinary musical skills. But such a child may experience comparatively few interactions with other children outside the home, may not master general motor skills of the sort that most children master at that time of life, and may have her spontaneous interest in a variety of life's activities interfered with.

My message: Beware of equating brightness with good development. Intellectual superiority is too frequently obtained at the expense of progress in other areas of equal or even greater importance.

Expensive Educational Toys

Everything I have said about overvaluing the importance of nursery school applies equally to expensive educational materials for Phase VII children. No matter what you receive in the mail or what you read in the newspapers, no toys have proven educational value for children of this age. Do not worry about the child next door who has every educational toy ever manufactured; he has no advantages over your child.

Unsupervised Play Groups

Particularly in the early stages of Phase VII, I advise you to be wary of play groups for your child—and, for that matter, of day care programs and nursery schools as well. You also have to be selective about your Phase VII child's first friends. The child of three is already a small person with a fair degree of mental and emotional maturity. As we have seen, however, the child of two is still a far cry from that kind of person; he is still capable of succumbing to primitive destructive emotions. It is painful to watch a relationship form between two children who play together regularly in which week after week the submissive child becomes resigned to intimidation by the other. This form of psychological pressure may not be as obvious as the occasional physical abuse that is often evident in such situations, but it may be of even greater long-term significance. I do not oppose group experiences for children under thirty months of age, but you should know that your child can undergo experiences of a relatively painful kind if supervision is not adequate and effective and if the children he interacts with are not yet fully civilized.

In our parent education program, most of the children have come through the attachment process of the first two years rather well. They have stopped testing their parents. They understand the rules they have to live by, and they are satisfied with them. They are ready for their first friendships with peers.

We warn parents, however, that the typical two-year-old is not usually as well developed and that they will have to be careful about who they get to play with their two-year-old child. We tell them they should look for another two-year-old who is equally socially mature, a very submissive one, or a three- or four-year-old. Until children reach at least thirty months of age, their capacity for friendship with your Phase VII child has to be determined on an individual basis, because the twenty-four- to thirty-month age range is a transition period.

Overindulgence

The third year of life is a time when children often show the unpleasant consequences of many months of overindulgence. Some children become very difficult to handle during Phase VII, particularly if there is a crawling baby in the home. Yet this is a time when firm discipline must be maintained. You do your child no service by routinely giving in to her or allowing her to engage in temper tantrums or other undesirable behaviors. (I must say candidly that if she is still given to such behaviors at two years of age, you will have your hands full for some time to come.) You should make a special effort to finish the basic socializing process as soon as possible. Do yourself and your child a huge favor by maintaining a loving but very firm hold on the life of your child in her third year.

A note of caution: In our otherwise very effective model programs in Missouri and Massachusetts, we have found that the single most difficult problem for first-time parents to cope with is avoiding overindulgence of their children. In spite of the finest educational support system I know of, first-time parents still tend to overcompensate to make sure that their children are happy and continue to love them. The result is overindulgence.

Let me reiterate a couple of tips that seem to help parents control their tendency to overindulge their children. First, a guiding principle for parents should be to teach their child that he is very special, but no more so than any other person, especially his parents. Second, parents should adopt an attitude of healthy selfishness. The people most likely to produce an overindulged young child are his own parents. We suggest that parents picture one circle within which are the rights of the child and another circle within which are their own rights. They should examine a child's behavior to make sure that while all of the child's legitimate rights are being respected, the child is not being allowed to intrude upon the circle bounding the rights of others.

9

An Overview of Educational Developments During the First Three Years of Life

General Remarks

The purpose of this chapter is to sum up the many aspects of early educational development that we have examined in detail in the preceding pages. You will find nine charts designed to provide you with overviews of the topics discussed and to serve as simple points of reference.

The charts are divided into three groups. The first is titled "Prerequisite Information," by which we mean information about the growth and development of children during the first three years needed in order to approach the task of education sensibly. The second, "Educational Foundations," deals with the development of the four major educational processes that have been referred to throughout the text. The third, "The Growth of Special Abilities or Competencies," deals with those characteristics that are especially well developed in outstanding three- to six-year-old children.

The term "special abilities" is used on the third chart because this book does not deal with all of the abilities that develop in the first three years of life. Some have been left out because, as far as we can tell, no special teaching methods or circumstances are necessary for their good development. For example, in our research we did not find that children developing poorly were usually less competent in the areas of perceptual or motor development. This statement will be perceived as controversial by people with a special interest in those processes. As you probably know, several books are available that offer guidance on how to develop your child's motor abilities in the first years of life; other books claim it is very important to guide a child's sensorimotor development—especially visual motor development—in the first three years of life. If you choose to follow the advice of such authors, that is, of course, up to you.

One of the key problems facing parents is confusion. This confusion is rooted partly in the long-term neglect of the need for dependable knowledge about early development, and partly in inadequate guidance from our educational system. If you follow the recommendations in this book, I am confident that your three-year-old will be off to a fine start in life and, most important, that she will be a happy child. If, however, you want her to play the violin, do push-ups, or read at two or three years of age, you will have to look elsewhere for guidance.

These charts are organized around a scale going from birth to three years of age and subdivided into quarter-year units. The age at which you should expect the typical child to exhibit the behavior in question is indicated by the point at which a short vertical line bisects the horizontal line. The horizontal line, in turn, is meant to describe the normal variability of the onset of that behavior or process. In some instances it is also meant to indicate that the process is ongoing from the beginning of the time indicated through the end of that time, as represented by the horizontal line.

In most instances the length of time a process is undergoing development will be evident. In Chart A-1, on motor development (page 244), you will see that the first entry is head control. The vertical and horizontal lines indicate that on the average you can expect a child to acquire head control, the ability to hold her head steady when held upright, at about four months of age. The horizontal line indicates that this ability first may be seen at any point from three to four and a half months of age. By way of contrast, if you look ahead to Chart C-1, "Social Abilities" (page 253), you will find that there is no vertical mark across the top line of the graph, labeled "Getting and holding the attention of adults," which stretches horizontally all the way from birth to three years of age. This lack of a vertical mark indicates that there is no brief period during which these abilities come into a child's repertoire, but that they are emerging and developing more or less continuously from the time he is born until he is at least three years or age.

Even though the horizontal line (in Chart C-1) representing attention-getting abilities ends at age three, this does not mean that after their third birthday children do no further learning in regard to such abilities. It means that the bulk of the learning process takes place during the first three years. Furthermore, the fact that Chart A-1 shows a central tendency and a range under head control does not mean that a child who acquires head control earlier or later is necessarily atypical. These charts are meant to describe how most children develop. Three-quarters or more of all normal children will probably fall within the ranges indicated.

PREREQUISITE INFORMATION

Chart A-1 shows the major motor developments as they appear during the first three years of life. Other motor developments also appear that are not shown—for example, the eye-blink to an approaching target during the first three months, and the focusing ability of the eyes that develops during the same period, give or take a week or two. Both behaviors are important, but Chart A-1 is intended to include only those motor achievements that have major learning implications.

Problems in motor development are much less prevalent than those in language, intelligence, and social skills. Given the average environment, most healthy children develop normal motor abilities. The topic thus has not received special emphasis in this book.

In order to educate a baby, and to enjoy her to the fullest, I believe you should know what she is likely to be doing from day to day. Chart A-2 (page 246) is complicated, as are the activities it deals with. For more detail, I suggest you refer back to relevant sections in the text.

Chart A-3 (page 247) deserves a few special remarks because the concept of shedding limitations was not, as such, focused upon in the preceding text. It is important for you to know what a child's natural limitations are as he goes from a state of total helplessness at birth to a state of miraculous accomplishment at age three. For example, a child under three months of age is a crib-bound creature with modest sensorimotor capacities. Looking at mobiles is one of the few activities he can engage in during those brief

A. PREREQUISITE INFORMATION   1. MOTOR DEVELOPMENT

Birth — 3 mos. — 6 mos. — 9 mos. — 1 Year — 3 mos. — 6 mos. — 9 mos. — 2 Years — 3 mos. — 6 mos. — 9 mos. — 3 Years

Head control
Turning over
Reaching
Sitting balanced
Crawling, scooting, etc.
Sitting up by oneself
Climbing six-inch units (including stairs)
Climbing twelve-inch units (including furniture and appliances)
Climbing down stairs
Cruising (walking while holding on to support)
Unaided walking
"Riding" small four-wheeled wagons
Riding simplest tricycles

A. Prerequisite Information   1. Motor Devlelopment

periods when he is awake. In this regard it is useful to know about the role of the tonic neck reflex, which predisposes the normal child under two and a half months of age to look to his far right or far left rather than directly overhead. If you want to provide an effective mobile for your two-month-old baby, you should not place it directly overhead.

Similarly, all children require some degree of control and guidance by older people in their first years of life, and most grown-ups tend to use language in controlling and guiding them; this means that basic information about the language young children can cope with is a prerequisite for effective parenting.

EDUCATIONAL FOUNDATIONS

Do not be confused by the fact that the first few entries on Chart B-1 (page 249) do not, strictly speaking, have to do with language per se. Since they do involve the child's earliest responses to sounds, they belong here. Note in particular the wide ranges in onset of the various language capacities. These can be observed in preceding charts as well, but language seems to be an area in which wide variability is normal, though it is worrisome to parents. Parents often become needlessly concerned by insignificant delays in the acquisition of speech. Speech, like walking, is a behavior that has a remarkably broad range of onset. During the first three years of your child's life, you should be concerned with the growth of his understanding of language rather than with his speech.

Nothing is more important for a child's educational development than a well-developed curiosity. The shifting directions of a child's development of curiosity are shown in Chart B-2 (page 250).

The only potentially confusing thing about Chart B-3 (page 251) has to do with special entries about a child's development in regard to an older sibling who is less than three years old. No information is given that pertains to relationships with siblings considerably older than the baby.

Chart B-4 (page 252) leans very heavily on the work of Piaget. For more information on this fascinating topic, I urge you to look at the Recommended Readings, particularly J. McVicker Hunt's book, *Intelligence and Experience.*

THE GROWTH OF SPECIAL ABILITIES

The two charts in this section point to particularly important educational abilities that can emerge during the first three years of life. These abilities

A. PREREQUISITE INFORMATION   2. TYPICAL EXPERIENCES

Birth — 3 mos. — 6 mos. — 9 mos. — 1 Year — 3 mos. — 6 mos. — 9 mos. — 2 Years — 3 mos. — 6 mos. — 9 mos. — 3 Years

Sleep/Sucking and gumming the fists/Brief visual interest/Arm and leg motions

Extensive visual interest (own hands and faces of others)/Batting with hands/Arm, leg, and head motions/Sucking and gumming anything handy/ Socializing with anyone, intentional crying (for company)

Extensive visual interest/Hand-eye activities (batting, feeling, reaching, and grasping/Arm, leg, and torso exercises (including turning over)/Sucking and gumming anything handy/Play with own sounds/Socializing, especially with primary caretaker

Extensive visual interest/Simple manual activities with small objects/Practice in sitting up/Leg exercises/Sucking and gumming anything handy/Play with own sounds and attending to words/Socializing, especially with primary caretaker

Extensive visual interest/Practice in emerging gross motor skills (crawling, climbing, cruising, walking)/ Socializing with, and getting to know, primary caretaker/Exploring the qualities of objects, especially small portable ones/Gumming anything handy/Attending to words/Practicing simple skills, e.g., closing and opening doors and covers, filling and emptying containers, standing objects up, etc./Learning about simple causes and effects, e.g., light switches, pushing balls, jack-in-the-boxes, TV switches, etc./Coping with a slightly older sibling (reactively)

Extensive visual interest/Listening to language/Practice simple skills, gross motor skills (running, "riding" wagons, etc.)/Exploring objects/Doing very little (idling)/Procuring objects/Getting and holding the attention of the primary caretaker/Going along with simple requests (cooperating)/Asserting himself and testing wills/Coping with a slightly older sibling (reactively and proactively)/Seeking assistance when needed/Practice in emerging gross motor skills/Emergence of late night sleeping problems

Extensive visual interest/Using and listening to language/Practicing motor skills gross and fine (including tricycle riding and scribbling)/Exploring new objects/Engaging in fantasy activities (make-believe)/Creating products (simple drawings and puzzles, buildings, etc.)/Getting and holding the attention of the primary caretaker and peers/Practicing leading and following peers/Going along with simple requests/Conversing/Seeking assistance when needed

A. Prerequisite Information 2. Typical Experiences

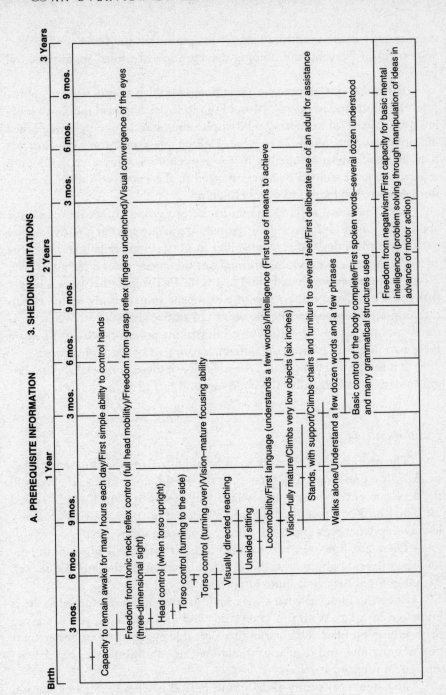

A. Prerequisite Information 3. Shedding Limitations

develop over many months. Note, for example, that the process of the development of "getting and holding the attention of adults" spans three full years.

A word about "expressing affection and mild annoyance when appropriate to adults and to peers": Most of the well-developed children we studied were capable of expressing mild displeasure or annoyance, although they did not do so very often. They were able to express affection easily, and this they did much more frequently. In contrast, children who were developing relatively poorly seemed to be constricted in the expression of their emotions, both to adults and to other children.

Like the social abilities shown in the preceding charts, the nonsocial abilities in Chart C-2 (page 254) typically are acquired over a fairly lengthy period of time. For example, the ability to notice small details and discrepancies is shown as developing throughout the entire three-year range. The moment the three-week-old child learns to discriminate between a nipple that contains milk and the adjacent parts of the human body, he has begun the long-term acquisition of the ability to notice differences. When he is thirty months old he may catch an adult making an error in logic. I believe these two instances of noticing differences are part of the same process.

It is interesting to note that the majority of these nonsocial abilities begin to develop shortly after the child's second birthday.

Fundamentals

The goals of the first eight months of life are the development of basic skills; the preservation of interest in the world (curiosity); and above all, the development of interpersonal security, or a sense of being loved and cared for. The likelihood that anything will go wrong in these three areas is very low. Doing what feels right will usually produce good results.

There are, however, two hazards during those first eight months: diminished hearing ability and the overdevelopment of the intentional cry. Avoiding those hazards is quite important.

Knowing in detail what your baby can and cannot do and what she is interested in is key. With this knowledge and understanding you can avoid the overdevelopment of the intentional cry and engage in the ongoing function of designing, and regularly redesigning, an educationally beneficial environment for your baby.

The eight- to twenty-four-month period is where the parenting job becomes much more stressful and more difficult to perform with the very best results. Guiding good development of language, intelligence, and curiosity is surprisingly easy, but helping your child become a healthy social

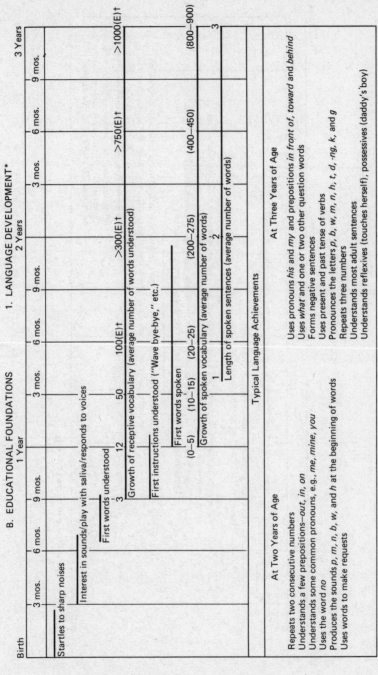

B. EDUCATIONAL FOUNDATIONS

1. LANGUAGE DEVELOPMENT*

| Birth | 3 mos. | 6 mos. | 9 mos. | 1 Year | 3 mos. | 6 mos. | 9 mos. | 2 Years | 3 mos. | 6 mos. | 9 mos. | 3 Years |

Startles to sharp noises

Interest in sounds/play with saliva/responds to voices

First words understood

Growth of receptive vocabulary (average number of words understood)
3   12   50   100(E)†   >300(E)†   >750(E)†   >1000(E)†

First instructions understood ("Wave bye-bye," etc.)

First words spoken
(0–5)   (10–15)   (20–25)   (200–275)   (400–450)   (800–900)

Growth of spoken vocabulary (average number of words)

Length of spoken sentences (average number of words)
1   2   3

Typical Language Achievements

At Two Years of Age

Repeats two consecutive numbers
Understands a few prepositions—*out, in, on*
Understands some common pronouns, e.g., *me, mine, you*
Uses the word *no*
Produces the sounds *p, m, n, b, w,* and *h* at the beginning of words
Uses words to make requests

At Three Years of Age

Uses pronouns *his* and *my* and prepositions *in front of, toward* and *behind*
Uses *what* and one or two other question words
Forms negative sentences
Uses present and past tense of verbs
Pronounces the letters *p, b, w, m, n, h, t, d, ·ng, k,* and *g*
Repeats three numbers
Understands most adult sentences
Understands reflexives (touches herself), possessives (daddy's boy)

† (E) = Estimate

B. Educational Foundations 1. Language Development

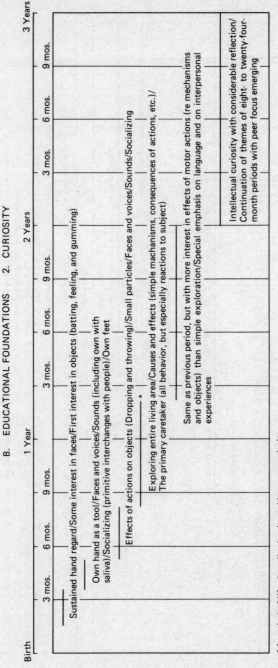

B. Educational Foundations 2. Curiosity

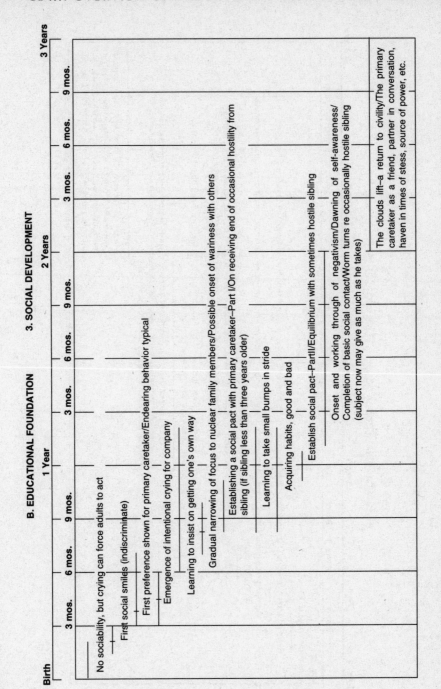

B. Educational Foundations 3. Social Development

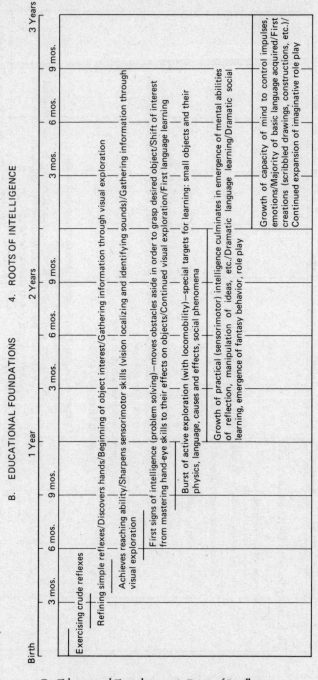

B. Educational Foundations 4. Roots of Intelligence

C. THE GROWTH OF SPECIAL ABILITIES (Competencies)   1. SOCIAL ABILITIES

	Birth	3 mos.	6 mos.	9 mos.	1 Year	3 mos.	6 mos.	9 mos.	2 Years	3 mos.	6 mos.	9 mos.	3 Years
Getting and holding the attention of adults (in socially acceptable ways)													
Expressing affection and annoyance (when appropriate) to adults													
Using adults as resources after first determining a job is too difficult to handle alone													
Showing pride in personal accomplishment													
Engaging in role play or make-believe activities													
Leading and following peers													*
Expressing affection and mild annoyance (when appropriate) to peers													*
Competing with peers													*

*Major development of this ability continues beyond 36 months of age.

C. The Growth of Special Abilities (Competencies)
1. Social Abilities

C. THE GROWTH OF SPECIAL ABILITIES (Competencies)   2. NONSOCIAL ABILITIES

	Birth	3 mos.	6 mos.	9 mos.	1 Year	3 mos.	6 mos.	9 mos.	2 Years	3 mos.	6 mos.	9 mos.	3 Years

The ability to notice small details or discrepancies *

Anticipating consequences *

Good language development *

Dealing with abstractions *

Making interesting associations *

Planning and carrying out complicated activities *

Using resources effectively *

Dual focusing—maintaining concentration on a near task, and simultaneously keeping track of what is going on nearby *

Putting oneself in the place of another person *

*Major development of this ability continues beyond 36 months of age.

C. The Growth of Special Abilities (Competencies)
2. Nonsocial Abilities

being is considerably more difficult. The key problem is nearly always the tendency to overindulge a baby. Overindulgence leads to poor social function, and it substantially diminishes the child's happiness. Being loving but very firm is essential.

Finally, the single greatest source of stress on families with more than one child is close (less than three years) spacing of children. No matter how able and energetic you are, close spacing in almost every case will make your job remarkably more difficult and less rewarding. Its consequences can be even less desirable for the older child.

Helping a child make the most of her first three years is extremely important for her future development and for full enjoyment of those years for all concerned. It is by no means beyond the capacity of most parents. Knowledge and occasional support make the job easier and more successful. It is unfortunate that parents still have to seek out these resources. They should be available to every family raising children by the country's educational system.

SECTION II

TOPICS RELATED TO CHILD REARING DURING THE FIRST THREE YEARS OF LIFE

Introduction

I have been involved in research on the development of the young child since 1957. Beginning in 1965 with the Harvard Preschool Project, my staff and I became involved in a type of activity that has not been common in the careers of child development research workers: we extended our research into actual work with young families. During the course of this work we always hoped we were providing useful services, but our principal goal was applied research for the purpose of creating the kind of knowledge about child-rearing that might ultimately benefit all parents and children.

At Harvard and in our Brookline early education project, our Missouri work, and our ongoing New Parents as Teachers model program, we have had the pleasure of working with literally thousands of families of all kinds. These families ranged from Boston-area couples, where both parents held doctoral degrees, on through a wide variety of families from all levels of society, including young people from rural Missouri with very limited education and very few resources.

As I look back on all these experiences I am enormously grateful for having been offered such an opportunity. As the years have gone by, our views about early development have been refined, sometimes corrected, sometimes reinforced. We have also learned a fair amount about how to prioritize issues. For example, in our work with families with two or more children, the factor that caused the most grief in a wide variety of families was having children spaced too closely in age—that is, less than three years apart. The finding was so routine that I have felt justified in spending a good deal of time in this book and elsewhere attempting to deal with it. Similarly, in work with first-time parents we have learned that the most difficult part of child rearing seems to be avoiding overindulging and spoiling a child. We have also been enormously impressed by the pervasiveness of the problem of undetected mild to moderate hearing losses during the first three years of life. Finally, the inflammatory topic of substitute child care for babies has, over the last twenty-five years, been the source of much controversy and guilt.

These experiences of the last thirty-eight years of study of human development and parenting are the basis for the arrangement, selection, and ordering of the topics presented in this section.

PART I: MAJOR ISSUES

How to Avoid Spoiling Your Child (or How to Help Your Child Become Delightful as Well as Talented)

Preventable spoiling begins to occur shortly after a baby is six months old. The mechanism that is at the heart of the process is the baby's cry, more specifically his demand cry. By fourteen months of age the signs of spoiling are often very clear. The baby has become a whiner who cries much more than well-developing babies and is clearly very often unhappy. Such a baby makes life miserable for the entire family during his negativistic period in the second year of life. By his second birthday he can be accurately labeled "spoiled." My colleagues and I have seen the process so often that there is no mystery about its reality.

Fortunately, we have also seen when and how spoiling can be prevented. Lest I mislead you about how easy it is to describe or prevent spoiling, I should point out that I have written a whole book on the topic (*Raising a Happy, Unspoiled Child,* Simon & Schuster, 1994).

Let me outline the most common way in which babies can develop into unpleasant three-year-olds. Spoiled children develop only in families that love their children very much. Neglected children do not become spoiled. The origins of spoiling lie in the natural and vitally important tendency of most parents to lavish attention, affection, and care on their babies in the first months of life.

I have described a cycle that begins soon after birth: a baby feels distress, he cries, the parent comforts him. This is a natural and necessary cycle. During the first half year of life, a crying baby must be promptly comforted so that he begins to acquire a sense of interpersonal security. The goal of this activity is to produce a child who, at six or seven months of age, has learned through thousands of experiences to associate someone out there with the sensation of feeling better.

Because of the natural learning that takes place when experiences and the people involved in them recur over and over again, by the time babies are five and a half to six months of age they learn to use the cry deliberately as a call for attention.

From that point on to the age when mobility surfaces (most often between seven and a half and eight months of age), babies very often find time hanging heavy on their hands. The six-month-old, for example, cannot do much more than lie on her stomach or back or sit in an infant seat while looking about and occasionally listening to sounds. Contrast that condition with what happens when the child is a nine- or ten-month-old crawler who is actively exploring every situation she can get into. It's not surprising that a six-month-old will use her cry in order to be picked up or at least have an older person come to entertain her. If this strategy succeeds, the usefulness of the cry becomes reinforced during this period. So far so good, no harm done.

But the situation may take a less than ideal turn a few months later as the nine- or ten-month-old begins to create problems for his parents when he is supposed to be sleeping. It is common for such a child to begin to wake up at anywhere from 9:00 P.M. on through 2:00 or even 3:00 A.M. and then begin to cry for company. Of course, he may be crying because he's ill or in physical distress. Very often, however, he's simply alone, usually in a dimly lit room, he's not sleepy, and he has nothing to do. Therefore, he brings into play the one tool that has alleviated boredom before—the cry. It is easy to see how the tendency to use the cry can become ingrained as a result of the beneficial experiences of response to his cries of distress during the preceding months. It is equally easy to see how it might be the beginning of a substantial inconvenience to parents.

Not long ago I had a long-distance emergency call from a dentist in Georgia who was mildly embarrassed to describe the lengths to which he and his wife were going to stop the nighttime crying of their eleven-month-old. They had reached a point where they were taking the child on a minimum of two automobile rides, after midnight and before six in the morning, nightly. No wonder they were beginning to see the situation as an emergency. They, like others in the same boat, were beside themselves. (I should mention parenthetically that they had discussed this problem with their pediatrician, who had told them that the baby was in fine shape physically and they should simply let the baby cry it out.)

The next observable step in the process of spoiling occurs when children are a little over one year of age. Now, for the first time, such children begin to skillfully use a whine to overcome resistance. We have observed many a thirteen- and fourteen-month-old child very effectively insist on getting his own way using this annoying tool. What has gone wrong is that between six and twelve months of age the parents have failed to teach the baby that the demand cry can be used with only limited results. They have, on the contrary, taught the baby that if she pushes really hard, her desire to have her own way will usually, or at least very often, overcome the initial objections of her parents. Put simply, they have done an inadequate job of setting and enforcing limits. Twelve-month-olds whine because they have been rewarded for doing so.

At fifteen or sixteen months of age, with negativism and self-assertiveness surfacing, another stress is placed on parents. Now they have to cope with a child who deliberately challenges their authority. Many a parent will habitually make too many allowances for the fact that the child is just a baby and will allow unpleasant behaviors, such as throwing of objects or kicking people. They seem to make these allowances partly because they love the baby, partly because they are afraid that the baby might not love them quite so much if they are firm, and partly because they just don't know how to cope with a child who repeatedly seeks out situations where he can challenge their authority. Whatever the reasons, a pattern of letting a child behave in an unacceptable manner becomes entrenched.

Closely associated with the problem of coping with negativism is the tendency of parents at this stage to allow the minor needs of the child to inconvenience them. In their zeal to make sure that the baby is always getting his needs satisfied, parents fall into the habit of chronically inconveniencing themselves.

Finally, there is the tendency of parents not to follow through when they set limits during the second half of the second year. A parent, seeing a Phase VI infant doing something objectionable, might say something firmly to end the behavior and then turn away and become reinvolved in cooking or a telephone conversation, ignoring the fact that the child is repeating the behavior. The child learns from such experiences that if she pays attention to her parents for a few moments when they are angry at her, they will soon turn away, and she can then continue to do whatever she wants.

The result of this very common path of development can be a two-year-old who may very well have a good mind and fine language and physical abilities but who is extremely unpleasant to live with. We have seen parents actually leave home for a couple of weeks to get away from such a child for a while.

The problem is aggravated by the tendency of a Phase VI child in the process of the final stages of early attachment to stick close to her parents throughout the day. Such a child is very likely to move into the third year of life without having fully resolved the question of what she can and cannot do in the presence of adults. This child is likely to routinely throw temper tantrums, especially during the first half of the third year, and she is likely, too, to cause maximum grief when it comes to a closely spaced younger sibling. For obvious reasons, this problem seems to be greatest in the case of first children. As you can imagine, such a child is not likely to be perceived by peers as an attractive possible friend.

Can you avoid this outcome? The answer is an emphatic yes. To begin with, you must bear in mind the difference in the evolutionary stages—the phases we have been discussing—for timing is important. You could, for example, guarantee avoiding a spoiled baby by neglecting him in the first months of life, but that would be extraordinarily ill-advised. It is essential that a baby receive, during her first six or seven months of life, the routine comforting and pleasurable experiences that we have described earlier in the book. But you can start to make a difference with spoiling at about four and a half months of age. Bear in mind that from about one month or so after that time your baby will begin to use crying intentionally to get company.

The key lies in the baby's interests. If you know what they are, and if you provide opportunities for your baby to pursue them for much of the day, she will be much less likely to become bored and frustrated than she would otherwise. She will have something to do much of the time. She will not begin to overdevelop her intentional cry for company. For the details of how to design a developmentally suitable day for your four-and-a-half- to seven-and-a-half-month-old, refer to the appropriate sections in Phases IV and V.

Once your baby can crawl across a room, make your home accident-proof and encourage exploration.

During the six- to fourteen-month period, teach her the three social lessons I have described, especially that she has a right to insist on getting her way, but that this is a limited right, and you determine those limits.

During those months, build your authority firmly by setting clear limits and sticking to them, even when tears are flowing down your baby's face. You have to keep in mind that some instances of unhappiness are inevitable if your baby is to develop realistic expectations about what she is entitled to in your family and in life. If you treat her with love, firmness, and understanding, she will cry less often between eight and twenty-two months of age, she will do less complaining during those months, and she will become the happiest two-year-old you will ever meet. Happiness at two requires occasional unhappiness between seven and twenty-one months of age.

It is a mistake to wait until your child gets to seventeen or eighteen months of age before beginning to set limits, for by then it is very much more difficult to do. Remember also that during this time a child should be taught that although she is indeed special, she is no more so than anyone else, especially you.

If you adopt these practices and if you avoid overly stressful conditions by spacing your children three or more years apart, I am willing to guarantee that your child will become a delightful companion by twenty-four months (and stay that way) and that you will not have to suffer through temper tantrums during her third year of life. How's that for a promise?

Sibling Rivalry and the Spacing of Children

There is little question that the difficulties associated with having closely spaced children under age three constitute the single most pressing concern for families with more than one young child. I pointed out this problem in the first edition of this book twenty years ago. I said then that we had found no way to help families deal with this problem that avoided large doses of stress for everyone concerned.

In the intervening years, many couples who have put off having children until their thirties or early forties have continued to seek advice that would make it possible to have very closely spaced children and not come to grief. After twenty years of searching, I haven't found anything better than what I suggested in 1975, and that advice only helps somewhat.

Aside from having a baby with a serious physical defect, no situation has moved women with high intelligence and talent to tears anywhere near as often as the day-to-day episodes of sibling rivalry caused by close spacing.

Many parents have said to me, "I'm in my late thirties. I can't wait three years for my second child. What can I do?" My answer has always been "I can help, but I can't change the rules." Two-year-old babies don't like one-year-old competition. No matter what you do, you can't change that.

Sibling rivalry problems do not begin during the second pregnancy or even soon after the second child is born. After all, a newborn sleeps most of the time, is very small, has a relatively soft cry, and spends most of his time stored in a crib in another room. The older child will probably maintain her good temperament until the new baby starts to crawl. At this point, however, the baby will not only need more of the parent's attention but may also get into the older child's toys as well, and the older child may then hit or otherwise hurt the baby. As the months go by, she may regress, become more babyish herself, take to crawling if she has been walking, go back to a pacifier or bottle, revert to negativism or tantrums, return to wetting herself if she is already toilet-trained. She may show marked signs of being unhappy, appear sad, cling excessively to her parents, or burst into tears for no apparent reason. In fact, the number of different ways in which children reveal their jealousy in such situations is remarkably large. That this is a thoroughly undesirable state of affairs is obvious; but if it exists, what can you do about it?

The first order of business is to protect your younger child. Understanding what is happening to your older child is essential. You cannot get anywhere if you do not know why your older child is behaving this way. Babies have been seriously injured by their older siblings, and you should not underestimate the risk. At the same time, you should be aware that it makes no sense to try to make the older child feel guilty about expressing his aggression toward the baby; after all, his dislike of the sibling is natural. But it must be made clear to him that aggression of any sort is unacceptable and will not be permitted.

The third task is to make life more bearable for the older child—the happier she is, the easier the life of the new baby and of the parents will be. Once the baby is home, you can reduce the upset by avoiding lavish praise of the baby in the presence of the older child. As soon as possible, provide out-of-home experiences for the older child. These help to relieve the pressure in the family situation. If the older child is over two and a half years of age, a regular play group could be an excellent idea. In any event, the use of a baby-sitter to take the older child to the park, the zoo, and the like would help.

It is extremely important for the older child to have a half hour or so of undivided attention from either parent every day, to reassure her in the only language that she can fully understand that she is loved just as much as ever.

Do not make the mistake that many parents make by placing extra demands on the older sibling. The older child is much more mature than the baby, but she cannot be expected to act with restraint and wisdom. She should not be asked to be extra grown up, to be a big sister, and so forth. Parents in these situations tend to overestimate the abilities of the older sibling. Hard as it is on parents, the fact is that when there are two very young children in the home, both need special attention, and the job of the parents is going to be much more demanding than it was before.

Many parents ask if there is a way to prepare a two-year-old for the arrival of a little sister or brother. Unfortunately, rational explanations of complicated future situations are useless when the listener is so young. The best way to prepare a child for the arrival of a new baby is to do a fine job of teaching her, before her second birthday, that she is very special and dearly loved but she is no more special than any other person in the world, especially her parents.

Finally, let me restate the blunt truth of the matter: though parents can do much to alleviate the problem of closely spaced siblings, there is simply no way of making the situation as easy as dealing with one child only or with widely spaced children. Both parents must understand and accept that fact. If the parent with the principal child-rearing responsibility comes to feel that her or his partner simply doesn't understand how difficult the job is, the stress level between parents can become very substantial.

Discipline

For first-time parents, only avoiding overindulgence is more difficult than the closely related problem of exercising effective discipline. Discipline problems do not surface until the child reaches crawling age, and they generally come to a head during a child's second and third year of life. Few functions of the parenting process are more important than performing the role of disciplinarian. It is, after all, through the early socializing process that parents can produce either a three-year-old who is a delight to live with or one who is a holy terror. It has been our experience that helping a child become intelligent and articulate is always considerably easier than helping him to develop a healthy capacity to get along well with other people.

WHEN AND HOW TO DISCIPLINE YOUR CHILD

I do not believe discipline is necessary for a child under seven months of age. People who concern themselves with making a child "mind" during that period are misinformed. A baby's actions during most of those months are not intentional. He is not trying to annoy or irritate anyone. When he cries, it is not a demand; he just feels uncomfortable.

From about seven to twenty months is the period when effective discipline becomes very important and, for many parents quite difficult to employ. I have described three styles of discipline. The first, for use during Phase V, eight to fourteen months, involves immobilizing the child for fifteen seconds. This technique works for all babies. It is, however, difficult for some parents. It does represent the use of force, and it is a form of confrontation. There is no denying that. I have no easy answer to this problem. Making sure that your baby gets your message is more important than the way you send that message.

If, at ten months of age, he has developed a habit of knocking your glasses off your face whenever you pick him up, he really has to be taught that he will not be allowed to do that. If you find the immobilization tactic too painful, I urge you to discourage the behavior some other way. Some parents use a brief period of confinement in a playpen. Your baby will still cry, but at least you won't have to hold him firmly. Others will withhold attention by turning away from him. Again, he still may cry. One thing that won't work is explaining why he shouldn't knock your glasses off or bite you. On the contrary, in dealing with a ten-month-old, explanations reinforce the bad habit.

Whichever method you choose will produce unhappiness at that moment for your baby, but that is unavoidable if you are aiming for maximum long-term happiness for him. Your goal should be to make sure that when you say no, nothing he does will change your decision.

During this phase, diapering is a classic opportunity for you to establish your authority, but once again, while distraction can help, talking will be counterproductive, and some physical force seems to be essential.

These same principles apply as your baby moves into Phase VI, fourteen to twenty-four months. If you have set limits and built your authority effectively in Phase V, you will get through the next phase much more easily than if your baby has become a poorly socialized fourteen-month-old. Confining the child behind a gate for fifteen to thirty seconds of unhappiness will work with just about every baby. Some parents prefer to use a spell in the crib or playpen. Once again, the most important factor here is the effectiveness of your authority, not the method of punishment. You do not want your baby to become a two-year-old tormentor. She won't if she is taught consistently during Phases V and VI that she will almost always get what she wants and promptly, but that when you say no, nothing she does will change your behavior.

It takes several months for this message to get through, but once it does, the results are glorious. I can also assure you that this firmness will neither reduce your child's love for you nor suppress her spirit or her spontaneity.

Once your child becomes able to reason, which will happen between twenty and twenty-three months of age, you can begin to use rational methods for discipline, but continuing to maintain firm control will remain essential.

In studying children in their own homes, some happily developing well and others not so satisfyingly, we paid special attention to discipline. We found that regardless of the family income, cultural background, and educational level, firm discipline always accompanied good social development. From the moment these children began to crawl, their parents took the time to make sure that when behavior was unsafe or otherwise unacceptable, the infant received a clear and persistent message to that effect.

In these homes, telling a child not to do something was ordinarily not repeated more than once, and the command was almost always followed up if the child resumed the forbidden behavior. Despite the real effort needed to follow through on such occasions, all of the successful parents we studied did so. In return, as the weeks went by, such parents had an easier time than most, and their children became happier than most.

WHEN DOES A CHILD FIRST UNDERSTAND THE MEANING OF THE WORD "NO"?

In the first six months of life children do not understand the meaning of any words whatsoever. By four months of age, you can expect your child to respond to his name, provided that he is in a good mood and not too preoccupied. Interestingly, such behavior does not indicate that he actually knows his name. You can prove this by waiting a few minutes and calling him again, only this time using some other name. Use the same bright, pleasant tone, but call him Godzilla instead of Gordon. You will get the same response: he will pause, turn to you, and smile. Why doesn't he discriminate? Because he does not yet understand the meaning of words.

Children begin to learn the meaning of words at about six months. Progress is slow for the balance of the first year and then accelerates at the beginning of the second. They normally acquire a basic understanding of the word and the concept of "no," which, by the way, includes a special tone of voice and a stern look, somewhere between the eighth and tenth month of life.

From that point on, you are going to be saying no with some frequency. This doesn't mean that it will always be effective, particularly if it is overused. Indeed, if you hear yourself saying no very frequently, stop and figure out what is causing the regular conflicts and then try to make changes that will reduce the source of trouble.

Between seven and a half and ten months of age, most babies begin to move about on their own. From that point on, you will occasionally have to set limits on his behavior. Some parents try to teach the baby the meaning of the word "no" at this stage. Babies can grasp the meaning of such prohibitions from about nine months on. I would urge you, however, to minimize the frequency with which you have to say no to your baby during Phase V, eight to fourteen months, by modifying your home so that the baby cannot easily reach most of your breakable and valuable items. When you discourage your baby from reaching for an object, you are beginning to associate disapproval, from the person who means more to him than anyone else in the world, with his natural tendency to explore. You run the risk of discouraging his curiosity if this kind of restriction is too regular a feature of his life.

In addition to modifying your home so that you won't have to say no very often, you can and should use distraction as an alternative between the ages of seven and twelve or thirteen months. A child of eight or nine months who has come across something you do not want her to play with, perhaps something dangerous or fragile, has no internal controls to prevent her from approaching the object. As soon as you notice such a problem, it is an easy matter to move the baby out of trouble's way—in effect, to distract her. You can give her a couple of plastic cups or a toy, draw her attention to the new items, and at the same time remove whatever it is that you do not want her to play with. Her strong interest in new experiences will result in immediate attention to the new objects, and her undeveloped memory and limited determination will preclude any complaints about the removal of the item that you took away. Distraction redirects curiosity; saying no discourages it.

This limit-setting is not the kind of discipline that one would apply to an eighteen-month-old. You are not trying to teach the Phase V baby self-control; you are only imposing external control. If, however, you do not begin to use effective controls at this earlier stage, the problem will become much more difficult to solve later on. It is easier to establish effective control in the earlier stage because of the weakness of the child's memory, the strength of his curiosity, and the absence of previous experience in overcoming your resistance.

It is important to keep two principles in mind: (1) that there is a line where the baby's legitimate rights end and those of other people begin, and (2) that you must follow through consistently in setting limits. As for the first principle, common sense will tell you when the baby is infringing upon the rights of others. She may be doing something as blatantly selfish as taking a toy away from a visiting baby, or something somewhat more subtle, such as asking for more and more of your attention when you are concerned with an older child.

You do a baby no favor by making too many allowances for the fact that he is just a baby. Some infants, by the time they are two years old, are convinced that nobody else in the world is quite as important as they are. That is usually a sign that they have been dearly loved and cared for, but if such an orientation persists, those babies will become accustomed to a self-centeredness that will in the long run be bad for all concerned. It is up to you to draw the line and draw it clearly. Both parents need to come to a common position on this basic issue, although it is the parent who spends the most time with the baby whose influence is the most important in shaping the baby's expectations.

As for the second basic principle, following through consistently, parents must persist when they want a child to behave in a particular way. If they get into the habit of following through and seeing to it that their commands are obeyed, then the negativistic behavior that emerges in the middle of the second year will be easier to handle.

This advice is at times difficult to follow because it requires patience and single-mindedness, and because it can be time-consuming. If you tell a fifteen-month-old not to pull on the drapes or not to climb up on the coffee table, you have to stick with that command for however long it takes to get the child to cease and desist. If, on the other hand, you relent or allow your attention to wander, the child will learn that if he stops doing the forbidden activity for a few moments and waits, he can go right back to it as soon as you turn away.

EXCESSIVE CONTROL

As important as it is to set limits, let me emphasize again that it is equally important for the child to have enough freedom to explore the world. If you find that your baby is very frequently getting into trouble, the problem may well not be that she needs more discipline but that the environment is unsuitable for her.

If you have either to be with her constantly or to confine her to a playpen, both you and your youngster are in for bad times. It really is essential to rearrange your home for your newly crawling baby. An occasional prohibition is not only much less work than chronic "don'ts," it is also likely to be much more effective. The parent who is constantly nagging at a child is usually unhappy, and the same goes for the baby, who either fights back—thereby setting up a pattern of conflict that may persist for years—or gives up, which is even sadder. Try to strike a just and sensible balance. Be firm and follow through, but do not fight about anything that is not worth a fight. And modify your home to minimize conflicts.

WILL FIRM CONTROL MAKE A CHILD FEEL LESS LOVED?

Many parents seem to feel that love and discipline are incompatible, that the more a child is disciplined, the less she will love and feel loved. This simply is not so. In my experience, if parents are consistent in setting limits from seven to eight months on, and if these limits reflect a fair distribution of rights between parents and children, the child will feel completely loved.

When you begin with elementary limit-setting, both parents and children become accustomed to basic egalitarian ground rules. A child does not feel less loved when she learns from her first experiences that she cannot always go when and where the spirit moves her. When her itinerary includes parts of the floor where you are sweeping up broken glass, or the top of the stairs when you have forgotten to close a gate, you won't think twice about the issue of control. You should be just as forthright when the baby is destroying an unread newspaper. Although the child is not in any danger, if you allow her to destroy the newspaper you are extending her rights too far into your territory. If this seems somewhat selfish, it is; but it is healthy selfishness. Bear in mind that if the child concludes during her first year that no one else is as important as she is, she may all too easily develop into the kind of person who really is less loved.

THE AGE OF REBELLION

From age fifteen to twenty-one months true negativism emerges and disciplinary problems escalate. Yet the same basic principles of discipline that you followed when the child was younger still apply now: you should stand your ground and do whatever is necessary, within reason, to make sure your child knows that when you say something, you mean it. By seventeen months of age, your toddler's memory has reached the point where distraction, unfortunately, will not work anymore. By the same token, his language and intellectual capacities are so much better that you can give simple commands and instructions and expect that he will understand them reasonably well.

Your toddler's receptive vocabulary will range from a minimum of a few dozen words up to a couple of hundred, and he will probably understand several dozen simple instructions. It is now that your earlier work on setting limits really helps. If your child has become accustomed to living with controls since he was eight or nine months of age, he is going to be comparatively easy—notice I didn't simply say "easy"—to handle during the negativistic period.

From twenty to twenty-two months of age we expect to see a decline in the almost reflexive negativism of the preceding five months. If things have gone well, the frequency of testing and defiant behavior begins to decline. Your child starts to become much more reasonable.

Two-year-old children can be delightfully reasonable and pleasant to live with. Or they can be entering a phase referred to as "the terrible twos." If your child moves into her third year without having learned that you run the home, then you are in for trouble. Remember that during her third year your child's power as an individual—her intellectual ability, her forcefulness, her imagination, her capacity for devious and difficult behavior—will grow at an impressive pace. If you are still having control problems at the start of your child's third year, you must get on top of them as quickly as possible.

The Critical Importance of Hearing Ability

Precisely because the symptoms of impaired hearing are not always obvious, parents should be especially alert to this danger. It is just about impossible for an infant to grow to his full potential if his hearing is impaired for much of his first years of life. The ability to acquire language depends on the ability to hear well, and children normally do their basic language learning during the early years. Retarded language development in three-year-olds is one of the most common symptoms of future educational difficulties in underachieving preschool children.

Severe hearing loss is defined as 70 or more decibels of loss. Mercifully, such losses are comparatively rare. Only one newborn in 100 is afflicted by such a condition. Far more common is the mild to moderate hearing loss of from 20 to 55 decibels. It has recently become clear that anywhere from one-quarter to one-third of all children, regardless of family income level, suffer from repeated intermittent hearing loss during the first few years of life. This, then, is a topic of vital importance to anyone responsible for raising a child.

For an older child, or for an adult, a moderate hearing loss might not be a major problem, since previous learning makes it possible for an older person to infer most of what he cannot actually hear. In contrast, when language is being learned for the first time, even a minor loss of hearing can be a significant obstacle to understanding and learning.

Not only is intellectual development likely to be impaired by reduced language capacity, the development of social skills is likely to be affected. The ability to gain someone's attention, to get information from an adult, and to exercise leadership depends in large part on the capacity of the child to use and understand words. We do not socialize our children through gestures or through grunts and groans.

An extremely serious situation exists in this country with respect to the early detection and treatment of mild to moderate hearing loss in children from all levels of society. Severe losses—for example, from nerve-cell or conductive deficits—are relatively rare, but mild to moderate losses arise frequently from respiratory distress, to which infants are particularly susceptible, especially when they spend many hours daily in group care, and from allergic reactions. Respiratory infections often lead to the middle-ear problems (otitis media) that are quite common during infancy and toddlerhood.

This condition is often accompanied by the presence of fluid in the middle-ear system and by hearing loss. To be sure, when the infection is cleared up, the fluid usually disappears and hearing returns to normal; but such episodes commonly occur repeatedly during the first two years of life, and for however long a child is unable to hear normally, he is experiencing a loss no less important to learning than if it were caused by congenital nerve damage.

In young children mild to moderate hearing losses often remain undetected for several years. If a child has a severe hearing loss (70 to 80 decibels), even as a newborn her behavior will be quite different from what people expect, and in any event, a severe handicap will usually be noticed early in the child's life during routine medical examinations. This is not the case with moderate hearing loss.

Mild or moderate hearing loss is usually easily detectable when an older child or an adult is affected. The affected person's speech may be slurred or louder than is necessary; he may be slow to respond, or he may misunderstand conversations. None of these signals is easy to detect in a child under two years of age, however. One does not expect a baby to speak clearly at a normal level or to understand speech well.

I wish I could tell you that your pediatrician will always alert you to symptoms of moderate hearing loss, but that may not be so. Pediatricians have to cope with many symptoms in infants that might indicate a developmental difficulty. At times, perfectly normal children behave in ways that suggest there could be something significantly wrong with them; yet often such symptoms vanish and the child develops normally.

Because of this peculiarity of the first years of life, and because of a desire to avoid needless anxiety in parents, medical practitioners often reassure parents by telling them that one or another worrisome behavior is not really serious and that the child will outgrow it. This practice infuriates people in pediatric audiology, for the consequences of inattention to suspected hearing loss during the first years of life can be serious.

WHAT TO DO

First, be on guard for mild or moderate hearing loss throughout your child's first two years. In the absence of adequate professional practice you may have to take on this responsibility yourself. Follow the procedures we recommend (see the checklist on page 274, and review the instructions for screening for hearing losses given in Chapter 4) to be sure that this part of your child's development is going well. A hearing loss should be treated with the same urgency as a high fever. If a pediatrician were to look at your baby and find his temperature significantly above normal, she would hardly shrug the matter off and tell you she would see the baby again in six months. On the contrary, she would do everything possible to see that the temperature returned to normal as soon as possible. From a learning standpoint we believe that the same policy should be followed with respect to hearing losses. If you are told, or if you suspect, that a child under three years of age may be susceptible to even a temporary hearing loss as a result of, for example, an ear, throat, or bronchial infection, have the condition assessed promptly by a pediatric audiologist.

The following checklist includes some of the signs that should alert you to a hearing problem in your baby. It is followed by the measures you can take if you discover such a problem.

The professional treatment of mild to moderate hearing loss consists of two major elements: medical attention, and special assistance to parents. Typical medical treatment includes the use of hearing aids for children as young as six months. It could also include minor surgery to relieve conductive difficulties—for example, the insertion of small tubes to cope with the buildup of pressure in the middle ear (myringotomy).

Even when nothing can be done medically, it is essential that parents be informed about a hearing loss immediately. If they accept the reality of the impairment and are willing to take guidance from specialists, parents can help enormously to minimize the consequences of a hearing handicap for the rapidly developing child.

Parents' Checklist for Detecting Hearing Loss in Babies

At Age	Danger Signals
Birth to 3 months	Baby is not startled by sharp clap within three to six feet; is not soothed by her mother's voice.
3 to 6 months	Baby does not search for source of sound by turning her head and eyes; does not respond to her mother's voice; does not imitate her own noises, *oohs, ba-bas,* etc.; does not enjoy sound-making toys.
6 to 10 months	Baby does not respond to his own name, to the telephone ringing, or to someone's voice when not loud; is unable to understand common words—for example, "no," "bye-bye."
10 to 15 months	Baby cannot point to or look at familiar objects or people when asked to do so; cannot imitate simple words or sounds.
15 to 18 months	Baby is unable to follow simple spoken directions; does not seem able to expand his understanding of words.
Any age	Baby does not awaken or is not disturbed by loud sounds; does not respond when called; pays no attention to ordinary crib noises; uses gestures almost exclusively to communicate her needs and desires rather than verbalizing; or watches parents' faces intently.

Steps to Take if Hearing Loss Is Detected

Step	By Whom
Pediatric assessment with particular attention to upper respiratory system.	Physician or pediatrician
Otologic and audiologic assessment to find out what is causal picture—physical condition of ears, nose, and throat. Is hearing involved, and if so, how much does the child hear? What course of treatment and education is indicated?	Pediatric audiologist

Steps to Take if Hearing Loss Is Detected (Continued)

Step	By Whom
Attention to factors including social and economic deprivation that affect developmental language and speech.	Parents and professionals in medicine and audiology
If irreversible loss is established, refer to agencies that can assist parents with an educational program.	Professionals in medicine and audiology; well-baby clinic; hospital or university speech and hearing center or health center; Easter Seal or Crippled Children Society; Alexander Graham Bell Association for the Deaf

Source: Compiled with assistance from the Alexander Graham Bell Association for the Deaf. For additional information from the association, write to 3417 Avolta Place, N.W., Washington, D.C. 20007.

But parents must face the reality of the situation. Some specialists report that some parents refuse to acknowledge a child's hearing defect. Such a response may be understandable, but it is no less mistaken or damaging to a child's welfare.

Plenty of difficulties are present in early human development that we still cannot overcome, but mild or moderate hearing losses represent an altogether different situation. The knowledge and techniques exist that enable us to deal successfully with the vast majority of children in need, and the cost of detection and treatment is small. All the more reason, then, why it is imperative that we should adopt more effective national policies with respect to this issue—and soon.

The Importance of Early Detection of Developmental Difficulties

You may wonder why I have been so insistent about the need to detect developmental problems as early as possible. The principal reason is that attempts to solve such problems later, from three years on, have proven stubbornly resistant to our best efforts. The same is true of the educational deficits such problems create. By the time a child reaches three years of age, professionals have only very limited power to make up for any previous delays in the natural evolution of learning.

Unfortunately for new parents, educational systems in most countries have been very slow to accept the importance of this reality. There are, to be sure, some encouraging signs. The state of Missouri, for example, has passed legislation requiring every school district to offer comprehensive educational services for all children less than three years of age. Some forty-three other states are also operating programs derived from the New Parents as Teachers Programs that I designed. Unfortunately, none has provided their personnel with adequate training, and funds are, for the most part, very limited.

In our model program we tell parents we will monitor the development of all major abilities in their children. Furthermore, if any potential problems surface, we will help the parents get any special help that might be needed. I firmly believe that the nation's education system should make and keep that promise to every family raising children.

We now proceed with the following schedule of screening practices:

Screening Abilities During the First Three Years of Life

Age	Procedures
3 weeks	Questionnaire: Family History of Hearing and Vision Problems and Information on Birth Process
4 to 5 months	The Denver Developmental Screening Test (modified) and the Ewing Hearing Test (modified)
8 through 30 months	The Harvard Preschool Project Social Competence Rating Scale (modified)
12 months	The Denver Developmental Screening Test (modified) and the Ewing Hearing Test (modified)
14 months	The Harvard Preschool Project Language Abilities Test (modified)
24 months	The Denver Developmental Screening Test (modified), the Ewing Hearing Test (modified), the Harvard Preschool Project Language Abilities Test (modified)
30 months	The Denver Developmental Screening Test (modified), the Ewing Hearing Test (modified), the Harvard Preschool Project Language Abilities Test (modified)

But what about those of you who do not have access to a first-rate program? Where do you go? What do you do? Since the early 1970s, numerous local programs devoted to good development in the first years of life have sprung up all over America as well as in many other developed nations.

The existence of these programs has raised the likelihood that parents can find some sort of assistance in this matter, particularly if they live in urban areas. Yet the fact remains that even if you can find a parent-support or early education program in your area, you will probably not find personnel who are adequately trained for these tasks. In other words, the task of early detection of developmental problems may still be left largely up to you.

This being so, let me review some of the key elements in our recommended procedures for detecting developmental difficulties so that you can get a better sense of the priorities you should attach to the different facets of the problem.

Any information gathered when your child is three weeks of age is not usually information you can or should act upon immediately. To know, for example, that the birth process was more difficult than it might have been does not usually indicate any action that a medical practitioner would not normally take. Such information is not likely to be clear enough to demand immediate action and may indeed not have any long-term significance. Any influence that a difficult delivery may have on the child's development will usually surface considerably later. If at one year of age, for example, a baby starts showing a developmental delay, a professional will want to know everything he or she can about the baby. The reason for seeking information about the birth process is to try to build as complete a picture of the child's history as possible to help distinguish between sources of difficulty that are rooted in something the baby was born with versus those that might be due to the baby's history of experience.

DENVER PEDIATRIC DEVELOPMENTAL QUESTIONNAIRE (PDQ)

At four or five months of age we use the PDQ to get an overall picture of how well the child is developing. The procedure is similar to what a pediatrician will do in a well-baby examination. The PDQ, however, is a relatively crude device and should not be thought of as providing precise answers to any questions. Built upon earlier tests like the Gesell Developmental Schedules, it allows a modestly trained individual to determine in a few minutes if a child is more or less normal or falling behind in any important way.

If we find a developmental delay with the PDQ at four or five months of age, we can be pretty sure, in a typical family sistuation, that the difficulty is due to a congenital problem rather than something that parents have been doing in their child-rearing activities.

EWING HEARING TEST

The Ewing Test, sometimes called the whisper test, can be used at four to five months of age to screen for mild to moderate hearing losses. (Information gathered when the baby was three weeks old can only help identify the child who was born with a reasonably severe hearing loss.)

SCREENING FOR THE DEVELOPMENT OF SOCIAL AND LANGUAGE SKILLS

I recommend regular screening for the development of social competence during the eight- to thirty-month period. Social competence, as we define it, has to do with interpersonal skills—how to get along with other people. You know, having read thus far, that I value the child who is socially skillful at least as much as the one who is bright.

Research in this particular area has been very sparse, especially in comparison to studies of the growth of intelligence, language, and physical skills. Nevertheless, we have done enough research on the emergence of healthy social functioning, and have had enough experience with families, to urge parents to do what they can to monitor the growth of social skills during the first years of life.

From the chart describing the development of social abilities (C-1) on page 253, you can see that we emphasize five types of behavior during the first two years of life, and three additional social skills during the third year of life. Unfortunately, it is unlikely that you will find early childhood professionals in your area who are knowledgeable about monitoring the development of these abilities. And equally unfortunate, few parents will have had the benefit of observing many other children go through these developments, nor will they be entirely free from bias. Yet that is far from saying that you, as a parent, can do nothing. Armed with this book you may be able to identify a professional who can do this job. And even in the absence of such a person, you can use this book as a guide on what to watch for at the appropriate ages. Should you find that some of your child's skills are not developing well, you will want to put more emphasis on them in your interactions with your child; this may well be all that is needed.

In addition, the social skills of a child whose social style★ is evolving in a less than optimal way will be affected negatively. The neglected child will become less likely to use an adult as a resource. The spoiled child will develop a much more elaborate collection of ways to gain and hold the attention of her mother. It will take a trained professional to identify such differences.

★There is an important difference between social skills and social style. Using an adult as a resource is a social skill. Behaving chronically as a tormenting, unhappy two-year-old is an unfortunate social style.

At one year of age we suggest a repeat of the Denver Test to reassure you that your child is developing well in an overall sense. Also, there should be a repeat of the hearing screening procedure, which you cannot do too often. And finally, at fourteen months of age, there should be a screening for receptive language development.

Receptive language development screening, which is somewhat similar to screening for mild to moderate hearing loss, is quite important and too often neglected. A long-standing tendency prevails in the field to equate early speech with early language. This is a mistake, and you should be well aware of the important differences. In the chart on the development of language abilities (B-1) on page 249, you will note that the onset of speech is extraordinarily variable, with the first words sometimes coming well before the first birthday and sometimes, even with normal development, not until the second. The onset and growth of receptive language (the understanding of words), however, is much more consistent.

A fourteen-month-old toddler who does not talk at all is quite likely to be normal, but if she does not understand at least two dozen words, it is likely that she has a developmental delay of consequence.

Until quite recently, procedures for screening a fourteen-month-old for receptive language abilities were of limited practical value. Fortunately, Dr. James Coplan of the State University of New York at Syracuse developed an excellent device he calls the Early Language Milestones Test, or the ELM. Your pediatrician may know of it. If so, he or she can use it, because it is remarkably easy for any child development professional to master. The procedure takes less than 30 minutes.

You may find yourself in the same situation when you try to monitor your child's receptive language growth as you do in respect to social skills: qualified professionals are scarce.

Once again your best asset is yourself. If you become knowledgeable about test procedures, not only are your chances of finding a properly qualified professional much better than they otherwise would be, but you can, if you are careful, do a bit of testing on your own.

A key requirement when testing for receptive language is to avoid using manual gestures. For example, if you want to know whether your one-year-old knows the words "Wave bye-bye," you mustn't wave at her as you ask her to respond.

In front of your seated one-year-old, set out a half-dozen common objects: a cup, some keys, a bottle, a doll, and a ball, for example. Without pointing at or glancing in its direction, ask him to give you the ball, or ask, "Where is the ball?" If he gives you one of the items, the correct one or not, praise him, replace the item, and ask for one of the others. You will probably not perform in a totally professional manner, but you will find the exercise interesting and informative.

Please don't let me confuse you. The growth of language is so central to good development in the first three years of life that I urge you to have your child checked by a qualified professional for receptive language ability at about fifteen and twenty-five months of age. Well before your baby is fifteen months of age, you might ask your pediatrician to be prepared to use the Early Language Milestones Test, or ELM (see above) with your baby at the appropriate time. An agency near you that is engaged in child development research or early education may have personnel who are familiar with this test or who are willing to procure it and test your child. It is both tragic and avoidable for a child to reach her second birthday without proper progress in language development.

At about two and two and a half years of age we repeat a number of screening tests: the PDQ procedure for overall development, the Ewing hearing screening, and the ELM for receptive language ability. Along with the continued procuring of information on social skill development, these tests round out our recommendations for comprehensive learning-focused early detection of developmental problems.

As children approach their third birthday, the likelihood of finding qualified professional help increases substantially. This is due to long-standing practices in early childhood work that favor examining children once they reach thirty months of age or so.

I cannot end this discussion on early detection of educational difficulties without mentioning once more the important subject of spoiling. In our work we find that it is usually the well-informed, caring parents—those who value their children more than just about anything else in life—who are most likely to run into problems in the areas of both undetected and untreated mild to moderate hearing losses and spoiling. In both cases, the parents' failure to spot developing troubles can doubtless be ascribed to a lack of objectivity bred of love, an unwillingness to admit that anything could be wrong with a child so cherished. It is a subtle danger, and one to which wise parents should be especially alert.

SUMMARY

Two powerful facts underline the necessity for paying close attention to early detection of educational difficulties. The first is thoroughly documented—our limited capacity to undo poor development once the child has reached three years of age. The second is the happy other side of the coin—to wit, that the child who at age three is functioning well on the various goals described in this book—intellectual, linguistic, and social—is very likely to be well launched toward excellent later development, including his performance in school.

These are the simple reasons why I have pleaded so vigorously in so many forums that the first goal of any public educational system should be to help each child get the most out of the first three years of life. Fortunately, the chances that your child will do so are vastly better today than they would have been as recently as thirty years ago.

The Benefits of Breast-Feeding

In my early experiences in the field of child development the question of breast-feeding versus bottle-feeding was of practical concern to professionals as well as to parents. Thirty years ago, the consensus among professionals was that there was little to choose from between the two methods. Although breast-feeding might have seemed more "natural," many took pains to point out that the climate of love associated with the process could just as easily be created by a bottle-feeding mother. As for nutrition, there seemed to be little medical concern about bottle feeding because of an abundance of apparently suitable formulas.

Of course, some concern was expressed about the impersonal kind of bottle-feeding often given infants raised in institutions. In such cases it was not uncommon for bottles to be propped up on pillows or blankets so that a staff member, who might have had eight or more infants to feed, could handle a large number of them at once. The work of numerous researchers, including René Spitz, on the dramatic harm that could come to children reared with minimal attention, served to alert professionals to the importance of close human contact during the feeding experience.

But this special situation notwithstanding, durng the 1950s and 1960s no special effort was made to laud the advantages of breast-feeding over bottle-feeding. Unquestionably, professional opinion was influenced by the desire to support women who, for any number of reasons, did not choose to breast-feed.

Sometime toward the end of the 1960s a change occurred. Medical studies began to provide evidence that breast-feeding really was superior to bottle-feeding in a number of important ways. While specifics of the argument are beyond my area of expertise, in essence breast-fed babies were found to be significantly healthier. Since then, most professionals, at least Western ones, have become increasingly firm in their advocacy of breast-feeding, and I too have consistently recommended breast-feeding on the basis of medical evidence.

About ten years ago, I participated in an annual conference of the La

Leche League. The league was started in the 1950s by seven midwestern mothers who wanted to breast-feed but were unable to find support among their friends and professional advisers. The La Leche League, by any standards, has become enormously successful, now having well over 100,000 members and branches in over two dozen countries. Ironically, members of the league currently are consulting in developing nations in an effort to help reinforce the concept of breast-feeding.

My prior contact with the La Leche League had been very limited. I had been aware of its existence and of the members' passionate devotion to breast-feeding; but their very passion had led me to be somewhat reserved about their work because it could easily lead to overstatements and unsubstantiated claims. Otherwise, however, from a distance, I valued the organization's humanistic goals and its emphasis on close, caring relations between parents and children.

After my presentation at the conference I had an opportunity to meet and talk with a number of the league's leaders. As we talked, I realized that they were surprised that I endorsed breast-feeding solely on the grounds of its proven medical advantages, not only from the point of view of nutrition but also with respect to preventing allergic reactions during infancy. Several members of the group insisted that there was much more to breast-feeding's advantages than that.

Soon after those meetings I was sent several research reports on the differences between breast-fed and bottle-fed babies. I now feel that this information is worthy of your serious attention, for something new, something of potentially great importance, has surfaced on this topic.

Over the previous decade in our work with families we had become particularly sensitive to the apparently widespread threat to the hearing of children under age two, arising from otitis media, or middle ear infection. There is little question that chronic episodes of this infection give rise to mild to moderate hearing loss in a goodly percentage of young children, with consequences that can be serious and long-lasting. Although these consequences usually are not life-threatening, they do pose problems for the acquisition of language, higher mental abilities, and effective social skills.

One of the most important research reports sent to me came from the University of Helsinki in Finland. Its main findings were as follows: some 237 breast-fed and bottle-fed children were studied. Recurrent otitis media was strongly associated with early bottle-feeding in contrast to prolonged breast-feeding (defined as six months or longer), which had a long-term protective effect up to three years of age. Interestingly, this benefit was found only with boys (boys have been found to be more susceptible to middle ear disease in infancy than girls). The authors were not clear as to whether the human milk actually gave protection against infections and allergies or whether these harmful effects were somehow associated with cow's milk.

This report—along with two more, of equally high-caliber research, reporting on the studies of Canadian and East Indian babies—made a strong case for the link between bottle-feeding and the frequency of mild to moderate hearing losses. This link, found in several countries, is potentially of great importance for the development of young children everywhere.

The studies also raised an interesting point about substitute care. Substitute care not only reduces the likelihood of prolonged breast-feeding but children in group care are exposed to infectious diseases to a much greater degree than is found in home-reared children.

Two articles on research in New Zealand seem to indicate that breast-feeding is strongly associated with improved speech clarity and better reading ability in five- and six-year-old children. In the New Zealand studies the benefits were limited to male children; and it has been found repeatedly, throughout this century, that girls are generally more advanced with respect to early language acquisition than boys.

It is possible, although at this point it's only speculation, that if we could reduce the frequency of mild to moderate hearing losses in boys during the first years of life, such differences in early language acquisition might also be reduced or even eliminated.

These and several related studies have led me to modify my previous stance and to recommend to all new parents that they attempt prolonged breast-feeding if it is at all possible. It must now be said that breast-feeding is clearly the preferred method. Benefits are not just confined to nutrition but very probably extend to learning as well. If for any reason you do not breast-feed, then you should be especially alert for a somewhat higher likelihood of middle ear problems, especially in boys.

Substitute Child Care

Ever since the summer of 1979 when I innocently responded to a *Los Angeles Times* reporter's question about substitute child care, I have been in the middle of a controversy. I stated then, and I will state again now, that full-time substitute care for babies under three years of age, and especially for those only a few months of age, does not seem to me to be in the best interest of babies.

Let me try to explain why I maintain what to some people seems such a controversial position.

Traditionally in our culture women have assumed the primary responsibility for raising their children, especially during the first years of the child's life. Today that tradition is being challenged. More and more infants and toddlers are spending the majority of their waking hours in the care of someone other than a member of their immediate family.

As one who has specialized in the study of the development of children, I have been, and I remain, disturbed by this situation. Of course, I worry most about the effects on children, but I also worry about the pressures being put on those women who do not choose to join the trend. Moreover, I am saddened by the thought that many adults are missing some of life's sweetest pleasures, those that parents receive when they spend time with their own babies.

I do not pretend to be an expert in all aspects of family life, but I do claim to have some special knowledge of the educational needs of young children. On the basis of that consideration alone I take my stand: simply stated, I firmly believe that most children get a better start in life when, during the majority of their waking hours of their first three years, they are cared for by their parents or other nuclear family members, rather than by a substitute caregiver.

However, from the time an infant acquires the ability to crawl across a room until she stops challenging her parents' authority, I don't believe it is in anyone's best interest for a parent to be at home full-time with a baby. I strongly recommend part-time substitute care—in other words, I suggest that the primary caregiver get away from the baby for several hours every day. The reason for doing this is simple: the stress and the emotional intensity of being with the Phase V and VI baby day in and day out invariably reaches very high levels and often stays there for months. This level of stress is not fair to anyone. Both the parent and the baby do better when they have regular relief from each other, especially during the fifteen- to twenty-four-month period.

In seeking substitute care you should first look for a warm, sensible, experienced, and highly recommended person to come into your home and care for just your baby. Credentials are not important; it is the person who counts. Try to have that person's hours overlap as often as possible with your child's nap time. Please understand that if you remain in your home, in the hope of relaxing or working in another room, your baby, if she is mobile, will try her hardest to get to you. It will be better if you leave.

Also, we have found families have better results with nannies in their twenties than those who are older. In the latter case, significant conflicts are not only inevitable but more frequent as well.

The second best option is to seek the same kind of person and have her care for your child only, in her home. The third best option is to use carefully selected family day care, where the ratio of children to adults is as small as possible. For children under eighteen months, three children to one adult is maximum. For eighteen to thirty months, I recommend no more than four, and for thirty months to five years, five. During the first two years of life, especially because of the problem of contagious diseases, I do not recommend any form of center-based substitute care.

THE NEEDS OF INFANTS AND TODDLERS

The first three years of life are like no other period. With regard to the emotional development of babies, a fundamental significance has long been accorded to the parent–infant bond, and that bond is formed during the first two years of life.

In this century many studies have been made of physically normal babies reared in institutions in which, as a rule, no single adult had primary responsibility for any individual baby. The studies have almost always revealed that the absence of a primary caretaker during a child's first few years produces serious emotional and psychological debilitation. Although few people advocate institutional child-rearing, these studies are not irrelevant on that account, for now we must go on to ask, what of lesser deviations from the norm of parental care?

Several forms of part-time substitute child care—from British nannies to Israeli kibbutzim—have existed long enough for us to learn something from them. Although these and related practices suggest that an adult outside of the baby's family can assume the primary caretaking role without any obvious harmful consequences, the exact consequences of different forms of such practices are not known. In both the British and Israeli systems, the selection and training of substitute caretakers is usually done with great care, and the caliber of treatment the baby receives in most such situations appears to be very good.

By way of contrast, studies of salaries for child-care personnel in the United States repeatedly indicate an average hourly rate of just over minimum wage, and staff turnover is notoriously high. The chances of finding first-rate care in a center are very low. Although many intelligent, well-trained, dedicated people undoubtedly work in substitute-care situations, it is equally clear that many others, probably the majority, do not meet that description.

We know that among other warm-blooded species whose offspring are initially helpless, the general rule is that newborns are cared for by their parents during the early stages. To me this apparent fact of nature, coupled with a tendency in many human societies for babies to be reared by their parents, strongly suggests that parental care is uniquely important. Although I grant that neither animal analogies nor widespread and long-standing custom is conclusive in itself, I take them as powerful indicators, as I do the fact that progressive programs in Western countries have almost always aimed at making it possible for parents to care for their babies at home.

Added to these facts is what I have learned from my own research in human development. I have had the privilege of being able to compare the everyday experiences of many children from many kinds of families, and my own observations overwhelmingly suggest that, all things being equal, a baby's parents and grandparents are far more likely to meet her most important developmental needs than are any other people.

One of the unique advantages those family members have is illustrated by one of the many inevitable achievements of all healthy infants: the first steps. Unaided walking usually first takes place when a baby is about eleven or twelve months old. When the baby is being raised at home, especially if she is a first child, both parents and everybody else in the nuclear family look forward to the event with anticipation and perhaps even some mild anxiety. When the time comes, the impact on the family is powerful and very exciting. Parents ordinarily become absorbed in the experience to a degree that friends cannot adequately understand unless they have been through it themselves.

The parents' typical response to those first steps is to envelop the baby in praise and enthusiasm, and such intense experiences seem to me to be extremely important. For the parents, they reinforce the commitment to the child in the family life. For the baby, they contribute to one of the building blocks of lifelong pride in achievement: her sense of personal security and worth.

Between seven and eleven months of life most babies learn to sit up, crawl, stand up, lower themselves to the floor, climb, walk while supported, and finally walk alone. All of these achievements and many more are occasions for parents to lavish attention and legitimate praise on the baby. In this very important part of the child-rearing process, parents have a natural advantage over other adults. Although loving child-care workers will usually enjoy and applaud a baby's achievements, they simply cannot match the enthusiasm and excitement expressed by most parents. After all, when one has seen two hundred babies take their first steps, one's reactions to the two hundred first cannot possibly contain the same enthusiasm typically shown by the baby's parents.

Another area in which parents have an advantage over substitute caretakers is in the encouragement and satisfaction of an infant's curiosity. Once a baby learns to crawl, she becomes capable of exploring a much expanded world. Over the next year and a half a major part of her day consists of closely examining small objects and their motions, wondering at the way simple mechanisms work, studying people, and physically exploring the space around her. To get the most out of these experiences, it is best if an infant has ready access to an older person who is especially interested in her and is eager to serve as a personal consultant. No one fits that description quite so well as a baby's parents or grandparents.

Substitute caregivers come in many styles; they can be well-trained, experienced child development specialists with master's degrees in early education (if so, the cost of their services will be very high); they can be high school graduates with special training in child development; or they can be aunts, cousins, or even older siblings. They may care for one baby or a group of babies, in an infant's own home, in their home, in a nonprofit center, or in a commercial center. As you might expect, the quality of care a baby receives varies as widely as the caretakers, from warm and knowledgeable to indifferent and unskilled. What the impact is on babies is not yet known.

The few studies of center-based care that have been done have produced mixed results, but I still would not endorse such care during a child's first two years, except for families with special needs. I am concerned not only with avoiding obvious harm but with encouraging every baby's very best development as well, and none of the few evaluations performed so far has addressed the question of what situations are actually good for children.

To put it bluntly, after more than thirty-eight years of research on how children develop well, I would not think of putting my own baby or grandchild in any substitute-care program, especially a center-based program, on a full-time basis during the first few years of life.

SITUATIONS WHERE FULL-TIME SUBSTITUTE CARE MAKES SENSE

There are two situations in which substitute child care may be a necessity: (1) when parents cannot raise their own children; and (2) when the parents simply don't want to rear their babies.

The first situation is likely to exist where alcoholism, drug abuse, or some other debilitating condition afflicts parents to such a degree that child-rearing is impossible. In such families the environment is so bad that the only hope for the children is to remove them from the family and place them in foster care. Nor does the situation have to be that extreme. Unfortunately not all of the parents of the approximately four million babies born in the United States each year are happy, intelligent, in love, and psychologically fit for parenthood. Many babies are born to mothers under eighteen years old who already have two or three other children. In some of these cases the prospects for the new baby may be so grim that full-time substitute care, if it is of good quality, may very well make sense. Some good government-sponsored programs are geared to such circumstances.

The second situation, when a family just does not want the job of child-rearing, is harder to define, but it is no less real. Some parents simply do not want the time-consuming, occasionally stressful job of raising a baby. This is a psychological matter, and one that I prefer not to comment on, except to say that in such situations I believe some substitute arrangement would be preferable.

PART-TIME CARE

To the surprise of some, I am a strong advocate of substitute child care on a part-time basis, for all families who would like it, from the time a child is seven or eight months of age.

In our research I have met parents for whom the concept of any substitute care during their baby's early years was unthinkable: they were having such a wonderful time with their baby that they dreaded separation. Although I am careful about urging such people to use substitute care, I believe that in order to avoid overattachment, the use of an occasional baby-sitter, at the very least, is good for most families right from the beginning.

Part-time care can free up the time of either or both parents to earn needed income. It can also give parents, especially the mother, the opportunity to pursue a career, studies, or the like. But from my point of view, the most important reason for part-time substitute care is that it gives parents a break from the continuous responsibilities of child-rearing.

Psychological relief, whether through outside work or relaxation, is very important for full-time parents. For years young women, by themselves, have carried the continuous responsibility for the well-being of their children. To many people this situation might seem perfectly normal and not worthy of comment, but if you observe women with infants in their homes, as we have done, you cannot help being impressed with the stress that is often generated, particularly when there are two or more closely spaced young children in the family.

One of the most popular features of some of our programs for young families is the opportunity for people to simply get away from their children for a few hours every week. When you combine that psychological relief with the opportunity to talk to other young parents in similar circumstances, you get some significant benefits.

FATHERS AND GRANDPARENTS MAKE GOOD MOTHERS, TOO

No study anywhere has indicated that mothers are the only people capable of raising babies. We have observed many fathers and grandparents who seemed well suited to the task and were willing and even eager to share the job. I have always thought it unfair that fathers and grandparents have limited opportunities to share in the many exciting and memorable everyday events in babies' lives. Babies begin life and get to know the world only once, and they grow up very fast.

SUMMARY

If you feel you have no option but full-time substitute care for your baby, so be it; but for those fortunate enough to have a choice, it is, I believe, best for most of your baby's waking hours to be spent with parents or grandparents during her first thirty months of life. Such an arrangement is usually the surest way to see to it that a baby gets a fine early education. Furthermore, child-rearing, especially when it is shared, can be one of life's most rewarding experiences. For further information on this topic, please refer to the Recommended Readings section of this book.

Variations in the Onset of Early Behaviors

When should children first begin to crawl, talk, stand alone, and exhibit each of the hundreds of other accomplishments we associate with normal development? Devoted parents often become anxious about when such behaviors will emerge in their preschool-age children.

Over the last few decades, with the increased awareness of the importance of early childhood development, such concerns seem to have become even more widespread. This anxiety is reasonable and indeed healthy to the degree that it indicates a sense of responsibility and an awareness of the importance of normal development during the first years of life. But much of the existing concern is also based on a lack of understanding of early development.

Everyone who studies young children agrees that one of the invariables of early human development is its variability. After all, children are not assembly-line products. You can expect that just about every Ford will look and perform pretty much like every other Ford. But that's not the case with a young human.

Take, for example, the age of walking. Children in various parts of the world, on the one hand, walk as early as six or seven months of age. A substantial percentage of perfectly normal children, on the other hand, do not walk before they are one and a half years old. Yet parents worry when their baby does not walk early.

The amount of anxiety a parent feels varies from none at all to a fairly significant quantity, depending upon the developmental rates of other babies they know. The date at which walking comes into a child's repertoire varies widely, but except in extreme cases that variation means absolutely nothing in terms of the child's educational future or physical well-being.

This is not to say that you never need worry about when your child starts to walk. If your child is eighteen months old and not walking, you should certainly have him examined by a medical person. But I still would not be especially concerned. Only if he still did not walk at the age of two would I think there would be some reason for serious concern.

Parents very often show even more concern about the age at which their baby starts to talk. The onset of meaningful speech—that is, using particular labels to routinely indicate one kind of object or person—can happen in normal babies at any time from seven or eight months to the second birthday. As with the emergence of walking ability, you can expect wide variability in the onset of speech in any group of normal babies.

If a child of nine to ten months already has a speaking vocabulary of several words, that may be taken as a good sign. But if after sixteen months your toddler still says not a word, I would begin to be concerned. A professional examination would be a good idea, starting with the child's receptive language ability, and if that is negligible, moving on to a thorough physical examination, especially of hearing mechanisms.

The growth of the understanding of language is much less variable and is a much more reliable indicator of developmental progress than speech during the first three years of life. The first understood words usually begin to appear shortly after the child is about eight months of age. Progress at first is generally slow, so that the one-year-old is likely to understand only five to ten words. But progress accelerates during the second year of life and even more during the third.

A fourteen-month-old who does not say anything is likely to be perfectly normal; but a fourteen-month-old who does not understand at least two dozen words is very likely to be suffering from a developmental delay of consequence.

Everyone responsible for rearing children should be well informed about the normal range in the dates of onset of certain landmark abilities and capacities. There is no reason why such information should not be common knowledge, and parents who have good medical care for their children will, in fact, inevitably be given some of this kind of support by their physicians. Unfortunately, other physicians lose credibility with parents by overusing an all-purpose answer to questions about the onset of children's abilities. Many parents have complained to me that their pediatricians routinely say of late onsets that the child in question is probably just a "late bloomer" and that there is no cause for concern. Up to a point, that is undoubtedly an appropriate verdict and the parent may be needlessly anxious. But beyond a certain point, such a diagnosis may be a substitute for a knowledgeable and useful response.

In summary, then, you should expect significant variation in the date of onset of a wide variety of abilities and other phenomena in the first three years of life. The charts in Chapter 9 indicate how consistently these variations are seen in development, where you can expect wide variation, and where in relation to other processes you should look for a narrow range of onset of the behavior in question.

Play

Children's play, a subject of great interest to parents, has received little attention from those who study the development of young children. (Two notable exceptions are the works of Brian Sutton-Smith and Dorothy and Jerome Singer, cited in the Recommended Readings section at the end of this book.) Babies don't have to earn a living, and therefore when people talk about the behavior of babies, the word "play" is used automatically to denote most of what they do. Thus babies are thought to play much more often than adults.

But do they? What do they do that meets a proper definition of the word? What is a proper definition of "play"? If playful behavior involves pleasure, lightheartedness, smiling, laughter, giggling, and so on, then babies don't play very much. They act that way only sporadically. They spend a fair amount of each day in various states of need or discomfort—for example, hungry or wet—and together these two types of activity amount to less than half of their waking hours. What about the rest of the day?

When a ten-month-old is trying to push a lever on a toy to make the cover pop up, the expresson on her face is likely to be quite serious. If she succeeds, probably no one will reward her for her efforts, and since what she's doing is not obviously useful anyway, we might be tempted to regard such activity as play. But I would suggest that the baby has every right to be serious, for what she is doing is probably quite important. In fact, Erik Erikson has persuasively argued that the play of babies is actually crucial to the growth of a healthy personality.

In his view, the play activities of babies give them a chance to try out experiences under circumstances that are safe. These rehearsals help to prepare the child for later challenges, much as the playful fighting of kittens and puppies helps them learn skills needed for survival when they become mature animals. Erikson also claims that simple successes in the play of babies help to establish a strong ego and sense of worth. It is hard to argue against such a position in the face of the universal interest healthy infants display in the sensorimotor achievements of infancy.

What, then, do we mean by children's play? The most conservative definition would be "an activity in which a child is clearly having fun while being active." A baby who is laughing or giggling but otherwise doing nothing, for example, would be considered happy but not actually playing. The problem with such a definition is that much of a baby's activity that we ordinarily consider playful would be excluded. Practice in hand-eye skills—an activity that occupies hundreds of hours, especially from the second month of life through the second year—is mostly a serious activity, often featuring purely sober facial expressions, regardless of whether toys are involved.

In addition to playing with toys and other objects, young children enjoy simple games with adults. Although such behavior often is more correctly categorized as maintaining social contact than as a structured game, the child's mood is definitely playful. Similarly, large-muscle activity is often done just for fun: jumping on a bed, running, climbing. And play may be involved during what we have labeled gain-pleasure experiences: being tickled, being swung in the air, turning somersaults. As the child grows older, these two kinds of play usually increase.

Any new environment may evoke exploratory play. Thus sand, water, or any sort of modeling material, such as Play-Doh, can stimulate play.

What about make-believe? Children pretend to be something or someone else only rarely during the second and third year of life—or 1 to 2 percent of all experience—in comparison to exploratory and mastery tasks, which together account for 15 to 22 percent of all waking time. Make-believe appears to be especially common in the behavior of unusually competent three- to six-year-old children. Pretending, or role play or make-believe, includes impersonations—being Batman, for example—and the ascription of unreal qualities to situations or materials—as in "baking" with Play-Doh. Such behavior first appears at about the middle of the second year and increases steadily on through the third year.

In our research, children who were developing very well consistently engaged in more of such behavior than children developing poorly. Parents, therefore, should encourage such behavior, especially when it first appears shortly after the first birthday. The fact that it is great fun for everyone else is a bonus.

During the first ten months of life interesting developments appear in the area of play. Given the opportunity, crib-bound infants six weeks to eight months old will engage in hand-eye activities for hours. I have observed many instances of two- to four-month-old babies totally absorbed with crib toys or entranced with their own reflection in a small mirror.

From eight to fifteen months of age, exploring the qualities of objects is more common than practicing simple skills with them. But between eighteen and thirty-six months there is a steady decline in the amount of time spent in exploratory behavior. During the same period, mastery experiences, especially hand-eye exercises, increase rapidly. This pattern of mastery behaviors taking the place of exploratory behaviors proceeds faster in children who are developing unusually well.

Children destined by three years of age to be very different in terms of achievement will seem very much alike in their primary behaviors at one year of age.

Our research indicates that development in the first three years of life is linked with the quality of the small-object activities of a young child. In this sense, the "play" of babies seems to be an important affair, and its quality appears to depend on many circumstances. These include the manner in which the primary caregiver handles the baby's curiosity, the freedom allowed for exploration, the responsiveness of adults to the baby's efforts to master his body, and the establishment of a stable social relationship with the central person in his daily life.

Looking at the larger process of the development of play during the first three years of life, it seems to me that exploration and mastery tasks are examples of learning-to-learn activities, which underlie the acquisition of skills and information. These in turn seem to lead to a new form of activity that surfaces toward the end of the third year of life: constructing a product. This activity, fairly common in three- and four-year-olds in nursery schools, may appear as early as the third birthday, but usually only in precocious children.

The first products constructed are simple and few in number—a tower of two or three blocks, a scribbled drawing, a simple puzzle put together—but they are developmental landmarks all the same. Piaget has brilliantly described and explained the significance of some of these developments. His work, along with that of others, enables us to see the strands of development that lead from little interest in the outside world during the first month of life; through practice in using the hands as reaching tools; on to mastery of other basic manual skills such as grasping, releasing, and throwing; and finally to an increasing interest in the world of objects, their qualities, and their paths of motion.

Toys

What role do toys play in this development? It would seem that their contribution is potentially significant, for our studies indicate that babies are involved in nonsocial experiences considerably more than half of their waking lives. Although some of that time is spent eating and a good deal is spent looking steadily at things or people, defending territory, or just idling, much of it—thousands of hours—is spent interacting with physical objects large and small. Furthermore, this involvement with objects leads to interchanges between infant and mother that generally set the stage for verbal and social learning. For a sense of how a child spends time, see the activity charts that follow.

The ideal toy would be safe, appropriate to the child's level of devel-

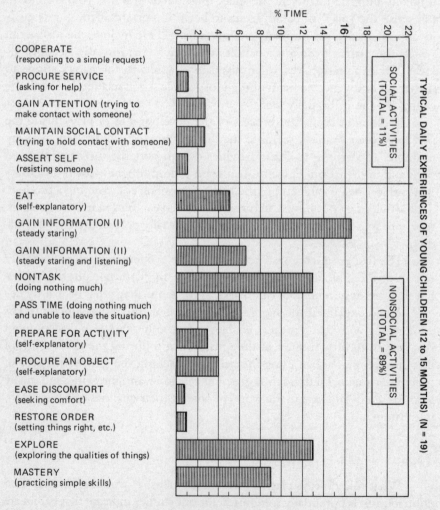

Typical Daily Experiences of Young Children (12–15 Months) (N = 19)

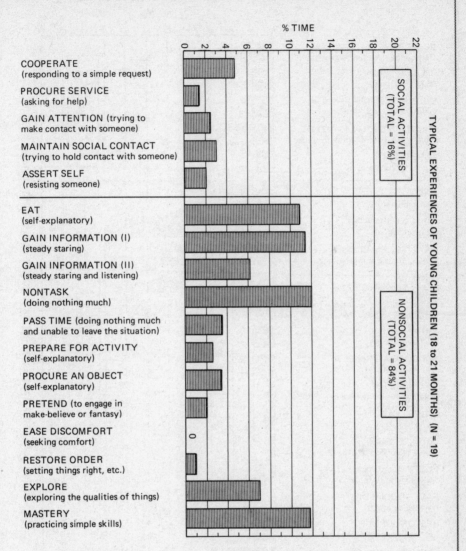

Typical Daily Experiences of Young Children (18–21 Months) (N = 19)

opment, fun, and even educational in the sense of stimulating the child's body and mind.

Until recently the challenge of creating even a good toy seems to have been too much for most designers in the toy business, but that situation is gradually changing. Now quite a few really good toys are available for children less than three years of age. You still have to be selective, and your best

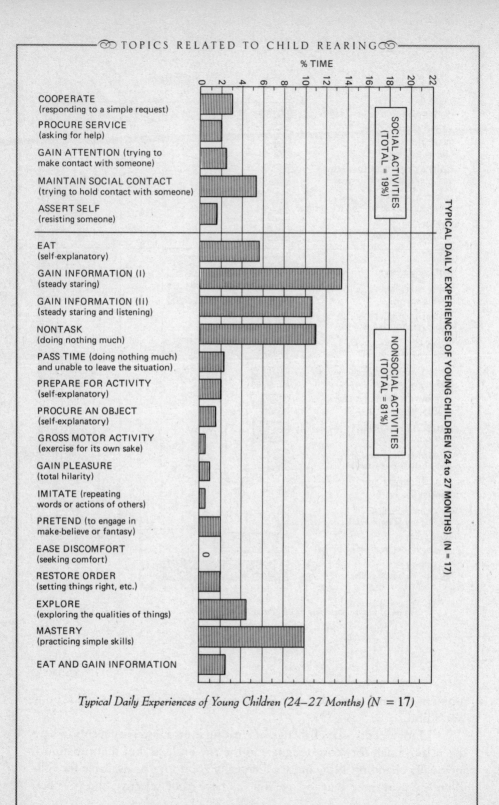

Typical Daily Experiences of Young Children (24–27 Months) (N = 17)

guide is a sure understanding of the rapidly evolving interests and abilities of your child.

Toys can be specially designed to be toys, or they can be any objects children play with regardless of their intended use. Either way, toys are part of the lives of children from very early on.

During the first three years of a child's life I see four distinct stages in respect to toys. In stage one, from birth to about seven months, babies get around little on their own, and toys can be very useful in helping to make the child's immediate surroundings interesting and instructive.

In stage two, from about seven to fourteen months, babies are normally excited and challenged by the process of mastering their bodies, especially in moving about and climbing. They find ever-new vistas for exploration, if they are allowed to, and social development begins to proceed rapidly. During this stage, toys, especially store-bought ones, play a smaller role in children's daily activities. There is simply too much competition for their attention.

The third stage covers the rest of the second year and corresponds to Phase VI of the child's developmental pattern. Social development in relation to the primary caregiver, usually the mother, occupies the center of the toddler's daily life. As a result, the toys of greatest interest to him are those that are useful in social activities, especially those involving the primary caregiver. The most conspicuous example is books.

Stage four corresponds to Phase VII, the third year of life. Because of remarkable developments in language, intelligence, and imagination, the role of toys is great in this period. Those that nourish the fantasy play of the two-year-old are especially effective during the third year of life.

In our research we routinely recorded what infants and toddlers did from moment to moment under natural circumstances in their own homes. We also kept track of their movements about the home and what objects they dealt with. At times over the years, I have worked for or consulted with most of the major manufacturers of toys for children under three. It is from this background that I provide the following information about toys.

MOBILES

For years parents have bought or received mobiles, along with rattles, as the first toys for their child. Mobiles, in fact, have legitimate uses for children. Toward the end of the first month, babies first begin showing substantial interest in exploring their surroundings. Since their abilities are very limited, a mobile is one of the few toys that makes sense for a baby less than one month old. Babies between three and nine weeks of age, when on their backs, lie in the tonic neck reflex (TNR) position, in which the head is turned to

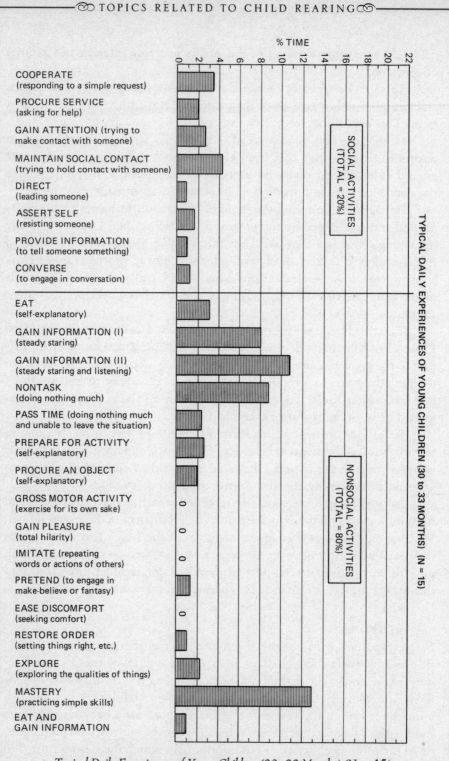

Typical Daily Experiences of Young Children (30–33 Months) (N = 15)

the side, usually the right, most of the time. It is rare for such an infant to spend much time looking directly overhead. Anything hung directly over the center of the crib is not nearly as likely to be looked at as something suspended above and to the far right or to the far left. An appropriate mobile should be designed so that its principal features are oriented toward the baby. Moreover, it should be interesting to the baby. We know that babies especially like to look at the upper half of the human face. A well-designed mobile should include a pattern of that sort.

Another consideration is how far away the mobile should be placed. When it comes to viewing their surroundings, babies do not do as well at three to nine weeks as they will when they are a few months older. In the three- to nine-week period, they are most comfortable looking at targets from seven to about sixteen inches away.

Another reason for placing mobiles at least seven or eight inches away is so that babies won't be able to reach them: these first mobiles are for looking only. When the baby gets to be eight to ten weeks of age she will become interested in more than merely looking; her interest will shift toward her own hands and the task of learning to use them. From that point forward your baby will need something that she can strike or handle.

A minority of the commercially available mobiles are now designed with some of these considerations in mind, but you can easily make a better one yourself. For detailed instructions, see the appropriate section in the treatment of Phase I (Chapter 2).

If you stand back and look at what you have created, it may not look like much, but over a period of days or weeks, chances are pretty good that your baby will spend a fair amount of time looking at the faces. An added tip: some people have found that mounting such a mobile over the changing table helps make diapering easier.

Whether or not you use a mobile is not likely to be of vital importance for the baby's development. It is, however, one of the very first steps in the process of designing a world around the baby that is appropriate to her rapidly changing interests and abilities.

RATTLES

Another perennial gift for the newborn baby, the rattle, is not suitable for the first months of life. Newborns cannot clearly see, reach for, or hang on to small objects. A new infant cannot even hold a rattle unless it is forced into her clenched fist. Once it is placed there, any baby under two months of age will ignore it.

Once your baby acquires some hand–eye skill and an increasingly strong tendency to gum objects, rattles become more useful. This usually happens from about four months on. Over the next several months, a rattle that offers a small challenge to your baby's limited hand-eye skill will be of interest to him. One of the best rattles consists of plastic keys on a ring and costs about two dollars.

FLOOR AND CRIB GYMS

Once your baby is ten or eleven weeks of age, he will enter a new stage. He will no longer be content with just looking: he will want to touch, handle, and hit as well. This desire to explore objects is part of the process that will eventually lead to reaching ability (by about five and a half months). In the beginning, however, touching consists mostly of striking or batting objects with a fist. Not until sometime during the third month are babies able to use their fingers effectively for exploring, because it is not until then that the innate grasp reflex relaxes its hold on her fingers. Nevertheless, from age seven or eight weeks or so, you should, at times when she is comfortable, provide your infant with objects within striking distance.

A number of toys can be used for this purpose. The central fact to remember is that a baby who has reached ten to twelve weeks of age will show a keen interest in batting objects and, as he gets a bit older, in exploring their shapes and textures with his fingers and, of course, trying to get them to his mouth. For this reason, objects suspended on strings are less appropriate for this stage than those that yield slightly when struck, then return to place. String-mounted objects can be frustrating to an infant just beginning to learn to reach.

For years, the best toy for batting and touching was the crib gym. During the 1980s crib gyms were mostly supplanted by floor gyms. Floor gyms are good toys for the two-and-a-half- to six-month-old. So are crib gyms, although they have become hard to find. Many floor gyms are narrow enough so that they can be placed in a crib over your baby.

A tip: When using a floor gym, place your baby in an infant seat (your car seat will do); babies lying beneath a floor gym have to fight gravity to reach up and touch the suspended objects.

BUSY-BOX TOYS

Millions of versons of the legendary busy box, or activity box, have been sold. In recent years, with the increasing interest in materials for very young children, three or four copies of the original busy box have been created by several toy manufacturers. While many continue to be sold, none of them is a good toy for babies.

Busy boxes are recommended by toy companies for babies six months to two years of age, but few such babies ever spend much time with them beyond a few minutes when they are first offered. For a toy to be worth buying it has to have enough intrinsic play value so that the child will go back to it at least once in a while and for at least a few minutes each time. That does not happen with the busy box. The sole power of such toys is, in my opinion, their appeal to adults—they look as though babies should like them.

A child a little older than two may use any kind of toy, including this one, as a device for engaging the attention of an older person. Nothing is wrong with this, but it does not mean that the toy has play value. My message is this: skip the busy box.

Twenty years ago, again on the basis of our observations in homes, I strongly recommended a related toy from the maker of the original busy box for babies between ten and twenty months of age. That toy was then called the Surprise Busy Box. The toy is still sold, but now it is called the Disney Busy Poppin' Pals toy. It consists of several compartments in a row with tops that spring open, each cover operated by a different mechanism. The toy is likely to appeal to most babies between eight and fourteen months of age. The infant less than one year old can operate only the simple lever mechanism, which is similar to a light switch, and then only if it is hair-triggered. But by age fourteen months or so, toddlers can usually work all of the switches. You can expect many episodes of baby-initiated play with this kind of toy during these six months, provided that it is easily operated by your baby.

The apparent reasons for this toy's appeal are the youngster's strong interest in tasks that challenge hand-eye skills, his interest in the abrupt release of the compartment covers, the universal popularity of hinged objects among children of this age, and the pleasure that comes from successfully relatching the cover. Furthermore, these toys are sturdy: they can be dropped from chairs and tables repeatedly without breaking. All in all, this is an excellent toy, except that the newer versions—at least the ones we have sampled—are too difficult for babies less than eighteen months or so to operate. Unfortunately, by that age, the toy is much less appealing.

Fisher-Price makes a good alternative. It is called the pop-up bunny. This is one of a large number of toys that have been designed over the last decade to take advantage of the success of the Busy Surprise Box. This one is the easiest model to operate. It is a square box with only one compartment. To get the cover to pop open the baby has to strike a horizontal roller. When it rotates it releases the top and voilà! Up pops a bunny or a bear. We recommend the toy for babies as young as seven months of age, especially if they can sit up unaided. Its appeal will last about two months.*

*We have found many of these toys do not work well. Also, the Mattel Company, which now owns Fisher-Price, may discontinue this toy.

The next easiest to operate is the version made by Shelcore, one of the more reliable companies offering toys for babies. It, too, has several compartments, but unlike current versions of the Busy Surprise Box, one or two are generally within the capacity of a nine- or ten-month-old to operate.

Why aren't more good toys available? For the same reason we don't have more fun and less stress raising our children: because it has taken a long time for reliable, detailed knowledge about babies to be generated, and though enough is now known, it is not known widely enough to be used routinely by toy companies.

I have spent many hours talking with leading toy designers. They are invariably very able people who understand the economic factors affecting toy design very well. They know how much individual pieces and whole toys are likely to cost to manufacture, and they have a good feel for whether or not that cost will get in the way of sales. They know a great deal about materials and manufacturing. And they know how to appeal to toy buyers— parents and grandparents in particular. They know how to make an attractive package and how to advertise a toy.

Toy companies have made lots of money selling toys for babies over the last several years. But they still don't understand as much as they should about the creature for whom they are designing the toys. Babies change very rapidly in the first three years, more rapidly than they do during the remainder of their lives. You cannot, for example, make a toy for a baby who is two months of age and expect it to be appealing to a baby who is two years of age, even though, from the perspective of the toy manufacturer, it would be very nice if you could.

In my mind there is absolutely no question that we could have better commercial toys than are currently available. During the last twenty-five years, much really useful information about babies has been developed through research. By making more use of this information, toy companies could do a valuable public service.

If what I believe about the educational significance of the first years is even partly true, the production of toys for the first three years of life may someday have to be considered a responsibility of the school system. In the meantime, however, responsible toy manufacturers could do a lot to fill the gap.

Safety should be your paramount concern when choosing materials for use with infants and toddlers. Beware of poorly made toys. Beware especially of small objects that might become lodged in a baby's mouth. Parts that can become separated from larger objects are just as dangerous as individual small items. No object with a major dimension less than one and a half inches is safe for an infant or toddler. You can also determine whether a small object is dangerous by testing it with a simple gadget called a no-choke tube. If the object fits into the tube, it is too small for a baby to play with safely. You can procure the device through the Toys To Grow On catalog (1-800-542-8338). Currently it costs about one dollar.

If you buy a used toy for your baby and it has been repainted, you must be sure that the paint is not toxic. If you have any doubt at all on this issue, don't buy the toy.

BASIC TOYS AND RELATED EQUIPMENT FOR THE FIRST THREE YEARS OF LIFE

1. A comfortable rocking chair for you, for use from birth on. Cost: $60 or more. To help you comfort a baby in distress, and for sheer enjoyment for both adult and baby. Close body contact while being moved rhythmically is enjoyable at all ages. It is particularly soothing to infants during the first months of life.

2. Six Nuk or other major brand of orthodontic pacifier, for use from birth to seven months or older. Cost: $1.50. To help you soothe an uncomfortable baby. Specialists in pediatric dentistry see nothing wrong with the use of a pacifier during the first years of life. Sucking, even when not followed by ingestion of fluids, is particularly soothing to infants during the first months of life. In my experience pacifiers have reduced more stress in infants and parents than can be calculated. Count me as an ardent advocate of pacifiers. You ought to know how to introduce them to your baby. See the appropriate passages in the section on Phase I (Chapter 2).

3. One or more mobiles, for use from three to nine weeks only. Cost in materials: $1. To provide something attractive for the baby to look at when she is alone. Babies begin to show interest in the outside world toward the end of the first month. A mobile can be very appealing for the next two months or so. To make your own see Chapter 2.

4. Two good-quality unbreakable mirrors, one about six inches across (circular or square), the other about eight by twelve inches, for use from three weeks to six months, with occasional use for several additional months. The small one should be attached to the side of the crib in a place where your baby can easily see herself. It should be tilted toward her at about a 10-degree angle so that her line of sight, when she is lying on her back, will be perpendicular to it. The larger mirror should be mounted vertically at the head of the crib, so that when she is placed on her stomach, five or six inches away from it, she can catch a glimpse of her upper body when she raises her head about 30 degrees. You can expect her to be able to do this at about four to six weeks of age. Cost: about $10 for the small one. Both Fisher-Price and Mattel make one with a built-in 10-degree angle. (You're not the only one who reads this book.) I do not recommend the convex type. Why distort the world for an infant who is trying to figure out what it's like? The larger mirror unfortunately sells for about $30.

5. A crib gym, for babies from ten weeks to six months. Cost: about $20. Very few crib gyms are being sold nowadays. One of the better ones is made by Ambi, a Dutch company that makes several good toys for babies. Use masking tape to prevent objects from rotating away from the baby and frustrating her. A crib gym will provide opportunities for your baby to explore his nearby world while also learning to use his hands under the guidance of his eyes. Avoid the kind that has objects suspended by strings, as this arrangement tends to frustrate infants. Note: a child who can pull himself up to a sitting position is too old for a crib gym.

6. A floor gym, for use from two and one-half to six months. Cost: about $20. More than half a dozen brands are now available. They are pretty much alike. I would avoid the one on which objects are suspended from plastic links. It is too difficult for the infant to grasp them. Also avoid the type that is too wide to place in the crib over the baby.

7. An infant seat, for use from birth to three months. Cost: about $20. Make sure that it is well made and stable. Babies over four months of age are often able to tip these seats over. Furthermore, such babies are better off on blankets or safe flat surfaces. Many models are available, and they enable you to move the small infant around the house with ease. As head control gets better, babies enjoy looking at more and more of their surroundings, and an infant seat also increases the opportunity for adults and babies to play face-to-face games. Car seats can take the place of infant seats and can be a bit better in that the angle of the typical infant seat is too shallow for a baby over three months of age.

8. A Jolly Jumper type toy. Cost: about $30. For use from about four months and one week to about eight months. Fisher-Price makes an excellent one. I don't recommend the all canvas seat, but rather one with a padded plastic frame. Babies enjoy the bouncing action and their parents' excitement as they watch. This toy will also help hold down the overdevelopment of the intentional cry for company.

9. A small, well-made walker, for use from four and a half months to the crawling stage. Cost: about $35. The Graco Totwheels II is very good. This device will relieve boredom and frustration by giving the baby mobility and will help keep down the overdevelopment of the intentional cry for company. It's an important device that should be used only under supervision.

10. The Fisher-Price pop-up bunny or bear, for use from seven to ten months. Cost: about $17. Widely available. This toy helps feed the baby's interest in operating simple gadgets and is a great toy to hold in reserve for emergency distraction. It is one of the very few commercial toys with great play value.

11. The Shelcore pop-up toy. Cost: about $16. This serves the same purposes as the pop-up bunny or bear for the nine- to fourteen-month period.

12. Just about any bath toy, for use from seven months to two years. Cost: about $10–20. The best do more than float. If the toy has a water wheel, a squirter, or a bubble-maker, it will have maximum appeal. Babies love water play, and the variations in toys are infinite. These items will help during bath time. This toy has lots of play value and is very sturdy. But don't forget to duck.

13. A bathtub support seat, for use from six to eight months when babies are not fully able to sit without support. Cost: about $20. Several makes are available. This gadget, which sticks to the tub with suction cups, makes the bath a time for fun rather than apprehension.

14. A Gertie ball. Cost: less than $4. Blow this soft, inflatable ball up to about six inches. Even a baby only seven months old can pick it up because of its softness. A best buy. Remove it when your baby is fourteen months old.

15. About six books with stiff pages (board books), for use from ten to fourteen months. Cost: about $1 to $3 each. At ten months of age, your baby will practice hand-eye skills by separating and turning the pages. He will also gum the book, and he will occasionally look at the pages. At fourteen months, he will spend less time practicing skills and gumming and more time examining the book's contents. As your baby enters Phase VI, at fourteen months of age, he will use books for more conventional purposes.

16. A toy telephone, for use from one to three years. Cost: about $8.00. This toy will enhance your baby's emerging interest in make-believe activity. (She will have even more fun with the real phone.)

17. Six to twelve balls, especially inflatable beach balls up to twenty-four inches in diameter—the bigger the better. Ping-Pong balls are useful too, but only for a child over fourteen months of age and only with supervision. For use from age one year on. Cost: $1 to $3 each. The ball is the single most popular type of toy during the second year of life. It is great for learning about the movements of objects; for practicing throwing, chasing, picking up, and carrying; and for getting someone else to play along. The epitome of elegance in babies' toys.

18. Pots and pans, as many as you can spare, for use from seven to fourteen months. No toy list would be complete without pots and pans to feed the child's curiosity about objects and sounds.

19. Three stair gates, for use from seven months to two years. Cost: $15–60. Install one gate at the top of the stairs. Place the second gate at the lip of the third step from the bottom, to allow stair climbing without anxiety or supervision. Place a cushion on the floor at the foot of the stairs in case of a fall. Supervise the baby's first attempts and make a big fuss over her successes. Climbing downstairs is mastered several weeks after climbing upstairs. It helps if you teach her how. The third gate will be necessary during the fourteen- to twenty-two-month period if you follow my advice on discipline.

20. A playpen. Yes, a playpen, for use from five to fifteen months. Cost: about $30. To fill the need for a safe place to put a baby for a few minutes when, for example, the floor is wet or when a pot is boiling over. Do not get into the habit of putting a child in a playpen or any other restrictive device for long periods of time, however. The second syllable, "pen," is much more accurate in describing this device than the first, "play." Manufacturers now call them playyards.

21. Plastic containers with lids, for use from seven to fifteen months. Empty ice-cream containers are also fine—the more the better. To feed a baby's strong interest in mastering hand-eye skills. These containers can also be used for water play. Babies in this age range are intrigued by their developing hand-eye skills. They enjoy removing and replacing the lids. Some frustration is likely, but you can keep it down by providing materials that are not too difficult for the baby.

22. A large plastic container filled, or partly filled, with at least a dozen small but safe objects such as large thread spools and plastic doodads, for use from seven to fifteen months. To facilitate exploration of small objects and practice of hand-eye skills. Your baby will examine these objects one at a time or, at other times, will dump them all out at once. Sometimes he will then put them all back. A small plastic laundry basket is ideal.

23. A small, low, four-wheeled toy with a handle like that on a supermarket shopping cart, to push or to sit on while moving here and there, for use from eleven to fifteen months. Cost: about $20. There are many good models on the market; Little Tikes makes an excellent one. For fun.

24. Large empty boxes, for use from one to two years. Purpose: having fun.

25. A children's wading pool. Cost: about $10. All babies love water, but your baby should use the pool only with supervision.

26. A sandbox. Cost: $50–75. Babies love sandboxes. Don't forget to cover the box when it's not in use.

27. A doll and doll carriage or stroller, for use from fourteen months to three years. Cost: about $25. To feed a rapidly growing imagination. This toy's worth has been validated by time.

28. An outdoor swing, for use from one to three years. Cost: about $35.00. Make sure the swing is sturdy. Most children love being swung through the air.

29. About forty story and picture books (the more the better), for use from fourteen months to three years. Cost: about $3 each. To support the development of language, curiosity, and a healthy social life. The child's language achievement level after fourteen months will be suited to storytelling. The strong social interest of the second year heightens the pleasure. You can start a bit earlier, but do not be surprised if the child shows very little sustained interest until eighteen or more months of age.

30. Electronic books. Cost: about $18. By pushing one of several pictures in a column on the side of the page, the baby can produce dramatic sound effects linked to the story. I like these books, and so do most Phase VI children.

31. Scribbling and drawing materials for use from eighteen months onward. Cost: about $10 for the basics. To encourage drawing and the use of writing implements. Get washable nontoxic crayons and markers. Representational drawing emerges during the third year. Do not be surprised if your baby uses the crayons on surfaces you would rather not see decorated.

32. Puzzles, for use from fourteen and a half months onward. Cost: $5–15 each. Get two or three, at least, at each of the four levels of difficulty. Puzzles provide a simple challenge to hand-eye skills, a sense of achievement, and an opportunity for parents to reinforce the child's pride of accomplishment. Be careful to match the level of difficulty with the child's ability to deal with frustration, especially during the seventeen- to twenty-month period. Some children get to be amazingly skillful at these, sometimes succeeding faster than adults.

33. The Fisher-Price family playhouse or garage, or any similar scenario toy (many are available) for use from twenty months to three years. Cost: about $20. To encourage imagination and fantasy activities. Babies are now ready for play that involves organization and themes. For this and other reasons, these toys work. All Fisher-Price toys are well made, and scenario toys are great for children of this age.

34. A slide and a climbing toy with ladder and play area under the platform, for use from eighteen months to three years. Cost: $50–60. Little Tikes makes a good one. For enjoyment of large-muscle activities. Interest in gymnastics is high throughout these first years. These toys are well made; too bad they cost so much, but remember, there is always something to climb at home.

35. A play kitchen, for use from eighteen months to three years. Cost: $50–80. Little Tikes makes a highly recommendable one. Of course, the kitchen should be equipped with play food, groceries, and pots and pans. This item feeds the child's interest in make-believe play. A real winner.

36. A low table and two chairs, suitable for "afternoon tea and snacks," for use from eighteen months to three years. Cost: about $35. A proper complement to the child's kitchen. These toys appeal to both boys and girls at this age.

37. A small tricycle, for use from two to three years. Cost: $16–25. After two years of age, you can teach most children to use the pedals.

TOYS AND EDUCATION

During the first three years of life toys vary in their attractiveness depending on the developmental level of the child. Before a baby can crawl, toys can hold his attention better than they will in the months that follow. This is because the very young infant can neither change his own location and scenery nor practice the various motor skills involved in crawling, climbing, walking, and so forth.

From early crawling to about fourteen months, the excitement and challenges associated with the new ability to move about overwhelm the appeal of nearly all toys. From fourteen to twenty-four months, most children become intensely interested in the person with whom they spend the bulk of their waking hours. While motor activities and visual exploration continue, social needs assume the highest priority. Toys that are conducive to social interchanges, therefore, become more appealing. Storybooks and fantasy tools—for example, telephones and dolls—gradually become more popular in the second half of the second year.

Finally, during the third year, the progress made in language and intellectual skills and the child's resolution of the power struggles of Phase VI combine to make toys much more enticing than they had been since the first months of life.

Throughout the first three years you should try to maintain a balance in the child's interests: give him not only the chance to play with toys, pots and pans, and the like, but also the opportunity to exercise and practice physical skills; and give him the opportunity to interact with other people in fantasy games, ball games, reading, and so on. There is no need to push a child from one activity to another. The best clue that learning is taking place is the child's interest in what he is doing. If he is fascinated by any activity, that probably means it has learning value.

Throughout these early years, regular lengthy periods of boredom are not a good sign. A basic feature of first-rate early development is that from the second month of life on through the third year the child is engaged in interesting activities most of the time. During this period it is the parents who make such regular involvement possible. Provided you learn about the evolving interests and abilities of your child, creating these opportunities is not a very difficult task. Toys can play a role in the process, but they are not vital.

"EDUCATIONAL" TOYS

I feel quite confident in telling you that to do a superb job of educating a child in the first three years of life you do not have to buy a single "educational" toy. Anything that genuinely interests a child, be it only an empty ice-cream container, is educational.

Many parents wonder whether certain toys will help to lengthen a youngster's attention span. Three factors determine the length of time a child devotes to one activity: (1) the basic ability of the child to maintain focused attention on any topic or object, (2) the attractiveness, or interest value, of a topic or object, and (3) individual differences among children.

As to the young child's basic ability to maintain steady attention, some professionals feel that young children are quite limited in this regard, and that, because of this limitation, they may not actually be ready for school even by their sixth birthday. Everyday observations tend to reinforce that view. Toddlers and preschoolers sometimes move from one activity to another more rapidly than older children and adults. But why a person at any age shifts her focus depends on more than the capacity for sustained attention. At the very least, it also depends on whether she is still interested in that activity. But attention also depends on physical circumstances such as fatigue or jitteriness, and on whether distractions are present. Phase I babies (birth to six weeks) rarely show sustained visual attention in anything. They may, of course, be pondering some subject within the mind's eye, but the burden is on someone to prove it, and that is not likely to happen.

From the end of Phase I on, however, the growth of the capacity for sustained attention is obvious. Three-month-old babies can and do study their own hand and finger movements for as long as ten continuous minutes. They do so apparently because it is very important for all humans to learn to use their own hands as tools. In other words, the basic capacity for sustained attention of impressive duration emerges very early in life.

This fact points strongly to the conclusion that lack of sustained interest by a two-year-old—whether it involves a toy, a story, or a television program—is not likely to be due to an inadequate capacity for sustained attention. But as for helping to expand a child's basic attention span, whether through toys or any other medium, I am afraid we know little about how we could do so or, for that matter, about whether we should try.

The only hint we have arises from two related research findings. In one study we found a strong positive correlation between the usual length of time young children spent in steady looking (at objects and people) and their later general level of achievement. In another study we found an even stronger positive correlation between the usual length of time spent in steady looking, while an adult talked about what was being looked at, and later achievement. Thus, talking to a baby about what she is attending to may help increase her ability to attend. We are not sure of this. We cannot even prove that greater attending ability of this kind is good. But if you suspect that it is, you are not alone: so do I.

Experience Versus Heredity: The Nature-Versus-Nurture Controversy

The relative contribution to achievement of experience versus heredity has dominated early childhood research throughout its history. From time to time this debate seems temporarily resolved, at least in a superficial sense, only to resurface a decade later just as vigorously as before.

During the late nineteenth century it was assumed that inherited characteristics were of the greatest importance with respect to achievement. The child's nature was believed to be pretty much brought into the world with him. The influence of Freud and his followers and of people in learning theory, starting with Ivan Pavlov, the Russian physiologist, rebutted this orthodoxy; and during the second and third decades of the twentieth century people became increasingly impressed with the importance of early experiences, particularly those of the first five years of life.

A counterreaction began during the 1930s, with Arnold Gesell, the Dr. Spock of the 1940s, among its leaders. The result was a host of experiments designed to show that there were limits to what early teaching could do for a child. For example, interesting studies were done in which identical twins were used to show the importance of maturation and the genetic timetable. In one case a twin was taught to roller skate earlier than he might ordinarily have been. But when the other twin was taught the activity at a more appropriate (later) age, he caught up quickly.

Similar experiments were done using scissors and stair climbing. The tide in the 1930s turned away from emphasis on the power of early experiences and back toward the importance of maturation and inherited traits.

We saw a reversal yet again in the 1950s and 1960s, as the work of Piaget became more influential and as the civil rights movement gathered power. The undying optimism that we always seem to have about the potential of children again pushed its way to the forefront. This resulted in more and more research and practical activity based on the notion that early experience was important. Thus the 1960s saw the establishment of such programs as Project Head Start, designed to help young children obtain better early educational experiences.

Today the controversy is far from over. We still do not have enough dependable evidence to make reliable judgments about how much achievement can be ascribed to experience and how much to innate competence. Perhaps the most succinct way to express my own judgment in this matter is this statement: what a child brings into the world sets an upper limit to the achievement level that he can attain, but it provides no guarantee whatsoever that any achievement will take place. A child with the best possible central nervous system and physical apparatus at birth will not achieve even average levels of competence unless the experiential requirements are there. The most perfectly endowed baby can be prevented from ever learning language simply by being prevented from ever hearing any. Such a child will never reach his intellectual potential, nor will he be a particularly effective social animal. Genes set the upper limits that each child can attain. Experiences determine just how much of the baby's potential is realized.

The responsibility of those of us who rear children is not really much affected by the nature-nurture debate. We are obliged to provide the best possible experiences that we can, particularly in the first years of life, regardless of the amount of inherited potential of a child.

Having a First Baby When You Are a Bit Older

We work with many families where the mother is having her first child when she is in her thirties. We work regularly with women who are in their early forties and having their first baby. These women are in a first-rate education and support program. They do very well. For the majority of such families, there is absolutely nothing worrisome to us about their capacity to do the job. Indeed, their maturity is almost always an obvious advantage.

One special hazard does seem to make the child-rearing task more difficult for some older mothers: a minority seem to have more of a tendency to overindulge their children than do younger women. This is no small consideration when it occurs. In addition, for obvious reasons, older mothers are more likely to feel they have to have their second child quickly, to minimize the likelihood of possible birth defects and other physical problems.

PART II: OTHER ISSUES

Programs That Promise Precocity

The Better Baby Institute, founded by Glenn Doman in 1978 and based in Philadelphia, promises parents smarter and more capable babies if the parents attend a four-and-a-half-day training program. Twenty years ago Doman was urging parents to help their children learn to read during infancy by using a specially prepared kit. National news magazines such as *Time* and *Newsweek* have also featured Doman's work.

Professionals have been either puzzled or enraged. Does Glenn Doman know a dramatically better way to raise a baby? Are parents making a mistake if they do not closely monitor and stimulate development from birth? Are the typical anxieties and keenly felt ambitions that some parents have for their children being exploited? The national YMCA was similarly upset about programs designed to teach swimming to infants.

On the other hand, many have been impressed by violin and piano skills shown by preschool students who have been exposed to the Suzuki training methods. What does it all mean?

The achievements people seek in their children range from the conventional to the extreme. Most parents want their children to develop free from handicaps, to become capable, well balanced, confident, and comfortable with other people. "Capable" usually means as far above average as their congenital potential will allow. Most parents' aspirations do not include professional skills in such areas as tennis, ice-skating, and music or genius levels in math. This is not to say that parents would not value such skills, but rather that they usually do not set such goals and pursue them avidly.

Some people, however, very much want very high levels of achievement for their children as soon as possible. Their ambitions range from reading before three years of age to acquiring a prodigious vocabulary early in life, learning to swim during infancy, and learning to play a musical instrument. Can anyone really produce such results? The most widely accepted study of the growth of intelligence during the first three years of life is the work of Piaget, but nothing in his work directly addresses the question of how to help a child become very bright very early. He simply was not interested in that subject. At present many studies of gifted children are taking place, but as yet no substantial knowledge exists on how to bring about giftedness.

One relevant study was our own Harvard Preschool Project. With a large staff and generous funds, we spent thirteen years examining the histories of children who developed unusually well during the preschool years. But we were interested in balanced development, and in fact we deliberately excluded intellectually or artistically precocious children who were not equally capable of interacting with others or who were weak in any other major area of development.

Our research taught us very little of consequence about how to produce precocious children. It has shown us that helping most babies become bright is rather easy to do, but we have always valued healthy social development at least as highly as any other goal. Interestingly, I do not believe any programs that promise precocity place social skills, compassion, and happiness at the top of their list of goals. Neither we nor anyone else can provide any direct basis in research for any program that promises intellectual giftedness.

Is there nevertheless a basis in well-established practice that would help parents encourage precocious development in their children? In Montessori preschools the successful teaching of reading and writing to preschoolers has been demonstrated repeatedly over the decades. At the University of Kansas preschool, teaching preschoolers to tie their own shoelaces (no easy task) has also been demonstrated repeatedly. These examples confirm what has been believed for many years: children can be taught some skills considerably earlier in life than is customary. The more complicated questions are these: Does it make sense to do so? And what are the costs?

Each program that claims success requires regular, extensive teaching and practice sessions. None has been subjected to controlled testing. In none has there been an examination as to whether a child's intrinsic interest in learning has been affected. In none has anyone examined the impact of less than expected progress on the feelings between parents and children. In other words, nothing is known about side effects.

Little is known about long-term effects as well. David Elkind, author of *The Hurried Child* and a respected child development researcher, has reported that early reading ability is often linked to later academic problems. He has been very emphatic in recommending that parents not seek to encourage precocious development in their children.

What about the Suzuki approach? Unlike Doman's Better Baby Institute, the Suzuki approach does not claim to produce extraordinary achievement in all major facets of development. The Suzuki method has been in existence in many locations with conspicuous success (in respect to musical training only) for many years, and there is nothing secretive about it: the procedures are available for examination by anyone.

What are the potential disadvantages of special teaching programs for the very young? If the program requires several hours of practice or study each day for parents and children over a long period of time, I believe that a child's spontaneous interest and pleasure in learning are likely to be jeopardized. If the child must spend large portions of time in any narrowly focused direction, such as tennis, ice-skating, music, or reading, I believe she will probably have to pay a significant price in other developmental areas as well as in motivation to learn. A child might come to be valued too much for what she has achieved or whether she has met certain goals dictated by a program rather than for what she is, and I feel that this could be a serious negative factor in any young child's life.

During the early years children learn to relate to people in fundamental ways. That learning takes a lot of time. They also learn to use their bodies, and that learning takes time.

We have studied many children who developed into happy and very talented preschoolers. All of them spent most of their time in experiences they chose for themselves. They even spent a lot of time relaxing.

Any program that promises precocity ultimately has to be evaluated in the light of how much it may subtract from other important, even crucial, learning opportunities; and for these reasons I cannot recommend any program that promises precocious development during the first years of life.

There are some good lower-intensity alternatives, however. Many of the thousands of parent-support programs that have sprung up over the last twenty-five years include attention to learning during the first years, but they are not really concerned with setting new records in infant achievement.

Teaching Infants to Swim: Beware!

As part of the dramatically increased interest in educating babies, a good deal of attention has been paid to teaching infants to swim, or at least attempting to drownproof them. Given my feelings about high-intensity early-achievement programs in general, you might not be surprised to learn that I am unenthusiastic about this type of program.

Actually, this topic is something of a special case, made more confusing because of the conflicting safety and enjoyment factors involved. No one would disagree with the desirability of helping to avoid infant drownings, nor would anyone object to an activity that brings parents and their young children together for the delightful shared experiences that programs of this nature promise.

But now a new consideration has surfaced, one that is of great importance and that must be brought to the attention of everyone concerned with infants. It is called *water intoxication*.

In an article in the YMCA magazine, *Discover* (May-June 1983), Marjorie M. Murphy, aquatic director of YMCA of the United States, and Charles Fiske, an editorial assistant, registered substantial concern about infant swimming lessons and cited several instances of serious harm done to infants during such lessons. In each case, harm was attributed to confirmed reports of an infant swallowing too much water, resulting in the condition known as water intoxication. Consequently, the YMCA has endorsed the policy of the Council for National Cooperation in Aquatics, as expressed in its statement that "Children under three should not be entered into organized swimming instruction classes." The CNCA has issued ten guidelines that characterize safe programs for children under three years of age. I consider this subject so important that I shall quote at length from the YMCA article:

> *Water intoxication occurs when a person swallows enough water to lower significantly the concentration of salt (sodium) in the blood. This causes the brain to swell, which in turn produces a decreased level of consciousness, progressing from lethargy to stupor to coma. Seizures may also occur. With appropriate treatment the condition is reversible, as long as there isn't oxygen deprivation due to prolonged respiratory arrest during seizures, vomiting, or choking. The symptoms included restlessness, weakness, nausea, muscle-twitching, convulsions, and coma.*
>
> *None of the children was noticed to be in trouble when in the water—choking or gasping. Doctors did not find water in their lungs.*
>
> *Adults and larger children cannot normally drink enough water to cause water intoxication. But small infants are vulnerable for two reasons: their lower body weight (and blood volume) and the natural reflex of an infant to swallow when anything enters its mouth. Swimming experts agree that an infant automatically holds its breath when submerged; but infants do open their mouths and swallow all the water that comes in.*
>
> *Doctors have identified water intoxication as a problem for years, but not until recently did they notice it could occur while swimming. The cases they saw usually resulted from improper feeding of an infant when, for whatever reason, the parents gave water or diluted formula to the child. Symptoms follow the swallowing by three to eight hours, so many instructors never see them. Mild symptoms of lethargy or irritability might be thought to be normal signs that the baby is tired. In such cases children had a fine time swimming—the problem came later. . . .*
>
> *Finally, it is not established that any of the goals of swimming lessons for infants can be reached in a lasting way. Children with very early exposure to water have not proved to do any better in the long run than children who start later. Drownproofing is pointless until a child is old enough to know what is going on—that is, to really know that if he propels himself he will go in a certain direction, that if he just floats he will stay in one place, and so forth.*
>
> *Any good that comes from infant swimming programs is certainly outweighed*

by the risks of water intoxication. Based on what we have seen so far there is a clear danger that water intoxication can occur during any [swimming] lesson. The YMCA strongly urges that programs for children under the age of three should include a parent, and that very small children should not be placed underwater or allowed to drink pool water.

I can only concur: any teaching program that includes submersion of the infant definitely is not recommendable.

The YMCA guidelines for infant swimming programs are available from local YMCAs, physical education specialists, and aquatic coordinators. You can also write to the YMCA of the United States, 101 Wacker Drive, Chicago, Illinois 60606. Telephone: 312-977-0031.

The Role of the Father

Several books have been published on the role of the father in the development of the young child. In addition, research reports in leading journals and statements at conferences and in the popular media have focused on how important the father is to the developing child. Unfortunately, many of the assertions made about this topic have been unsupported and contradictory.

The most fundamental question is whether the absence of a father makes a significant difference in the development of a very young child. Since women have traditionally had the responsibility for most of the direct child-rearing activities with infants and toddlers, it is reasonable to ask whether a father or some other man is necessary in early child-rearing in order for the process to be fully successful.

If the father is expendable, all succeeding questions take on a different degree of importance, and the many women raising babies alone can breathe a collective sigh of relief. If, on the other hand, the father has a significant role to play, either directly with the child or indirectly through the mother, a whole host of other questions will surface. For example, are the child-rearing styles of a father different from a mother's? How much direct influence should the fathers have? How does the impact of the fathering style affect the mothering style and, in turn, the child's development?

Where do I stand on these questions? As with full-time substitute care for infants, existing research on this subject is simply too scarce for anyone to be dogmatic. Some older research has been used to claim that prolonged father absence leads to sexual problems for both boys and girls, with boys becoming less masculine and girls less feminine. That claim has not evolved into a generally accepted principle, however; it remains only an interesting speculation.

In our Harvard Preschool Project research a few of the children developing very well were being raised without fathers at home, but the number was too small to allow for generalizations. In succeeding years, I have become convinced that a woman can do a superb job of raising a child without a man, but that like any job that gets to be highly stressful and extremely exciting at times, it is better when you share it with someone.

Although men have not been much involved in the less pleasant aspects of child-rearing—such as diapering, discipline, and everyday stress—they have also had far fewer opportunities to share in the day-to-day rewards. Living with a healthy baby brings lots of absolutely wonderful pleasures, in great quantities, to the primary child-rearer.

In our model parent education program, we have had a fair number of role-reversal situations, where the father has been the principal child-rearer. As far as I can see, the only difference is that the father cannot breast-feed. Otherwise, the knack of good parenting does not seem to be restricted to women.

Full-time parenting of babies is for most people a very difficult job at times. For many reasons, I am strongly in favor of equally shared parenting. From my point of view the ideal child-rearing situation would consist of (1) equal time for both parents to share the job, (2) part-time work—perhaps as much as two-thirds time—for both parents once the baby reached seven or eight months of age, and (3) occasional use of high-quality substitute child care.

A Look at the Subject of Bonding

The concept of bonding came to the attention of the public as well as professionals about twenty years ago as a result of the work of two physicians at Case Western Reserve University (Cleveland, Ohio): Drs. Marshall K. Klaus and John H. Kennell. They reported that when mothers were given sixteen extra hours of contact with their children immediately after birth, the relationship between those mothers and their infants soon became more beneficial for both mother and child than under the normal procedures. In the more common situation a mother of a newborn spends very little time with the infant during its first day of life.

Klaus and Kennell reported that several years after birth, those mothers who had spent extra time in close contact with their newborn babies during the lying-in period tended to be more affectionate, more interested in, and less harsh with their children. Thus arose the concept of bonding: the (very) rapid development of an intense and healthful attachment between a newborn and her mother in the first hours of life.

This dramatic announcement, which seemed to offer exciting new information, immediately received great publicity. Quite a number of hospitals rapidly modified their practices so as to allow young mothers and their newborn babies to enjoy as much close contact as possible during the postnatal period.

The mothers in the original study of the bonding phenomenon were women of low-income families living in the Cleveland area. An attempt to repeat the findings with middle-class mothers was performed at Stanford University. The Stanford study found that in the first month of child-rearing, mothers who had the extra contact with their newborn babies were more inclined to cuddle their infants and be physically affectionate with them. They also seemed more confident as mothers. Yet by the end of the first year of the child's life, there seemed to be no differences between the behavior of mothers who had been given the extra contact and those who had not. More important, no differences were found in their children. The Stanford project concluded that factors such as the socioeconomic status of the parents and the sex of the infant were considerably more powerful in respect to child-rearing styles than the amount of early contact. When another attempt to repeat the original finding was conducted at the University of Colorado Medical School Center, this time with lower-middle-class mothers, the results were similar to those of the Stanford study.

Beyond these three studies few direct tests have been conducted of the concept of bonding. If only for that reason we should be all the more cautious about accepting the original claims.

When researchers are deciding whether to accept a new finding, they look to see how it fits in with other known evidence. A good deal of available information bears indirectly upon the issue of bonding. Some of this evidence concerns the general attachment process that takes place during the first two years of a child's life. Others deal with the nature of both the newborn child and the mother.

In regard to the attachment process, we have evidence from many studies of children and also of the young of other animals which clearly indicates that early experiences are important for lifelong emotional and social health and that a good early attachment is vital for physical, emotional, and educational growth. Yet by the same token, there is also much evidence showing that during the first three to four months of life babies are quite primitive. By that I mean they lack the mental equipment to understand what is going on around them or to identify any individual with any accuracy. It would appear that newborn babies will become attached to any older human who spends much time with them. For survival it is so important for them to become attached to an older human that from about two months on, they will respond with affectionate signs to just about anybody.

It is not until about the fourth month of life that babies begin to be selectively responsive to the people with whom they have been living, usually the mother. From that point on, the attachment becomes more focused, and toward the end of the second year the baby's entire day revolves around his mother or other primary caregiver.

This general picture of the process of developing attachments does not fit very well with the notion that the first few hours of life are especially significant from the baby's point of view. That could, however, be a special time from the point of view of the baby's mother. Although newborns are quite simple, undeveloped creatures from an intellectual, emotional, and social standpoint, that is not the case with respect to their parents. It is possible that a mother undergoes some uniquely important experience during the first day after the birth of her child that will somehow have a lasting effect on her child-rearing style and on her feelings for her baby.

What, then, of the original claim about the crucial importance of bonding in the first day of life? In favor of the claim we have only one study on a small group of mothers. But we have two other studies that fail to support the first one. Also casting doubt on the claim is a whole host of other evidence that points to the notion that bonding should be considered a subheading under the larger subject of attachment, a process that takes the better part of the first two years of life in most cases, and one that is so important to the survival of the species that it is not likely that its success depends heavily on the events that take place over a few days.

What would happen if we acted as though bonding did depend heavily on the events of a baby's first days of life? If this merely caused parents to spend more time with their babies in the first hours of their babies' lives, no harm would be done. Indeed, the experience would probably be quite enjoyable for everyone concerned. But then any mother who was prevented from having close contact with a new baby might very well come to fear that there would be no way she could ever have a first-rate relationship with her child.

Since many young mothers are unable, for a variety of reasons, to be with their babies during the first few days, the consequences of such fears would be widespread and harmful. The same would be true for adopting parents, who are almost never present during the first hours of their child's life.

In the interest of all such parents, I think it is important that we treat the entire concept of bonding with reserve. It is no more than a hypothesis, and not a very well supported one at that.

I might add here that in the thirty-eight years that I have been studying early human development I have seen the rise of any number of unusual ideas about birth and child-rearing, most of which could not be validated.

Some years back, for example, an obstetrician from Africa was treating his patients with a depressurization machine, a sort of inverted metal kettle within which the air pressure could be reduced. It was designed to fit over the abdomen of a woman late in pregnancy, and the lower pressure would reduce the external pressure on the abdominal walls. The woman would remain in this device for about a half hour, and this treatment would be repeated several times during the third trimester of pregnancy.

The claim of the doctor, published in legitimate journals, was that babies born after such a fetal experience were healthier, more alert, and generally better off. Further, he reported that when the babies were a year of age they had achieved higher developmental levels.

You can imagine the impact of such a report. People everywhere wanted to know where they could find doctors who had depressurization machines. Yet the depressurization fad soon evaporated, and today you never encounter information on this particular procedure. It is possible that in times to come we shall hear no more about "sudden" bonding, either.

In summary, the more physical contact babies have in the first months of life the better for all concerned. But clearly, the failure to have sixteen extra hours of close bodily contact in the first day of life should in no way jeopardize the growth of a healthy attachment relationship between parents and children.

Play Groups for Infants and Toddlers

A play group is a group for babies too young for nursery school. Traditionally this has meant children less than two and a half years of age, although lately some nursery schools have been accepting children as young as two years. Indeed, with shifting ideas on the importance of education during the first years of life, new "educational" programs are being created for even younger children.

Most people who get involved in play groups do so on a cooperative basis, with responsibility for the group taken by each family in turn. Children involved may range widely in age, but I would like to confine my comments to play groups for children between twelve and thirty months of age.

In studying children under thirty months of age, we have seen repeatedly that it is wrong to expect them to play together civilly. They are not ready for civility. Children between twelve and twenty-two months of age possess negligible social skills. Most of their social experience has usually been with only one or two very special caring adults. Not only do they lack social sophistication, but their age-mates are equally inexperienced. Left unsupervised, toddlers will behave more like small monkeys than small angels, using force to determine who is in charge. Moreover, children with siblings, especially those close in age, are more likely than only children to be either aggressive or wary as preschoolers.

Absolutely no justification exists for letting a baby be abused by another child. If your child encounters hostility from another preschooler, do not try to teach her how to deal with aggressive peers. Instead, avoid contact with such children. If your own child is being aggressive, put a stop to the behavior and limit her contact with her peers to those times when an adult can supervise closely what is happening.

If your child attends a play group, you must keep in mind that the only way to prevent some children from suffering and others from indulging in cruelty is to maintain close supervision. Do not assume that such supervision is taking place. If your child seems unhappy and there are signs that others are pushing her around, check out the situation and remove her if necessary.

Do children get any benefits from participating in a play group? One current view is that experience with age-mates promotes social development. Another is that babies can be helped intellectually by the stimulation of group activity. No one has as yet generated any evidence to support either claim, and in my view, parents should not expect such benefits from play groups.

Ordinarily, sometime during the third year of life, children begin to turn their attention away from an intense focus on the home, their parents, and their siblings and toward the exciting world of peers. That new interest grows ever stronger as the child grows older, but for children under two and a half years, the benefits of a play group are questionable at best.

Do parents get any benefits from play groups for children under thirty months? Undoubtedly. A parent can always profit from a regular brief respite from the continuous responsibility for a baby, especially during the second year of life. But if you do decide to place your twelve- to thirty-month-old child in a play group, be clear about what the hazards may be.

When Two Languages Are Spoken in the Home

Many parents have asked me what they should do about language learning when a child is being raised in a bilingual family. Since I am not an authority in this area, I consulted some language-learning specialists. I found that although no one has done research on the effects of one or another approach to language acquisition in a bilingual home, language-acquisition experts were in almost unanimous agreement on some points. They said that if both languages are spoken well, then both should be used with the child from the beginning in a natural way. Furthermore, they suggested that one parent use one language consistently and the other use the second language consistently.

The result, they theorized, should be as follows: during the first two to three years of life the child will be a bit slower than a monolingual child of comparable ability in the acquisition of language; but by the fourth or fifth birthday the child not only will have caught up but will be bilingual.

In the absence of any more substantial information, we have been passing that advice on to families we have worked with. Two dozen members of our New Parents program have followed that advice, and guess what? Not only did every one of their children become bilingual, but in every case the children developed faster in both languages than did our generally fast-developing monolingual children. A few of our children have even acquired three languages by their second birthday.

Not long ago, one such child, who had been exposed regularly to English, Persian, and Arabic, became unhappy about what a visitor was doing. This twenty-six-month-old child angrily told her, in Persian, to stop. When she didn't, he told her to stop in English. She didn't. He then told her to stop in Arabic. To his father's friends he speaks only Arabic, the family's primary language. At times, when he is addressed in Persian, he will answer correctly in English.

I find all of this behavior remarkable. And this child is not all that different from others we have worked with. Infants and toddlers apparently have a far greater capacity to learn languages than we have given them credit for. By the way, the parents of this trilingual child made no special effort to teach this child any of the three languages. They simply followed the standard advice we give all our parents and that you will find in the opening paragraph of this section, above.

On a related note, I have been told by knowledgeable people that children of hearing-impaired parents routinely acquire far more words in sign language before their first birthday than the hearing child in a typical family situation acquires receptive vocabulary.

How Amazing Is the Newborn?

About a dozen years ago a research report appeared with the claim that babies less than two months of age are capable of several types of imitation including tongue protrusion. At about the same time, other reports indicated that newborns would turn accurately to look for sounds and coordinate their looking with their parents' behavior. A sensational book on learning in the womb appeared. It claimed that the fetus listened to and stored specific thoughts and words for many months before birth. Does that mean that newborns are much more capable than we previously thought?

Before the 1960s, newborns were generally thought to live in what William James called a world of "buzzing, booming confusion." Today some students of human development would have you believe that babies are already busy "tuning in" on their mother's thoughts and feelings well before birth. Others talk of active appreciation of experiences by babies as they undergo the birth process. Still others insist that infants see, hear, compare, make decisions, and behave intentionally within their first weeks of life.

What can fetuses and very young infants do? What goes on in their minds between conception and their first birthday? Analyses of these subjects can, and have, filled several books. Even so, most of what we would like to know remains to be learned. Such evidence as does exist comes from several sources: anatomical studies of the growth of the central nervous system; studies of problem-solving by babies, older children, and animals; Piaget's studies of the growth of intelligence; and observational studies of the behavior of the human fetus and infant.

The prevailing picture of early human abilities was first modified significantly by studies of vision, especially those of Robert Fantz, published in the early 1960s. Fantz demonstrated that babies could "discriminate" among targets during their first months of life. But whether they were comparing targets or only looking at those they could make out was not clear. Nor was it clear whether they were perceiving "faceness" or just complexity. In any event, Fantz convinced most people that babies could see better than William James thought they could, especially after they were two months old.

Two and a half months seems to be a turning point in regard to the development of vision. My own early research produced findings that enlarged this picture and tended to confirm the work of Fantz.

At about ten weeks of age visual convergence and tracking become functional, and focusing ability becomes adequate for processing nearby details. At about the same time, children begin to study their hands. For the first time, they move their gaze back and forth over the features of a target while looking at them. But although this behavior is impressive, it can hardly be called sophisticated.

As for hearing, although it is true that the newborn can turn toward the source of a sound given highly restricted conditions, do not expect much behavior of this kind before the fourth or fifth month. Unless held in the prone position and exposed to a particular kind of sound, infants during the first weeks of life routinely do no more than blink, startle, or pause in their activities in response to sound.

For most people who study human development, Piaget's analyses of intellectual development remain the most accurate. The picture he created from his continuous observations of his own three children has been supported by many studies over several decades. Although it is true that tongue protrusion in the first month of life, now confirmed, contradicts his views, that single contrary finding is clearly offset by hundreds of studies that support his detailed picture of intellectual development. And in any event, imitative behaviors with the tongue in the first weeks of life are not followed by a continuous growth in imitation behaviors; they simply die out by the time the infant is two to three months of age.

Imitation does begin again shortly thereafter, but it is what Piaget called *quasi-imitation*. For example, the baby can sometimes be induced to continue playing with her own saliva if her parent tries to duplicate that sound during a lull in the activity. True imitation surfaces in the third quarter of the first year, as Piaget reported, and from then on, it increases in quantity and type, especially during the second and third years of life.

Imitative tongue protrusion is indeed amazing. Such inexplicable behavior is, however, but one of many present at birth. A variety of innate organized behaviors, in humans and other animals, inspire awe but do not require that we ascribe mature mental abilities to the creature. As we have seen, the red kangaroo fetus, on its own, leaves its mother's uterus early in fetal development and, though blind and weighing less than one ounce, makes its way through the cervical canal, out the vaginal opening, up the abdominal wall, over the lip of the pouch, and into the pouch. It then finds a nipple, attaches itself to it, and resumes fetal development. Shall we consider this creature to be of high intelligence?

In Piaget's view, babies start pretty much from scratch at birth. They do not think or process specific experiences in the aware, conscious style of older children or adults. They have no inborn memories or appreciation of the world around them. They make no decisions and perform no intentional acts for several months. The first intentional problem-solving appears at about six or seven months when a baby moves an obstacle aside in order to procure another desirable object. Not until eight or nine months do babies begin to develop short-term memory. Then, by eighteen to twenty-four months, they begin to solve problems by thinking about them.

This picture of the developing mental capacities of the infant is far more consistent with a great deal of evidence that exists than any other that is claimed for the fetus and the young infant. Claims of the amazingly capable newborn may be seductive, but to accept such claims without due regard for legitimate and substantial evidence to the contrary makes little sense. Indeed, uncritical acceptance of such claims could have harmful consequences for new or expectant parents.

The film *The Amazing Newborn,* which shows newborns engaging in imitative behavior such as tongue protrusion, and a few other behaviors that are clearly atypical, has a brief disclaimer at the end informing viewers that they should not expect to elicit such behavior from their own babies at home.

However, I cannot imagine new parents *not* attempting to repeat various demonstrations shown in the film and not being disappointed when their baby fails to respond.

My strictures of exaggerated claims on behalf of the newborn go double for claims on behalf of the unborn. The assertion that the fetus is capable of perceiving his mother's thoughts and feelings in utero, and that these perceptions will have significant long-term effects on the child's mental and emotional health after birth, is not only unproven but highly improbable, to put it mildly. And the same potential for needless worry over unrealized expectations exists here as for the "amazing" infant claims. I urge you to be skeptical of claims about "amazing" mental and emotional capacities in newborns and fetuses, and to be very slow in incorporating revolutionary new ideas into your child-rearing style.

Toilet Training: When and How

Toilet training is another child-rearing issue about which there is a surplus of opinion and a shortage of evidence. According to Freud and a large number of psychoanalytically oriented professionals who succeeded him, toilet training can be a source of enduring emotional problems and personality traits.

In the opinion of many people, including this author, Freud was a genius whose views on the causes of emotional illness and the motives that guide human lives have unquestionably advanced our knowledge. But I do not believe his theories about infantile sexuality have ever been substantiated in any but minor ways.

Freud believed that toddlers are at the stage in psychosexual development when primary gratification is obtained through the pleasurable sensations experienced in the anal region. Disturbance of, or conflict involving, the periodic rewards of anal gratifiction is likely to cause lasting damage to the growing psyche. Parents who communicate feelings of shame and guilt while toilet-training their babies can, said Freud, easily cause serious and lasting emotional damage.

Toilet training attempted at age twelve to twenty-four months confronts the normal willfulness of a child of this age. A child tends to resist the adult, and according to Freudian theory, the result for the child might be lifelong internal conflicts concerning the anal function.

Naturally, psychologists influenced by Freud's thinking have been more than slightly concerned with the issue of toilet training. In the 1950s and 1960s Erik Erikson continued in the Freudian tradition to emphasize the significance of toilet training. Nevertheless, such theoretical analyses have never been supported by any evidence.

Given what we know today, no justification exists for elaborate treatises or dire concern about toilet training. It is simply one of a large number of necessary chores that are required of all parents.

In the studies we have done, the majority of children developing well were not toilet-trained before their second birthday. That may well have meant an abundance of diapers to change and clean or purchase, but the result was, on balance, less stress for everyone when training began after the child was two. It is easier to deal with diapers than with endless accidents involving clothing, linens, furniture, and so on. Around age two most children spontaneously show an interest in learning to use the toilet. A potty on the floor that the child can use himself encourages this interest. If there is an older sibling in the home, the younger child's desire to imitate may be stimulus enough, and he may virtually train himself. Much praise from the parents for every success helps the process. Scolding for accidents doesn't.

A GUIDE TO PROFESSIONAL SERVICES

Many different kinds of professionals work in the area of early childhood education, but I shall restrict my comments to those who work with children under three years of age.

PARENT EDUCATORS

In regard to early educational development, you might immediately think of professional educators, but until the 1970s there were no professionals concerned with learning during the first years of a child's life. I am happy to report that times have changed.

As major efforts like Project Head Start matured, an accompanying growth occurred in the public's interest in learning during the first years of life. Since the early 1970s, many programs that have focused on learning during the first three years have come into existence throughout the developed world.

Unfortunately, parents may still find it difficult to locate a well-trained and qualified parent educator in their area. The number of institutions that train such personnel is small, and very little government support has been provided for the practice. But at least the chances of finding such a professional are considerably better today than they were before 1970.

The greatest need is for well-trained professionals who can teach parents how to educate their own children. You cannot, however, have extensive numbers of people trained adequately to educate parents without institutional support, at least not until jobs in the field pay better than they do now. For a time during the early 1970s we seemed to be moving fairly steadily toward such institutional support, but more recently interest in that movement among federal administrators and major philanthropic organizations has declined strikingly.

The apparent success of the Missouri's New Parents as Teachers Project has led to similar activities in forty-two other states, but unfortunately, nearly all of the personnel involved have had less than one week of training. That won't help you much.

In many parts of the country the Junior League has vigorously endorsed and sponsored parent education programs that focus on learning during the first years. They are generally of high quality, but unlike what we do in our model program, they do not attempt to provide comprehensive parent education and support services.

I remain convinced that the field will continue to grow and that institutional support will ultimately be a routine government responsibility. In the meantime, thousands of programs, most of which are sponsored by grassroots organizations, do focus on learning in the first years, and substantial numbers of professionals in early education are devoting themselves to the subject. As inadequate as the current situation is for meeting the needs of all new parents, it is light-years ahead of any time before in history. I am not discouraged.

THE PHYSICIAN

Probably the most common kind of parent educator is the physician. Pediatricians nowadays are not as worried about rickets and malnutrition and other infant diseases as they were forty or fifty years ago. Instead, they seem to spend most of their time coping with the management problems of new mothers. After all, until very recently, and in many instances even today, the pediatrician was the only professional with whom new parents had routine contact. Unfortunately, except for brief exposure to the subject of child development during medical school training, and whatever they may have gleaned from children's parents, most physicians have not been adequately trained for this particular task.

That picture, too, seems to be changing, and there are signs of a move within pediatrics to improve training in early education. For the time being, however, you would probably be wise to consider pediatricians, physicians, and nurses best qualified to help with your child's medical needs, narrowly defined, instead of looking to them for information on language acquisition, personality growth, and discipline.

Also note that pediatricians vary extensively in their approach to educational issues. Some, for example, have a strong psychiatric orientation and offer psychological guidance about the emotional well-being of the baby. Will this guidance be entirely appropriate? Possibly, but you can see that in such cases the role of educational and medical professionals might become somewhat blurred.

When in doubt, I suggest you seek guidance from a variety of sources rather than from a single practitioner.

SOCIAL WORKERS AND RELATED PROFESSIONALS

People in social work also provide professional assistance in child-rearing. Since social workers become intimately involved in the problems of a large number of families, young parents often ask them for advice. Public health nurses, visiting nurses, homemakers, and members of the Child Study Association, a volunteer group that advises parents, all offer guidance from time to time, but it is highly unlikely that they have had high-caliber training in parent education.

Even if someone in one professional capacity or another claims to have been exposed to all of the information available about early educational development of children, that exposure may have taken place more than twenty years ago. If so, the chances are high that he does not still have a substantial background in this field.

DEVELOPMENTAL DAY CARE PROFESSIONALS

A new kind of professional has been surfacing in recent years as a result of the growth of day care. Although day care was not primarily intended for children under three years of age, many such children are now in day care, the majority of them in small groups in a private home—a practice known as family day care.

Day care was conceived to serve the purposes of parents not children. Until fairly recently, as long as a child was safe and reasonably happy, the day care experience was considered adequate. In the last twenty years, with the growing interest in early learning, however, safety and happiness are no longer always considered adequate, and the result has been what is called developmental day care.

Family day care providers do not generally claim that they are operating a "developmental" program. It is the larger, more visible programs, based in universities, government installations, and large industries, that make this claim.

The definition of developmental day care not only includes but has as its highest priority the educational development of the child. So far so good, but though increasing numbers of talented professionals are now involved in developmental day care, the caliber of training most have received still suffers from the general immaturity of the field. If you are fortunate enough to get your baby into a developmental day care operation attached to a university or a government facility, your child will probably receive much better care than she would get in most unaffiliated day care situations.

CHILD PSYCHIATRISTS

Child psychiatrists do not often work with children under three. A modest number of programs do exist for the treatment of actual or potential emotional handicaps in infants and toddlers. Many of those, however, are experimental in nature, and this field is a very difficult and comparatively young one in which "cures" are hard to come by. A two-year-old child with a significant behavior disturbance is a difficult case for any professional.

If you have a child with a behavior disturbance that could be significant, you should of course consult and work with your physician or other health professional; but you must not look for the same type of prompt recovery that you might expect in, say, the area of orthopedics or infectious disease.

I suggest you be very cautious about placing your faith in any child psychiatrist. Make sure that he or she is highly recommended by several reliable sources.

To help you cope with the special nature of this subject area, I recommend the book *A Parent's Guide to Child Therapy,* by Richard Bush (Delacorte Press), which offers a well-written commonsense approach to the subject of behavior disorders and emotional difficulties in early childhood. Bush provides guidance for parents whose child may have emotional difficulty, who are unhappy with the help they are getting from their physician, and who feel they have nowhere else to turn. He gives a full picture of the various behaviors that worry parents, and he distinguishes those that have significance from those that do not. Bush also discusses the different kinds of professionals who can help parents deal with different problems. All in all, this book is a very valuable contribution to the literature.

In 1977 the National Center for Clinical Infant Programs was established to improve and support professional initiatives in infant health, mental health, and development. This multidisciplinary group with headquarters in Washington, D.C., was started by a wonderful physician named Reginald Lourie. Today it sponsors a good deal of the best research and training in the subject of the very young child and mental health. From organizations such as this we can expect to see the growth of a very substantial resource for parents as the years go by.

Then, too, do not overlook the counsel you might get from someone who has raised several children and has, along with a good memory, a great deal of warmth and common sense. You may well find that such a veteran parent will be better able than most professionals to help you deal with your concerns about the first years of life.

A Guide to Information About Children

Where can you go to get the best information about children? First of all, you can make use of the materials found in this book and of the advice of reliable friends who have already faced some of the problems that you now confront. In addition, you can resort to a huge number of books, both technical and nontechnical, droves of magazine articles, many publications from the U.S. Government Printing Office, an occasional TV program, and films and videotapes that can be rented. You can also seek advice from various professionals of the sort mentioned in the previous section. Never depend solely on any single authority. The more information you can get, the better, so consult more than one source, and try to get the best materials available.

BOOKS

First-time parents should have three kinds of books. One kind should deal with the physical well-being of the child. This book should be written by a qualified physician or group of physicians. The classic of the field is, of course, Dr. Benjamin Spock's *Common Sense Book of Baby and Child Care.* But there are other equally valid treatments, such as *The Child Health Encyclopedia,* by the Boston Children's Medical Center and R. I. Feinbloom, and a new book by Laura Nathanson called *The Portable Pediatrician.* Please note that I recommend these books principally for the practical information they provide about the physical well-being of the child; they excel on topics such as nutrition, disease, and growth of the body. If a subject like discipline is included, as it often is, I would suggest that you skip that part of the book. Also skip any chapters that have to do with learning or education.

The second useful kind of book is the sort that Penelope Leach specializes in. She is sensitive to the classic sources of emotional stress that parents experience, and she is also sincere, very capable, and totally dedicated. Another type of book in this second category also provides effective support for new parents, but from the point of view of parents themselves. Two excellent examples are *The Mother's Book* and *The Father's Book,* both edited by R. Friedland and C. Kort. These volumes contain several dozen candid personal accounts by mothers and fathers of the emotional aspects of parenthood. Some of the topics are pregnancy, postpartum changes, breast-versus bottle-feeding, and redefining relationships. Both books are well written and exude genuine compassion. You should also know about a book called *Discovering Motherhood,* a marvelous volume from an organization named Welcome Home. This, too, is a collection of essays by lay people. Its focus is on support for the practice of parenting by parents. I strongly recommend it.

The third category of book is about behavior and learning. These books tell you what babies are like during the first years, how they learn, what obstacles might hinder learning, and how you can help. Behavior and learning are, of course, what this book is about.

Although these are the basic kinds of books most needed by young parents, there are many other books that you might find interesting and informative.

Konrad Lorenz's *King Solomon's Ring,* for example, has an absolutely marvelous description of behaviors of other animal species, many of which help cast light on the behavior of human babies.

Parents who want to pursue the fascinating subject of the development of intelligence in children further should look into the research and writings of Piaget. The best single introduction to Piaget's work can be found in *Intelligence and Experience* by my old friend of many years, J. McVicker Hunt.

Of Piaget's own writings, the most important is *The Origins of Intelligence in Children,* but I would first recommend Hunt's book; one by D. Singer and T. Revenson called *A Piaget Primer: How Children Think;* or another by Maryanne Spencer Pulaski called *Your Child's Mind and How It Grows.* (Piaget is not easy reading.)

For more specifics on these and other books, please see Recommended Readings.

FILMS AND VIDEOTAPES

You can rent good films and videotapes on the development of the young child from university-based libraries. Pennsylvania State University has a particularly extensive collection. The price is about $20. You can call 800-826-0132 for a catalog, or you can get information on such materials by writing to us at the Center for Parent Education, 81 Wyman Street, Waban, Massachusetts 02168. We also offer literature that contains reviews of such materials. From the Center you can also obtain our TV series, *The First Three Years,* on videotape or film.

MAGAZINES

For years magazines have existed that specialized in the subject of parenting, and for good reason, since there is no more interested, motivated, and open-minded student of early childhood than a first-time parent. Magazines for new parents are of decidedly uneven quality, however. The best of them in my opinion is *American Baby,* a copy of which most new mothers receive in the hospital.

But even in the case of *American Baby,* you must never assume that something is true simply because it appears in print. A recent edition of that leading magazine had an article entitled "Is Your Baby Gifted?" According to the criteria cited, about 85 percent of all American babies are gifted. Because our center was mentioned as a resource, we received hundreds of calls from many parts of the country. The most common one started with the statement, "I have just read an article in *American Baby* magazine, and it seems that my eighteen-month-old is gifted. Can you give me some help in guiding his development?" The most impressive call was from a woman with a four-month-old. She too began, "I have just read an article in *American Baby* magazine and it seems that my baby is gifted."

The author of that article is by any standards a much better than average writer. Her article contained a good deal of valid, detailed information. Unfortunately, it contained a good deal of inaccurate information as well.

Highly variable accuracy is the norm in books by professionals, including some very well known leaders in the field; in television programs from commercial and public networks; in newsletters and magazines; and, in fact, in just about any form of communication about babies that you will be offered.

One of the core reasons I admire writers like Joseph Stone of Vassar and Jean Piaget is that they knew when *they didn't know something.* Among professionals in early human development work, this kind of respect for truth and accuracy is surprisingly rare. Because of the uneven quality of the available materials, your search for information will be much more difficult than it ought to be. My bottom-line advice to you: be a skeptic in this subject area.

GOVERNMENT PAMPHLETS

The U.S. Government Printing Office has produced a series of pamphlets on raising young children. *Infant Care,* the best known of these, is available for about $2. Along with the Bible and Dr. Spock's books, it is one of the best-selling publications in this country. Still, though such pamphlets are adequate beginners' texts, you will have to look elsewhere for many important details.

Since early education is basically a responsibility of government, the federal Department of Education or your local school system ought to provide the child-rearing information that you need. I predict that sooner or later they will.

Professional Testing of Young Children

The testing of young children for educational progress during the first years of life is of absolutely fundamental importance. We must be able to spot something going wrong as soon as possible if we are to give each child the best possible chance to make the most of whatever he brings into the world. Unfortunately, this is yet another area that has been adversely affected by the scarcity of useful research. For example, I have emphasized repeatedly the role of curiosity in early learning development. Yet to this day we have next to no scientific knowledge about its day-to-day development. Nevertheless, we do have enough information and experience to make this promise: With a proper program of screening we can spot anything important that is going wrong in most of the major areas of development. We developed screening procedures for the Missouri project, and we have improved them in our model program activities at the Center for Parent Education. This kind of help for a family can be provided for less than $200 a year during the first three years of life.

THE IMPORTANCE OF THE WORK OF ARNOLD GESELL

Dr. Arnold Gesell did pioneering work on the general development of young children in the 1930s. From his research, done with the children of 109 middle-class families in New Haven, Connecticut, he was able to describe the general shape of early development. On the basis of that early research Gesell produced a test that any pediatrician could use to screen children for normality, in about fifteen minutes during an office visit.

His test, which has been in widespread use for decades, has proved to be extremely valuable in research studies and private practice all over the world. Shortly after Gesell's test came into general use, new and supposedly improved tests of a similar nature began to be produced; we now have a fair number of them. They include the Bayley Test of Infant Development, the Cattell Test, and the Denver Screening procedures.

Significantly, all of these newer tests depend largely on the work of Gesell, with each of them using items that very much resemble those of the original Gesell Schedules. If these later tests have any advantages over Gesell's original test, they lie solely in the realm of technical improvements. For example, the Griffiths Scale from England, created by Ruth Griffiths, is technically much better, but its items very closely resemble those of Gesell.

The last twenty-five years have seen some progress in early assessment and general developmental testing, but much more basic work still needs to be done. Given what we know today, we could, however, provide effective early detection services for all children. All it takes is informed and determined educational leadership.

THE NECESSITY OF VARYING EVALUATION SYSTEMS

A consideration to be kept in mind in early testing is that at about thirty months of age, a child changes from one kind of testee to another. The child over thirty months old is assumed to have enough language skill so that language can be used in instructing him during the testing process. The child under thirty months, on the other hand, is unreliable in language skills and is, therefore, generally tested as if he had little or no language. Testing of a very young child more closely resembles evaluation of the abilities of simpler animal species, while testing of older children more closely resembles the kind of testing you may remember from your own school days.

Testing of infants has traditionally involved both the mother's reports of what a child can do and the use of machinery such as the electroencephalograph, which produces records of brain activity that can be examined for signs of abnormal development, or optical instruments like the retinoscope or the ophthalmoscope to check vision. Mothers' reports are also essential, even though it has been repeatedly found that their reports of the capabilities of their children, particularly in the realm of learning achievement, are seldom as reliable as those generated by less partial observers. But mothers, nevertheless, have important information about their children that no one else could possibly have.

THE PROBLEM OF FALSE POSITIVES

A problem that complicates the testing of young children is that of false positives. Put simply, a false positive is a symptom or a behavior that suggests there is something wrong with the baby but that eventually proves not to have been meaningful. This is so common that pediatricians and other child development testers have adopted a very conservative attitude toward the significance of occasional symptoms during the child's first year.

The problem of false positives puts the professional into a dilemma. If she conscientiously reports every anomaly, or unusual element of behavior, to the baby's parents, she can cause the parents much needless anxiety. Yet if she ignores such signs, she runs the risk of paying insufficient attention to the earliest point at which a real problem has begun to develop. Parents should therefore be patient and understanding with their physician or a psychological or educational tester when it comes to the evaluation of behavior during the first two years of life.

GENERAL DEVELOPMENT TESTS

By far the most common procedure that could be called educational testing is the testing of general development. The Gesell Schedules are still used for that purpose, in spite of their age, as are many newer tests. In our early work, for example, we routinely used the Bayley Scale to test all of our children under two years of age. Such scales generally produce at least two and sometimes as many as four scores. From the Bayley the tester calculates a mental and a physical score. The Gesell generates four subscores and a fifth overall score called the development quotient, or DQ, so called to distinguish it from the intelligence quotient, or IQ.

For many years professionals have acknowledged that children under two years of age do not show the same forms of intellectual capacity that older children and adults do. The Bayley Scale does have a mental index, though what kind of mentality it measures is unclear.

The Gesell Schedules enable a tester to gauge a child's overall DQ. The tester also calculates a motor score, a personal social score, a language score, and an adaptive score. The testing on these general developmental tests, particularly for the child under two years, is predominantly a matter of eliciting performance by the baby through the use of attractive materials or by asking the mother to report on the child's behavior at home. The examiner may also present the baby with one-inch red wooden cubes; the examiner then moves aside and watches the baby's behavior with these cubes. The behavior can range from ignoring the cubes to building towers with them.

On the basis of typical behavior of the children in this original sample, Gesell created a framework within which the behavior of other children might be placed and compared. Other items on such tests involve eliciting reflexive behavior. For example, you can determine how much head control a baby has by placing him on his stomach and waiting awhile; he will generally produce the behavior in which you are interested: head-rearing. During the thirty minutes an examiner sees the baby, he will not hear many of the words that a baby of eighteen months might occasionally use at home. Even if he hears them, he might not recognize them. This is where the mother's knowledge of her child's vocabulary comes into play.

These developmental tests are widely used, and some people use them to test children right up through entry into kindergarten. Generally speaking, scores on these tests with children under one year of age do not have any predictive value, with one important exception: if a child repeatedly scores very low, you probably have something to worry about. By "very low" I mean somewhere below 85 on tests where the average score is 100. Scores slightly below average are not usually significant.

Consider two one-year-old babies, one who scores 95 on one of these general tests and another who scores 115; at three years of age, the low scorer is no more likely to score under 100 on an intelligence test than is the high scorer.

TESTING THE FOUNDATIONS OF INTELLIGENCE— LANGUAGE DEVELOPMENT

In a crude sense, the general developmental scales can be used to generate information about a child's language development. A language subscale is within the Gesell, but such tests are neither powerful nor very reliable. The Harvard Preschool Project developed a good scale for assessing language development starting when a child is around seven months and extending to his third birthday. It assesses the development of receptive language, not speech. It depends very heavily on what the child does in response to situations and verbal instructions. This scale, though experimental, is useful, and we used it in monitoring language acquisition in our Missouri project. We found children who, at fourteen months of age, scored well on the Denver Developmental Test, but who in fact were significantly delayed with respect to early language development.

I now strongly recommend the use of a new scale called the Early Language Milestones scale, or the ELM. This instrument was developed by a research pediatrician named James Coplan, of the State University of New York at Syracuse. Dr. Coplan's goal, like Arnold Gesell's, was to provide the pediatrician with a procedure that was easy to learn and use and that could be performed in less than fifteen minutes. He did a good job. With the ELM, we can now identify the toddler who by fourteen months of age has begun to fall behind or move ahead significantly. This is an important advance. Previously, we could not make such a determination until about two years.

Both screening and testing (which provides more precise information than screening) are invariably fairly difficult procedures with children less than thirty months old. In addition to the fact that such children often have very limited language skills during the period from fourteen to twenty-four months, the typical child's reluctance to interact with unfamiliar people may interfere with any procedure of this kind. Interestingly, it is easier to test a three-year-old or a one-year-old than it is to test a child of twenty months.

Clearly, then, in trying to interpret the meaning of the screening or testing procedure for children under two, one has to be cautious. Repeated indications that a child knows something can usually be depended on, but if a child fails on some test item it is often not because of inability but rather because he is simply not cooperating.

TESTING SOCIAL DEVELOPMENT

Social development is assessed in the same generally crude manner, by general developmental tests. It is also assessable using experimental instruments that our Preschool Project has produced. We have, as this book has indicated, identified eight qualities of interaction with people that can properly be called social skills and that seem to have substantial importance in terms of normal social development. The Preschool Project instruments do a fair job of judging how well a child is proceeding in these areas. Nevertheless, they are still crude, unfinished instruments that leave much to be desired.

Unfortunately, even to this day no other choices of consequence are available. Several other procedures are labeled tests of social ability or status, but none of them focuses on such interpersonal skills as effectiveness in getting someone's attention, ability to use another person as a resource, and so on. This lack of suitable tests is directly linked to the absence of fundamental research in this vital area of human development. Until now intelligence, language, and perception have been more popular than social development as topics for research in infancy. Given time, the situation will improve, but for now much more work is needed in this area.

TESTING CURIOSITY
We draw nearly a total blank when it comes to testing curiosity, especially during the first years of life. Difficult though it may be to believe, no basic research has been done in this area. We have no standardized tests for assessment, nor do we even have any well-developed experimental instruments.

MEASURING THE DEVELOPMENT OF INTELLIGENCE
The development of intelligence may be crudely assessed using general developmental tests. The Bayley Mental Index is related in some sense to the growth of intelligence, as are the Language and Adaptive scales of the Gesell. How they are related is not precisely known.

The Bayley Mental Scale begins to relate well to later, more established tests of intelligence once the child reaches her second birthday, and very high or very low scores on the Bayley Mental Scale from age two on generally indicate underlying stable patterns of development. These extremes, however, only help us to identify the intellectual status of a relatively small portion of two- to three-year-old children.

For the first two years of life the most sophisticated treatment of developing intelligence has to be based on the work of Piaget. A few tests are now available that have been drawn directly from his basic research. Although these tests are nowhere near as technically well developed as some of the older developmental tests, they are the most promising with respect to monitoring intellectual growth in the first two years. These tests of sensorimotor intelligence, like the tests for general development in the first two years of life, only identify whether a child is progressing normally or is falling behind.

In a population of children who are free from pathology and are growing up in average families, you rarely will find delays on tests of sensorimotor intelligence in the first two years. The situation changes, however, once children reach two years of age, the age at which abstract thinking ability usually emerges.

For a long time about the only instrument that could be used to test the intelligence of a two-and-a-half-year-old child was the Stanford-Binet. The Binet has never been considered very powerful when used with such a young child, but it was the best we had until recently. Then, in the 1980s, a new test appeared that seems to be considerably better, the Kaufman Assessment Battery for Children, or the ABC test. Using the Kaufman, we are now able to do a much better job in assessing intelligence from thirty to thirty-six months on.

TESTING FOR VISION AND HEARING ABILITY

Vision and hearing are such important prerequisite capacities underlying learning that they should be monitored closely during the first years of life. In fact, they are tested only rarely, though that situation appears to be changing.

All physicians who have responsibility for health care do some sort of visual examination of children beginning shortly after birth, but this examination is generally cursory. A small number of highly trained pediatric ophthalmologists do considerably more. Some assess visual ability in babies less than six months old, looking to see if their eyes focus well on nearby objects, whether they track moving objects well, and so forth. Most children do not get reasonably sophisticated visual assessment, however, until they enter school. That is much too late.

There has long been a disagreement between ophthalmologists and optometrists about visual care in early development. The ophthalmologist is a physician who specializes in diseases of the eyes. The optometrist is not a physician. He focuses on visual performance. The two territories overlap, but instead of cooperating, these professionals tend to quarrel.

Most ophthalmologists are more inclined to focus on the health of the eyes than on visual functions such as tracking moving targets or focusing. Indeed, the ophthalmologist characteristically uses drugs to put the eyes into a state where the focusing mechanism is not working.

A small minority of leading optometrists do considerably more, even in the first months of life. They assess the infant's capacities in such areas as three-dimensional vision, convergence, and tracking.

There is, however, some good news. The frequency of deficits in vision during the first few years of life is remarkably low, probably less than 1 percent of all children. In addition, many of the defects that do occur are so obvious that almost any cursory examination will detect them.

As bad as it is to have a child with undetected but significant visual deficits, it may even be worse developmentally for a child to have an undetected hearing deficit. Hearing usually is crudely tested at birth and at regular pediatric examinations, but the typical test does not amount to much more than determining whether a child is deaf. Obviously this is not enough; babies can respond to fairly loud noises and still have very substantial deficits in hearing ability.

It is now clearly within our capacity to do sophisticated hearing screening from the time a baby is four or five months of age. Since language development begins at about six or seven months and undergoes its major development over the following two years, it seems obvious that any baby who has a correctable hearing deficit should be assisted before he gets to be six or seven months of age. Although this is not now being done routinely in this country, I predict that it will be in another decade or two.

Recently, new instruments like the acoustiscope have been developed that make screening for early hearing ability simple enough for almost anyone to do, with very little training required.

Because of the development of better instruments and because of the rapidly growing awareness of the importance and the prevalence of mild to moderate hearing losses in the first two years, I am confident that we will eventually see this problem properly tended to. In the meantime, I urge you to make sure that this particular part of your child's functioning is looked after properly.

For more information on this very important topic, see the section on the importance of early detection of hearing losses.

What Happens After Thirty-six Months of Age?

Sometimes when I present my views about the importance of the first three years of life I notice sad looks coming over the faces of parents. These sad expressions are usually followed by the same questions: "Is it all over after three? Is there nothing further I can do about my child's development? Is there no way I can compensate for the mistakes that I probably made?" Answering these questions is rather difficult for me because to some extent I really do believe it is too late after age three. But the qualifications I place on this statement are important.

Of course children continue to develop after age three. Indeed, I am inclined to agree with psychologists like Erik Erikson who hold that human beings continue to develop in important ways until they die. Based on almost four decades of studying human development, however, I do believe the degree of flexibility that humans have, their capacity for fundamental change in lifestyles and intellectual ability, all decline steadily with age. This has been the theme of any number of studies of child development, and I do not know of anyone who has studied human development in any serious way over the years who disagrees with it.

What is at issue is the degree of flexibility that remains at various stages of life, as well as our capacity as individuals and as a society to make optimum use of that flexibility. In this respect, Hollywood may have misled us.

During the golden years of Hollywood, when so many of us spent so much time at the movies, a thematic staple was the sudden and dramatic conversion of someone headed the wrong way in life. On the screen, before our very eyes, we would see adult human beings changing from nasty, vicious, small-minded people to enlightened, wonderful human beings, all thanks to a single dramatic event. Often the principals were teenage boys and girls who seemed to be on the wrong track but who, as a result of meeting up with somebody like Spencer Tracy or Edmund Gwenn, suddenly "found the way."

When a movie like *The Bad Seed* was made, in which a young child was portrayed as completely evil from the earliest days of her life, audiences were shocked. Such a point of view seemed inconsistent with American principles such as "hope springs eternal"; "there's always room for change"; "we can always aspire to the best"; and "it's never too late." The truth is less consoling.

My feeling is that once a child reaches two years of age, his primary social orientation has been established and from then on, it becomes increasingly difficult to alter it significantly. For example, if a child has been taught that the world revolves exclusively around him, that if he insists on having his way he will always find his parents' resistance crumbling, he will be predisposed to operate in a self-centered fashion in his subsequent interpersonal relationships.

This does not mean that a spoiled three-year-old child cannot be changed; but it does mean that changing him probably will not be easy and that it will become progressively less easy—and at some point probably impossible—as the child grows older. Nowhere in child development research has anyone demonstrated the capacity to alter early personality traits, social attitudes, or levels of intelligence in a major way. Of course, despite this lack of demonstrated ability to make fundamental improvements after the early years, we have to keep trying.

It seems to me that each person responsible for influencing the growth and development of young humans has no choice but to continue to do the best he can, at all times, to induce the most beneficial course of development for every child in his care. Indeed, I believe, though I cannot prove it, that the capacity for important change exists, even including dramatic improvement, after the child is three years of age. But the burden of evidence, along with common prudence, compels me to put most of my faith in the prevention of difficulties rather than in the hope of being able to remedy them later on.

In our research on the first six years of life we found that children who were doing remarkably well at three years of age already demonstrated the major elements of competence that distinguish the outstanding six-year-old. Between the ages of three and six years we found a process of refinement of abilities already in place, rather than the emergence of new abilities. Thus the description in this book of the special attributes of the well-developed three-year-old applies just as well to the six-year-old, the differences being only of degree.

Another aspect of the three- to six-year-old range that deserves reemphasis is the growth of interest in peer activities during this period. True social interest in peers seems to begin at about two years of age and to continue to grow steadily, so that by the time children enter adolescence you frequently find that what peers think about a child has become considerably more important to her than what her parents think. This seems to be a developmental fact that accompanies the shifting of interest away from the nuclear family, a long-term process wherein a human being goes from total dependency to as much independence as any of us ever achieve.

Piaget claims that children reach one particularly important plateau somewhere between six and eight years of age, as they leave egocentric modes of thought behind and move into what he calls *socialized thought*. As a child comes to value her peers, she becomes very much interested in being understood when she speaks to them. By seven or eight years of age this need to be understood causes her to start thinking about how to frame her ideas so that another person can deal with them. In contrast, the three-year-old does not go through such preparatory steps. After all, at home she didn't have to be careful about what she said to have her needs met by her parents.

In Piaget's system a later plateau occurs in early adolescence, when children achieve adult styles of thought and become mature, reasoning individuals. Interestingly, Rousseau advised several centuries ago that the best we could do about early education was to guard against it until children reached early adolescence and their "reason matured." Some modern educational theorists believe he was probably correct.

Nursery School

A nursery school generally accepts children between two and a half and five years of age. Programs ordinarily operate five days a week for three to four hours daily during the school year. Nursery programs vary in what they promise, but most offer enjoyable, challenging group experiences with modest claims for educational benefits. The majority of schools focus more on creating a good transitional social experience between the home and the elementary school than on training for academic readiness.

But what about nursery schools that promise lasting educational gains to those many parents who believe that a successful academic career requires a good nursery school experience?

Certainly a well-run nursery school can provide many interesting experiences for a young child. The equipment, the routines, the other children, and the teacher can be fascinating and great fun for a child. In addition, much learning can indeed take place. Children can be taught to read and write before they enter elementary school. Most can even be taught to tie their own shoelaces. And of course they also learn a good deal about the people with whom they interact.

But do these experiences have a long-term effect? Does a child who goes to a first-rate nursery school do better in later school programs than one who does not? The answer is no. No nursery school curriculum yet devised has been shown to bestow any lasting educational advantage on children, not even superiority in social adjustment. Is there, then, no reason to use a nursery school?

No shame should be associated with a parent's desire to take an occasional break from raising her children. As a means of giving parents, especially mothers, some time for themselves, nursery schools are important. My late wife and I sent all four of our children to nursery school. We did so not because we thought it would help them to excel later but because we sometimes felt we were drowning in children. We had access to well-run schools that were staffed by loving and knowledgeable people, and we were confident that our children would enjoy themselves and be exposed to interesting people, materials, and activities. And so they were.

CONCLUDING REMARKS

For the most part, information about the education of babies wasn't of serious interest to many people before the late 1960s. Even parents and grandparents who have always been excited by the many new developments of the first years of life were not particularly oriented toward the long-term educational significance of such early achievements. We all just loved our babies. Over the last thirty years or so, however, the situation has changed. We still love our babies, but now most people, especially those who are well informed, are convinced that babies are not just playing and growing but are learning a lot as well. Furthermore, many people have been persuaded that a baby's early experiences influence later learning in important ways.

Parents and grandparents aren't the only people who've acquired new ideas about this subject. Research workers, book and magazine editors, radio and television producers, toy manufacturers, and school and political personnel are among the newly interested parties. Many politicians, even including presidents, have spoken out about the importance of experiences during the first years of life. There is no doubt that society's views have shifted in this respect.

Some societal concerns surface and then quickly disappear. Interest in learning during the first years of life, however, shows no sign of abating. With so many parties involved, new information and trends continue to appear. In order for a book on the subject to remain accurate and timely, new editions are periodically necessary. That does not mean that all of the information in previous editions becomes obsolete. After all, babies still face the same developmental challenges: to achieve mastery over their bodies, to explore the world, to learn to communicate, and, most important, to commit to and receive commitment from at least one older person. This edition of *The First Three Years of Life* appears some twenty years after the first. It contains much that is new and, I am confident, useful. I have also found it necessary to change some things from earlier editions. I am totally comfortable with the material in this book. In fact, writing it has given me great pleasure.

How Tough It Is to Know

The public needs and wants information that will guide their child-rearing practices. Unfortunately, some of the facts they seek do not lend themselves to simple, clear answers, and there is a lot to know. I can't count the number of times radio and television people have seriously asked me to describe large parts of the story of human development in a six-minute segment of a program. If a writer or a television producer were to ask a qualified expert how to design a new automobile or, perhaps less ambitiously, how to cope with the demands on the tires, the expert would in all probability say something like "That's a strange kind of question to ask me. In order to answer it in any responsible way, I'd have to get into subject matter that you, as a lay person, simply wouldn't understand, so you can either have a very superficial answer or you can drop the subject, because you would have to do quite a bit of preparation before you would ever understand the complexities of the situation, and you certainly wouldn't have a ghost of a chance of communicating what you have learned to the public." While the comparison may at first blush seem farfetched, I don't believe it is that far off the mark.

People who write books about early child development come in all shapes and sizes. They are physicians, lay people, academic psychologists, and so on. Some authors write for a living and have little or no professional training in education or psychology, but they are of above-average intelligence, and they seek to explore the newest and best information in order to prepare their books or other products for the public. Television research people are in the same category.

Over the years I have dealt with several dozen such people. Invariably they are very smart and studious, and they usually operate with large budgets. Their task is complicated by the fact that in a half-hour or even a full-hour program that also has to make room for commercials, they have to teach about or explain issues ordinarily dealt with in a graduate school over a period of a year or more. I submit that their task is impossible.

People from television, magazines, and newspapers, people who write books, politicians, and indeed the majority of practitioners in related fields having to do with young children all face the same task, and more often than not, in my judgment, they end up failing at it. The problem to which I refer is that of coming up with the most accurate and reliable judgment about what to do in respect to real problems such as child care during the first years of a child's life, and special teaching to help a child get a head start in life.

Recently I read a review of a new book written by people working at Harvard with support from the Carnegie Corporation, one of the major foundations that tries to deal with the needs of children. The book includes analyses of various facets of the problem, along with suggested remedies. One remedy is intervention for educationally disadvantaged preschoolers. So far, so good. I quote: "The long-term effects of Project Head Start and other preschool programs are now exceptionally well documented. Assessment of the longitudinal impact of the experimental Perry Preschool Project (a small two-year program for three-year-olds) initiated in 1962 in Ypsilanti, Michigan, and partially supported over the years by the Corporation, revealed that at age nineteen those who were enrolled in the program were found to be twice as likely as a randomly assigned control group to be employed, attending college, or receiving training."

I don't know how many times, since the first evaluations of Head Start in 1968, I have heard observers and interpreters point to the "success" of the project and then cite the Perry Preschool Project as evidence of that success.

In order for the Perry Preschool Project results to prove that Head Start is successful, the project would have to have been *typical* of Head Start activities across the country, yet nothing could be further from the truth. In all probability, the Perry Preschool Project was markedly superior to 95 or more percent of the existing Head Start centers. The teachers were very carefully selected, trained, and supervised; the budget was far more generous than those of most Head Start centers; and so forth. For the other, more representative 95 percent of all Head Start centers, there is no evidence of success even remotely resembling that of the Perry Preschool Project.

Another example comes from the world of books. Take, for instance, the Johnson & Johnson book, *From Baby to Toddler,* by John J. Fisher (New York: Perigee Books, 1988), a follow-up to two earlier successful Johnson &

Johnson ventures. This is a considerably better than average book, and the writer is obviously very capable. Yet I found reason, in several places, to note in the margin "uncritical thinking." What happens is that the author, in searching for the newest and best research results, finds something that appeals to him and then uses it. It is possible, of course, that there was some activity between the discovery of the report and its use in the book, but I am inclined to doubt that there was much.

What kind of activity could there have been? Well, one could examine the quality of the research, the reputation of the researcher, and the relationship of that research result to existing information on the same subject. That is the kind of inquiry that any well-trained child development professional would be expected to perform. But that type of critical evaluation is not within the capability of people outside the field, no matter how clever they are.

This particular book is not as oriented toward new research findings as some. Several books we have looked at during the last ten years have cited dozens of research findings, and the same criticisms apply. Indeed, in our parent training programs, we advocate posting a reminder on the wall: "Simply because it's in print does not mean that it's true!"

What determines truth? One of the standard requirements in most scientific fields is replication. Many of the problems I see in books that shoot from the hip in terms of "new findings" is singularity. When something is reported by one research team—something different, exciting, dramatic—it should pique one's interest, but one should not immediately believe it. If the same sort of finding is reported by three, four, five, or ten independent research teams, then the likelihood of validity is increased dramatically.

Other indicators are also useful in determining the validity of a claim, such as the reputation of the person making the claim. One note of caution: some of the most visible and prominent authors make claims on the basis of grossly inadequate evidence or possess shaky research qualifications even though their public visibility is substantial. Unfortunately, knowing the difference between a celebrated figure who is respected by his colleagues as a solid scientist and one who is privately considered of borderline competence or honesty is just about impossible unless you operate within the field as a professional. There are no restrictions or safeguards, however, on whose views are offered to the public.

Another indicator of relevance is whether the claim is consistent with existing information in the field. Of course, if it is a subject about which comparatively little is known, it is much easier for the unsupportable dramatic claim to prevail, sometimes for an extended period of time. For instance, interest in the behavior of babies during the first months of life blossomed in the early 1960s. Reports of remarkable benefits of close physical contact during the first days of life swept the medical community. Later studies did not support the earlier claims, but it was years before replications were performed to test those claims. Today no one in the research community insists that a "superglue" type of bonding results from close physical contact during those first days. As a result, large numbers of adoptive parents have breathed a sigh of relief.

Research on the effects of early childhood education programs is a complex and confusing affair. Very few people who write for television are aware of something called "the self-selected sample." If a researcher is looking for a substantial number of families to participate in an educational enrichment study, the easiest way to gather that sample is to ask for volunteers through posters, word of mouth, radio programs, newspaper advertisements, and bulletin boards. People in the community will hear about your efforts and sign up for your program.

The problem with this procedure is that any good post-program test scores the children achieve cannot fully be attributed to the effectiveness of your program. Families who volunteer for these kinds of programs are generally those who are most knowledgeable, most aware of what's going on in the community, and most interested in children and education. They are therefore not representative of the entire population. This is known as a self-selected sample.

This particular problem caused all sorts of grief in connection with one apparently very successful parent education project that made its appearance in the late 1960s. This particular project seemed to be producing large benefits for the children, and it was much less expensive than other programs aimed at solving the same problem. The initial reports of success led to the rapid expansion of the program to several sites across the country, and no doubt influenced a good number of professionals in early childhood education.

A few years later, the project was obliged by its funders to assign families in a random fashion either to the experimental treatment or to the alternative activities. When random assignment was achieved, the differences between the groups of children disappeared. A few years later the same program was tested again in the same careful manner. Once again, when the sample was not self-selected, no benefits were found. In the intervening years a large number of communities had adopted the program, thinking it was effective. Sadly, this kind of problem is not all that uncommon in the field of educational research.

This situation was one of the rare instances in which a highly visible project was revisited and a significant flaw was identified and reported. Ordinarily this sort of reevaluation simply doesn't get done, for the same reason that replications are rarely made: because few organizations that fund educational research are willing to pay for such replications. In other scientific fields this conduct might be considered scandalous. In early childhood education it is the norm.

One more example: I recently consulted for a Fortune 500 company interested in producing toys for infants and toddlers. They were spending millions of dollars to explore this venture, they had assigned some very able people to the project, and they were making a substantial effort to "research" the field of early childhood development. Actually, their research amounted to a completely self-taught introduction to early childhood development. They tried to identify all of the important, relevant research reports, organize them, and milk them for information relevant to the toy industry. In my judgment, this was an admirable but totally hopeless venture.

They also sought out expert advice in a peculiar way. They went to people who were teaching courses in the relevant areas at the local university and asked these people to be their advisers. They recruited two or three people this way. However, the people they recruited explored only narrow segments of the subject areas and, in general, did a woefully inadequate job. This company was faced with pretty much the same task as the television network news reporter and the gifted lay writer—a task that, after thirty-eight years in and around such efforts, I am convinced is hopeless.

What, then, can people rely upon? I can see only one answer. If they are seriously looking for successful results, they are obliged to depend upon authorities. But they'd better be quite exhaustive in their efforts to identify those few who really know what they are talking about and are aware of what is and what is not known. The best effort of that kind I have ever seen was made by the Children's Television Workshop, the group that created *Sesame Street* and other educational television programs. They sought guidance, over a period of many months, from a large number of highly respected academic researchers in and around the subject of early education.

After a long series of meetings, some of which spanned several days, their core staff of CTW spent many more months sifting through the gathered information for consistent agreement versus shaky claims, and so forth. These extraordinarily talented people spent more than a year getting some sense of what was really known about language and intellectual learning in three- and four-year-old children. Only then did they begin to design their first television programs.

What does all of this mean to you? For one thing, it is intended to give you a sense of what I have learned about operations in a variety of important areas having to do with early childhood. What I have just described is relevant to the modern child-care scene, early intervention, parent education programs, toys, government policy, books, and magazines—in other words, this analysis is applicable to just about any activity associated with infants and toddlers. Second, it points to a thought I have had in my mind for many years; the importance, in the training of leaders in early childhood education, of high-quality exposure to problems in that branch of philosophy known as epistemology. Epistemology has to do with the quality of knowledge, and its study helps people evaluate the validity of proposed information. That, along with familiarity with a particular kind of educational or psychological research, is, in my judgment, absolutely indispensable for first-rate practice in this field. Without it, there is no way to be sensitive to the effects of self-selected samples, dishonesty in research, inadequate replication, inconsistency of evidence, and inadequate weight of evidence.

A Hot Potato That Sooner or Later Will Have to Be Considered

In a recent issue of *Empathic Parenting,* Dr. Elliot Barker's journal of the Canadian Society for the Prevention of Cruelty to Children, an article worthy of attention was reprinted from the *Toronto Globe and Mail* of October 2, 1987. The title is "Time to License Would-be Parents?" The author is Marvin Glass.

In the article, Professor Glass suggests that it is time to license parents. He is rebutted by Dr. Morton S. Rapp, a psychiatrist at the University of Toronto. I don't believe their debate settles the issue one way or the other, but I do believe that in the next thirty to forty years we may very well see the licensing of parents. If it is indeed true that what parents do with their very young children has lasting, powerful effects, then it seems that licensing may not be such a farfetched notion.

The Three Toughest Parts of the Job

Parents with only one child face two especially difficult chores: avoiding overindulgence and disciplining the child. For those with two closely spaced children (less than three years apart) sibling rivalry becomes a third difficult challenge. These conclusions have emerged from my thirty years of research in homes.

Helping a child acquire excellent language skills appears to be rather easy. The same can be said for enhancing the development of intelligence. Of course, heredity also plays a role. Some children will never achieve the highest levels of ability even though they appear to be just as normal as other infants at birth.

Helping a child to master his body and hand-eye coordination doesn't seem necessary. Nor is any special effort needed for vision or hearing skills to develop. Almost any way you rear a child—excluding, of course, abuse and neglect—will result in good development in those areas. They are either self-taught or maturationally based.

Avoiding overindulgence is another story. Most loving parents have trouble in this area, especially with their first children. A description of the problem and advice on how to deal with it have been offered in this book. These words are only meant to report that avoiding overindulgence remains at or near the top of the list of especially difficult aspects of parenting.

The same is true of the other two topics: discipline and sibling rivalry remain problematic. All three, moreover, seem to be complicated by another recent societal trend: delaying parenthood until women are in their thirties or even older.

If you are thirty-six years old at the birth of your first child, the tendency to overindulge and to be in conflict concerning discipline is greater than it might be for a younger parent. When you are thirty-six and have a one-year-old, the urge is sometimes strong to have a second child quickly (remember the biological clock). But unfortunately, no matter how you feel about the biological clock, two-year-olds don't like one-year-old siblings. Many young couples have asked anxiously how they can manage very close spacing, clearly hoping to hear that I don't really mean what I say about the extent of the hazards. The sad fact is that regardless of their needs or my empathy, the rules stay the same. For understandable reasons, slightly older children become jealous and unhappy about the new baby. As a result, everyone—the older baby, the younger baby, and both parents—has to pay a high price.

First-rate parent education can help, but it cannot eliminate the powerful effects of sibling rivalry. By not overindulging your first child, you make life easier for all concerned. A child who becomes accustomed early to having to wait, on occasion, for what she wants, who at times is turned down when she asks for things, and who is taught from the beginning to respect the rights of her parents will have less difficulty adapting to a younger sibling than one who has been overindulged.

New Parents as Teachers

MY CENTRAL FOCUS

I left an engineering career and became a psychologist more than forty years ago because I wanted to help more people become decent and capable. I wanted to improve the world. I still do. My subsequent career in psychology and education allowed me to pursue the study of human development continuously over those years. Determination was a factor in my longevity. An awful lot of good luck was, perhaps, even more important. I had the good luck to be born in the United States. I had the good luck to be born to a family that lived in the Boston area. I had the good fortune to be working in the Boston area when interest in early learning mushroomed during the 1960s. If any one of these circumstances had not been in place, my work could not have been done.

In the late 1960s I had been directing the Harvard Preschool Project for a few years when the first opportunity arose to put what we had been learning to the test in the public schools. Robert Sperber, superintendent of the Brookline, Massachusetts, school system asked if I would help do something with them aimed at learning in the preschool years. I agreed, and within a year we had established the Brookline Early Education Project (BEEP), a joint project of the Harvard School of Education, the Harvard School of Medicine, and the Brookline public school system.

BEEP's goal was to test this question: should the public schools help guide a child's learning from birth rather than from kindergarten age? It was a large, expensive project funded by the Carnegie Corporation, the R.W. Johnson Foundation, and the federal government at more than a million dollars a year for more than ten years. The staff was multidisciplinary and numbered more than fifty people.

After helping to plan the project and procure the money for it, I was faced with a problem: I could not continue to work for both the Harvard project and BEEP; I had to choose. I chose to stay with the university. We hired a director for BEEP, and I became the senior consultant.

The Brookline project was a failure. It didn't recruit the right kinds of families. It was inundated with affluent well-educated people who were quick to see its potential benefits. That kind of a population was a prime example of self-selection, and moreover, given the parents' advantaged status, the project had less room to deliver benefits to the children.

Furthermore, the guidance offered parents wasn't sufficient, and members of the home visiting staff failed to maintain their identity as educators. They became all-purpose social service workers. In addition, the new director rejected my strong suggestion that the results of the project be evaluated by outside experts. When it became clear that my advice wasn't going to be followed on basic matters, I quit.

Though BEEP was a very expensive failure, it received a lot of publicity, as would any sizable education experiment associated with Harvard, and hundreds of people came to visit. One visitor was of particular importance—the newly appointed director of elementary education in Missouri, Mrs. Mildred Winter.

Mrs. Winter liked what she saw at BEEP. In particular, she liked two aspects of the program: the fact that the ideas to be taught to parents were based on the Harvard Preschool Project's studies of successful families, and the fact that the program was offered to all families, not just to the poor. She returned to Missouri, teamed up with a remarkable woman, Jane Paine, from the Danforth Foundation, and spent a good portion of her time over the next twelve years trying to convince people that BEEP would look good in Missouri.

Mrs. Paine was and remains one of the most impressive professionals I have ever met. Highly respected, she worked hard to build support across the state of Missouri in political, medical, business, and community spheres. She succeeded brilliantly. Mrs. Winter convinced the state commissioner of education, Dr. Arthur Mallory, of the potential value of the work, and Dr. Mallory then lobbied hard and effectively for the program. It also helped that Missouri governor Christopher Bond and his wife were expecting their first child (the governor was in his early forties at the time).

We called the Missouri project New Parents as Teachers (NPAT). It was my second chance. Two of my associates and I provided nineteen days of preservice training to the staffs of four proposed sites during late 1981. We began to recruit and serve 320 families in January 1982. Parents were treated as teachers. They were given the best information we could find about the learning process during the first three years of life. They were taught what babies were learning as they developed rapidly, what tended to get in the way, and which teaching tactics seemed to be effective. The first edition of this book was the principal source of information. That book, written in 1974, was a more mature and accurate source of information than had been available for the BEEP project in 1970.

The program featured group get-togethers and home visits. We averaged nineteen contacts each year with each family from just before the birth of the child until his third birthday. (For more details on NPAT, see *Educating the Infant and Toddler,* Lexington Books, 1987.)

In June of 1984, fifteen months before the results were known, the Missouri legislature, flush with enthusiasm and extensive flattering publicity about the program, passed a law mandating the program statewide as part of the education system. This law was and remains the first of its kind. I had mixed emotions. It was potentially a wonderful development, but we had no proof that the program was helping children develop into better-educated three-year-olds than they would have become anyway.

Throughout 1984, as talk of expansion began, I urged caution and special attention to quality control. Of the nine staff members we had trained, perhaps five could become trainers of new staff, with some help from my associates and me. That small team might be able to start another twenty to twenty-five new sites in late 1985. In 1986 we might be able to expand to sixty or eighty additional sites, and so on.

Unfortunately, the state department personnel weren't listening. They were planning to start all 539 new sites in 1985! I was dismayed. What to do? I argued for more than a year. I got nowhere. Once again I quit.

An independent agency evaluated a sample of seventy-five children as they turned three years old in 1985, comparing them with seventy-five non-project children on measures of language, intelligence, and social behavior. The measures of language and intelligence were quite powerful, while the measures of social competence were weak. There were then, and are now, no strong measures of social competence in three-year-olds. The project children looked great socially—better, in the minds of the independent testers, than the comparison group—but solid test results would have impressed me more.

In language and intelligence, the program children were at the 75th percentile nationally on one measure and at the 85th percentile on the other! These results were and are sensational and unique. What an opportunity for public and private education! How gratifying to all of us who were involved! That's the good news. Unfortunately, there is also bad news.

Since 1985 the state of Missouri has been making a mess of the program and, worse than that, exporting the mess to forty-two other states and four other countries! The successful pilot program cost about $800 per year per family. The state allocated $165 and hoped that some communities would add more, although that was not likely to happen in many places. The state required five contacts per year with each family, versus our original nineteen. Staff members were overworked and usually poorly paid. Turnover was high.

The pilot program staff received nineteen days of preservice training plus two days of in-service training every six weeks for the next three years, 95 percent of which was directly from me. For the statewide programs and for out-of-state people, Missouri offers thirty hours of preservice training and, at most, one to two days per year of in-service education. The quality of that training is good, but the quantity is obviously nowhere near adequate.

In the pilot programs, we worked only with first-time parents, the easiest to work with. The state offers the program to everyone with one or more children less than three years old. There's more, but surely you can see why I'm deeply disappointed. I'm afraid that in a few years evaluations will show few benefits or none at all and that the movement toward universal parent education and support will be set back ten to twenty years.*

In 1989 we began a model program at the Center for Parent Education in Newton, Massachusetts, in order to demonstrate what the pilot projects were like as well as to train people. At the center, three of us work with about sixty families at a time.

Where, then, do we stand? The ideas in this book were the sole basis

---

*The first of such reports from PAT programs in Texas has just been published. No benefits were found.

for the NPAT curriculum. They are therefore the only ideas on raising infants and toddlers that apply to most families and have actually been shown to be effective. To be fair, few authors ever see their ideas tested. It should be of some comfort to you to know that there has been some confirmation of the general validity of this book. That is not to say that the entire contents of this book have proved to be valid. There are bound to be errors. There is still a long way to go before we reach anything resembling a complete science of early human development.

How does the NPAT experience affect you? Interestingly, at this time very few parents have access to excellent training and support such as that offered in the NPAT pilot programs. Perhaps in a very few places in Missouri high quality has been maintained. If you live in or near Newton, Massachusetts, you might call us and see if we have an opening. In the meantime, all I can do is wish you and your children well.

The original edition of *The First Three Years of Life* concluded with a few final comments. First, as I observed then, it seemed to me that no job was more important than raising a child in the first three years. Likewise, no job—indeed, no other experience in life—could offer deeper satisfaction. Finally, I said that our research, and that of many others, seemed to show that most parents had the resources to do a fine job, provided that those personal resources could be supplemented with information and support. I still feel the same way.

Back in the early 1970s there seemed to be a new consciousness of the importance of early experience. Parents, child development specialists, medical professionals, administrators of programs for children, and even legislators seemed to share a new enthusiasm for measures that would promote a more healthful and stimulating life for young children and their parents. I began to feel that important changes would soon take place, that more and more people would begin to treat the raising of a baby as the vitally important activity it is, and that public school systems would soon begin to assume some responsibility for guiding educational development in the first years of life by providing training and other services to new parents.

Well, it has been more than twenty years since that hopeful time, and it is now clear that I was too optimistic. The excitement of the early 1970s has not yet led to dramatic improvements for very many families with young children. For the most part, our educational system still operates as if no important learning takes place until a child reaches her sixth birthday.

Nevertheless, there are many tangible signs of a continuing and, indeed, growing commitment to the importance of early learning on the part of many individuals and organizations—that is, professionals, foundations, state government agencies, publishers, toy companies, and, most of all, parents. Parent education programs numbering in the tens of thousands have sprung up throughout the developed world. In the United States they have been sponsored by schools, community colleges, churches, mental health centers, hospitals, and grassroots organizations such as Junior League groups. These programs, along with what seems to be a more informed generation of new parents, are now our strongest indicators of progress. There are, however, other factors that complicate the picture.

Difficult economic circumstances, along with the growth of the feminist movement, have resulted in a sharp increase in the number of mothers who work out of the home. Unfortunately, this powerful and understandable trend conflicts directly with the message of this book. What do you do when the needs of the parents do not coincide sufficiently with the needs of children? Are there ways to reconcile the conflicting needs? I believe there are, and in the Recommended Readings section of this book I have cited books that provide guidance to modern young parents as they try to reconcile the apparently conflicting needs of mothers, fathers, and babies.

As I said earlier, I have been embroiled in the controversy about substitute care ever since 1979, when I remarked to a newspaper reporter that I felt the trend toward transferring primary responsibility for raising a child from the family to others was probably not in the best interests of most children. Controversy notwithstanding, I remain totally convinced that, to get off to the best start in life, babies need to spend a great deal of their waking time during the first three years of life with older people who are deeply in love with them. Although this ideal circumstance certainly does not always prevail in families, it is much more often found there than in any substitute-care arrangement.

Where do we stand in terms of knowledge and techniques for dealing well with the first years of childhood? First of all, we are, in general, much better informed than at any other time in history, thanks largely to the research of the last thirty years or so. Second, that improved knowledge base is enabling parents to increase the pleasure of raising children and to reduce the inevitable stress of the process. Third, I believe many babies are getting off to a much better start in life than they would have without this understanding.

I believe the prospects for universally available programs, such as the New Parents as Teachers Program, to prepare and assist new parents in child-rearing remain good, though not as good, perhaps, as they appeared to me in 1973. But my strongest hope for better programs for families with babies arises from my abiding faith in human nature and in the desire of all normal adults to want the best for their children. Raising children well is best accomplished when parents are well prepared and ably assisted in this most cherished function.

RECOMMENDED READINGS

This section introduces what I believe to be the most useful books currently available on the development of young children. This list is not complete, since there are undoubtedly writings of excellence that I do not know about, and many popular books are missing from the list because I cannot endorse them.

As I noted earlier, only a small fraction of the many books available contain detailed, reliable facts about the rapid development of children during the first years of life, mainly because comparatively few people until recently have sought and discovered such information. Gesell and Piaget are among that exclusive group who have made major contributions.

Though accurate and detailed information about infants and toddlers has been scarce, reliable ideas about how to rear a child have been even scarcer. Notice that I say *reliable* ideas. There has been no shortage of opinions and writings on the topic.

Child Development

Stone, J., and J. Church. *Childhood and Adolescence: A Psychology of the Growing Person*. New York: Random House, 1984. This book remains the most readable introductory textbook in college child development courses. The very practical and knowledgeable authors present a humanistic view of early child development. Other texts may be more informative from a technical standpoint, but no other text gives a better general appraisal of development of the young child. The late Joseph Stone was one of the rare child development authorities who was aware of what he didn't know.

U.S. Department of Health, Education and Welfare. *Infant Care*. Government Printing Office, Superintendent of Documents, Washington, D.C. A Children's Bureau publication that is reprinted and updated regularly, *Infant Care* has, for the better part of this century, been distributed widely to families in this country and is the single most popular document that the Government Printing Office has ever made available to the public. The fee for the pamphlet has always been nominal (about $1.00). Within its pages you will find a distillation of the conventional wisdom of each decade concerning the management of the infant. Historical analyses of the contents and ideas of *Infant Care* have shown that its recommendations to parents have shifted with whatever ideas were prevalent in child development research at any point in time. In fact, the directions to parents on some topics in *Infant Care* have taken a 180-degree turn in the space of only a few years. This vacillation on fundamental issues in child-rearing reflects the immaturity of the knowledge base in the field.

White, Burton L., B. Kaban, and J. Attanucci. *The Origins of Human Competence.* Lexington, Mass.: D. C. Heath, 1979. The concept of competence includes intelligence but is considerably broader. Competence comprises all of the significant abilities that a child uses in coping with his environment, including language, perceptual and motor abilities, and social skills. This volume is the final report of our long-term research on well-developing children in the first years of life. Though written for the scientific community, much of it is comparatively nontechnical. Parents who are especially interested in the research bases for my recommendations might find it worthwhile.

White, Burton L. *Raising a Happy, Unspoiled Child.* New York: Fireside, 1994. Avoiding overindulgence seems to be the most difficult part of the child-rearing process for the parents my colleagues and I work with. This book focuses on social learning during the first two years of life, and especially on preserving and enhancing happiness in infants and toddlers.

Stone, J. L., H. T. Smith, and L. B. Murphy. *The Competent Infant: Research and Commentary.* New York: Basic Books, 1973. This encyclopedic work is a compilation of most of the major approaches to the study of the young infant. It contains selected readings that, when put together, provide a rather complete, if fairly technical introduction to modern research on the very young baby.

Erikson, E. *Childhood and Society.* New York: Norton, 1950. Erikson has had enormous influence on the thinking in fields having to do with the motivation and personality of the young child. Erikson was a psychoanalyst, teacher, writer, artist, and, by any definition, a virtuoso. If for no other reason, you should read this book for the author's beautiful writing style. Beyond a gift for words, however, he weaves fascinating theories of the relationships among early child-rearing practices and the growth of personality and character in the young child. Erikson, heavily influenced by Freud, went considerably beyond Freud's early orientation to include many other factors, giving due respect to the complexity of the human personality. Though there is little evidence to validate Erikson's ideas, this is a rich book, a classic, and well worth reading.

Murphy, Lois. *Personality in Young Children.* Vol. 2. New York: Basic Books, 1956. Lois Murphy, working with four colleagues from related disciplines, studied the growth of personality in a group of nursery school children at Sarah Lawrence College some forty years ago. This entire book is devoted to the ups and downs of a single relatively well-adapted child from age two and a half to five and a half. The book remains unique in that it focuses on the development of a healthy child during the third and fourth years of life. The scene is usually his nursery school class, and the result is a rich documentation of normal personality development.

Chess, S., A. Thomas, and H. Birch. *Your Child Is a Person.* New York: Viking Press, 1965. Reprint, New York: Penguin Books, 1976. This book deals with the temperament of the young child with special emphasis on individual differences and characteristics that the baby brings with her into the world. It tries to make the case that many of the problems of raising children are due to the inherited characteristics that children bring with them into the world. Although I am by no means totally unsympathetic to the authors' position, I believe their case is somewhat overstated. Nevertheless, they have done high-quality research on the early development of personality in young children, and the book is therefore well worth reading.

Piaget, J. *The Origins of Intelligence in Children.* 2d ed. New York: International Universities Press, 1952. (May also be available in paper.) Without question Piaget has been head and shoulders above the rest of the field with respect to knowledge about how intelligence develops. His writings are classics. *The Origins of Intelligence,* dealing with the first two years of life, is extremely difficult reading, however. I advise you to read J. McVicker Hunt's interpretation of this book (see below). The extremely courageous, however, may find Piaget's own version a worthwhile challenge.

Hunt, J. McVicker. *Intelligence and Experience.* New York: Ronald Press, 1961. A portion of this book is devoted to a translation into understandable terms of Piaget's original work on mental development during the first two years of life. Other chapters relate Piaget's work to other research on the same processes. This book is well worth reading, but you may have to borrow it from a library, as it is now out of print.

Pulaski, M. Spencer. *Your Baby's Mind and How It Grows: Piaget's Theory for Parents.* New York: Harper & Row, 1978. The work of Piaget unquestionably contains the most valid and useful introduction to the mind of a baby, but until very recently very few professionals had access to understandable treatments of his work. Pulaski has done a great service by making these brilliant and fascinating ideas available to parents.

Singer, D., and T. Revenson. *A Piaget Primer: How a Child Thinks.* New York: Plume Books, New American Library, 1978. This book is another valuable introduction to the work of Piaget. I have often pointed out that if it were not for Piaget's work we would still be largely uninformed about how the mind of a baby works. I still believe that is true. It is therefore quite important to be able to make use of his findings, a need that is difficult to fill by reading his original works, which are too obscure and confusing for most people—including many professors—to cope with. The examples that Singer and Revenson use to illustrate Piaget's ideas are just wonderful. I strongly recommend this book.

Stallibrass, A. *The Self-Respecting Child.* New York: Pelican Books, 1977. Stallibrass has had extensive experience with play groups for two- to five-year-old children in England. She is also an avid student of the child development literature, especially the works of Piaget, Robert White, and others dealing with the subject of play. She makes a powerful case for the importance of play during the first two years of life, emphasizing the numerous physical activities that occupy so much of the time of infants and toddlers, particularly as they relate to mental and social development. In her view, the best conditions for the growth of self-respect allow two- to five-year-olds many opportunities to choose their own activities while learning to interact with other children. This is a notable book.

Play and Toys

Sutton-Smith, B. *How to Play with Your Children.* New York: Hawthorn Books, 1974.

Singer, D., and J. Singer. *Partners in Play.* New York: Harper & Row, 1977. Sutton-Smith and the Singers are, in my judgment, three of America's foremost analysts of the play of young children. Those with special interest in this topic probably cannot find more valid or thoughtfully presented work.

Butler, D. *Babies Need Books: How to Share the Joy of Reading with Your Child.* New York: Penguin Books, 1982. This is one of the finest books about the very young child that I have encountered. The author is described as a mother, a grandmother, a teacher, and children's book seller. Her position, magnificently presented in this paperback, is that books are more than just desirable and useful, they are mandatory for the very young child, starting with the first months of life. The author of this extraordinarily well-written book is not only knowledgeable and intelligent but also extremely passionate about the subject. She has a remarkable grasp of the nature of the very young child—especially as related to the child's interest in sounds, words, themes, and stories, all placed within the parent-child relationship.

Kimmel, M., and E. Segal. *For Reading Out Loud!* New York: Dell, 1991. This is an update of a very useful book first published in 1988. It serves the same purpose as the Butler book, above, in helping parents choose developmentally suitable books for children from infancy to adolescence. This one is also very well written and you will find it a great help if you bring it along when you visit a children's bookstore or a library.

Allison, C. *I'll Tell You a Story, I'll Sing You a Song: A Parents' Guide to the Fairy Tales, Fables, Songs, and Rhymes of Childhood.* New York: Delta, 1991. The subtitle explains why this book is valuable. Many classics can be found in this wonderful book.

Burtt, K., and K. Kalkstem. *Smart Toys for Babies.* New York: Harper Books, 1981. This is a pleasant and useful book. The authors borrow extensively from *The First Three Years of Life,* and they are at their best when they stick to the subject at hand—how to make interesting and appropriate toys at home. They do not do so well when they write about the educational implications of the toys, sometimes extrapolating inappropriately from the knowledge base. Although they cover most main points in regard to toys for children from birth to two, there are a few noteworthy omissions, such as the value of water play in the first year. Nevertheless, this book does contain a great deal of useful information and many good ideas.

Special Assistance for Parents

Brennan, H., P. Goresh, and C. Myers. *Discovering Motherhood.* Vienna, Va.: Mothers at Home, 1991. This is one of my favorite books, published by one of my favorite organizations. Mothers at Home is a grassroots organization dedicated to support for parents who are determined to play the major role in raising their own children. It contains a large number of short essays and poems by lay people. It radiates warmth and love.

Cahill, M. A. *The Heart Has Its Own Reasons.* Franklin Park, Ill.: La Leche League International, 1983. This is another constructive contribution to the continuing furor over substitute care for infants and toddlers.

Dreskin, W., and W. Dreskin. *The Day Care Decision: What's Best for You and Your Child.* New York: M. Evans, 1983. The Dreskins bring to this important topic the perspective of people who not only have been professionally involved in early childhood education for some time but also have participated in the evolution leading to the popularity of substitute care. They modified their nursery school to also become a provider of substitute care, but after almost two years of such experience they were so uncomfortable that they felt they could not continue to offer that kind of service. Furthermore, they became highly motivated to write about the issues involved. The result is this book.

Loman, L., *Of Cradles and Careers: A Guide to Reshaping Your Job to Include a Child in Your Life.* Franklin Park, Ill.: La Leche League International, 1984. This book is a serious attempt to encourage women to "have it all" but in a realistic way. The book documents the possibility of continuing a career and retaining primary responsibility for one's own children, including successfully breast-feeding. There are extensive and convincing case studies of women who have managed to succeed in this impressive achievement, along with discussions of such concepts as flextime, a reduced workweek, job-sharing, self-employment, the role of the father, decision-making, and selecting child care. The book is very well organized and written, and the appendix contains an excellent and extensive list of resources.

Maynard, F. *The Child Care Crisis.* New York: Penguin Books, 1986. The late Fredelle Maynard was a brilliant and dedicated woman. I believe her treatment of the dangers involved in the extensive use of substitute care for infants and toddlers is the most accurate and sophisticated treatise on this very important subject. Parents who have options should read this book before they decide whether or not to use child care during their baby's first years of life.

Bush, R. A. *A Parent's Guide to Child Therapy.* New York: Delacorte Press, 1980. For many years I have been concerned with and frustrated by the problems surrounding young children with emotional difficulties. Until recently I have been unable to advise parents, with any degree of confidence, what to do should their very young children begin to show such signs. This book is, in my opinion, an extraordinary breakthrough. Bush provides a remarkably rational and comprehensive introduction to the whole subject of child therapy. Witness, for example, the practical title of Part I: "When, Where, and How to Get Help," a promise which Bush goes on to amply fulfill. The book is written in a realistic yet reassuring tone. The author reveals a remarkable degree of common sense and a capacity for dealing with subjects in a concise and accurate way.

Friedland, R., and C. Kort, eds. *The Mothers' Book: Shared Experiences.* Boston: Houghton Mifflin, 1981. This is a superb, well-edited collection of interviews with and essays by sixty-four mothers who frankly discuss their feelings about various aspects of motherhood. The range of topics is broad, covering both popular issues—for example, breast-feeding and staying at home—and unusual topics, such as having triplets and dealing with the Oedipal triangle. Their concerns also cover a wide range of other topics, from everyday hassles to political commitments. The views expressed are equally varied and well balanced.

Kort, C., and R. Friedland. *The Fathers' Book.* Boston: G. K. Hall, 1986. This book is a companion to *The Mothers'-Book.* It is equally well done and delightful. I recommend it highly.

Lapinski, S., and M. D. Hinds. *In a Family Way: A Husband's and Wife's Diary of Pregnancy, Birth, and the First Year of Parenthood.* Boston: Little, Brown, 1982. You might ask what is so special about this sort of book. The answer is that if you are about to have your first child, reading this book will be extraordinarily entertaining. Lapinski and Hinds write beautifully, feel deeply, and have a tremendous capacity for love. Give yourself a treat.

Physical Health

Nathanson, L. *The Portable Pediatrician*. New York: HarperCollins, 1994. This is an unusual encyclopedic work focused on the first five years of life. Like many pediatric authors Nathanson attempts to cover conventional medical topics such as illness, injury, and well baby examinations as well as child development and parenting issues such as abilities, toys, equipment, and discipline. I am, of course, not qualified to comment on the medical topics, nor can I say much about the fourth and fifth year of life. As for subjects that have to do with understanding and guiding the child between birth and three years of age, however, I am pleased to say that this is the most sophisticated and comprehensive treatment of the subject by a pediatrician that I have ever read. There is no question but that Dr. Nathanson is a fine writer with high intelligence, compassion, and humor. In addition she is quite knowledgeable about the classic sources of stress that parents of babies must cope with, and she is an excellent observer. That does not mean, however, that the book is worthy of an unqualified recommendation. It does leave a good deal to be desired in respect to behavior and learning. Nevertheless, it is clearly the best I have seen written by a medical practitioner.

Metzger, M., and C. Whittaker, *The Childproofing Checklist*. New York: Doubleday, 1988.

Stewart, A., *Childproofing Your Home*. Reading, Mass.: Addison-Wesley, 1984. Infants and toddlers are vulnerable to accidents. Accidental poisonings and falls peak in the period shortly after the onset of crawling and continue through to about twenty months of age. Infants and toddlers love to explore and climb. The result is that parents must make their homes accident-proof. Among the several good books available on the topic, we recommend these two. Brief and inexpensive, they take you, room by room, through your home's child-safety needs in a clear, concise way. Definitely worthwhile investments.

Nursery School

Swift, J. W., "Effects of Early Group Experience: The Nursery School and Day Nursery." In *Child Development Research,* ed. M. L. Hoffman and L. W. Hoffman. New York: Russell Sage Foundation, 1964. There is a fair amount of confusion in the minds of parents about the benefits of nursery school for children. I can see no important educational reason to send an average or above-average child to any nursery school. Many nursery school personnel will argue that point. For some rare, solid, unbiased information on the topic, read this review chapter by Swift. This is the only reliable, fairly comprehensive treatment of research on the topic. Though it is now some three decades old, this book is still the only authoritative treatment of the subject. Until something better comes along—and don't hold your breath—it remains the last word on the subject.

Giftedness

Shore, B., F. Gagneau, S.T. Lariveaue, and R. E. Tremblay, eds. *Face to Face with Giftedness.* New York: Trillium Press, 1983. For those with a special interest in the topic of giftedness, this paperback volume should be of special interest. It contains selected presentations from the Fourth World Conference on Gifted and Talented Children, convened in Montreal in 1981. There are well over two thousand members of the World Council for Gifted and Talented Children, and more than a thousand attend the periodic world conferences. This collection of papers will provide the reader with insight into the diverse approaches to the fascinating topic of giftedness. The authors, from many countries around the world, present the most authoritative research on the topic.

Alvino, J., and the editors of *The Gifted Child Monthly. A Parents' Guide to Raising a Gifted Toddler.* Boston: Little, Brown, 1989. I have on several occasions recommended *The Gifted Child Monthly* newsletter, edited by Mr. Alvino. Indeed, when questions about giftedness have surfaced over the years, *The Gifted Child Monthly* and the International Organization on the Gifted and Talented have been our two principal sources of information. They have consistently shown good sense with respect to issues involving this interesting topic. Sadly, the newsletter could not be sustained. However, Mr. Alvino has assembled a large number of articles previously published in the newsletter into a fascinating and extensive book on the subject. This is no mere treatise on how to raise a bright child but a work of considerably more inclusive scope. I feel reasonably comfortable recommending this book. A principal reason is that, like the book by Zimbardo and

Radl on the shy child (see below), there simply is no better book on issues of giftedness. Bear in mind that more than half of the book is oriented toward children over three, but in this case I don't think that should deter anyone from buying it. What the reader should understand is that, like many in the field, it is uneven. I advise you, once again, to be slow to believe what is written by any single author. If you find a section of the book that looks interesting, by all means consider it a starting point. Any recommendations, whether they be in respect to bilingual education or emotional nurturance or any of the other important subjects dealt with on this subject, should be taken with a large grain of salt and followed up with explorations of second, third, and fourth opinions before implementation is considered.

Important Related Readings

Montessori, M. *The Absorbent Mind.* New York: Holt, Rinehart and Winston, 1967. Although Marie Montessori did not provide the last word on all topics in early education, she did have an interesting and original view of the growth and development of the young child. Indeed, many of her observations, so remarkably to the point, were not discovered by the general research community until almost a century later. This well-written book is worth your time. It is a classic.

Ulich, R. *Three Thousand Years of Educational Wisdom.* Cambridge, Mass.: Harvard University Press, 1961. Robert Ulich was one of the great thinkers in modern Western education. In this beautiful book he presented many invaluable writings on the subject of education. Though it is not primarily oriented toward early education, there is much here that has influenced the evolution of the field. Pay particular attention to the writings of Plato, Pestalozzi, Froebel, Comenius, and others who do refer to learning in the early years. This fine book should be in the library of everyone who reads and thinks at all about the human condition.

Lorenz, K. *King Solomon's Ring.* New York: Thomas Y. Crowell, 1952. I have always believed firmly that the study of other animal creatures helps us to understand our own condition. This book, by the founder of the science known as ethology, is absolutely delightful. Lorenz will introduce you to the fascinating study of growth and development in the young of other animal species. It would not surprise me at all if, from reading this book, you became interested in pursuing the topic of ethology.

Fraiberg, S. *The Magic Years.* New York: Scribner's, 1959. Although Fraiberg first published this book in 1959, it retains its magic and delight for contemporary readers. It describes the young child from birth to six years of age, dealing largely with psychoanalytic concerns buttressed by Fraiberg's clinical experience. The author's fresh, creative style overcomes most shackles one might associate with the psychoanalytic tradition. The sections dealing with sex identity—on being a boy and not a girl—however, do challenge the contemporary reader to rethink sexual assumptions. This is an excellent book for parents and professionals. It can enlighten and sensitize adults to the very special perspective of the young child. Another classic.

Zimbardo, Philip G., and Shirley L. Radl, *The Shy Child.* New York: McGraw-Hill, 1981. Shyness is a concern for many parents, but the subject has not been studied as extensively as others in this field. The authors, highly respected in the research community, direct the shyness clinic at Stanford University. This is the most authoritative book on the subject.

INDEX